11

CUBA IN THE WORLD

CUBA IN THE WORLD

COLE BLASIER • CARMELO MESA-LAGO

Editors

University of Pittsburgh Press

F
1788.2
C82

Published by the University of Pittsburgh Press, Pittsburgh, Pa. 15260
Copyright © 1979, University of Pittsburgh Press
Feffer and Simons, Inc., London
Manufactured in the United States of America

Library of Congress Cataloging in Publication Data

Main entry under title:

Cuba in the world.

  (Pitt Latin American series)
  Includes bibliographical references and index.
    1.   Cuba—Foreign relations—1959-
—Addresses, essays, lectures.   I.   Blasier, Cole,
1925–   II.   Mesa Lago, Carmelo.
F1788.2.C82   327.7291   78-53598
ISBN 0-8229-3383-7
ISBN 0-8229-5298-X pbk.

Contents

vi

Contents

Acknowledgments

Early versions of many of the chapters in this book were first presented at an international conference, "The Role of Cuba in World Affairs," at the University of Pittsburgh, November 15-17, 1976. The Rockefeller Foundation provided support for the conference, which brought together thirty-five specialists on Cuba in various academic disciplines from the United States, Latin America, Canada, Australia, Europe, and Israel. Conference sessions were devoted to Cuba's Revolution and foreign policy, Cuba's international political role, and Cuba's international economic role. Most of the papers in the volume have benefited from the comments of discussants and of other conference participants.

Support for preparation of some of the chapters was also received from the Department of State as part of a contract awarded to the University of Pittsburgh for research on the role of Cuba in hemispheric and world affairs in the second half of the 1970s. Responsibility for the content of the chapters, of course, rests solely with the authors; neither the Rockefeller Foundation nor the State Department is responsible for opinions, findings, or conclusions.

The staff of the Center for Latin American Studies at the University of Pittsburgh has played an important role in the preparation of this book. Carmelo Mesa-Lago organized the 1976 conference and directed execution of the State Department contract. June Belkin, managing editor of *Cuban Studies/Estudios Cubanos,* managed the conference and has worked closely with the editor of the volume. Shirley Kregar has been responsible for the financial and other administrative aspects of these efforts. Erma MacPherson, Carolyn Wilson, Lori Stuart, and Linda Yazvac have supplied secretarial services. The University Center for International Studies, under the direction of Carl Beck and Paul Watson, has provided important financial and administrative support.

The chapters by Jorge I. Domínguez, Yoram Shapira, Theodore H. Moran, and Archibald R. M. Ritter previously appeared in *Cuban Studies/Estudios Cubanos* 7 (July 1977) and 8 (January 1978). They have been substantially revised for inclusion in this volume.

CUBA'S POLITICAL ROLE IN WORLD AFFAIRS

EDWARD GONZALEZ

Institutionalization, Political Elites, and Foreign Policies

The "institutionalization of the Cuban Revolution" since 1970 has been acclaimed by outside observers and the Cuban leadership alike as marking a new, decisive stage in Cuba's political order. Indeed, the Cuba of the late 1970s is strikingly different from the Cuba of a decade earlier. Institutionalization has brought about the depersonalization of governance, the strengthening of the party and governmental structures, and the greater efficacy and rationality of the economy. Additionally, the state and governmental system has undergone a major reorganization under the new socialist constitution, leading to the creation of new leadership posts and organs of representation, and culminating in island-wide elections in late 1976. Yet it is not only Cuba's domestic order that experienced major transformations: Cuba's foreign policies also were dramatically altered in the post-1970 period.

On the foreign policy front, the strained relations between Cuba and the Soviet Union from 1966 to 1968 have given way to a new and mutually supportive harmony. Nowhere was this relationship more apparent than in the direct support given by the USSR to Cuba's military incursion into Angola beginning in late 1975 and in Cuba's furtherance of Soviet objectives not only in Angola, but also later in Ethiopia and other African states. Elsewhere the Cuban government had moved to diversify its economic ties with Japan, Canada, Western Europe, and other non-Communist countries in an apparent effort to lessen the island's economic dependence on the Soviet Union. In 1974, 41 percent of Cuba's total trade turnover was accounted for by these countries as opposed to 32 percent during 1971-1973.[1] Havana's stance toward much of Latin America also underwent a fundamental change from the 1960s. The Cuban government seemed far less interested in promoting violent revolution in the hemisphere than in restoring diplomatic ties and developing closer relations with a host of Latin American countries, including Venezuela and Colombia which only a few years earlier had been theaters of guerrilla activity. Indeed, Havana's new moderation paved the way not only for the lifting of sanctions by the Organization of American States (OAS) at the San Jose conference in August 1975, but also for the visit of Mexican President Luis Echeverría to Cuba that same month, marking the first visit of a ruling, nonsocialist Latin American president to Communist Cuba.

Most astonishing of all, however, were Havana's moves to normalize rela- 3

EDWARD GONZALEZ

tions with Washington despite Fidel Castro's earlier and repeated insistence that his regime would never approach the "imperialist" government of the United States. During 1974 and 1975, the Cuban government publicly and privately signaled its interest in working toward some kind of accommodation with the Ford administration. As a result, informal talks were held by representatives of the two governments between late 1974 and late 1975, only to lapse at the time of Cuba's rapid military buildup in Angola. But the new Carter administration quickly resumed the talks in March 1977, with both governments announcing on June 3 that they had agreed to exchange diplomatic officials who would set up "interests sections" in their respective closed embassies in Washington and Havana the following September.[2] These subdiplomatic ties seemed to signify that the state of mutual hostility and acrimony that had existed between the two countries for over seventeen years was coming to an end.

It can be argued that Havana's foreign policies in the 1970s simply responded to developments internal and external to Cuba. After years of Fidelista mismanagement of the economy, for instance, the near ruinous drive for the ten-million-ton sugar harvest in 1970 left the Castro regime with no alternative but to synchronize Cuba's foreign policy with that of the Soviet Union, to integrate Cuba's economy more closely with that of the Soviet Union and with the countries of COMECON (Council for Mutual Economic Assistance), and to reorganize the administration of the economy along Soviet lines. The extraordinary rise in world (and Soviet) sugar prices beginning in 1973 enabled Cuba to increase greatly its trade and credit with the advanced capitalist countries. Meanwhile, the demise of the guerrilla movements in Latin America after 1967, along with the emergence of nationalist leaders such as Velasco in Peru, Allende in Chile, and Peron in Argentina, had made it opportune for Havana to shift from a revolutionary to a diplomatic offensive in the hemisphere. The new international leverage and cohesiveness of the Third World, dramatized by the success of the Arab oil embargo and the Organization of Petroleum Exporting Countries (OPEC), also marked a decisive change in the international balance of forces and emboldened Cuba to extend its global reach to the Middle East, Angola, and elsewhere in Africa. Finally, the Castro regime no longer confronted a highly antagonistic United States following the termination of the Nixon presidency, as Ford and especially Carter became more receptive to ending the deadlock with Cuba. This development, it can be argued, together with the sharp decline in world sugar prices after 1974 and the resulting adverse effects on the Cuban economy, persuaded Havana to improve relations with its archenemy to the north.

While these and other factors became major determinants of Cuban foreign policy in the 1970s, the contextual explanation tends to view the Cuban regime as essentially a unitary and reactive actor in world affairs, or simply as a dutiful surrogate of the Soviet Union. What is overlooked is the internal complexity of the Cuban regime and the ways in which different tendencies within the regime interact with external developments in the shaping of Cuban foreign policies. In

the analysis that follows, I will examine not only the impact of external developments on the regime, but also how the institutionalization process of the 1970s
and the resulting changes in the distribution of political elites and power within
Cuba have themselves affected the regime's foreign policies. In so doing, I hope
to provide a more adequate explanation concerning the dynamic, seemingly
volatile character of recent Cuban global behavior which ranges simultaneously
from close alliance with the Soviets and militant activities in the Third World, to
steps toward normalizing relations with the United States.

Before proceeding, I need to state certain fundamental assumptions central
to the analysis. First, while there exists a high level of elite consensus, I do not
hold the Cuban regime to be monolithic. Rather, there are divisions within the
Cuban leadership which stem from differences among political elites in their
ideological and issue orientations, power considerations, and bureaucratic and
organizational interests.[3] Second, I believe there are linkages between these
political elites and policy outcomes. For example, Cuba's more pragmatic
policies on the domestic and foreign fronts can be traced in part to the rise in
influence of more moderate technocratic elites since 1970. Finally, I hold that
both the internal elites and elite-policy linkages can be identified by means of
careful analysis. Such analysis must necessarily be inferential owing to the nature
of the Cuban system, just as it is in Soviet and Chinese studies. But there is
evidence of elite groupings and of occasional conflict within the Cuban regime.
The position of these elites can be tracked by reading the Cuban press and by
analyzing changes in the composition of the party, state, and government. Similarly, elite-policy linkages can at least be imputed on the basis of what is known
about specific elite groupings and from both policy statements and policy actions.

This study is divided into three parts. The first examines the ways in which
the institutionalization process has both broadened Cuba's ruling coalition of
political elites and reconcentrated power in Fidel and Raúl Castro and their
following. The second discusses how three elite tendencies—the technocratic,
the revolutionary, and the military—have affected the regime's foreign policies
in recent years. The conclusion is a speculative analysis of Cuba's future foreign
policy postures in light of the internal constellation of elite forces within Cuba
and of developments occurring on the international front.

The Reconcentration of Power

Institutionalization and Broadened Leadership

There are three major aspects of the institutionalization process that has
altered the composition of the Cuban leadership since 1970.[4] The first is the
depersonalization of governance—the delegation of effective decision-making
powers from Fidel Castro and his immediate entourage to new and more technically qualified appointees and to governmental agencies that could now function
in more regularized and orderly fashion without the interventions of the *líder*

máximo. This step was initiated immediately after the 1970 harvest when some of Fidel's closest associates were replaced by new personnel drawn from more qualified civilian and military circles.

The second aspect involves two major administrative reorganizations. Carried out in November 1972, the first change established a new Executive Committee attached to the Council of Ministers, with seven deputy prime ministers to supervise and coordinate clusters of ministries engaged in related activities. This reorganization gave further impetus to the post-1970 tendency of appointing new personnel to leadership posts, with no less than four army majors—then the highest rank in the Revolutionary Armed Forces (FAR)—being appointed deputy prime ministers and another becoming a minister by the end of 1972. The second and more sweeping institutional change has occurred since February 1976, with the implementation of Cuba's new socialist constitution. As will be seen subsequently, it has led to the remodeling of Cuba's state and governmental structure similar to that of the Soviet Union, with a new National Assembly of People's Power, Council of State, and Council of Ministers being established in December 1976.

The third aspect of the institutionalization process concerns the Communist Party of Cuba (PCC): A stepped-up recruitment drive more than doubled its membership from 100,000 in 1970 to 202,807 in September 1975; new leadership was introduced at the highest levels through the expansion of the old six-man Secretariat to include five additional members in February 1973; and finally, a new Political Bureau, Secretariat, and Central Committee were unveiled at the party congress. In sum, the PCC was being transformed in Leninist fashion and accorded heightened political legitimacy as Cuba's ruling institution.[5]

These and other measures had the full support of the Soviet Union and were acclaimed by Leonid Brezhnev as evidence of the growing maturity of the Cuban Revolution. They were also matched by significant increases in Soviet support for the Cuban economy. Indeed, not only organizational reforms but major policy changes as well appear to have been the price the regime had to pay for ensuring high levels of Soviet bloc support after 1970. Major ideological and political concessions were announced at the thirteenth congress of the Central Organization of Cuban Trade Unions (CTC) in November 1973, signaling the wholesale replacement of Fidelista policies by a new, Soviet-style orthodoxy in Cuba's economic and labor affairs.[6]

In the meantime, the institutionalization process initially weakened the position of Fidel and his followers, particularly as it came on the heels of the devastating 1970 harvest shortfall when Fidel's charismatic authority had been severely shaken. For the first time in over a decade, other elite elements—among the "old Communists" from the Popular Socialist Party (PSP) and the new generation of technocratic managers—could now avail themselves of Soviet backing to seek greater power within the regime and the imposition of formal constraints on the Fidelistas.[7] Indeed, there were some former PSP leaders who gained influence and prestige in the post-1970 period. Carlos Rafael Rodríguez, for example, after long service as minister without portfolio, was named chairman of Cuba's delegation to the Intergovernmental Soviet-Cuban Commission for Economic, Scientific, and Technological Cooperation in December 1970 and became deputy prime minister in charge of foreign economic and diplomatic relations in November 1972; he was elevated to membership in the Political Bureau of the PCC in December 1975. Other ex-PSP members who also gained in prominence include Blas Roca and Arnaldo Milián as new members of the enlarged Political Bureau (1975), Isidoro Malmierca as member of the expanded Secretariat (1973), and Joel Domenech and Major Flavio Bravo as deputy prime ministers (1972).

In retrospect, the slippage in Fidel's position appears to have occurred between 1970 and 1973, with the CTC congress in November 1973 perhaps marking the nadir of Fidelista authority. But in 1969 Richard Fagen noted prophetically that, "while hardly consistent over the years in some of his policies and public pronouncements, he [Fidel] has been extremely consistent in reasserting his dominance over the shifting revolutionary power struggle."[8] To this end, Fidel employed three strategems to turn the institutionalization process to his advantage prior to the PCC congress in December 1975 and to refashion a new broader coalition of political, technocratic, managerial, and military elites dominated once again by Fidelistas and by Raulistas associated with the Ministry of the Revolutionary Armed Forces (MINFAR).[9] First, by accepting organizational and policy reforms, and by delegating decision-making authority to others within the top leadership, Fidel ensured the continued support of those civilian and military elites who might otherwise have opposed him had he insisted on clinging to the old personalistic order. Second, he pulled nine senior or high-level officers from the MINFAR who were loyal to him and to Raúl and placed them in the expanded PCC Secretariat, the Executive Committee of the Council of Ministers, and at the top of several ministries. In doing so, he limited the extent to which others without Fidelista or Raulista affiliations—such as the postrevolutionary generation of civilian technocrats and former PSP cadres—would occupy new positions in the party and government. And third, he and Raúl, as minister of the FAR, strengthened their position by making extensive personal appearances before troops and combat units and by ensuring that party organizational activities were conducted by personally loyal officers. This entrenched basis of support within the FAR provided strong leverage with which to assert their leadership over the party and government.

The 1975 PCC Congress

The party congress confirmed these changes in regime leadership whereby a broader coalition of elites now rules, but the two Castro brothers and their followers form the dominant, cohesive core (table 1.1). Fidel and Raúl were reelected as first and second secretaries, respectively. The original eight-man Political Bureau was enlarged to include five additional members, of which three come from the ranks of the PSP (Blas Roca, Carlos Rafael Rodríguez, and Arnaldo Milián). But the other two new members are followers of Fidel and Raúl (Pedro Miret and José Ramón Machado), while the original Fidelista and July 26

TABLE 1.1
The Cuban Leadership and Its Major Responsibilities: January 1976

	Political Origins and Allegiances [a]	Political Bureau [b]	Secretariat [b]	Other Party Positions	Principal Current Government Posts
Fidel Castro	M-26-7	1st sec.	1st sec.	—	Prime minister; commander-in-chief; pres. of Executive Committee, Council of Ministers
Raúl Castro	M-26-7	2d sec.	2d sec.	Pres., Commission on Security and Armed Forces	First dep. prime minister; min. of armed forces
Juan Almeida	M-26-7:F	Member	—	Political Bureau delegate to Oriente Province [c]	—
Osvaldo Dorticós [d]	M-26-7	Member	—	Pres., Commission on Economy	President of the Republic; pres., Central Planning Board (JUCEPLAN)
Guillermo García	M-26-7:F	Member	—	—	Dep. prime minister (transportation, communications)
Armando Hart	M-26-7:F	Member	—	1st sec., Oriente Province	—
Ramiro Valdés	M-26-7:F	Member	—	Member, Commission on Security and Armed Forces	Dep. prime minister (construction)

Name					
Sergio del Valle	M-26-7:F	Member	—	Member, Commission on Security and Armed Forces	Min. of interior
Blas Roca	PSP	Member (1975)	Member	Pres., Commission on Legal Studies	—
José Ramón Machado	M-26-7:R	Member (1975)	—	1st sec., Havana Province	—
Carlos Rafael Rodríguez	PSP	Member (1975)	Member	—	Dep. prime minister (foreign relations); pres., National Commission for Economic, Scientific, and Technological Cooperation, and chief Cuban delegate to Soviet-Cuban commission in this field
Pedro Miret	M-26-7:F	Member (1975)	Member (1973)	—	—
Arnaldo Milián	PSP	Member (1975)	—	1st sec., Las Villas Province	—
Isidoro Malmierca	PSP	—	Member (1973)	—	—
Jorge Risquet	M-26-7:R	—	Member (1973)	—	—
Antonio Pérez	M-26-7:R	—	Member (1973)	—	—
Raúl García	M-26-7:F	—	Member (1973)	—	—

(Continued on next page)

Notes to Table 1.1

Sources: Granma Weekly Review, January 4, 1976, p. 12; U.S. Central Intelligence Agency, *Directory of Personalities of the Cuban Government, Official Organizations and Mass Organizations*, A (CR) 74-7, March 1974; and ibid., *Chiefs of State and Cabinet Members of Foreign Governments*, A (CR) 75-46, December 1975. The CIA sources are available through the Documents Expediting (DOCEX) Project, Exchange and Gifts Division, Library of Congress, Washington, D.C., 20540.

Note: This table is adapted from Edward Gonzalez, "Castro and Cuba's New Orthodoxy," *Problems of Communism*, January–February 1976, p. 17.

a. The abbreviations used in this column are: M-26-7 = July 26 Movement; F = Fidelista; PSP = Popular Socialist Party, or "Old Communists"; R = Raulista.

b. Incumbents since 1965 unless appointed recently, in which case the year is indicated in parentheses. Membership in the political bureau and secretariat are listed in the order and form presented in *Granma Weekly Review*, January 4, 1976.

c. Almeida was appointed delegate from the Political Bureau to Oriente Province on September 23, 1970, perhaps a reflection of its great economic importance as a sugar producer, its political complexities, and Almeida's personal ties to the area.

d. Dorticós's removal in December 1975 from the Secretariat, where he had served since 1965, may have been for reasons of health. He was not named as a vice-president in the new Council of State that was unveiled in December 1976, however, which may have been for political reasons.

Movement core remains intact (see the first eight names in table 1.1) and was listed first by *Granma*. The new Secretariat was pruned to nine members with the dropping of President Dorticós and Faure Chomón, but otherwise this body remains unchanged from February 1973. As a result, Fidel, Raúl, and four of their followers emerged in firm command of the top organs of the party.

The new lineup of the Central Committee is similarly weighted in favor of the two Castro brothers, but is also is a more representative body that reflects the broader coalition that now rules Cuba. The membership of the Central Committee was increased from 91 to 112, with 12 alternates, with considerable renovation having occurred in the election of the new body. Excluding the 17 members of the new Central Committee who occupy positions in the Political Bureau and Secretariat, there are 46 new members (43 percent) and 61 continuing members (57 percent) among the remaining 107 members and alternates in the new body. Furthermore, the new Central Committee is a somewhat more balanced body when compared with the old in terms of political and institutional affiliations.

Although I have been unable to identify the former political affiliations of all the Central Committee members, table 1.2 does indicate that the share of the July 26 movement in the new body has increased in absolute numbers but has declined in percentage terms, whereas the PSP's share has remained fixed numerically and has declined even more sharply in percentage terms. These figures on political affiliation, of course, are affected by the large number of unknowns—23 (21 percent) of the 107 members. (This in itself might be suggestive of the declining importance of former political affiliations dating back two decades ago, or it may only reflect the incompleteness of data available to this author.) More conclusive is the data on institutional affiliations.

As table 1.3 shows, the largest institutional blocs consist of the active duty officers attached to MINFAR and the civilian ministries and agencies taken as a whole. At the time the new Central Committee was elected, the representation of

TABLE 1.2

Composition of the PCC Central Committee According to Political Affiliations

	July 26 Movement		Popular Socialist Party		Revolutionary Directorate of March 13		Unknown		Total	
	No.	%	No.	%	No.	%	No.	%	No.	%
New body	63	59	17	16	4	4	23	21	107	100
Old body	54	71	17	22	5	7	0	0	76	100

Sources: Granma Weekly Review, January 4, 1976, p. 12; U.S. Central Intelligence Agency, *Directory of Personalities of the Cuban Government, Official Organizations and Mass Organizations*, A (CR) 74-7, March 1974; and idem., *Chiefs of State and Cabinet Members of Foreign Governments*, A (CR) 75–46, December 1975.

Note: Members of the Political Bureau and Secretariat are excluded, but the twelve alternate members of the new body are included. Percentage figures are rounded out.

the MINFAR increased numerically from twenty-four to twenty-seven regular members (and three alternates), although its share slipped from 31.5 to 28 percent owing to the larger size of the new body. (By fall 1976, two of these active duty officers had become civilians, with one being appointed to the newly created post of minister of higher education.) The biggest gain was seemingly registered by the civilian ministries, whose numerical representation increased from twenty-eight to forty-one members and its share from 27 to 39 percent. But these bloc figures are deceptive in that the MINFAR representation may be larger than it seems if one counts former FAR-MINFAR officers now serving in civilian posts. In this regard, ten of the representatives from the civilian ministries were former ranking officers on active duty with the FAR before 1972, with two serving as deputy prime ministers and eight heading civilian ministries and agencies at the time the new Central Committee was named. If one adds—to use Jorge I. Domínguez's concept—the ten "civic soldiers" who occupied civilian posts, then the direct and indirect MINFAR representation runs to forty members or 37.0 percent of the Central Committee.[10]

The composition of the Political Bureau and Central Committee at the December 1975 PCC congress thus revealed the greater elite diversity that had come to characterize the post-1970 Cuban leadership. But it was clear from the outcome of the congress that Fidel and Raúl, together with their closest followers, remained very much in control of the party organs. Indeed, not only the two Castro brothers, but also veteran Fidelistas and Raulistas from the guerrilla campaign were accorded the greatest prominence on the pages of *Granma* in the nine months following the party congress.

Elites in the New State-Government Structure

As unveiled in December 1976, the reorganization of the state and government under the new constitution fully conformed to and formalized the existing

TABLE 1.3
Composition of the PCC Central Committee According to Institutional Affiliation

	Ministry of the Revolutionary Armed Forces		Ministry of the Interior		Civilian Ministries		Mass Organs		Party Professionals		Unknown		Total	
	No.	%	No.	%	No.	%	No.	%	No.	%	No.	%	No.	%
New body	30	28	5	4	41	39	8	7	13	12	10	10	107	100
Old body	24	32	4	5	28	37	3	4	10	14	7	8	76	100

Sources: Granma Weekly Review, January 4, 1976, p. 12; U.S. Central Intelligence Agency, *Directory of Personalities of the Cuban Government, Official Organizations and Mass Organizations,* A (CR) 74-7, March 1974; and idem., *Chiefs of State and Cabinet Members of Foreign Governments,* A (CR) 75-46, December 1975.
Note: Members of the Political Bureau and Secretariat are excluded, but the twelve alternate members of the new body are included. Percentage figures are rounded out.

distribution of political power.[11] As table 1.4 shows, Fidel and his brother were, not unexpectedly, elected by the deputies to the National Assembly of People's Power as president and first vice-president, respectively, of the Council of State and the Council of Ministers. The top leadership of the Council of State, in turn, corresponds to the party's Political Bureau: thus, along with Fidel and Raúl, the five vice-presidents and the first six members of the Council of State make up the Political Bureau. The remaining seventeen members, apart from the secretary, hold top government posts, control the mass organizations, head specialized institutes or associations, or otherwise represent important political groups. All but two of the thirty-one members of the Council of State are in the Central Committee. It thus represents a prestigious political body in which the original revolutionaries—among them veteran Moncadistas and Sierra Maestra combatants—once again predominate: twenty-one of the members are from the ranks of the July 26 Movement, eight come from the PSP, with the two remaining unknown to this author. Significantly, the MINFAR is represented not only by Army General Raúl Castro, but also by Division General Senén Casas—next to Raúl, the top man in MINFAR since 1971—and Division General Abelardo Colomé who was acclaimed for his role in leading victorious Cuban troops·in Angola.[12]

The eight vice-presidents named to the Executive Committee of the new Council of Ministers were chosen by Fidel in his capacity as president. They had been deputy prime ministers forming the Executive Committee on the previous Council of Ministers (or president as in the case of Dorticós). Hence, no change has occurred with the naming of the new body: Fidel and Raúl remain flanked by five close associates; the ex-PSP members continue with three members, the most prominent of whom remains Carlos Rafael Rodríguez (see table 1.4). The agency heads and ministers who are included in the Council of Ministers, but not its Executive Committee, provide somewhat greater variation.[13] Of the twenty-two ministers, excluding Raúl Castro and Sergio del Valle, sixteen are holdovers, five are new appointees, and one has been promoted by virtue of the office being elevated. Still, the political pattern remains the same: At least eleven ministers were affiliated with the July 26 Movement, only two with the PSP, two with the Revolutionary Directorate of March 13, and five are unknown to this author. Furthermore, the "civic soldier" remains very much in evidence in the new Council of Ministers: Excluding Raúl and Sergio del Valle, no less than nine ministers originally came from the FAR or MINFAR, the most recent being former Major-General Fernando Vecino Alegret who was appointed to the new post of minister for higher education in August 1976.

On the other hand, there are fewer civilian technocrats or managers heading the ministries and state committee within the Council of Ministers than perhaps might have been expected. Of the twenty-two civilian ministries, only five appear to be headed by civilians with technocratic and managerial qualifications: Agriculture (Rafael Francia); Sugar Industry (Marcos Lage); Foreign Trade (Marcelo Fernández); National Bank of Cuba (Raúl E. León); and Electric Power Industry (José L. Beltrán). Instead, recruitment often seems to have favored the

TABLE 1.4
The Cuban Leadership, December 1976

	Political Origins & Allegiances	Post in B or S	Post in Council of State	Post in Council of Ministers	Other Posts
Fidel Castro	M-26-7	1st sec., PB, S	President	President	Commander-in-chief
Raúl Castro	M-26-7	2d sec., PB, S	1st vice-pres.	1st vice-pres.	Min. of armed forces
Juan Almeida	M-26-7:F	Member, PB	Vice-pres.	Vice-pres.	—
Ramiro Valdés	M-26-7:F	Member, PB	Vice-pres.	Vice-pres.	—
Guillermo García	M-26-7:F	Member, PB	Vice-pres.	—	
Blas Roca	PSP	Member, PB, S	Vice-pres.	—	Pres., National Ass.
Carlos Rafael Rodríguez	PSP	Member, PB, S	Vice-pres.	Vice-pres.	—
Celia Sánchez	M-26-7:F	—	Sec.		—
Pedro Miret	M-26-7:F[b]	Member, PB, S	Member	Vice-pres.	—
Osvaldo Dorticós	M-26-7:F	Member, PB	Member	Vice-pres.	—
Armando Hart	M-26-7:F	Member, PB	Member	Min. of culture	—
Sergio del Valle	M-26-7:F	Member, PB	Member	Min. of interior	—
José Ramón Machado	M-26-7:R	Member, PB	Member	—	—
Arnaldo Milián	PSP		Member	Vice-pres.	—
Diocles Torralba	M-26-7:R[b]		Member	Vice-pres.	—
Belarmino Castilla	M-26-7:R[b]		Member	Vice-pres.	—
Flavio Bravo	PSP[b]		Member	Vice-pres.	—
Joel Domenech	PSP		Member	—	—
Luis Orlando Domínguez	M-26-7		Member	—	1st sec., Communist Youth League
Roberto Veiga	M-26-7		Member	—	Sec. gen., Confederation of Cuban Workers

Name	Affiliation	PCC Secretariat	Council of State	Council of Ministers	Position
Jorge Lezcano	M-26-7	—	Member	—	National coordinator, Committees for the Defense of the Revolution
Vilma Espín	M-26-7:R	—	Member	—	Pres., Federation of Cuban Women
José Ramírez	PSP	—	Member	—	Pres., National Association of Small Farmers
Haydée Santamaría	M-26-7:F	—	Member	—	Dir., Casa de las Americas
Osmany Cienguegos	M-26-7	—	Member	Sec.	—
Juan Marinello	PSP, Died, March 1977	—	Member	—	Pres., Peace and Sovereignty Movement
Severo Aguirre	PSP	—	Member	—	—
Reinaldo Castro	—	—	Member	—	—
Marta Deprés	—	—	Member	—	Sec., Federation of Cuban Women
Senén Casas	M-26-7:R	—	Member	—	1st vice-min., MINFAR
Abelardo Colomé	M-26-7:R	—	Member	—	Vice-min., MINFAR
Isidoro Malmierca	PSP	Member, S (to 1977)	—	Min. of foreign affairs	—
Jorge Risquet	M-26-7:R	Member, S	—	—	—
Antonio Pérez	M-26-7:R	Member, S	—	—	—
Raúl García	M-26-7:F	Member, S	—	—	—

Sources: Granma, January 14, 1976, p. 12; ibid., December 12, 1976; U.S. Central Intelligence Agency, Directory of Personalities of the Cuban Government, Official Organizations and Mass Organizations, A (CR) 74-7, March 1974; and ibid., Chiefs of State and Cabinet Members of Foreign Governments, A (CR) 75-46, December 1975.

Note: Names are listed in the order given in Granma for the PCC Secretariat. On June 10, 1977, the Political Bureau designated Arnaldo Milián (Cuba's foreign minister from 1959 to 1976) as a new member of the PCC Secretariat. In its first regular session held July 12–14, 1977, the National Assembly of People's Power elected Raúl Roa to fill the post on the Council of State left vacant by Marinello's death.

a. The abbreviations used in this column are: M-26-7 = the July 26 Movement; R = Raulista; F = Fidelista; PSP = Popular Socialist Party, or "Old Communists"; In column 2: PB = Political Bureau; S = Secretariat.

b. Formerly attached to FAR-MINFAR.

military officer or civilian with political qualifications, even in ministries and agencies dealing with more technical matters. Thus, a former military attaché to Chile (1972–1973) continues to head the Ministry of Mines and Geology.

Elite Coalitions and Reconcentrated Political Power

By the mid-1970s there existed a broader distribution and diversity of political elites in the Cuban leadership than at any time since the mid-1960s. The "old Communists" from the PSP were now included in the supreme organs of the party, state, and government. Carlos Rafael Rodríguez became the most prominent of the ex-PSP notables by virtue of his membership in the Political Bureau and Secretariat and his vice-presidency in both the Council of State and Council of Ministers. Isidoro Malmierca also stands out as a rising ex-PSP member due to his 1973 appointment to the Secretariat and to his December 1976 appointment as minister of foreign affairs. Additionally, civilian technocrats and managers have gained somewhat broader representation at the highest levels of the government, both by heading individual ministries and participating in the Intergovernmental Soviet-Cuban Commission for Economic, Scientific, and Technological Cooperation which Rodríguez leads on the Cuban side.

Despite this greater elite diversity, the Cuban leadership remains limited. To begin with, the "old Communists" are becoming an aged and passing leadership generation as exemplified by Blas Roca, Severo Aguirre, and Juan Marinello (who died in March 1977). For political and symbolic reasons, they are represented in the prestigious Council of State, and Blas Roca has been named president of the National Assembly. But these are not decision-making bodies; and in such bodies where the ex-PSP members do have representation, as in the Political Bureau and the Executive Committee of the Council of Ministers, they remain a small minority. Furthermore, the ascendancy of the civilian technocrats and managers has been checked by the appointment of ex-military officers to civilian posts. The FAR-MINFAR officers—whether in civilian posts or on active duty—constitute the most important elite grouping within the new Cuban leadership. Not only have they come to occupy vice-presidential posts in the Executive Committee of the Council of Ministers, to control individual ministries, and to hold membership in the Council of State. They also have provided the key element in Fidel's successful coalition-building, coalescing to form a Fidelista-Raulista core within the top leadership organs and providing institutional backing to the Cuban leader.

While a broadening of elite representation has occurred, this coalition-building has thus led to a reconcentration of political power in the two Castro brothers and their following. They clearly dominate the key organs of the party, state, and government in terms of sheer membership numbers and control over the most sensitive or powerful ministries. But more than that, Fidel's position as the supreme *líder máximo* has now been institutionalized in his multiple roles as first secretary, president of both the Council of State and Council of Ministers, and commander-in-chief. As president of the Council of State, moreover, he is empowered not only to name the first vice-president, vice-presidents, and other members of the Council of Ministers, but also to replace them with substitutes.[14] Institutionalization has thus reconcentrated power even though it has also resulted in a broader distribution of political elites in the present leadership.

Political Elites and Foreign Policies

Fidel's successful coalition-building, together with the favorable outcome of the institutionalization process, has affected Havana's foreign policy postures on several fronts. This strengthened power base at home has evidently emboldened Fidel to embark upon new foreign policy ventures toward Latin America, the Third World, and Washington since 1973. Additionally, the very diversity in the makeup of Cuba's new ruling coalition, along with Fidel's resurgence, now makes Cuba's foreign policies far more complex than was the case before or immediately after 1970.

Diversity and complexity do not necessarily mean that there is intense inter-elite conflict or an absence of consensus within the regime. On the contrary, the Cuban leadership of the 1970s appears to enjoy a basic agreement on such major foreign policy goals as maintaining Cuba's independence from the United States; assuring adequate levels of Soviet economic and military support while minimizing Cuba's client-state relationship; acquiring trade, advanced technology, and training from capitalist countries; and forging strong links with the Third World.[15] But different elites are likely to emphasize some goals over others or to favor a particular strategic line for the attainment of a goal. Accordingly, I shall argue below that three foreign policy tendencies emerged in Cuba after the early 1970s which generally reflect the basic policy interests, mentality, or organizational mission of the major elite actors within the new ruling coalition. Further, I will contend that two of these tendencies—those associated with Fidel, and with Raúl and the military—have now become predominant owing to the highly favorable outcomes of Cuba's military victory in Angola. The internal elite composition has affected foreign policy outcomes, but the success or failure of the latter has also had a major effect on the final balance of elite forces within the regime.

Foreign Policy Tendencies

Three foreign policy tendencies can be identified in the new ruling coalition. These are (1) the pragmatic economic tendency (Rodríguez), the revolutionary political tendency (Fidel), and (3) the military mission tendency (Raúl-MINFAR).

The Pragmatic Economic Tendency. The impulse toward greater pragmatism on the economic, political, and diplomatic fronts reflects the new influence of the civilian technocratic and managerial elites. It also stems from the greater Soviet involvement in Cuban affairs since 1970 which, in turn, has reinforced the position of the more pragmatic leadership within Cuba. This group

18

EDWARD GONZALEZ

is led by Carlos Rafael Rodríguez, whose continued prominence was confirmed
by his selection for the vice-presidency of both the Council of State and Council
of Ministers in late 1976. His allies, as in the past, include Vice-President
Osvaldo Dorticós, Foreign Trade Minister Marcelo Fernández, Sugar Industry
Minister Marcos Lage, Hector Rodríguez as head of the State Committee for
Economic Collaboration, as well as other specialists in charge of agencies dealing with technical, financial, or economic matters. These pragmatists, in turn,
tend to find support among the "old Communists" from the PSP who have risen
in influence within recent years. As befits their role specialization, the pragmatists attach highest importance to the primacy of economics. Consequently,
they emphasize the need to promote Cuba's rapid and sustained economic development through rational methods of socialist planning, cost accounting, and
financing at home, and by greater trade and technological ties with the advanced
countries of the socialist and nonsocialist worlds.

In this respect, the pragmatic leadership is painfully aware of Cuba's underdevelopment and its dependence on the more advanced countries for continuing
modernization of her economy. In September 1974, for instance, Dorticós
lamented Cuba's "scientific and technological poverty" which could be overcome only through the importation of what he termed capital-intensive "vanguard technology" for the modernization of Cuban agriculture and industry.[16]
Similarly, Cuba had to expand its ties with advanced capitalist countries because,
according to Rodríguez in early 1975, "a whole range of technologies is not yet
available in the socialist camp."[17] Indeed, the cruel dilemma of global inter-
dependence confronting Cuba and other underdeveloped countries was strikingly
put forth by Rodríguez at the FAO World Food Conference in November 1974.
Rising oil prices, he observed, threatened to plunge the capitalist countries into a
catastrophic economic crisis which would confirm the Marxist prophecy regarding the ultimate collapse of capitalism. Nevertheless, Rodríguez flatly rejected
the advisability of this development because such a catastrophe would involve
"the risk of a prolonged period of backwardness for the peoples struggling for
development. Therefore, we cannot declare ourselves in favor of such a dooms-
day solution to the economic and social contradictions. . . . This is why we are
willing to work with all those who are trying to avert such a world economic
crisis."[18]

The pragmatic tendency, therefore, proceeds from a set of economic assumptions and strategems that partially explains Cuba's foreign policies in recent
years. These are that (1) Cuba remains economically and technologically underdeveloped; (2) this underdevelopment must be attacked by exploiting Cuba's
economic and technological dependence on the more advanced socialist and
capitalist countries; and (3) the resulting dependency can be eased in the short run
by the diversification of Cuba's economic ties and in the long run by ultimately
attaining higher levels of development. Since 1970, with respect to socialist
countries, Cuba has gained admittance to COMECON (July 1972), signed new
and highly favorable long-term economic agreements with the Soviet Union

(December 1972), obtained a new trade, economic, and technical agreement for 1976-1980 with the Soviets (April 1975), and coordinated a new five-year plan with that of the Soviet Union for 1976-1980. But to balance this heightened dependence on the USSR, Rodríguez also began to negotiate new trade agreements, long-term credits, and investment contracts with numerous non-socialist countries after the early 1970s, when the booming sugar prices of 1974 and early 1975 greatly strengthened his negotiating position with western countries.[19] Rodríguez also appears to have been the driving force in seeking a new opening with the United States in hopes of securing elusive U.S. agricultural equipment, technology, computer facilities, among other items.

The Revolutionary Political Tendency. The second tendency impels Cuba toward the return to more revolutionary postures in its foreign policies. This more combative line bears the personal stamp of Fidel and is backed by veteran Fidelista revolutionaries and close associates who occupy top leadership posts in the party, state, and government. It stems in large measure from Fidel's greatly strengthened political power base at home after 1973. But is also derives from his perception that detente between the superpowers offered Cuba heightened security and that U.S. imperialism was increasingly weak and defensive as evidenced by the war in Vietnam, Third World solidarity, and especially the international capitalist crisis of the mid-1970s. In Fidel's eyes, therefore, "capitalism and imperialism are living in a crisis hour. . . . For many, the capitalist world is on the brink of the most serious disaster it has confronted since the somber periods of the great depression of the '30s."[20] Both his success in gaining control over the institutionalization process and his perception of the shift in the global balance emboldened him to take more aggressive foreign policy postures on several fronts.

Fidel's assertive policy of confrontation and defiance is aimed at U.S. imperialism and, as such, it is reminiscent of the Fidelista line of the 1960s. But the old line also appears to have been tempered by realization of Cuba's continued underdevelopment and dependence and by concern that post-1970 economic recovery could be jeopardized by adventuristic policies. Thus, Fidel evidently has been inclined to apply his revolutionary line somewhat more selectively than in the 1960s in an effort to reconcile it with the island's economic, technological, and political needs. Hence, he apparently favored the development of closer ties with Western Europe and Latin America and overtures toward Washington in 1974-1975.

While Fidel is concerned with Cuba's underdevelopment and dependence, he is far more ideological and political than are the pragmatists. The imperialism of the United States is to be combated through active solidarity with the Third World and by espousing Latin America's unity and separateness from the United States. Hence his affirmation in September 1974: "The United States on one side and the peoples of Latin America and the Caribbean on the other side form two worlds as different as Europe and Africa: they do not belong in the same community."[21] Within Cuba, in the meantime, the purity of the Revolution will be maintained by combating the foreign viruses of "ideological diversionism," represented by the non-Soviet Left, and "consumerism," represented by capitalist societies.

Above all, the Fidelista mentality is highly political in its world outlook and modus operandi: As in the past, Fidel is most concerned with disparities in power, and he is the master practitioner of leverage politics for redressing or reversing adverse power relationships. Unlike the pragmatists who emphasize economic strategies, Fidel employs leverage politics as the principal means by which his otherwise vulnerable, dependent island is to be made secure and great. Its extreme vulnerability to the United States, for example, is offset through long-standing protective and supportive ties with the Soviet Union. But more recently, Fidel sought to augment the island's limited power capabilities through closer association with the Third World. In particular, in September 1974, he called for the unity of the OPEC countries with the less developed world as the primary means by which to ease dependency and fundamentally alter the global balance in favor of the Third World: "If the petroleum countries stand united and firm, if they do not allow themselves to be intimidated by the threats of the United States, and if they seek the alliance of the remainder of the underdeveloped world, the industrialized capitalist countries will have to accept as inevitable the disappearance of the shameful and unjust terms of trade that they have imposed on our peoples."[22] Later he warned that "any playing around with imperialism by any Arab country is dangerous, because political opportunism cannot replace frank, open, and revolutionary diplomacy—and sometimes it leads to flagrant betrayal."[23] Even before the large-scale incursion into Angola, Cuba was extending military and economic assistance to Middle Eastern and African nations in an apparent attempt to solidify Cuba's Third World links and thereby augment its global influence (see chapter 3 of this volume).

Latin America provided another region in which Cuba could generate international leverage. In early 1975, Fidel observed that there were fundamental changes in Latin America toward "greater independence with respect to the United States, greater national awareness . . . and a greater understanding of what imperialism is and a willingness to confront that imperialism."[24] In fact, Cuba had already moved to capitalize on these trends through increased economic, political, and military relations with a number of countries. The Caribbean became the principal arena for considerable Cuban activity and the region in which Cuba began to emerge as a second-order power. Havana cultivated close ties with the regimes of Torrijos in Panama, Burnham in Guyana, and especially with the Manley government in Jamaica. There, the Cubans began training members of the prime minister's palace guard, stepped up Cuban economic and technical assistance, and otherwise cemented close political ties with the Manley government (see chapter 6 of this volume). Elsewhere, Cuba greatly improved its relations with Mexico, as demonstrated by President Echeverría's visit to Havana in August 1975, followed by Raúl Castro's return visit to Mexico City in September. Cuba had meanwhile reestablished diplomatic relations with Venezuela

in 1974 and subsequently sought closer relations with the Andrés Pérez government as the latter became more assertively nationalist in its foreign policy postures. Further affirming its Caribbean presence, Cuba joined the Latin American
Economic System (SELA), cosponsored by Mexico and Venezuela in October
1975, and became an active member of the Caribbean Multinational Shipping
Enterprise (NAMUCAR). Finally, Cuba has provided active support for the
Puerto Rican independence movement in recent years, culminating in the sponsorship of a proindependence conference in Havana in September 1975. Such
support, in turn, could provide the Castro regime with additional leverage in the
event of future negotiations with Washington. (For further discussion of these
activities, see chapters 5 and 14 of this volume.)

The Military Mission Tendency. The third foreign policy tendency is
headed by Raúl Castro and other MINFAR officers and involves the external,
professional role of the Cuban armed forces. To a large degree, this tendency
also is a product of a more institutionalized order. Not only has the FAR emerged
as a major political actor within the Cuban regime, as suggested by the results of
the party congress and the makeup of the new Council of State and Council of
Ministers, but the institutionalization process has strengthened the capacity of the
civilian sector to carry out administrative and economic activities that were
previously assigned to the Cuban army because of its higher level of professional
competence, technical training, and organizational skills. The strengthening of
the civilian sector, combined with lowered perceptions of external threat from the
United States, meant that the Cuban army could be pared down to a highly
professional standing force of about one hundred and twenty thousand and devote
itself primarily to military tasks beginning in the early 1970s. In the process, the
army has expanded its traditional military mission from one of internal defense of
the homeland, to a new external mission in support of Cuba's foreign policy objectives. Indeed, the high levels of professionalization and institutionalization attained by the army may have impelled it to search out and identify new organizational missions abroad.[25]

In Latin America, the role of the FAR has been confined to the establishment of professional military-to-military relations with the friendly governments
of Peru, Panama, Guyana, Trinidad and Tobago, Jamaica, and Mexico. Even so,
Havana held out the prospects of rendering conventional military assistance to
Latin American governments beginning in the early 1970s. To military delegations from the above named countries, Fidel declared that "the experiences of
our armed forces are at the service of the progressive governments and peoples of
this continent."[26] Meanwhile, Cuban military units were already being sent
overseas to the Middle East and Africa beginning in the early 1970s.

During military exercises in November 1974, Fidel could proclaim with
some justification that the Cuban armed forces were at the service "of our sister
peoples of Latin America in their struggle against imperialism, and we are on the
side of the peoples who face up to imperialism in all parts of the world."[27] The
Cuban armed forces worked to improve their combat readiness and develop their

offensive capabilities by engaging in new mobile defense operations during military exercises in 1974 and 1975. As will be seen below, the end result of the army's expanded military mission and capabilities was the embarcation of an estimated one thousand Cuban soldiers to Angola by mid-September 1975. Later, with the rapid buildup of the Cuban military presence to over fourteen thousand combat troops, the FAR became the decisive factor in the victory of the Popular Movement for the Liberation of Angola (MPLA). (See chapter 4 of this volume.)

Policy Contradictions

The three foreign policy tendencies described above presented contradictions in Cuban postures by the mid-1970s, and they imposed internal constraints on policy initiatives as well. To be sure, the revolutionary and military mission tendencies of Fidel and Raúl-MINFAR, respectively, tended to cohere and be mutually supportive. Still, Fidel's line of heightened confrontation with imperialism could come in conflict with the organizational interests of the FAR were the Cuban military to suffer serious reverses in one of its overseas operations. In any event, both stood in obvious contradiction to the pragmatic tendency aimed at broadening Cuba's economic, technical, and political ties with Western countries. As was illustrated by the so-called Carlos affair in Paris in mid-1975, both these more militant foreign policy tendencies could have undermined the Rodríguez line.[28] That they did not do so prior to Angola was due in large measure to Havana's success in divorcing its revolutionary and military postures in the Third World from its more pragmatic policies toward Latin America, Japan, Western Europe, and Canada.

The three elite tendencies imposed internal policy constraints, however. This was particularly true of any major Cuban effort to break the deadlock between Havana and Washington. As has been argued, the pragmatists would push for such a breakthrough. But even though it would provide undeniable economic and technological advantages for Cuba, the restoration of even limited ties with the United States might also entail costs unacceptable to the elites led by Fidel and Raúl. That such was in fact the case is illustrated by the outcome of the secret high-level talks held between the United States and Cuba during 1974 and 1975.

The round of talks were conducted quietly by U.S. and Cuban officials in Washington and New York on four occasions between November 1974 and November 1975.[29] Although initially exploratory, the talks soon led to a reduction in tension between the two countries. Secretary of State Kissinger declared on March 1, 1975, that the U.S. government saw "no virtue in perpetual antagonism" with Cuba, while Fidel later responded by describing Kissinger's statement as "positive" and went on to note that there had indeed been a lessening of tension. Moreover, each side followed with more substantive gestures. Cuba turned over a hijacker of an American plane and returned a $2 million ransom that had been seized in another hijacking. For its part, the U.S.

government voted for the removal of OAS sanctions against Cuba in July; and on September 23, Assistant Secretary of State William Rogers announced that the United States was "prepared to improve our relations with Cuba," and "to enter into a dialogue with Cuba." Within weeks of that announcement, however, Cuba was already deeply involved militarily in Angola. In the fourth and final session held in November 1975, Rogers registered strong U.S. opposition to the Cuban involvement. Nevertheless, he also urged the continuation of talks and proposed that Cubans be allowed to travel between the two countries for purposes of visiting relatives. According to Rogers, the Cubans never responded and the talks lapsed.

Conceivably, the Castro regime discontinued the talks because it calculated that further progress with the Ford administration was unlikely in an election year. Even so, the absence of a Cuban response suggests that the regime placed a higher and more immediate priority on Cuba's militant activities in the Third World than on the long-run and as yet uncertain prospects of resuming trade ties with the United States.[30] Such a policy priority, in turn, conformed to the new dominance of the Fidelista and Raulista elites. In late August 1975, prior to Cuba's large-scale military incursion, the foreign minister Raúl Roa, had stressed to the Conference of Nonaligned Nations in Lima, Peru, that Angola was crucial to the decolonization of southern Africa, and he urged the nonaligned nations to act "in whatever manner required."[31] The following month, Havana held a solidarity conference for the Puerto Rican independence movement, not-withstanding the considerable progress being made in the secret talks with State Department representatives. In any event, Cuba's ever increasing military incur-sion into Angola rendered a resumption of the talks virtually impossible. On December 20, 1975, President Ford declared that Cuba's action in Angola and Puerto Rico "destroys any opportunity for improvement of relations with the United States."[32] Fidel replied two days later at the party congress by announcing that "there never will be relations with the United States" if the "price" had to be Cuba's abandonment of its "solidarity" with anti-imperialist movements in the Third World.[33]

Angola and the Consolidation of Policy

The internal tension in Cuba's foreign policies in the mid-1970s was thus resolved by Cuba's large-scale military involvement in Angola. This is not the place for a detailed analysis of how and why Cuba committed itself deeply to the Marxist-oriented MPLA in Angola, all the more so because of the incomplete information surrounding the Cuban involvement. Three points need to be em-phasized, however.[34] First, the balance of evidence available indicates that Cuba was not acting as a Soviet surrogate in Angola. Rather, the Cubans were pursuing their own Third World interests which coincided with, and were supportive of, Soviet interests in southern Africa. Second, the available evidence again suggests that the massive Cuban military buildup in Angola that began in late October was not the product of a grand design on the part of Havana or Moscow. Instead, it stemmed from a hurried tactical response to a deteriorating military situation on the Angolan battlefields and from strong political and organizational considerations within the Cuban regime. And third, the triumphant outcome of the Angolan venture greatly strengthened the revolutionary and military mission tendencies within the regime, and above all the leadership position of Fidel Castro.

There were three stages to the Cuban military intervention in Angola during the latter part of 1975, with the Cubans evidently becoming more deeply drawn into the Angolan struggle than even they had originally anticipated. In the first stage, Havana responded to MPLA requests for assistance by dispatching the first 1,000 troops by mid-September, thereby augmenting the 250 Cuban military advisors already in Angola. What triggered the second and larger stage was the sudden South African incursion into southern Angola beginning on October 23, which was followed a few days later by the combined Zairian and FNLA (National Front for the Liberation of Angola) offensive in the north. Both of these movements threatened to overrun the MPLA forces and the first contingent of Cuban troops. The sudden military deterioration thus endangered the vital interests of the Revolutionary Armed Forces, the most powerful institution within the Cuban regime. Politically as well as militarily it was imperative for Fidel and the Cuban leadership to respond to this crisis. Accordingly, reinforcements were hurriedly airlifted across the Atlantic in Soviet and Cuban transport planes leaving Cuba three times a day; some two thousand to three thousand additional Cuban troops had arrived in Angola by the time of its independence on November 11. The third and final stage commenced soon afterward when the battlefield situation began to shift in favor of the FAR and MPLA forces. It was then, according to Fidel, that "Cuba sent the men and weapons necessary to win that struggle."[35] With stepped-up Soviet logistical support, the Cuban military buildup was rapidly increased to some seven thousand troops by the end of December 1975, rising to an estimated fourteen thousand or more by the following February when the war was concluded.

Within Cuba, the immediate and long-run effect of the Angolan triumph has been the strengthening of the revolutionary and military mission tendencies. Conversely, the pragmatic elite was weakened not only by the African development, but also by the precipitous drop in world sugar prices to under eight cents per pound by fall 1976, which in turn greatly restricted Cuba's capacity to trade with the non-Communist countries. Indeed, the apparent demotion of Dorticós from president to a vice-presidency in the Council of Ministers but not in the Council of State (see table 1.4) may have stemmed from his failure to prevent the sharp drop in Japanese purchases of Cuban sugar in 1976.[36] In any event, evidence for these conclusions can be found in the personnel of the current Cuban leadership: Save for Rodríguez and Dorticós, the technocratic and managerial elites remain underrepresented in the new Council of State, the Executive Committee of the new Council of Ministers, and the PCC Political Bureau. In contrast, veteran Fidelistas, Raulistas, or ex-MINFAR officers dominate the last two bodies. A year after Angola, moreover, two of the MINFAR generals who played key roles in the Angolan operation were appointed to the prestigious Council of State (Senén Casas and Abelardo Colomé).

Further suggestive of the heightened importance of the armed forces in the aftermath of Angola was the establishment of a new international ranking system for members of the FAR. It replaced a system which had been in existence for only three years and which itself had first established the rank of general (instead of major). Made effective on December 2, 1976, the new system promoted the top FAR-MINFAR officers to army general (Raúl Castro), army corps general, division general (Senén Casas, Abelardo Colomé, and others), and brigadier general, thereby replacing the previous two-tier system of lieutenant general and major general.[37] But the awards rendered to the FAR were by no means only symbolic. In his report to the PCC congress in December 1975, Fidel had declared that in the years ahead the FAR would be supplied with a "considerable amount of even more modern combat equipment characterized by increased firepower, maneuverability, and automation."[38] Scarcely a year later, on the occasion of the twentieth anniversary of the FAR, Army General Raúl Castro confirmed that the Cuban armed forces were being outfitted with "new and modern arms which will be viewed by our people for the first time."[39] Cuba's active promotion of "proletarian internationalism," its military success in establishing a new Marxist regime in southern Africa, and its instrumental role in furthering Soviet as well as Cuban objectives in Africa thus appear to have been rewarded militarily by Moscow.

Most of all, the Cuban triumph in Angola further strengthened Fidel's leadership position, as shown by political developments at home, and consolidated the revolutionary tendency as the predominant force in Cuban foreign policy. To begin with, the successful Angolan incursion not only resulted in increased international prestige and leverage for the Cuban leader in Third World circles. Even more importantly, it produced tangible rewards from the Soviet Union as Cuba proved itself to be an invaluable ally and asset in the promotion of Soviet global objectives. In addition to extending new military assistance, the USSR concluded a new five-year agreement with Cuba for 1976–1980 which appears extremely advantageous for Havana. Signed on April 14, 1976, the new agreement calls for a 250 percent increase in Soviet-Cuban economic and technical collaboration over the previous five-year period, and it provides for the installation of Cuba's first nuclear power plant and steel mill and the indexing of Soviet crude oil prices with Cuban sugar prices. By means of Angola, therefore, Fidel had simultaneously achieved two fundamental objectives in Cuba's relations with the USSR: He had cleared Havana's debts to the Soviet Union while recommitting the latter to still higher levels of economic, technological, and military support.

Elsewhere, too, the revolutionary tendency appeared on the ascendancy, closely supported by the military mission tendency. As before, Havana pursued aggressively its policy of alliance with Jamaica and other small states in the Caribbean in an apparent effort to consolidate Cuba's position as a second-order power within the region. On October 15, 1976, Fidel cancelled the 1973 anti-hijacking agreement with the United States. He did so on grounds of alleged complicity by the Central Intelligence Agency in the act of terrorism by Cuban exiles which had caused the death of seventy-three persons, fifty-seven of them Cubans, on a civilian airliner earlier in the month, charging that "there can be no form of collaboration between the aggressor country and the country under attack." In December 1976, he again called on the oil producers to unite with the less developed countries of the Third World in "one single front in the common struggle against their historical exploiters." Three months later, in March 1977, he embarked upon an extended tour of the Middle East, North Africa, and the "front-line" black African states around Rhodesia, overlapping the visit of Soviet President Nikolai V. Podgorny. Both Fidel and the Soviet leader pledged military aid for the guerrilla war against the white regime in Rhodesia.[40] Elsewhere, a large contingent of Cuban military advisors was reported in early summer to have been dispatched to aid the Marxist regime in Ethiopia.[41] These and other developments seemed to testify to the dominance of the revolutionary and military mission tendencies and to Cuba's growing assertiveness and global reach.

Future Policy Inclinations

Given the present alignments and policy inclinations of the different elites, and projecting from Cuba's new global position, what directions are the regime's foreign policies likely to take in the future? Why has the regime moved with such swiftness toward improved relations with the United States if the revolutionary and military mission tendencies are indeed dominant? Are there, in fact, other factors that might impel the dominant elites to adopt policies they would not otherwise accept? I shall address these questions by first focusing on what are likely to be Cuba's policy inclinations toward the United States, the Soviet Union, and the Third World, and conclude by exploring how various external factors might effect or alter Cuban behavior.

Limited Ties with the United States

With the advent of the Carter administration, considerable headway was soon made toward improved relations between the two countries. On April 28, 1977, following talks in New York and Havana, the Cuban and U.S. governments announced they had reached an agreement governing commercial fishing boundaries and reciprocal fishing rights under the 200-mile fisheries zones set earlier in the year by each country. Next, on June 3, both governments announced agreement on establishing "interests sections" in each other's capitals, with the exchange of diplomats to take place the following September. The Castro regime also embarked upon what seemed to be a major public relations campaign in the United States: U.S. tourism was being encouraged, U.S. business delegations were being invited in considerable number, and U.S. television and newspapers were being given access to Cuba and its leaders on a scale unprecedented since 1959. Behind these moves appears to be economic necessity: Cuba has experienced depressed sugar prices and a slowed-down economy, with Cuban officials now anticipating a 4 percent annual growth rate instead of the 6 percent earlier scheduled for the balance of the 1970s.

Despite the thaw and Cuba's economic needs, Fidel himself cautioned in a television interview with Barbara Walters that the establishment of full diplomatic relations could be long in coming: "I don't even think they could be reestablished during Carter's term. Maybe in Carter's second term, between 1980 and 1984." [42] In considerable measure, of course, progress toward full diplomatic relations is contingent upon the U.S. position. Still, there are at least three major factors which incline the Cuban leadership itself toward only limited, selective ties with United States, principally of an economic nature, and possibly no further movement beyond agreement on "interests sections" if the U.S. government ultimately demands major political concessions from the Castro regime.

First, by virtue of their primary objectives and organizational interests, the dominant Fidelista and Raulista-MINFAR elites are not likely to advocate other than limited or instrumental ties with the United States that serve Cuba's developmental needs. Because Fidel is concerned with greatly enhancing Cuba's international status and leverage with the Soviet Union and the Third World, he would be willing to accept improved relations as long as Washington does not require that Cuba cease those global activities which provide it with international leverage. Similarly, the other dominant elite tendency associated with Raúl and MINFAR is concerned with expanding the military proficiency, prestige, and mission of the Cuban armed forces. Again, such organizational interests can only be advanced if the quid pro quos with the United States does not call for Cuba to restrict its military activities abroad. Thus, the very interest structure of the dominant leadership may well limit the extent to which relations can be significantly improved.

A second factor limiting relations is Cuba's depressed trade position and resulting weak bargaining position vis-à-vis the United States: Cuba is in much greater economic need of the United States than the United States is of Cuba. Fidel himself conceded in a lengthy interview with Benjamin C. Bradlee, executive editor of the *Washington Post,* in late February 1977, that Cuba would benefit enormously from the resumption of direct trade ties with the United States. [43] In a discussion with a U.S. newspaperman four months later, Foreign Trade Minister Marcelo Fernández drew up a shopping list of manufactured goods and commodities that Cuba wants to purchase directly from the United States. [44] But the problem is that the glut of sugar has depressed the world market price from a high of sixty-six cents per pound in November 1973, to a level of around seven cents per pound in June 1977. This, together with the state of the Cuban economy and limited size of its internal market, gives Havana little economic leverage for bargaining with Washington regarding long-term credits and access to the U.S. sugar market. The latter is especially essential if Cuba is to

EDWARD GONZALEZ

purchase U.S. goods, and it may well be imperative for Cuba's economy owing to expected surpluses of Cuban sugar—which could amount to well over one million tons by the late 1970s—following scheduled deliveries to the Soviet Union and to other more limited socialist and nonsocialist markets.

To strengthen Cuba's bargaining position, therefore, such technocrats as Vice-President Rodríguez, Foreign Trade Minster Fernández, and Hector Rodríguez, head of the State Committee for Economic Collaboration, have sought to enlist allies among influential business circles in the United States with the apparent aim of pressing for the removal of the U.S. trade embargo. To this end, they have held out prospects of large-scale U.S. sales in the Cuban market if two-way trade is restored. In the aforementioned interview, for instance, Fernández observed that 30 percent of Cuba's total trade volume of $6 billion per annum was now accounted for by Japan and Western Europe and that this $1.8 to $2 billion market ought to be enticing to the United States. But he also made clear that the United States will have to compete with other foreign suppliers and will obtain only a portion of that market. According to Hector Rodríguez, furthermore, there will be other than economic reasons for limiting the U.S. share of the Cuban trade volume: "Even if we go back to trading with the United States, we could not abandon our trade with the socialist countries and the other nations of the Western world. There are other reasons, including purely moral consideration, because it would be a betrayal of friendly countries who have stood by us in very difficult times."[45]

Rather than possessing substantial economic bargaining power, Cuba's real and potential leverage is ultimately political. Most importantly, it stems precisely from those global activities—in Puerto Rico, the Caribbean, and Africa—which the U.S. Congress may insist Cuba relinquish in exchange for trade normalization. In view of the breakdown of the 1974–1975 secret talks, however, it does not appear that leading elements within the Cuban leadership are prepared to forego those activities from which the regime gains its international leverage.

The third factor working to limit relations is the Cuban perception of current and long-range global trends. It is quite clear that the Cuban leaders, particularly Fidel, view U.S. imperialism as weakening, and the global balance as radically shifting, in favor of the Soviet-aligned countries and the Third World.[46] The basis for such a perception came first with Hanoi's victory in Vietnam, the success of OPEC, and the international economic crisis in the capitalist world. But more recently, the stunning Cuban-Soviet success in Angola, the emergence of new Marxist regimes in Africa, and the Third World solidarity of the more radical nationalist regimes in North Africa and the Middle East all provide further confirmation of the changing correlation of international forces. In the words of Antonio Pérez Herrero, member of the PCC Secretariat, "The imperialists can no longer, as in the past, send out armed expeditions with impunity to crush peoples' rebellions in any part of the world."[47] For Fidel, Raúl, and their followers, Cuba's future does not lie with the United States, but with the Third World and the Soviet Union. On March 21, 1977, at the conclusion of his four-day visit to Tanzania, Fidel ruled our Cuba's acceptance of U.S. conditions for improving relations and instead reaffirmed his own:

> They [the United States] say we must stop giving our solidarity to the revolutionary movement in Africa. We feel *these issues are not matters for negotiation. . . .*
>
> We haven't organized subversion against or sent mercenary invaders to the United States. They are the ones who must stop this kind of operation, they must lift the blockade and this kind of activity against Cuba. These matters must be the political basis for any negotiations. *We will not make any concessions on matters of principle in order to improve relations with the United States.* [48]

Stripped of its rhetoric, Fidel's statement again suggests that his regime will concede to the United States only those issues that do not affect Cuba's leverage in Africa and elsewhere in the world. In bargaining with Washington, Cuba may be willing to release U.S. prisoners, to allow increased travel between the two countries by Cubans and Cuban exiles, and to agree to long-run compensation for the $1.8 billion in nationalized U.S. properties, in exchange for access to the U.S. sugar market and long-term credits with which to purchase U.S. goods. Insistence by Congress or the White House on a different mix of *concessions* which would diminish Cuba's heightened global role is likely to be rejected however, as Fidel indicated on several occasions during and following his African journey. [49]

Closer Alliance with the Soviet Union

In contrast to its limited dealings with the United States, Cuba can be expected to move into an even closer relationship with the Soviet Union through the foreseeable future. In part, this heightened integration stems from Cuba's increased economic dependence on the Soviet Union under the new five-year trade and economic-technical agreements which call for a 250 percent increase in economic cooperation between the two countries in 1976–1980. Soviet preferential pricing for Cuban sugar (thirty cents per pound) and Soviet crude oil (an estimated six dollars per barrel) also acts as a tether on the Cuban economy, making it disadvantageous for Cuba to shift its trade to other countries. Another factor contributing to closer political ties lies in the Cuban leadership's reading of international developments, including the growing might of the Soviet Union vis-à-vis the United States.

There is still another, equally important political reason for Cuba to develop an even closer relationship with the USSR: Cuba's standing within the Soviet bloc and its international leverage with the Soviet Union itself have been immeasurably strengthened since Angola. Both have been attained by Cuba's military prowess in advancing Soviet political and possibly strategic interests in Africa. Fidel Castro received a prolonged standing ovation—led by Brezhnev and other Soviet leaders—at the twenty-fifth congress of the Soviet party held in

February 1976 at the conclusion of the Angolan war, while heightened military and economic support to Cuba followed. In its relationship with the Soviet Union, therefore, Cuba possesses a status and leverage capability that it cannot obtain with other powers: in brief, Cuba can now command high levels of Soviet and Soviet bloc support for its services as a political and military paladin in the cause of "proletarian internationalism."[50] The role of paladin, rather than surrogate, denotes Cuba's autonomy and her value as a separate global actor in the Soviet-Cuban relationship.

Cuba's value as an ally of the USSR—and her leverage capabilities—are likely to increase further if the Soviet Union embarks upon a harder, more expansive foreign policy in the new post détente era as suggested by stepped-up Soviet interest in Africa.[51] Such an international role, in turn, further strengthens the revolutionary and military mission tendencies within the Cuban leadership, with both developing a strong political and organizational interest in exploiting the new Cuban-Soviet relationship.

Meanwhile, Fidel's month-long African tour in March 1977 already gives some evidence of the kind of political service he can render for the Soviets. He visited both Ethiopia and Somalia, two East African states where the Soviets have military support facilities, in what some observers believe was a Moscow-inspired effort to resolve the bitter conflict between the two countries. In Somalia he called for greater unity: "The revolutionary peoples must struggle together, the revolutionary peoples, who for centuries were subjected to colonial oppression, must strengthen our alliance with the world revolutionary movement, the socialist countries and especially with the great Soviet Union. . . . The Soviet people is the firmest and most loyal ally of those of us who struggle for independence and revolution, the firmest and most loyal ally of Somalia and Cuba and of other independent countries."[52] Following his African tour, Fidel arrived in Moscow in early April, reportedly for high-level strategy sessions concerning ways in which Cuba and the Soviet Union could best aid black nationalists fighting white minority governments in southern Africa. The importance of his visit was underscored by the presence of the top Soviet leadership upon his arrival at the airport—Party Secretary Brezhnev, Premier Alexei Kosygin, President Nikolai Podgorny, and Foreign Minister Andrei Gromyko. The Cuban leader had indeed achieved heightened international stature not only in the Third World but in the Soviet Union as well.

Concentrated Involvement in Africa and the Caribbean

While working in tandem with the Soviets, the Cuban leadership will also concentrate its attention on the Third World for its own ends. As explained earlier, the Third World offers the revolutionary tendency of Fidel an arena in which to seek additional international leverage through concerted action with other nationalist regimes and through his role as a Third World spokesman and champion of revolutionary solidarity.[53] By the same token, the Third World offers the military mission tendency of Raúl-MINFAR opportunities in which to engage in further missions abroad. Perhaps more so than in the past, however, Cuba's Third World activities are likely to be concentrated in Africa and the Caribbean, with a lower priority being assigned to the (non-Caribbean) Latin American states.

There are several reasons for a heightening of Cuban involvement in Africa in the near future and over the long run. To begin with, Cuba has gained a political as well as military presence in Africa that is unmatched elsewhere in the Third World and that could increase in momentum in the future. Cuba's military role in Angola, of course, is largely responsible, but there are still other factors working for an increase in the Cuban presence in Africa. Among these are the new Marxist and radical nationalist regimes on the continent that are receptive to Castro's Cuba. (The Marxist regimes are Angola, Congo, Ethiopia, Guinea-Bissau, and Somalia; Algeria and Libya are radical nationalist.) Conversely, there are the white minority governments of Rhodesia and South Africa which serve to legitimize Cuba's involvement in African affairs. In addition, Africa is likely to attract Cuba because of the region's rising importance to the USSR, which will thus assure high levels of Soviet economic and military backing for Cuban activities. Indeed, Cuba's growing links to Africa will not be exclusively military in nature, but will also involve—as they now do—economic and technical assistance. Finally, Africa presents the Cubans with a target of opportunity to which the United States remains largely uncommitted, thereby minimizing the risks of a direct Cuban–United States confrontation in those instances where Cuba extends its military presence. In Fidel's eyes, therefore, "Africa is the weakest link in the imperialist chain today.... There are excellent perspectives there for going directly from tribalism to socialism."[54]

Fidel demonstrated Africa's increased importance for Cuban foreign policy by his journey in March 1977 to Algeria, Libya, Somalia, Ethiopia, Tanzania, Mozambique, and Angola, along with a side trip to the People's Democratic Republic of Yemen. In Tanzania, the Cuban leader categorically denied the Zairian government's charges that Cuban personnel were aiding the Angolan-based Katangan rebels in their invasion of Zaire. He also insisted that in the struggle by the black nationalist forces against white rule in Namibia and Zimbabwe (Rhodesia), "the greatest part of solidarity must come from the African peoples, from the so-called front-line countries." Still, he pledged Cuban support for these struggles: "We sympathize with them and we will support them as we have done with other revolutionaries."[55] Later, in Mozambique and then in Angola, new cooperation agreements were signed by which Cuba will step up its levels of economic, technical, and other aid to these countries. Finally, by June 1977, fifty or possibly as many as four hundred Cuban military advisors were in Ethiopia to help train the regular army and people's militia of the Marxist regime struggling against the Eritrean independence movement and other guerrilla armies.[56]

While Africa looms as the major theater of Cuban military, economic, and technical activity in the Third World, the Caribbean region most certainly will continue to be a high priority region for the Cuban leadership. Not only is the region of intrinsic importance, but Cuba has already established its presence as a second-order power and has taken an active role in regional associations such as NAMUCAR and the Caribbean Development and Cooperation Committee. She has found receptive allies in Guyana and especially Jamaica. Still, Cuba's involvement is likely to be more circumspect in the Caribbean than in Africa. Not only is the Caribbean a region of critical importance to the United States, but also the Soviet Union can be expected to act as a further external constraint on Cuban activities in order to avoid being drawn into a confrontation with the United States. Hence with the exception of Puerto Rico, Cuba's Caribbean activities most likely will continue to take the form of government-to-government programs and multilateral ventures for regional development. Additional cooperative programs include the possibility that the Cuban leadership will render conventional military assistance programs to Caribbean governments if such aid is requested. Therefore all three foreign policy tendencies—not only the revolutionary and military mission, but also the pragmatic tendency—tend to cohere in the Caribbean.

What of the rest of Latin America? Here, the prospects for increased Cuban influence and leverage seem to have diminished since the mid-1970s. While maintaining a nationalist posture, the new military regime of President Morales Bermúdez in Peru is far less strident in its policy toward the United States than was the Velasco regime; the new regime has also veered to the right in its domestic affairs. Mexico has similarly become more conservative and favorable to the United States under its new president, José López Portillo, in marked contrast to the last years of the Echeverría administration. With the reorientation of these former potential allies, and with similar developments in post-Perón Argentina, the Cuban leadership is likely to relegate most of Latin America to lesser importance in its foreign policy calculations.[57]

Constraints on Cuban Inclinations

The foregoing analysis posits the probable policy inclinations or preferences of the Cuban regime. There could well be external constraints upon Havana, however, or other considerations that might force alterations in behavior. For instance, Angola generated very high returns for Cuba. But the likelihood that the Angolan situation with all its peculiarities can be replicated elsewhere in Africa would appear slim indeed, if only because the United States, Western Europe, and particularly the more moderate African states will seek to forestall the expansion of the Cuban presence, as was demonstrated by the Zairian situation. Even more critical, Cuba's international leverage as a paladin would decline appreciably if the Soviet Union turns out to be more a reactive or status quo power than an expansionist one.[58]

There are also intrinsic limits to Cuba's military capabilities owing to its size and the demands of the Cuban economy for human and material resources (see chapter 3 of this volume). Despite the level of professionalization and the combat experience of FAR, therefore, Cuba may find it difficult over the long run to sustain the role of an international paladin in the Third World. Further operations of the Angolan type, with heavy losses to Cuban troops, could conceivably strain the relationship between Cuba's military and political leadership. Finally, the needs of the Cuban economy, together with Soviet desires to ease the burden of assistance to Cuba, could strengthen the hand of the more pragmatic, technocratic leadership in pushing for an accommodation with the United States that would ensure two-way trade. Were this to occur, the Castro regime might be constrained from embarking upon new global activities that would jeopardize these trade ties.

Still, there are also constraints that could prevent Cuba from disengaging from its paladin role and its close alliance with the Soviets and from moving toward more normalized relations with the United States. In respect to the latter, economic, social, and cultural ties with the United States, unless closely controlled, could pose a subversive threat to Cuba's revolutionary society. Most importantly, the very structure and logic of Cuba's international position may force it to maintain its distance from the United States and to enhance its pro-Soviet and paladin role; through the latter, Cuba can obtain far more in terms of concrete economic and military ties, and in international status and leverage, than it ever can through the United States. Cuba's value to the Soviet Union, and its prospective returns, are likely to be higher still if Moscow embarks upon an even more activist global policy in the future. Hence, President Carter's announced intention to ''aggressively challenge'' Soviet influence in Cuba (and elsewhere in the Communist world) will probably make little headway owing to the high convergence of Cuban and Soviet interests at present and possibly over the long run.

NOTES

I wish to express my appreciation to Dana Sweet, who graciously gave of his time to provide information on the Cuban armed forces, and to David Ronfeldt for this collaborative efforts on earlier studies which have provided a partial basis for the one presented here. I would also like to thank Isidro Sepulveda and Melanie Speir for their research assistance and Teddi Malonado and Becky Herrera for their careful typing of the manuscript.

1. See the data presented in chapter 9 of this volume.

2. *Los Angeles Times,* June 4, 1977, pp. 1, 7.

3. I have explored these divisions in earlier studies. These are Edward Gonzalez, Luigi R. Einaudi, Nathan Leites, Richard Maullin, and David Ronfeldt, *Divisions Within the Cuban Leadership: Their Implications for Cuba and the United States* (Santa Monica: The Rand Corporation, 1971, for internal distribution only); and my later study, ''Political Succession in Cuba,'' *Studies in Comparative Communism,* Spring–Summer 1976, pp. 80–107, reprinted in Irving Louis Horowitz, ed., *Cuban Communism,* 3d ed. (New Brunswick: Transaction Books, 1977), pp. 537–69. An opposing view, relying primarily on quantitative data, is presented by William M. LeoGrande,

34

"Continuity and Change in the Cuban Political Elite, 1959-1976" (Paper presented at the Annual Meeting of the New York State Political Science Association, Albany, New York, March 26, 1977). I have not employed the term "political elites" or "elites" perjoratively, nor do I use it to refer to a particular socioeconomic strata. Rather, as applied to Cuba as well as to other communist societies, it refers to those individuals or groups who, by virtue of their authority, office, skills, functions, and control over the means of coercion and production, wield political power and directly affect policy making at the highest levels.

4. On these and other post-1970 developments, see Carmelo Mesa-Lago, *Cuba in the 1970's: Pragmatism and Institutionalization* (Albuquerque: University of New Mexico Press, 1974); Leon Gouré and Morris Rothenberg, *Soviet Penetration of Latin America* (Coral Gables, Fla.: Center for Advanced International Studies, University of Miami, 1975), pp. 19-80; and Edward Gonzalez, "Castro and Cuba's New Orthodoxy," *Problems of Communism*, January-February 1976, pp. 1-19. See also Nelson P. Valdés, "Revolution and Institutionalization in Cuba," *Cuban Studies/Estudios Cubanos*, January 1976, pp. 1-38; and Jorge I. Domínguez, "Institutionalization and Civil-Military Relations," ibid., pp. 39-66.

5. Fidel himself had earlier underscored this transfer of political legitimacy to the PCC: "In the early years of the revolution, individuals played a decisive role, a role now carried out by the party. Men die, but the party is immortal." *Granma Weekly Review*, August 5, 1973, p. 5.

6. Ibid., January 14, 1973, pp. 2-3; ibid., November 25, 1973, pp. 7-11.

7. See Edward Gonzalez, *Cuba Under Castro: The Limits of Charisma* (Boston: Houghton Mifflin, 1974), pp. 206-21; Edward Gonzalez and David Ronfeldt, *Post-Revolutionary Cuba in a Changing World* (Santa Monica: The Rand Corporation, December 1975, R-1844-ISA), pp. 13-21; and Gonzalez, "Castro and Cuba's New Orthodoxy," pp. 2-14.

8. "Revolution for Internal Consumption Only," *Trans-Action*, no. 6 (April 1969), p. 13.

9. While the Fidelistas and Raulistas were almost without exception members of the July 26 Movement, they fought at the side of either Fidel or Raúl during the anti-Batista struggle, or soon after attached themselves to one of the brothers as personal followers. In general, the Fidelistas tended to occupy high posts in the party and government, whereas the Raulistas were more concentrated in the armed forces throughout the 1960s. There are Fidelistas who hold top commands in the FAR, however.

10. According to Domínguez, Cuba's civic soldiers "have actually ruled over large sectors of civilian and military life . . . have civilianized and politicized themselves by internalizing the norms and organization of the Communist Party, and have educated themselves to become professionals in military, political, managerial, engineering, economic, and educational affairs. Their civil and military lives have been fused." Domínguez, "Institutionalization," pp. 40-41.

11. See *Granma Weekly Review*, December 12, 1976, p. 5. *The Latin American Political Report*, January 7, 1977, p. 507, also contains a convenient summary of the new leadership, including a combined listing of party, state, and government officials.

12. *Granma Weekly Review*, December 12, 1976, p. 6.

13. The agency heads comprise those directing the Central Planning Board (JUCEPLAN), and nine state committees charged with specialized functions related to economic, technical, scientific, and other social activities. For lack of personnel data, I have been unable to determine the political, professional, and institutional backgrounds of several of the appointees. A complete listing of agency heads and ministers is given in ibid., p. 5.

14. These powers are granted in the new Law on the Organization of Central State Administration, articles 7-9. The text of the law is in ibid., December 19, 1976, pp. 9-12.

15. For a comprehensive analysis regarding these and other foreign policy issues, see Gonzalez and Ronfeldt, *Post-Revolutionary Cuba*, pp. 51-78. Much of the following discussion of elite-policy tendencies draws on this study.

16. *Granma*, September 14, 1974, pp. 2-3.

17. *Le Monde*, January 16, 1975, pp. 1, 4.

18. *Granma Weekly Review*, November 24, 1974, pp. 9-10.

19. For instance, in December 1974, Rodríguez obtained $900 million in Spanish credits; in January 1975, he visited Paris and obtained $350 million in credits; in March, Canada extended $155 million in credits; and in May, he secured an Anglo-Cuban cooperation agreement worth $580 million in British credits.

20. *Granma Weekly Review,* October 27, 1974, p. 3.

21. Ibid., October 6, 1974, p. 3.

22. Ibid.

23. Ibid., March 30, 1975, p. 3.

24. Interview with Mexican newsmen, Radio Havana, January 10, 1975.

25. See Domínguez, "Institutionalization," pp. 47–55, 61–62; and chapter 3 of this volume.

26. *Verde Olivo,* January 8, 1974, p. 6.

27. *Granma Weekly Review,* December 1, 1974, p. 7.

28. The French government expelled three Cuban diplomats from the Paris embassy in June 1975, accusing them of being Cuban intelligence (DGI) agents with ties to "Carlos," the notorious Venezuelan international terrorist, who had shot down three French security agents investigating a Palestinian terrorist ring.

29. The following is based on David Binder's account in the *New York Times,* March 29, 1977, pp. 1, 8.

30. According to an unnamed U.S. official close to the talks: "On the one hand you had the technocrats, who wanted wider contact with the United States. On the other, you had the old-line Cuban revolutionaries who knew that improved relations with Washington would destroy some of their revolutionary elan. I believe Fidel couldn't decide which side of the argument to support, so he just let the contacts stop." *Los Angeles Times,* March 30, 1977, p. 4.

31. See *Granma Weekly Review,* September 7, 1975, pp. 8–9.

32. *New York Times,* December 21, 1975, p. 1.

33. Radio Havana, December 22, 1975.

34. The following summary analysis is based on Edward Gonzalez and David Ronfeldt, "Castro's Cuba: From Surrogate to Superclient," draft article, May, 1976; and Gerald J. Bender, "Kissinger and Angola: Anatomy of Failure," draft article, September 1976. An extensively researched analysis of Cuba's overseas activity has been written by William J. Durch, *The Cuban Military in Africa and the Middle East: From Algeria to Angola,* Professional Paper no. 201, Center for Naval Analyses, Arlington, Va., September 1977. In it Durch also finds that Cuba's involvement in Angola was independently motivated rather than Soviet-directed, and that the military build-up occurred in stages in response to changes in battlefield conditions.

35. *Granma Weekly Review,* May 2, 1976, pp. 4–5. Along with the FAR, the Ministry of Interior (MININT) also participated in Angola, dispatching its Special Troops Batallion. See Fidel's speech in ibid., June 20, 1976, pp. 2–5.

36. Fidel thus complained that Japan's purchase had dropped from as much as one million tons in recent years to only 130,000 tons in 1976, causing Cuba to apply "drastic restrictions" in its imports. See ibid., December 12, 1976, p. 3.

37. The new nomenclature of ranks is in ibid., December 5, 1976, p. 12.

38. Radio Havana, December 22, 1975.

39. *Granma Weekly Review,* December 12, 1976, p. 12.

40. Ibid., October 24, 1976, p. 3; *ibid,* December 12, 1976, p. 2; ibid., March 27, 1977, p. 1; and *Los Angeles Times,* April 4, 1977, p. 4.

41. Western sources differ on the size of the Cuban advisory force in Ethiopia. See n56 for further details.

42. "Fidel Castro Speaks," ABC television, June 9, 1977.

43. Benjamin C. Bradlee, "Castro Fears Carter Will Come Unstuck on Cuba," *Manchester Guardian-Washington Post-Le Monde Weekly,* March 13, 1977, p. 16.

44. See the aptly titled article, "Havana's view: Rich Potential Seen for U.S., Cuba Trade," *Los Angeles Times,* July 4, 1977, pp. 1, 14.

EDWARD GONZALEZ

45. Ibid., p. 1.

46. See Gonzalez and Ronfeldt, *Post-Revolutionary Cuba,* pp. 32–38.

47. *Granma Weekly Review,* April 17, 1977, p. 5.

48. Ibid., March 27, 1977, p. 1 (italics added).

49. In an interview for *Afrique-Asie,* for instance, he declared that Cuba's solidarity with Angola "will never be subject to negotiation with the United States. This is something that can't be negotiated." Ibid., May 22, 1977, p. 3.

50. Cuba thus represents a classic example of a small state that is able to employ international leverage in its relations with the patron-state to further its own national interests. On the concept and usage of international leverage, see Richard W. Cottam, *Competitive Interference and Twentieth Century Diplomacy* (Pittsburgh: University of Pittsburgh Press, 1967). For an examination of Cuba's pre-1970 employment of leverage in dealing with the USSR, see Edward Gonzalez, "Relationship with the Soviet Union," in Carmelo Mesa-Lago, ed., *Revolutionary Change in Cuba* (Pittsburgh: University of Pittsburgh Press, 1971), pp. 81–104.

51. See the analysis by Peter Vanneman and Martin James, "The Soviet Intervention in Angola: Intentions and Implications," *Strategic Review,* Summer 1976, pp. 92–103. For the Soviet view, see V. Kudryavtsev, "A U.S. 'Plot Against Africa'," *Izvestia,* August 14, 1976, along with other Soviet articles, as translated in *The Current Digest of the Soviet Press,* September 15, 1976, pp. 1–3. See also the *New York Times,* March 13, 1977, p. 3.

52. *Granma Weekly Review,* March 27, 1977, p. 2.

53. See, for example, his address to the Libyan regime of Colonel Muammar El Khadafi, ibid., March 20, 1977, p. 2. On the other hand, as a Third World spokesman, he sharply indicted some of the OPEC countries of the Middle East for not sharing more of their oil revenues with the less developed countries, and for squandering their oil earnings on sophisticated armaments and ostentatious life-styles. See his speech to the new National Assembly of People's Power, ibid, December 12, 1976, pp. 2–3.

54. Ibid., May 22, 1977, p. 2.

55. Ibid., March 27, 1977, p. 1.

56. According to the *New York Times,* diplomatic sources reported that there were 50 Cuban military advisors in Ethiopia (June 21, 1977, p. 3). The *Observer,* however, reported new shipments of Russian weapons and "the arrival of 400 Cubans to advise and train the much heralded 'Peasant Army'" (June 26, 1977, p. 6). (After completion of this study, Somalia declared war on Ethiopia—in July 1977—and Cuba subsequently dispatched an ever increasing number of combat troops to aid Ethiopia. As of April 1, 1978, the U.S. government reported the Cuban buildup at between sixteen and seventeen thousand in addition to the estimated twenty thousand troops in Angola.)

57. See, for instance, Fidel's pessimistic appraisal of Latin America, in contrast to that of Africa, in *Granma Weekly Review,* May 22, 1977, p. 2.

58. Thus, the leverage that Cuba can derive as an international paladin is heavily dependent upon the motivations underlying Soviet foreign policy. I am indebted to Professor Richard W. Cottam, University of Pittsburgh, for pointing out this problematical aspect of Cuba's leverage situation.

2

COLE BLASIER

The Soviet Union
in the Cuban-American Conflict

The Soviet presence in Cuba has been among the most vexing and misunderstood foreign policy problems in the United States for a generation. Many Americans do not understand how and why Soviet influence was established in Cuba, the nature of the relations between Castro and Soviet leaders, or where Cuba fits in the pattern of Soviet aims and priorities. It is no wonder then that there is so much confusion and disagreement in the United States about what U.S. policy toward Cuba should be.

Some recent shifts in Cuban foreign policy and changes in the global situation contribute to this confusion. Castro has now broken out of his isolation in the hemisphere and in the world and has reestablished Cuba's relations with many Latin American and other foreign governments. Progress toward rapprochement with the United States under Presidents Ford and Carter culminated in the exchange of "interest sections" in Washington and Havana in September 1977. Cuba's Soviet-sponsored military operations, first undertaken in Angola in 1975, spread to Ethiopia in 1977. In order to understand these developments and assess the Soviet role in Cuban-American relations, three fundamental matters deserve mention.

First, the Eisenhower administration and the Castro government were responsible for the Soviet presence in Cuba initially. By taking extreme economic and military sanctions in an effort to depose Castro, the U.S. government made the survival of the Revolution dependent on Soviet help. Castro himself was eager, for good and sufficient reasons of his own, to seek Soviet assistance; Soviet models suited his personal and political objectives. Without U.S. sanctions, Castro would have had a harder time breaking with the United States and attracting Soviet support. The punitive policies of the United States and Castro's need and desire for Soviet aid provided the USSR with an irresistible opportunity to extend her influence in the Americas.[1]

Second, although the Soviet government exercises great influence in Cuba and seeks to have her way there as in other parts of the world, Castro has shown time and again, most particularly in the 1960s, that he is not a Soviet puppet but a formidable negotiator and useful ally. While Cuban and Soviet interests are by no means identical, the two governments have found many areas for mutually beneficial collaboration in recent years, especially in the Cuban economy and in Africa.[2]

Third, while the Soviet record in Cuba is one of the brightest achievements of Soviet foreign policy since 1945, Cuba is not a top Soviet priority. The security of the Soviet leadership, the well-being of the Soviet economy, and Soviet relations with Eastern Europe, Communist China, and the United States, are all far more important to the USSR than relations with Cuba. Any assessment of Soviet intentions in Cuba should take into account the origins of her influence there and her more pressing national interests elsewhere.

The Soviet position on Cuba's role in the world, and particularly on the latter's expanding relations with the United States, is important to both Havana and Washington. How does the USSR view Cuban-U.S. rapprochement? What effect would Cuba's resumption of diplomatic and economic relations with the United States have on Soviet interests? Will the USSR attempt to obstruct or delay the resumption of these relations? How can a better understanding of Soviet interests and motives in Cuba help shape a more effective American policy? Such questions are, of course, pertinent mainly if the tentative and cautious efforts of the United States and Cuban toward rapprochement continue. That may depend partly on Cuba's military operations in Africa (see chapters 3 and 4 of this volume), or Cuba's policies elsewhere, such as toward Puerto Rico (see chapter 5).

In order to illuminate these and other issues, this chapter will concentrate mainly on assessing the costs and benefits to Soviet political, economic, and strategic interests of the long-standing relationship with socialist Cuba. An understanding of the impact of Cuban-U.S. rapprochement on those interests makes it easier to understand the Soviet role to date and to predict its future direction.

Political Benefits

The Castro government's main benefit to the USSR has been political. Since the great Communist victory in China and the extension of Communist power into North Vietnam, the international Communist movement has had few gains to boast about. Beginning in the early 1950s the tide of events seemed to run against the Soviet Union: Tito strengthened Yugoslav independence of Stalin and rebelled against Soviet ideological orthodoxy; the USSR and China headed toward a split; Albania joined the Chinese; there were political upheavals or unrest in East Germany, Hungary, Poland, and, in 1968, Czechoslovakia; and Communist liberation movements around the world suffered one defeat after another. In those years, until Vietnam was united, Cuba was the only country to "go Communist" and provide fresh evidence to support the Soviet claim that Communism is the wave of the future. In fact, Cuba is still the only Communist country not contiguous to the socialist countries of Europe or Asia. Cuba's demonstration effect has thus been important to Soviet political strategies and propaganda efforts around the world.

In spite of tensions in the Cuban-Soviet relationship, Cuba has been a major supporter of the USSR in the international Communist movement, especially in recent years. Although more restrained than Moscow in criticizing Communist

China, Cuba consistently supports the USSR in the Sino-Soviet conflict. More-over, Cuba's qualified approval of the Soviet invasion of Czechoslovakia in 1968 was especially welcome in Moscow, although Castro made it clear he supported the Warsaw Pact's military operations for reasons of his own.[3]

Castro has also been a major supporter of Soviet policy in the Third World, particularly in the nonaligned movement (see chapter 7). At the same time Castro has not been effective in promoting Communist revolutionary objectives in Latin America, but not for want of trying. He believed for many years that the time was ripe, or could be made ripe, for national liberation movements to seize power in Latin America. Soviet leaders were skeptical, as were many local leaders of the Moscow-oriented Latin American Communist parties. Moscow felt obliged to go along rhetorically so as not to be outflanked on the left. Castro and the guerrilla leaders he supported came into open conflict with many of the old Communists. None of the Latin American guerrilla fighters gained power, and most were wiped out. Time proved Moscow right. By the early 1970s Castro had shed his revolutionary romanticism in Latin America and even urged caution on his Chil-ean comrade, the socialist president, Salvador Allende.

Angola was the first country where the Cubans were successful in helping a revolutionary movement come to power. Castro's Angola operation was a great political victory; at the same time it involved open-ended costs and risks. Like the United States in its own military operations abroad, Castro found it far easier to land troops than to evacuate them.

Observers in the United States have rushed to assert, or simply assume, that the Cuban military operations in Africa and their Soviet sponsorship pose a threat to the United States, but often they do not explain how, or the extent to which, this may be so. Cool and comprehensive evaluations of U.S. interests in Africa have been rare. Cuban and Soviet interference in various parts of the world may or may not hurt U.S. interests, just as U.S. interference in other countries may or may not have damaged the Soviet cause. Both sides suffer from time to time from self-inflicted injuries.

A major question here is whether Cuba's developing relations with the United States threaten the political benefits the USSR has enjoyed in Cuba so far. What that new role would not seem likely to do, certainly not in the foreseeable future, is lead to the demise of Marxism-Leninism in Cuba. Cuba now appears to be safely socialist. There appears to be no organized opposition to Castro on the island now that most of his bitterest enemies are either in exile, dead, or in prison. Many of the anti-Castro leaders abroad, particularly in Florida, have tended to become less militant and to be integrated into American society with more to lose and less to gain by repatriation to Cuba. And as the years have passed, the prospects of U.S. support for such groups and of U.S. armed action against Castro have gradually diminished.

In fact, Castro's more secure hold over the island and the less threatening posture of the United States appear to be important reasons why normalization between the two countries is now possible. Neither Castro nor the USSR has much reason to fear that normalization, *carefully orchestrated,* need threaten the security of the Castro regime in the near or medium term. Both governments can now view closer relations with the United States with more equanimity.

Yet a strong case can be made that closer relations with the United States will make Cuba more independent of Moscow, at least in the long term. The effect that such a development will have on the political benefits the USSR has derived from its Cuban association needs to be examined carefully. For example, Castro's support for the USSR in the international Communist movement may owe less to Soviet pressures than to genuine coincidence of views. Moreover, Communist China will probably not be able to compete effectively with the Soviet Union for Cuba's attentions for a long time, whether in the economic or military field. Cuba, too, may continue to support Soviet primacy in Eastern Europe and the latter's defense there of socialist orthodoxy. If there ever should be serious political disturbances in Cuba, however unlikely at the moment, Cuba might welcome Soviet assistance, particularly if this could be credibly linked to "imperialism." That surely is one of the reasons Castro reluctantly approved Warsaw Pact intervention in Czechoslovakia in 1968.

Unlike the Communist leaders in Western Europe, Castro is in power and does not need to woo an electorate in the western sense. Similarly, he is likely to support Soviet views on Eurocommunism, whose revisionist doctrines if applied in Cuba might challenge his authority. And unlike the Eastern European governments who find the Eurocommunists' independence of Moscow beguiling, Castro, without the near presence of Soviet military and police power, already enjoys more autonomy than they do.

In supporting national liberation movements in the Third World, Castro's policies are likely to parallel those of Moscow whether Moscow pressures him or not; in fact, Castro's tendency to rush ahead of Moscow there is well known. But if Cuba does develop closer economic and political relations with the United States and other market economies, Cuba would then have some of the same reasons to exercise restraint that Moscow already has.

What all this adds up to is that even though closer relations with the United States are likely to increase Castro's independence of Moscow, such a development is not likely to have a very adverse effect on the political benefits that Moscow enjoys. Castro's Marxist-Leninist regime seems relatively secure, which is the main point. In foreign policy, Cuba is likely to follow the Soviet line or something close, whether Moscow has great leverage or not. United States policymakers should not deceive themselves on these points. What is clear, however, is that Cuban-U.S. rapprochement seems to be the best, perhaps the only, opportunity for loosening Cuban and Soviet ties in the long run. The main reason for this is that the greater the conflict between Washington and Havana, the greater Havana's dependence on Moscow.

Economic Burdens

The fact of Soviet aid to Cuba is well known in the West, but its volume and significance are not fully appreciated. Bilateral economic assistance is often viewed as a kind of supplemental boost to a recipient economy for constructive humanitarian, social, or developmental purposes. In this sense it is logical that the Soviet Union, as the leading Communist power, would lend a hand to a Third World country like Cuba which has gone so far and so fast in establishing a Marxist-Leninist society on the Soviet model.

In the absence of further elaboration, such a view of Soviet assistance to Cuba is casual and superficial. It would be hard to find any society in history which, in the absence of war, was subjected to more abrupt, far-reaching, and severe revolutionary shocks than Cuba. In addition to the profound social and political havoc of revolution, Cuba's domestic economy, and its foreign economic relations, were completely restructured. It is a kind of miracle that Castro and his regime survived.

The Castro government and the new society it sponsored were able to survive only because of massive Soviet assistance. That assistance meant far more than simply helping Cuba develop a little faster and a little better. (Chapter 11 of this volume describes the nature, scope, and impact of Soviet and other socialist economic assistance to Cuba.) Since 1962 when the full repercussions of the Revolution began to be felt throughout the society, Cuba has had a deficit economy, saved from bankruptcy only by Soviet aid. Cuba has been unable to export enough goods to pay for the imports she has needed to feed and clothe her people and operate the economy. That deficit has been reflected in high negative foreign trade balances from 1962 through 1973 (see table 9.5). The trade deficit has usually been several hundred million pesos, in fact some 555 million pesos in the worst year. The deficit that year, 1969, was more than 80 percent of exports, and the deficit has often run from 25 percent to 50 percent of exports, or more. Castro's critics will be quick to blame these deficits on low output caused by poor economic policies or poor management, and surely both have been responsible in more than a small way. A broader and fairer view, however, would also take into account the huge economic costs that are inevitable in any radical revolution as well as fluctuating demand and prices for Cuba's exports.

Sugar has continued to be Cuba's principal export, comprising betwen 74 percent and 88 percent of the total (table 9.9). Yet Cuban output of sugar has only occasionally risen much over 6 million tons, which is only slightly above the last prerevolutionary years' output (table 9.2). Meanwhile, except for the period 1973–1975 (table 13.5), sugar prices on the world market have not been much above prerevolutionary prices, particularly when compared to the substantial increases Cuba has had to pay for imports. Cuba's other exports, which account for a relatively small part of her export income, have had only a mixed performance in output and prices compared to before the Revolution, with the fishing industry performing well and other traditional exports like tobacco, disappointingly.

Since the Soviet Union has provided more than half of Cuba's imports during many of these years, it is not surprising that Cuba's largest trade deficits have been with the USSR (see table 2.1). In fact, about 85 percent of Cuba's cumulative trade deficit has been with the Soviet Union—3.5 billion out of 4.1

COLE BLASIER

TABLE 2.1
Cuba's Balance of Trade and the USSR

	Global Balance	Soviet Balance
1959	− 38.8	+ 12.9
1960	+ 28.4	+ 23.3
1961	− 12.3	+ 41.1
1962	−237.0	−189.5
1963	−322.2	−297.1
1964	−304.5	−135.0
1965	−175.6	−105.9
1966	−327.7	−247.3
1967	−294.1	−215.9
1968	−450.9	−382.2
1969	−555.0	−436.0
1970	−261.5	−161.5
1971	−526.3	−427.1
1972	−418.9	−490.3
1973	−314.9	−301.3
1974	− 3.7	−214.5

Sources: Prepared from tables 9.5 and 9.7, in millions of pesos.

billion pesos (table 9.7). Cuba and the Soviet Union do not publish balance-of-payments figures, but the two countries have announced that repayment of most of this debt (except for the accumulation 1973–1975) will not begin until 1986. Thus, Soviet absorption of trade deficits on which payments have not yet begun constitutes a major part of Soviet economic assistance to Cuba.

Cuba's large and continuing trade deficits, however, do not fully reflect weaknesses in Cuba's foreign trade, nor the true measure of Soviet economic assistance. That is because the Soviet Union has long been paying Cuba more than the world market price for two of her important exports, sugar and nickel, and charging less for an important import, oil. As table 12.5 shows, the Soviet Union paid Cuba about 6 cents per pound for sugar from 1963 to 1972, a price as much as 4 cents above the world market price in some years. Since sugar was Cuba's major export, this differential price constituted a huge Soviet subsidy during most of the revolutionary period. Similarly, the USSR has paid Cuba more than the world market price for her nickel exports, in recent years sometimes nearly 50 percent more.[4]

The USSR has also sold Cuba petroleum, one of her most costly imports, at prices below the world market price, particularly beginning in 1973 when oil prices began to skyrocket (table 13.5). (It is not possible to calculate the extent to which these various price subsidies are offset by the pricing of Cuba's imports from the USSR under "tied" assistance.)

All of these forms of economic assistance—balance-of-payments aid, sugar and nickel subsidies, and petroleum subsidies—came to over $8 billion by 1976 (see table 2.2). Since Cuban sugar output is not likely to increase significantly (sugar prices are far below the historic high of 1974 and are not likely to advance much soon) nor are most other exports likely to grow dramatically, Soviet assistance will have to continue at high levels.

The total of economic assistance to Cuba by 1976 shown in table 2.2, $8 billion, does not include certain other types of Soviet assistance. For example, Cuba and the Soviet Union have elaborate arrangements for scientific, educational, and cultural cooperation (see table 11.5). In some cases, both sides participate in the financing.[5] Because Cubans have a far greater need to study in the USSR than Soviet specialists in Cuba, however, and because the USSR is likely to have more equipment than Cuba, no doubt the Soviet Union tends to pay the largest share of the costs of this cooperation.[6] Such expenses must run into millions of dollars.

Soviet expenses in the scientific, educational, and cultural field are, however, far less than the costs of Soviet military assistance to Cuba. Since 1960, when Castro began to receive Soviet military assistance, the USSR has provided most, if not all, the equipment for the Cuban army, navy, and air force. The Cuban armed forces are now among the strongest in Latin America, and their military manpower is inferior in numbers in Latin America only to the armed forces of Brazil and Argentina.[7] The army, for example, has over six hundred Soviet tanks, as well as other armored vehicles, personnel carriers, artillery, and so forth. The navy, comprised mostly of smaller warships, has eighteen Soviet submarine chasers, twenty-five Soviet fast patrol boats, and some fifty coastal defense surface-to-surface missiles. The air force has some twelve squadrons of different Soviet MiG aircraft plus Soviet helicopters. The air force also has twenty-five Soviet-equipped surface-to-air missile battalions.[8]

It is difficult to calculate what it costs the Soviet Union to provide virtually all the modern equipment of the three Cuban military services. Official U.S. sources calculate the value of this equipment from 1961 through 1975 at $933 million. The dollar costs ascribed to this equipment must necessarily be arbitrary. Nor do U.S. figures include the costs of training, services, or construction which were an important part of the Soviet military assistance to Cuba.[9] As chapter 3 indicates, the U.S. estimates are only part of total Soviet military assistance.

Detailed authoritative reports on Soviet military assistance are not, however, available in either Soviet or Cuban sources. Castro did put the value of Soviet military aid to Cuba up to 1970 at 1.5 billion pesos.[10] At the end of 1975, he calculated the value of military equipment given to Cuba "free" at "several billion pesos."[11] The actual figures must then be at least 2 billion pesos and could be considerably higher than that (pesos were calculated at par with the U.S. dollar until the latter was devalued). Castro called attention to Soviet training services which presumably came on top of the equipment figures. It seems likely that, estimated conservatively, military assistance to Cuba has cost the Soviet Union *at least* the equivalent of $2 or $3 billion.

The grand total of Soviet assistance to Cuba through 1976 includes (1) the $8.3 billion in table 2.2; (2) millions of dollars of scientific, educational, and

TABLE 2.2
Soviet Economic Assistance
(million U.S. $)

	1961–67	1968	1969	1970	1971	1972	1973	1974	1975[a]	1976[b]
Balance-of-payments aid	1,393	432	494	231	509	632	437	294	65	110
Trade deficit	1,180	382	436	162	427	535	404	259	30[c]	75[c]
Interest charges	59	28	34	45	57	69	—[d]	—[d]	—[d]	—[d]
Other invisibles	154	22	24	24	25	28	33	35	35	35
Repayable aid	1,393	1,825	2,319	2,550	3,059	3,691	4,128	4,422	4,487	4,597[e]
Subsidies										
Sugar[f]	632	150	86	150	56	-22	154	4	365	897
Petroleum[g]	—	—	—	—	—	—	—	370	300	375
Nickel[f]	—	—	—	—	—	—	48	40	27	22
Total cumulative aid	2,025	2,607	3,187	3,568	4,133	4,743	5,382	6,090	6,847	8,251

Source: U.S. Central Intelligence Agency, Research Aid, *The Cuban Economy: A Statistical Review, 1968–1976* (Washington, 1976), p. 14.
a. Provisional.
b. Estimated.
c. Clearing account deficit, i.e., trade deficit excluding Soviet hard currency purchases of sugar.
d. A Cuban-Soviet agreement of December 1972 exempted Cuban debt from further interest charges.
e. Estimated Cuban debt to the USSR consisting of (1) an estimated $4.05 billion in direct balance-of-payments assistance and (2) an estimated $550 million in development aid. The USSR has agreed to postpone initial repayment of this debt until 1986.
f. The sugar and nickel subsidies are estimated as the difference between the values of sugar and nickel exports to the USSR and the value of these exports if sold on the world market. They are considered a grant and are not subject to repayment.
g. The petroleum subsidy reflects the difference between the value of petroleum purchased from the USSR and the value of these imports at world prices. It is considered a grant and is not subject to repayment.

cultural assistance which has not been estimated; and (3) military assistance worth several billion dollars. Thus it seems likely that Soviet assistance to Cuba through 1976 must have been about $11 billion, or more. I have not constructed a table of total Soviet assistance to Cuba because so many of the figures are informed estimates with numerous qualifications and reservations. As a result, these global figures are not strictly comparable to figures on Soviet aid to other countries, nor to reports of foreign assistance in the West.

Authoritative figures on Soviet economic assistance are not generally available, and the percentage figures shown in table 11.2 are of limited use. The U.S. Central Intelligence Agency's estimates of Soviet aid to less developed countries (excluding Cuba and any other socialist countries) show that total Soviet aid to all such countries comes to $10.9 billion. The largest recipients during this period were India ($2.4 billion) and Egypt ($2.2 billion). Thus, even though the figures may not be comparable, it is likely that Soviet economic assistance to Cuba alone is probably not very much less than all Soviet assistance to developing countries outside the socialist orbit (see chapter 11, n. 1).

With the reservations about comparability in mind, it is also interesting to compare Soviet assistance to Cuba with U.S. assistance to selected countries. Table 2.3 lists the countries in Latin America whose cumulative, bilateral economic assistance from the United States exceeded $500 million through 1976, as well as three small or medium-sized countries outside the hemisphere who have

TABLE 2.3
Selected Recipients of U.S. Aid, 1962–1976

	Population (millions)	Loans and Grants (million U.S. $)		
		Economic	Military	Total
Latin America				
Bolivia	5.5	505	70	574
Brazil	104.2	2,218	433	2,651
Chile	10.4	978	158	1,136
Colombia	24.0	1,372	130	1,457
Dominican Republic	4.6	550	32	582
Peru	15.4	386	144	530
Other				
Israel	3.3	1,860	5,912	7,772
South Korea	33.5	2,622	5,299	7,921
South Vietnam	18.3	6,013	16,191	22,203

Sources: Population figures are 1974 estimates (rounded) of the U.N. Demographic Yearbook 1974 (New York, 1975), pp. 109–11. South Vietnam figures are 1970 census. Aid figures are from U.S. Overseas Loans and Grants and Assistance from International Organizations, U.S. Agency for International Development (Washington, D.C.: 1977).
Note: Figures are rounded and cover the period through September 30, 1976. The Latin American countries listed are those in the area which received during 1962–1976 in excess of $500 million in total U.S. aid.

COLE BLASIER

been exceptionally favored recipients of U.S. aid. It is striking that Soviet economic assistance to Cuba at $8 billion is greater than U.S. economic assistance to all these countries, even South Vietnam and Israel. Note, too, that the estimate of all Soviet aid to Cuba at $11 billion exceeds the totals of all these countries except South Vietnam.

The reader is cautioned not to take these figures or comparisons too seriously. No doubt the U.S. figures are low and do not, of course, include U.S. contributions to the World Bank, the Inter-American Development Bank and other international agencies or the private sector. But the figures suggest that Soviet assistance to Cuba has been immense, in the same high order of magnitude as U.S. assistance to its most favored small countries. Such aid constitutes a heavy economic burden on the USSR. My conversations with informed Soviet citizens suggest that there is knowledge of this burden in Moscow, that many Soviet citizens would like to see it reduced, and that there is even some grumbling about it.

Strategic Ambiguities

The USSR's close relations with the Castro regime have long had a bearing on Soviet strategic and military interests. Not only is most of Cuba's military equipment of Soviet manufacture, Soviet officers have long been Cuba's principal military advisors, many of them stationed on the island. Although Cuba is not a member of the Warsaw Pact, Cuban leaders participate as observers in Warsaw Pact military maneuvers as did Raúl Castro in Poland in September 1976.[12] There are frequent exchanges of visits between the Cuban military and their counterparts in the socialist countries. For example, General of the Army Heinz Hoffmann, Politburo member and minister of defense of the German Democratic Republic, visited Cuba in September 1976.[13] Raúl Castro was received by the general secretary and the Soviet minister of defense in February 1978; a photograph of the meeting appeared on the front page of *Izvestia*.[14] There are apparently exchanges of military information and joint or coordinated military planning as well, most particularly regarding Africa.

Cuba is not strategically indispensable to the Soviet Union because the USSR has the capabilities to destroy targets in the United States with ballistic missiles launched from Soviet territory or from submarines operating off U.S. coasts. Nonetheless, as the Soviet effort to install missiles with nuclear warheads in Cuba in 1962 shows, Cuba appears to have been perceived as having some strategic value; rockets launched from Cuban soil could be delivered with greater accuracy and speed on U.S. targets. In any case, the USSR removed those missiles from Cuba after the October crisis, and there appear to have been no land-based strategic missiles in Cuba since that time.[15]

Nor is Cuba essential for the operation of Soviet submarines armed with nuclear missiles. These have long operated in the Atlantic from northern Soviet ports. Yet the island is a convenient location for servicing Soviet submarines.

Provision of fuel, supplies, and rest for the crews permits such submarines to spend more time on their Atlantic stations and less time in transit to and from distant Soviet ports. Concern about this strategic advantage in 1970 led President Nixon to protest that preparations to establish a Soviet submarine base at Cienfuegos were in violation of the Kennedy-Khrushchev understanding of 1962 that the USSR would not place offensive weapons in Cuba. The protest was successful, and there appears to have been no subsequent establishment of Soviet submarines or other bases on the island. Nor have Soviet missile submarines visited Cuban ports since 1974.[16]

Soviet surface naval craft, including light cruisers and destroyers, and Soviet aircraft have also paid repeated visits to Cuba, the latter to the José Martí Airport near Havana. At repeated intervals recently, the USSR has deployed several Bear reconnaissance aircraft from Cuba for a month or six weeks at a time.[17] Soviet ships on hydrographic, intelligence, and scientific missions have been operating in Caribbean waters. Through these various activities, the Soviet armed forces have now acquired extensive experience in, and knowledge of, the area and established a military presence there.

It is easier to describe these activities than to assess their significance. As long as the 1962 agreement remains in force, the USSR will be unable to use Cuba as a base for launching a strategic attack on the United States. Cuba's own air and naval forces are primarily defensive and are not suitable for attacks on the United States; the navy is comprised mainly of small craft, and the air force lacks long-range bombers.

While it would not be technically difficult for the Soviet military to establish bases in Cuba quickly, it would seem even easier for U.S. forces operating from Florida to prevent their ever becoming operational. Cuba is thus not likely to be of great benefit to the Soviet Union in the event of a nuclear war with the United States. In the unlikelier event of a conventional U.S.-Soviet conflict in the Atlantic, similar reasoning also applies since Cuba is so vulnerable to U.S. air strikes.

For these reasons, the Soviet military presence in Cuba now seems significant more for political and psychological than for military reasons. Both sides in the East-West conflict marshal their forces for bargaining. The Soviet presence in Cuba offsets the U.S. presence in Europe, but only symbolically—the United States, unlike the USSR in Cuba, has operating bases in Europe.

How then might Cuban rapprochement with the United States affect the marginal political-military advantages Cuba offers the Soviet Union? Cuba's military ties with the Soviet Union are not likely to be affected in the short and medium term, less likely, for example, than her economic and political relations. First, Cuba is heavily dependent on the Soviet Union for spare parts for its major equipment for all three armed services. Second, just as a matter of common prudence, the Cuban leaders probably find military dependence on a distant power a lesser evil than military dependence on the nearby United States. Castro may also prefer to have his main military ties with the USSR rather than with the

United States in the event of a domestic political upheaval. If Cuba were to develop military ties outside the Warsaw Pact, the United States is not the most likely candidate. Thus, some Soviet leaders might view U.S.-Cuban rapprochement as leading to a smaller Soviet military presence in Cuba, but not necessarily to the replacement of the Soviet Union by the United States.

U.S.-Cuban rapprochement does, however, offer one not widely recognized advantage to the Soviet strategic posture. The USSR has long posed as the protector of Cuba, trying to give the impression that Soviet armed forces would rush to Cuba's defense if she were attacked by the United States. Yet the USSR has been careful not to commit herself formally to do so, and Cuba's exclusion from the Warsaw Pact is not an accident.[18] In fact, Soviet military ties with Cuba could be an awkward burden for the USSR and place her in a potentially untenable situation. If a military conflict between Cuba and the United States were to break out, the Soviet leadership would have two main choices with respect to the use of armed force, neither of which is acceptable. The first would be to commit Soviet military forces in the defense of Cuba, which almost certainly would lead to a nuclear holocaust. This is a choice the USSR is most unlikely to make, as her conduct in 1962 shows. The second choice would be not to enter the conflict; but if she did not spring to Cuba's defense, and thus virtually guaranteed Castro's defeat, the damage to her political and strategic position in the world would be immense. As a result, one of the best ways to avoid either of these two most undesirable outcomes from the Soviet perspective is to support some kind of *modus vivendi* in the Caribbean which will not force the Soviet hand. Like the United States, the USSR can benefit from reducing tensions and the prospects of war that accompany them.

The Soviet Position

Some westerners continue the cold-war tradition of viewing the Soviet Union as monolithic; they doubt there could be disagreement within the Soviet Union about Cuba. The history of intraparty struggles and group behavior, East and West, belie that view. Soviet citizens also let it be known, informally and perhaps unintentionally, that there are different views in the Soviet Union about Cuba. To date, official sources do not reveal any significant or concerted Soviet opposition to Cuban rapprochement with the United States.

In any case, if the Soviet government opposed rapprochement, it should have blocked Castro's initiatives in this regard long ago. The process has already gone so far that the Soviet government would have difficulty ending it unilaterally. No doubt the Soviet leadership has profited from U.S. mistakes in Cuba and may be cautious about ever pushing Castro so hard that he would fall into the arms of the United States as a last resort. All this may seem too remote a possibility for serious discussion; what it does suggest is that there are limits on Soviet behavior.

Another possibility is that the dominant view in Moscow may be to regard U.S.-Cuban rapprochement as, on balance, in the Soviet interest. Published

Soviet statements about the normalization of relations between the United States and Cuba tend to avoid expressing explicit approval or disapproval. One reason for this may be that the Soviet government wishes to appear faithful to the principle that the resumption of normal relations between these two countries is their own business and is not a subject upon which the USSR should assume the position of judge. Another reason may be that, presumably, socialist countries usually favor normal relations between all countries in spite of differences in their social systems. No doubt too, Soviet leaders may believe that discretion is advisable in this matter for reasons directly related to their quite separate set of bilateral dealings with Cuba and the United States. Moreover, Soviet commentaries are almost invariably cautious about substantive elaborations on policies that have not previously been spelled out already.

A positive treatment of the Carter administration's policies on normalization of relations with Cuba, however, was a front-page commentary in *Izvestia* on February 17, 1977, under the headline, "Common Sense Prevails." Strong criticism of previous U.S. policies toward Cuba comment about the widespread recognition in the United States that these policies have failed, permitted the inference that the Carter administration's greater flexibility on the Cuban question marked a step forward. The clearest indication of the Soviet position came in the statement that "political circles in Washington are coming more and more to understand that normalization of relations with Havana is in the interests of both countries," a statement that seems to indicate Soviet approval. The author was also quick to approve as sound Cuba's policy of developing relations with all countries, including the United States.

The Soviet academic journal *Latinskaia Amerika* devoted an article to U.S.-Cuban relations in its third number in 1977. Most of the text was a retrospective critique of past U.S. policies toward Cuba, of the growing criticism of those policies in the United States, and a descriptive account of recent developments. The author, N. V. Dmitriev, strenuously opposed any U.S. conditions on normalization affecting Cuba's relations with other socialist, African, or Latin American countries. The article seemed to imply that normalization could be a good thing if the United States would give up its policy of "blackmail and pressure," but the article did not formulate or quote any formal Soviet position on the matter.

If the February 1977 *Izvestia* commentary is authoritative, the Soviet government would seem to favor rapprochement. When I asked a Soviet official, who is in a position to know government policy and is scrupulous about sticking close to the official line, what he thought about the United States reestablishing relations with Cuba, he replied: "Why don't you try it out?"

The cloud suspended above U.S.-Cuban rapprochement in early 1978 was the Soviet-sponsored Cuban military involvement in Africa. The consequences of these operations depend on how far and how long military collaboration continues and how the Carter administration perceives its effect on U.S. interests. Some resolution of this issue, if only an uneasy resolution, would seem to be necessary before further progress in rapprochement can occur.

The Soviet "military industrial complex," as one Soviet citizen once commented only partly in jest, may regard Cuban rapprochement with the United States as a net loss to the Soviet strategic position in the Caribbean. Soviet leaders who take a broader view, however, are likely to conclude that the significance of the decline of the Soviet military presence there, now at best a possibility rather than a probability, should not be exaggerated in view of Cuba's peripheral strategic value to the USSR. Those who hold this view may also welcome a reduction of tensions between Cuba and the United States as making less likely their ever having to face two unacceptable choices: participating in military operations against the United States in the defense of Cuba or, more likely, watching the demise of the Castro regime from the sidelines.

The main price of U.S.-Cuban rapprochement is, if anything, political, but not in the sense that it threatens the Soviet Union's main interests there, namely the survival of the socialist regime. Rapprochement in the long term is likely to mean some decline in Soviet political influence in Cuba, particularly with respect to foreign policy. For the foreseeable future it would probably involve political uncertainty but not a rapid deterioration of the Soviet position. In fact, tensions between Cuba and the United States have a negative impact on progress toward U.S.-Soviet agreements on arms control and on East-West trade. The establishment of viable and enduring relationships with the United States in both these areas may well be viewed in Moscow as far more important than a marginal loss of influence in Havana.

The main advantage of rapprochement to the Soviet Union is that it is probably Cuba's best opportunity to get on her feet economically and reduce the need for Soviet assistance. From both the Cuban and Soviet perspective, the Cuban economy must prove itself, which it has so far failed to do without massive foreign aid. For Communists above all, the test of their system and their ideology is ultimately economic. Another obvious advantage of Cuban economic viability would be a reduction in the Soviet Union's burden.

It is ironic that just as Soviet prospects for overtaking capitalism, if ever, may lie in strengthened economic relations with the West, Cuba's best opportunities for making her economy work better lie in rapprochement with the United States.

NOTES

1. Philip W. Bonsal, *Cuba, Castro and the United States* (Pittsburgh, 1971), pp. 150–56; Cole Blasier, *The Hovering Giant: U.S. Responses to Revolutionary Change in Latin America* (Pittsburgh, 1976), pp. 189–200.

2. In addition to pertinent chapters in this volume, such as 3, 4, 9, and 11, there are a number of recent, western studies dealing with Cuban-Soviet relations including Herbert G. Dinerstein, *The Making of a Missile Crisis: October 1962* (Baltimore, 1976); Leon Gouré and Morris Rothenberg, *Soviet Penetration of Latin America* (Miami, 1975); Jacques Levesque, *L'URSS et la revolution*

cubaine (Montreal, 1976); William E. Ratliff, *Castroism and Communism in Latin America, 1959–1976* (Washington, 1976); Morris Rothenberg, *Current Cuban-Soviet Relationships*, An Occasional Paper of the Center for Advanced International Studies, University of Miami (Miami, 1974); James D. Theberge, *Russia in the Caribbean* (Washington, 1973); and the related work of such scholars as Edward Gonzalez and David Ronfeldt.

3. *Granma Weekly Review*, August 25, 1968, pp. 2 ff.

4. See chapter 12, n. 30.

5. Joint financing was provided, for example, in technical cooperation in television and in collaboration between the Academies of Sciences. See documents 25 and 31 in the appendices of A. D. Bekarevich and N. M. Kukharev, *Sovetskii soiuz i Kuba: ekonomicheskoe sotrudnichestvo* (Moscow, 1973).

6. This applies, to give some examples, to the training of Cuban specialists in the Soviet Union, the provision of equipment in soil conservation, and in atomic power. See appendices in ibid., documents 4, 11, and 23.

7. U.S. Arms Control and Disarmament Agency, *World Military Expenditures and Arms Transfers 1966–1975* (Washington, D.C. 1976), p. 26.

8. International Institute for Strategic Studies, *The Military Balance, 1977–78* (London, 1977), pp. 69–70.

9. For the years 1961 through 1964, see *The International Transfer of Conventional Arms*, A Report to the Congress from the U.S. Arms Control and Disarmament Agency, Committee on Foreign Affairs, U.S. House of Representatives, August 12, 1974, p. 8. For later years, see annual issues of the same agency's *World Military Expenditures and Arms Transfers*, including the issue published in December 1976 covering the period 1966–1975, p. 61. The figures are in current dollars. The largest transfers were made in 1962, 1963, and 1967—$455 million, $76 million, and $82 million respectively. The assistance of Colonel Norman M. Smith, then of the ACDA, in collecting and interpreting this information is gratefully acknowledged.

10. *Granma*, May 3, 1970, p. 3, column 2.

11. Fidel Castro, *La primera revolución socialista en América* (Mexico: Siglo Veintiuno Editores, S.A., 1976). This is the report of the Central Committee to the first congress of the Cuban Communist Party. Castro said that the USSR "nos ha entregado gratuitamente los modernos medios de defensa con que están dotadas nuestras unidades y cuyo valor es del orden de varios miles de millones de pesos" (p. 210).

12. *Granma*, October 3, 1976, p. 1.

13. Ibid.

14. *Izvestia*, February 14, 1978, p. 1.

15. U.S. authorities have periodically provided reassurances that there are no nuclear weapons in Cuba. An authoritative discussion of the Soviet military presence in Cuba is contained in *Soviet Activities in Cuba*, Hearings before the Subcommittee on Inter-American Affairs, House of Representatives, 93rd Cong., Parts 4 and 5, October 31, 1973, November 20 and 21, 1974 (Washington, 1974), pp. 5 and 57. The latest U.S. official denial that there is no Soviet submarine base in Cuba was reported by the *New York Times*, March 28, 1978, p. 9.

16. H. R. Haldeman, *The Ends of Power* (New York, 1978), pp. 85–88. See also appendices of Theberge, *Russia in the Caribbean*. The information on missile subs is from a telephone interview, April 10, 1978, with Wayne Smith, coordinator of Cuban Affairs in the U.S. Department of State.

17. Wayne Smith, interview.

18. For interpretation of this slippery subject and the events leading up to the missile crisis of 1962, see Dinerstein, *The Making of a Missile Crisis*, esp. pp. 232–38. Note that when Brezhnev made his historic visit to Cuba in January 1974 (and cabled President Nixon a greeting en route) he said that Cuba did not stand "alone" and participated in the brotherhood and camaraderie of the socialist countries. Yet he did not mention any military commitments. In fact, his talk stressed peace, opposed "the export of revolution," and supported improvement of Soviet-American relations. Fidel Castro and Leonid Brezhnev, *Cuba-URSS: amistad indestructible y anti-imperialista* (Lima, 1974), pp. 38, 42, and 47.

3

JORGE I. DOMÍNGUEZ

The Armed Forces and Foreign Relations

The development of the armed forces is one of the success stories of the Cuban Revolution. They defeated the internal and external armed opposition to the revolutionary government; they provide a substantial deterrent to another attack, from internal enemies or from abroad; they are able to inflict considerable costs on those who may seek to overthrow the revolutionary government. Providing effectively for the national defense and for the defense of the incumbent revolutionary government has been their principal contribution to Cuban foreign relations. But the armed forces have also helped to spread the influence of Cuban foreign policy beyond the country's shores. This was done most spectacularly in Angola, where Cuban troops were committed to front-line combat and successfully defeated their enemies and those of the Popular Movement for the Liberation of Angola (MPLA) which became Angola's government in Luanda. The armed forces have also conducted an extensive military assistance program which increases Cuban influence overseas and affects the quality of Cuban relations with a great many countries, and they helped Ethiopia defeat the Somali invasion.

This essay concentrates on the international aspects of the behavior of the Cuban armed forces. In the first section, however, as well as in parts of subsequent sections, I shall consider some internal elements to the extent that they shed light on the potential for further Cuban military operations overseas.

The most striking feature of Cuban foreign military policy in the second half of the 1970s is the justification of military intervention abroad on the grounds that it bears no relationship to more common conceptions of the national security. The Cuban leadership explains its military intervention in Angola as unselfish internationalist solidarity, not in terms of narrower national interests. The facts that Angola is geographically distant, that it has not been a long-term central concern of Cuban foreign policy, and that it is difficult for Cuba to benefit economically from influence in Angola, are cited as evidence of the purity of Cuba's motives.[1] This kind of justification may mean a Cuban willingness to intervene militarily anywhere in the world. Except for the United States in Indochina, no other state today has made such a claim or has been willing to shed the blood of its citizens to implement that claim on such a large scale, far from its borders, and independent of the narrower formulations of the national security. To make this commitment credible, Cuba must maintain a military establishment equal to the task and pursue a foreign policy close enough to that of the Soviet

JORGE I. DOMÍNGUEZ

Union to make overseas military intervention politically feasible. It is argued that the actual threat posed by Cuba to other countries is not so great as may be suggested by its justification of the military intervention in Angola; Cuba may be more moderate in the future in the implementation of these broad claims because of the costs borne by the armed forces in their successful conduct of that war.

Capabilities

The Cuban armed forces have very substantial economic resources for the pursuit of their ends. The military budget peaked in the early 1960s at approximately 500 million pesos; it declined in the late 1960s, to rise again in the early 1970s. On the eve of Cuba's entrance into the Angolan civil war, Cuba's military budget was at least 400 million pesos, and it may have been somewhat higher. These budgetary estimates include only those publicly admitted expenses directly attributable to the armed forces, excluding large-scale Soviet weapons donations and some costs in maintaining the critical reserve forces.[2] The highest budgetary commitment occurred at the time of the greatest threat to the survival of revolutionary rule in the early 1960s; the next highest has occurred in the mid-1970s, when Cuban regular armed forces have entered overseas combat. The military establishment was labor-intensive in the 1960s, becoming more capital-intensive in the 1970s. The rise in military expenditures in the 1970s, therefore, is explained in part by the higher costs of military professionalization and of the modernization of inventories and facilities for which Cuba is responsible. Cuba's military capabilities are also linked to the state of its economy. (This subject is addressed in other essays in this volume.) The Angolan intervention occurred in the immediate aftermath of the large scale expansion of internal economic resources and improvement in Cuba's balance of payments in the first half of the 1970s.[3] The projected 40 percent slowdown of the economic growth rate in the five-year plan for 1976–1980, compared to the previous five years, compounded by the continued slide of the international price of sugar outside of preferential agreements, leaves fewer resources for military and related purposes in the years ahead compared to the recent past.[4]

Cuba's resources for war are also enhanced by Soviet assistance. The Soviet Union supplied Cuba "free of charge" with weapons worth "several thousand million pesos" between 1960 and 1975.[5] Of course, the Soviet Union has provided many other things—credits to finance bilateral trade deficits or to promote economic development, subsidies to Cuban sugar exports and petroleum imports, technical assistance—but two elements need to be highlighted.[6] First, the Soviet Union apparently increased the rate of weapons deliveries to Cuba in the 1970s, particularly by providing costly, modern equipment to the air force. Soviet deliveries of weapons free of charge from 1960 to 1970 were worth about $1.5 billion; by 1975, the amount may have doubled.[7] Soviet deliveries are planned to continue in the late 1970s.[8] Second, the intensity of Soviet technical advice to Cuba—including military technicians—has also increased in the 1970s. Through

1971–1972, between three thousand and forty-five hundred Cubans had been trained in the Soviet Union; in 1974 alone, over eight hundred were studying in the Soviet Union, or more than twice the annual rate that had prevailed in the 1960s. The number of Soviet specialists in Cuba increased from about one thousand in the early 1970s to "several thousand" by 1973, and possibly six thousand (half military) by 1975.[9]

No other Latin American country commits as high a proportion of gross product to military expenditures. The absolute sum of Cuban military expenditures—including estimates of free Soviet weaponry—exceeded that of every other neighboring country, though Venezuela and Mexico approximated it. Cuban military expenditures were no less than ten times those of the Dominican Republic, and twenty times Nicaragua's. Among the countries bordering on the Caribbean and Gulf of Mexico, apart from the United States, Cuba was the preeminent military power. The only Latin American country whose absolute military expense probably exceeded Cuba was Brazil.[10] Cuba's military efforts are, of course, not surprising. It is the only Latin American country whose defense has been seriously threatened (by the U.S.), and it is the only one to have undertaken a major contemporary overseas military effort.

According to Prime Minister Castro, the Revolutionary Armed Forces had a standing global membership of about 300,000 at their peak in the early 1960s. By 1970, this global number had declined to 250,000 and by the latter part of 1974 to about 100,000. The Institute for Strategic Studies estimated that Cuba's regular armed forces in 1975 amounted to 117,000 and the ready reserves, mobilizable within forty-eight to seventy-two hours, to about 90,000 (additional reserves were not estimated).[11] Thus the change in the Cuban armed forces from 1970 to 1974 can be attributed to a shift of personnel from semiprofessional full-time military activity to the military reserves. The size of the truly professional forces has apparently remained constant. Moreover, the total number of people under the authority of the Armed Forces Ministry has, in fact, increased through such programs as the reserves and the Army of Working Youth, which are excluded from these estimates of global standing forces.

The defense of Cuba, in practice, rests with the navy, equipped to intercept landings and prevent hit-and-run raids. Estimates of the navy's size have varied from 6,000 to 7,500 between 1970 and 1975, in part because its officers and crew have exchanged roles regularly between the navy and the merchant marine, so that the navy's standing size is difficult to estimate. The air force, with its air and antiaircraft defense forces, is equipped to intercept exile attacks, and also has principally a defense role, although it is also available for overseas combat. Its size has risen from 12,000 in 1970 to 20,000 in 1975. Defense also rests with the Frontier Corps (a regular military unit under the Ministry of the Interior, not the Armed Forces Ministry) which has about 3,000 members. Thus about 30,000 troops are concerned principally with defense.

Cuba's other military capabilities are not necessary to the daily practice of defense, although they are a critical part of the Cuban deterrent against the

United States. The size of the professional army has been estimated at 90,000 for several years—excluding all reserves and the Army of Working Youth and its predecessors. The army's ready reserves have been estimated at 90,000, yielding a total of 180,000 troops available for internal security, defense, or overseas combat. They are reinforced by the elite Special Forces Battalion under the Ministry of the Interior; this unit was sent to Angola in the fall of 1975 to resist the South African advance pending further reinforcements. There are also 100,000 troops in the Army of Working Youth, but they are mainly engaged in production and have only nominal military training.[12] There are more than 500,000 reservists, including the ready reserves, at various levels of combat readiness. The ready reserves must be included in the Cuban order of battle: they have constituted a majority of all Cuban troops engaged in war exercises in the mid-1970s, and 70 percent of the Cuban troops in Angola were reservists.[13] The internal security units of the Ministry of the Interior amount to an additional 10,000 troops. There are also several tens of thousands of civilian workers providing logistical support under the direct commands of the Armed Forces Ministry and the Ministry of the Interior. Their number increased 23 percent between 1971 and 1975. Thus the total number of troops under the command of the two ministries, but excluding the non-ready reserves, the civilian workers under direct military command, and the civil defense, was no less than 321,150 in the mid-1970s. This should be considered the minimal order of battle (see table 3.1). There is substantial variation in the level of combat preparedness and readiness within this number, and additional reserves are available for extended military operation. The 100,000 in the Army of Working Youth, and substantial portions of the forces allocated to defense and internal security, should be subtracted to estimate the numbers available for overseas service.

The weapons structure of the Cuban armed forces has remained stable since 1968, the turning point in Soviet-Cuban relations. Cuban-Soviet collaboration since then, so important in the economy and in politics, has brought only marginal or incremental changes in Cuban weapons structure.[14] The principal change in the army's weapons structure up to the Angolan war was the doubling of the number of tanks by adding light tanks and increasing the number of medium and heavy tanks. After the Angolan war, Cuba also added T-62 tanks, of which fifteen were shown in published photographs for the first time in December 1976, and several BM-21 multiple rocket launchers. The fast patrol-boat force has been increased and qualitatively improved. There was also a modest qualitative improvement of the surface-to-surface short-range ground rocket force and an increase in the number of training aircraft. The major change was the replacement of the 1948 MiG-15, especially by the supersonic MiG-21, and the introduction in the early 1970s of the more modern MiG-21MF.

Though there have been no fundamental changes, the Soviet Union has strengthened and modernized Cuban capabilities. The light tanks give greater mobility. The MiG-21, introduced in 1965, was the first supersonic military aircraft in Latin America.[15] The changes in the MiG force reflect not only the

TABLE 3.1
The Order of Battle, 1976

Defense	
Air Force	20,000
Navy	7,500
Frontier Corps	3,000
Internal Security	
Interior Ministry troops	10,000
National and International Purposes	
Army, regular troops	90,000
Army, ready reserves	90,000
Special Forces	650
Forces with Low to Nominal Combat Readiness[a]	
Army of Working Youth	100,000
All non-ready reserves	410,000
Minimal Order of Battle,	
first 8 categories	321,150

Sources: International Institute for Strategic Studies, *The Military Balance, 1975–1976* (London: International Institute for Strategic Studies, 1975), p. 64; *Granma Weekly Review,* December 12, 1971, p. 6; ibid., December 1, 1974, p. 7; ibid., September 28, 1975, p. 7; *Granma,* June 8, 1976, p. 4; ibid., April 20, 1976, p. 2; and Gabriel García Márquez, "Colombian Author Writes on Cuba's Angola Intervention," *Washington Post,* January 10, 1977, p. A14.

a. In addition to those listed below, there are the civilian workers of the Armed Forces Ministry, numbering several tens of thousands.

modernization of inventories but also the most substantial modification of weapons doctrine. Bombers with long flying ranges (the MiG-15 has a range of 560 miles) are replaced by fighter interceptors with short flying ranges (98 miles for the MiG-21). The bombers, though old, had a fundamentally offensive purpose; the fighter interceptors have a variety of purposes, but their combat radius sharply limits offensive utility for an island country. Thus the changes in the weapons structure of the air force emphasize a more defensive posture, within a general weapons structure that has changed only marginally and predictably. The announced plan for further changes fits the view that modernization is the principal aim, rather than a drastic change of posture.

The Soviet Union has maintained an important limitation on Cuban weapons structure: Transport facilities have remained small and constant. The prerevolutionary Bristol Britannia BB-218 turboprops can only transport a few troops at a time, slowly and at considerable risk because of their age and their limited flying range and carrying capacity. Although all of Cuba's transport aircraft acquired since the Revolution have a flying range of at least 325 miles, their transport capacity varies only between fourteen and fifty passengers per flight. These tend to be older Soviet aircraft (1947, 1953, and 1962 models). Their capacity is even more limited than the Bristol Britannia's—one reason for the use of the latter in transportation to Angola. Changes in the navy have improved Cuba's naval defensive capability through more and better fast patrol boats, but they have done little to improve Cuba's offensive capability. Cuba used its merchant marine to transport troops to Angola; yet it lacks the ability to ship medium-to-heavy combat weaponry. Thus Cuban offensive military operations can only occur as they have—with the concurrent, active, and steady support of the Soviet Union to supply the Cuban armed forces with the appropriate weaponry for overseas combat.[16]

In conclusion, Cuba has sufficient military resources to deter any invasion from the United States which is not the result of a formal U.S. declaration of war. And even if the U.S. government were to commit massive resources to an invasion, the Cuban forces would inflict extraordinarily high costs on the invaders. Cuba has a large, professionalized, well-equipped, and battle-tested military force, in close alliance with the Soviet Union. The size of its forces, and the willingness of the Soviet Union to provide additional supplies for overseas operations, enables the Cuban government to pursue an active foreign military policy. Even at the peak of the Angolan war, less than a tenth of the Cuban order of battle was engaged. This analysis indicates that Cuba has a substantial potential for overseas military operations so long as the USSR is willing to participate in the implementation.

Military Doctrine

Cuban military doctrine exhibits both continuity and change from the mid-1960s to the mid-1970s. Concerning weapons structure and expenditures, it has remained basically unchanged since the second half of the 1960s, after the survival of revolutionary rule was assured. The military doctrine on these subjects was modified primarily by the shift of the air force to a more defensive posture, by the acceleration of military modernization, and by efforts to reduce the military burden on the economy.

By the end of the 1960s, the Cuban armed forces, in increasingly close cooperation with the Soviet Union, began to modify the implementation of military personnel doctrine. These changes accelerated during the early 1970s. There has been a decline in the personnel in the standing regular armed forces, especially in the army, an increase in military professionalization not only in the remaining standing armed forces but also in the reserves, coupled with a modernization of weapons inventories, a new focus on the role of the reserves, and an increase in military mobilizational capabilities.[17]

The general rationale for the military establishment has been the most variable feature of military doctrine. It has had four phases since the Revolution. Until 1965, when the last internal insurgencies of any consequence were defeated, the Cuban military was a large conglomerate at a low level of professional competence, concerned with assuring the survival of revolutionary rule. Cuba has had full control over the surface-to-air missiles on its territory since early 1965.[18]

The second phase, in the late 1960s, was premised on substantial fears of foreign attack and distrust of the Soviet Union. In July 1967, Armed Forces Minister Raúl Castro presented two national security reasons for the maintenance of a large military establishment (in addition to other internal social, economic, and political reasons). One was the potential military threat to Cuba from its neighbors, principally the United States. He reviewed published reports of U.S. military contingency plans, the record of clashes around the Guantanamo naval base, CIA covert operations including plots to assassinate his brother, and press reports that the United States had never agreed not to invade Cuba as part of the bargain to solve the missile crisis of October 1962. Cuban security, Raúl Castro believed, should not rest on U.S. willingness to respect an agreement. He also reviewed possible military threats to Cuba from Venezuela and other Latin American countries in retaliation for Cuban "solidarity" with revolutionary movements operating in those countries.[19] This was the peak of Cuban support for such movements.

The second national security reason was stated thus: "Should the national security, which is our very existence in this case, depend exclusively on foreign support? We think not. Why not? Because that would ill accustom our people to depend on others for the resolution of our problems. Do we have that support? Yes, we do. Is it good? It is. Should we depend on it exclusively? No." Fidel Castro put it more bluntly, also in July 1967: "We must say realistically that we are thousands of miles away from any country that can give us any kind of help and in case of invasion here, we must learn to accustom ourselves to the idea that *we are going to fight alone*."[20] This reflected the increasing strain in Cuban-Soviet relations which reached the boiling point in the winter of 1967–1968, when a "microfaction" was uncovered within the Communist Party of Cuba (PCC), including its Central Committee, in coalition with Soviet and East European party and government personnel, seeking to change Cuban government and party policy. The Soviet Union also slowed down the level of petroleum deliveries to Cuba, so that rationing of petroleum products had to be tightened severely.[21] Given great uncertainty about Soviet-Cuban relations, and facing an aggressive United States, the armed forces minister and the prime minister made a prudent case for military self-reliance. Raúl Castro concluded that Cuba would even have to sacrifice aspects of its development, especially in construction, to "prepare the country for a war although we do not know when it will begin." The new military budget was the highest of the second half of the 1960s, both in absolute terms and as a percentage of gross national product, reflecting Cuba's greater commitment to support revolution in Latin America and the greater strain in Cuban-Soviet relations.[22]

Those national security policy decisions, though very expensive, bore some correspondence to the remaining objective threat. By the mid-1970s, the objective threat to Cuba had declined even further. Relations with the Soviet Union improved after Prime Minister Castro endorsed the invasion of Czechoslovakia in 1968 and have become warmer ever since.[23] While self-reliance may remain the determining ingredient of Cuban military doctrine, it need no longer be justified by serious doubts concerning Cuban-Soviet relations. Relations between Cuba and many Latin American countries have also improved markedly since 1968. By 1975, Cuba had diplomatic relations with Argentina, Barbados, Canada, Colombia, Guyana, Jamaica, Mexico, Panama, Peru, Trinidad-Tobago, and Venezuela.[24] As for the threat from the United States, the prime minister called the U.S. government steps of August 1975 to remove those aspects of the embargo policies toward Cuba affecting third parties, "positive steps, and we have received them with satisfaction." He outlined an agenda for U.S.-Cuban negotiations once the embargo was fully lifted, including "compensation (the compensation they would demand from us, and the compensation we could demand from them because of the fifteen years of blockade), and the occupation of a part of our territory, the Guantanamo naval base."[25] In short, Cuban government perceptions on several national security policy elements had changed much between 1967 and 1975.

Despite many changes in objective conditions and in some elite perceptions, certain themes of Cuban national security policy changed little in this third phase of Cuban military doctrine. On November 22, 1974, Prime Minister Castro asserted that "our country will need, therefore, over an indefinite period of time, greater and greater defense capacity." The national security reasoning had been reduced to the following: "Even if one day there should be economic and even diplomatic relations between us [Cuba and the United States] that would not give us the right to weaken our defense because our defense can never depend on the imperialists' good faith." [26] Seven months later, Raúl Castro stressed the "essential need to increase our military power constantly." The government planned to adhere to this "firm commitment . . . despite the fact that the present correlation of forces favors the socialist camp and despite the positive advances made in international détente."[27]

The Angolan war opened the fourth phase of military doctrine, adding a new dimension to elite perceptions. Prime Minister Castro's main report to the first party congress in December of 1975 noted that "the starting point of Cuba's foreign policy, according to our Programmatic Platform, is the subordination of Cuban positions to the international needs of the struggle for socialism and for the national liberation of peoples." This position was reaffirmed by the foreign policy resolution of the congress. Both the prime minister and the congress committed themselves open-endedly to participation in the Angolan civil war.[28] Therefore, in addition to the hypothetical threat to Cuba which formerly had justified the existence of a large military establishment, there was a new element: the present and future commitment to send the Cuban armed forces to fight overseas.

Although Cuba had supported revolutionary movements in many countries of the world in the 1960s, those commitments had never been formally tied to the role and purpose of the Cuban armed forces. Cubans who had fought abroad, expressing their internationalist duties and commitments, had been said to have acted on their own, though with the warm support of the Cuban people, party, and government. For example, Ernesto (''Che'') Guevara had renounced formally all his positions in Cuba before embarking on his career as a revolutionary in Bolivia. Since 1970, small numbers of Cuban officers and troops had been sent overseas, ordinarily as a part of Cuba's growing military assistance program. The most important commitment had been the contingent sent to Syria during and after the 1973 Arab-Israeli war. The commitment of such forces, which generally operated only in supportive and logistical roles and not in front-line combat, required no modification of existing Cuban military doctrine. The number of Cuban casualties from these programs was apparently quite small and accidental. Never before Angola had the Cuban armed forces been formally committed to front-line overseas combat as a formal part of their military mission. The Cuban armed forces had been justified for national defense; internationalist solidarity for combat roles had been open to military people, though formally as individual, not institutional, actions; non-combat roles had not required a change of mission. Since the Angolan war, however, there is a new rationale for the Cuban armed forces, which is no longer merely defensive. Engagement in front-line overseas combat is now to be rewarded publicly and explicitly within Cuba. Prime Minister Castro noted that this was one of the reasons why individuals were judged worthy to enter the Central Committee of the PCC. At the party congress in 1975, 8 percent of the 3116 delegates present had won merits because of their active participation in actions of international solidarity.[29]

The change in the justification for military doctrine in the mid-1970s had substantial implications for both Cuban foreign policy and its armed forces. The standing of the military in the Cuban political system had been buttressed by internal political and economic needs, as well as by the need to deter the United States; the armed forces had not played a central role in Cuba's support for revolution abroad in the 1960s. The decline in the credible threat from the United States, and in a credible threat of internal insurrection or exile attack, reduced the need for a large-scale military establishment. The shift toward a more economically efficient economy in civilian hands—away from the ''command'' economy of the late 1960s—also circumscribed, though it did not eliminate, the military's economic role. Foreign military activities, however, add a new doctrinal justification for the Cuban armed forces and relate to the Cuban government's foreign policy objectives, including normative internationalist solidarity, political influence, and a redefinition of Soviet-Cuban relations. The standing of the military in the Cuba of the late 1970s is linked directly, for the first time, to overseas performance. Were the military component of Cuban foreign policy to decline, the internal political and budgetary pressures on the Cuban armed forces might increase. Thus the Cuban military have come to have an institutional stake in the continuation of a vigorous Cuban foreign policy abroad, especially in Africa.

Foreign Military Aid

During the 1960s, Cuba actively supported revolutionary causes and movements in many countries, especially in Latin America. With the defeat of a number of insurgencies and the victory of others, and with increasing economic difficulties at home, Cuba's engagement in insurrection declined. The Cuban government now deals more actively with governments than with their oppositions.

In July 1969, Prime Minister Castro opened a new page in the history of Cuba's Latin American relations by supporting publicly many of the actions of the Peruvian military government. This support was offered without an evident quid pro quo, even though Cuban internal policy was still very radical, and many in the Latin American left remained skeptical of the Peruvian military's commitment to change.[30] The beginnings of Cuban foreign aid programs, in their current public government-to-government setting, may also be linked to Peruvian-Cuban relations. In 1970, notwithstanding the absence of diplomatic relations, the Cuban government sent aid to Peru in the wake of a devastating earthquake. That aid had program characteristics important ever since; they are common to civilian and military aid programs, with obvious exceptions:

1. The amount of aid, measured in pesos or dollars, is relatively modest, as one might expect from a small country that is not wealthy.

2. The aid usually consists of technicians, often assisted by nontechnical skilled personnel, who provide specific services such as medical care or building a school; they also train host country personnel. There were 4,100 Cuban civilians stationed overseas in this program in mid-1977, scheduled to rise to 6000 by year's end (90 percent of them were in Africa).

3. There is no necessary prior agreement on Cuban influence in the recipient country for nonmilitary programs; there is no obvious or immediate quid pro quo; it is not even necessary that there should be diplomatic relations; it is, of course, expected that this donation will serve Cuba's interests in the long run.

4. The Cuban government rewards its foreign aid personnel with public exposure and support and takes this service into consideration in promotion decisions; it also encourages foreign governments to reward Cuban personnel.

5. Cuba has been especially forthcoming in natural disasters; its quick, useful response, without rushing for short-term influence gains, has often opened the way for gains in the long run.

6. Aid has been mostly government-to-government; Cuba has no programs to bolster the private sector. Aid to insurgents has been reduced to services that can be offered in Cuba itself (conferences, some training, radio broadcasts, printed literature, etc.), and it is given openly, not secretly.[31]

Cuban foreign aid programs in the Americas have nonmilitary purposes, as in Jamaica and Guyana, or the natural disaster relief in Guatemala, Nicaragua, and Honduras. Cuba has provided foreign assistance even when it has led to some hardships at home. Its efforts to heal the sick and teach the illiterate do not pose a threat to other countries. What is, however, the military content of Cuba's foreign aid programs?

Cuba and Angola

Cuban aid to the MPLA began in the early and mid-1960s and was expanded spectacularly by the sending of up to twenty thousand Cuban troops in 1975–1976 to ensure its victory and to repel the South African armed forces. The Angolan operation highlighted the effectiveness of the procedures to upgrade the quality of Cuban armed forces; it also stressed the close military link between the Soviet Union and Cuba. The Cuban forces were flown over equipped only with light weapons; medium and heavier weapons were supplied on the spot by the Soviet Union. Cuban weapons inventories were not substantially drawn upon. Cuban Bristol Britannia air transports were used, as well as the Cuban merchant marine, to take military personnel to Angola. Apart from the Special Forces of the Ministry of the Interior, Cuban troops included artillery, motorized, tank, rocketry, air force, and infantry units. Cuban troops may have begun to withdraw from Angola in the spring of 1976.[32]

The war in Angola had significant costs—in human lives, resources, the employment of personnel who might have otherwise been used in Cuba toward development. Very little is known about these costs. There were also costs incurred by the military institutions.[33] There was a much higher demand for personnel, leading elite civilians responsible for production to obstruct the withdrawal of personnel from their production tasks. This was the first time the government has acknowledged substantial elite civilian unwillingness to contribute to military activities. There was some troop insubordination during the Angolan war, although its extent cannot be determined and was probably limited. There was also a manifestation of widespread unhappiness among the people concerning compulsory military service, contrary to the impression given by the government that the only ones who did not wish to serve were religious fanatics. Military service was perceived by parents, sons, teachers, and even government agencies as undesirable and coercive. The Angolan war also worsened relations between the party and some professional military officers, leading to an exacerbation of political strains within the armed forces.

There is, however, no reliable evidence of substantial opposition among the Cuban elite or the masses to the decision to send troops to Angola; neither the general principle of committing troops for the sake of internationalist solidarity, nor the specific decision to implement that principle in Angola, was challenged in or outside the government, in so far as one can tell from public sources. Most people in Cuba probably supported the Angolan policy. Nevertheless, the indirect costs incurred by the Cuban armed forces as an institution during the Angolan war can be and have been documented. The main impact may have been to exacerbate an ordinary problem. When Gregory Treverton asked in Havana whether there had been unhappiness with the Angolan intervention, he was told that there was no "ideological disenchantment" but that "some people had reacted in a human way to the departure of husbands and sons to a distant war.''[34] The ordinary fear and dislike of military service was probably compounded by the reality of war overseas. Husbands and sons were departing not merely for a few weeks of reserve training, but for months of war; they were not to learn a trade, but to engage in combat. An inference is that the costs have been high enough to persuade Cuba not to commit its troops lightly to another operation on the scale of the Angolan war, but that the benefits are sufficiently high to seek to continue its influence through foreign military assistance short of combat.

After independence, the Cuban foreign aid program to Angola has included military and nonmilitary aspects. The Cuban-Angolan 1976 military agreement committed Cuba to the unlimited defense of Angola against hostile neighbors. Although the treaty requires only the "Cuban military units and weapons necessary to support the People's Republic of Angola in case of aggression from outside," the Cuban government's interpretation is that the guerrillas opposed to the Luanda government are agents of outside forces, extending the effect of the treaty to internal counterinsurgency operations.[35] Thus about three thousand Cuban troops are stationed in several bases in the Cabinda enclave; they have been described as an "army of occupation" over a territory which wished to secede from Angola and did not support the MPLA in the civil war, but which is crucial to the survival of the Luanda government because it has the principal petroleum wells.[36] Through the first half of 1976 there were only several hundred Cubans in civilian roles in Angola, but the Angolan demand for them rose faster than anticipated. Their number was planned to rise to more than three thousand in 1977, but it had already reached five thousand by April 1977. Cubans in Angola are truck drivers, bricklayers, or construction foremen, as well as professionals. There are Cuban foreign aid projects in public health, construction, community development, furniture production, communications, sports, culture, education, labor, poultry farming, fishing, sugarcane farming, sugar refining, and coffee farming. Of course, Cuba will also "organize and train their armed forces, helping to train cadres for the struggle against sabotage and counterrevolution." Thus Cuba is likely to organize Angola's armed forces, police, and internal security forces, to aid in the organization of its external and internal trade, and of the MPLA as a Communist party, as well as to design and develop mass media and propaganda instruments.[37]

The Angolan case exemplifies another aspect of Cuba's foreign aid program: the use overseas of the "civic soldier."[38] The same individual may have both civilian and military background, competence, and goal orientation; someone who is sent overseas to build a school may also be able to engage in military activities, while someone who first goes overseas as a soldier may become a construction worker. Prime Minister Castro announced in June 1976 that Cuban troops were being withdrawn from Angola; he also noted that, while the numbers of military personnel in Angola would decline, civilians would increase. Some Cuban troops have returned home, but some who went to Angola as soldiers have now begun to perform in civilian rather than military activities. There is nothing sinister about this, no repudiation of the commitment to reduce the military presence. Yet it becomes impossible to tell to what extent Cuban military capabilities have actually been reduced in Angola. The health personnel and military instructors who arrived in early October 1975 also engaged in front-line combat. Cuban construction workers were also under military command. President Castro said that they "must be workers and soldiers at the same time." Cuban civilians in Angola can be called back into active military service, should the fortunes of the Luanda government take a turn for the worse, without the need to call up and transport troops from Cuba.[39]

Cuban Aid to Other Countries

Prime Minister Castro has stated that "no Latin American country, regardless of its social system, has any reason to fear the Cuban armed forces," adding that only the people of each country can make a revolution. "Never has the Cuban government thought of carrying the revolution to any country of this hemisphere with the weaponry of its military units," and "no country of black Africa has any reason to fear from Cuban military personnel."[40] Thus the Angolan experience has been presented as a specific response to a concrete historical situation, not to be repeated easily or frequently.

There are many other possibilities, however. First, the Cuban armed forces may be sent overseas to help an incumbent government suppress an insurrection described as the result of foreign intervention. Second, they may be sent to repel a conventional military invasion of one country by another. Third, the assurances to incumbent governments are imited to the regular and reserve armed forces: They do not include support extended by the Ministry of the Interior and other Cuban government organizations to opposition forces, nor direct assistance by Cuban civilians to opposition forces elsewhere. Thus elements of subversion policies remain within the scope of the Cuban government's foreign policy. Fourth, the armed forces might provide training and supplies to forces in one country that may then invade another country without additional Cuban participation. This appears to have been the case with Cuban support to the Shaba or Katangan rebels who invaded Zaire in 1977-1978, and to the Polisario Liberation Front's fight against Morocco over the former Spanish Sahara. (President Castro has denied that Cuba "armed or trained" the Katangese, although they fought with Cubans alongside the MPLA in the closing months of the Angolan civil war.)[41] Fifth, the assurances to African countries are limited in two ways: They exclude Rhodesia and South Africa, and they leave open the possibility of Cuban engagement in Northern Africa (for instance, between Morocco and Algeria). Therefore, Cuba's declared foreign military policy still presents a possible threat to other countries.

Civic soldiers have also been used in other countries. They formed the construction brigades sent as a part of the foreign aid program to Guinea (building roads and airports), Vietnam, Peru (building hospitals), and Tanzania (building schools) in addition to Angola.[42] Because Cuban foreign aid personnel performing civilian tasks in Indochina were sent there while wars were being fought, it is likely that they, too, were civic soldiers. If all construction brigades are composed of civic soldiers, Cuban personnel in Jamaica may have been under the direct supervision of the Armed Forces Ministry; however, the government of Jamaica has denied any military or police links with Cuba, so the matter is uncertain. The construction program in Tanzania, including 226 Cubans, required not only actual building by the Cubans, but also the training of Tanzanians by Cuban personnel. Obviously these Cubans have skills well beyond those possessed by simple construction workers: They can teach as well.[43]

Some Cuban foreign aid programs, however, have clearly emphasized military features (see table 3.2). The size of Cuba's military aid program is difficult to determine; Fidel Castro reported to the party congress in 1975 that "the men of the army [sic], in keeping with international solidarity, cooperated in organizing the armed forces and militias of other progressive nations; they gave unhesitatingly firm support to countries threatened by imperialist aggression. On more than one occasion, they have shed their generous blood in other lands of the world." Armed Forces Minister Raúl Castro told U.S. Senator George McGovern that Cuba had military missions of ten to fifty men in several African countries. While that may be the modal size of Cuba's current African programs, the size of the Cuban foreign military aid missions—in Angola and elsewhere—has often been larger.[44] One of Cuba's oldest allies in Africa, in the mid-1960s as well as in the mid-1970s, has been the Congo (Brazzaville). The Congo played a crucial role facilitating Cuba's participation in the Angolan civil war; ten years earlier, Cuba had an active foreign aid program in the Congo. Cuban military personnel advised the Congolese government on civil and military defense procedures and structures; Cuba awarded 220 scholarships for Congolese to study in Cuba.[45]

Cuba's principal contribution to North Vietnam and Laos during the Indochina war was the sending of antiaircraft and antimissile military personnel, medical brigades, and an undetermined amount of other modest material assistance. After the end of the Vietnam war, Cuban assistance to North Vietnam became more diversified. Thus, by the end of 1975, some Cubans were sent to Hanoi to train Vietnamese in hotel and restaurant management; a Cuban construction brigade of 900 construction workers has helped in war reconstruction. Postwar Cuban aid to Laos also emphasized construction work; Cubans were building airports in Laos in December 1975.[46]

In the 1970s, Cuba has paid special attention to the successor states of Iberian empires; it had assisted the rebellions against the Portuguese in most of them. Cuba assisted the rebels in Guinea-Bissau by sending military and medical personnel; the most famous Cuban captured by the Portuguese in Guinea-Bissau was Pedro Rodríguez Peralta, promoted to the central committee of the PCC in December 1975 as a reward for his international solidarity. After independence, Cuban aid continued with the sending of medical teams and others to train personnel in defense, economics, education, and public health. Guinea-Bissau played a crucial role in support of the Cuban war effort in Angola; Cuban support for Guinea-Bissau, including military aid, apparently increased after the Angolan war.[47] In 1976, Cuba sent four doctors to São Tomé and Príncipe, almost doubling the number of doctors there, and agreed to a foreign aid program that would include education, fishing, agriculture, and cattle raising, all through the sending of Cuban technicians.[48] In the fall of 1973, Cuba sent forty intermediate level teachers to the Republic of Equatorial Guinea (former Spanish Guinea); it was apparently the "first time that such a large group of Cuban teachers will be going outside the country" in a foreign aid program.[49]

One of the more interesting military aid programs had developed in Somalia. Cuba and Somalia established diplomatic relations only in July 1972. Until early 1974, Cuban aid was limited to public health and the sugar industry. Since then, Cuban military personnel assumed important responsibilities for Somali military and political training at several bases. Cuban-Somali agreements in 1976 extended the Cuban foreign aid program for a longer period of time, but the agreements were terminated, and the Cubans expelled from Somalia, as a result of Cuban assistance to Ethiopia in the Somali-Ethiopian war that began in 1977.[50]

The Cuban Middle Eastern program developed in the late summer of 1973. On September 9 in Algiers, two days after his controversial defense of the Soviet Union at the meeting of heads of state of nonaligned countries, Prime Minister Castro announced that Cuba would sever diplomatic relations with Israel. Cuba then increased its military aid program in Somalia and Southern Yemen.[51] A brigade of fifty-two health personnel arrived in Syria on 13 October 1973 to support the Syrians during the second half of the October war with Israel; it is likely that these were civic soldiers. There is some uncertainty concerning the total size (from several hundred to thousands) and the activities of the regular Cuban military units sent to Syria after the 1973 Arab-Israeli war; yet there is agreement that they were the only substantial non-Arab military force in Syria, that their principal contribution was to operate relatively complex Soviet military equipment (such as tanks and MiG-23 aircraft) and to instruct others on how to do so, and that most of them departed by 1975. One result of Syria's participation in the Lebanese civil war, and of its combat against Palestinian forces in Lebanon, was a cooling of Syrian-Cuban relations throughout 1976, though the Cuban government never publicly broke with the Syrians.[52]

At the end of 1975, the domain of the Cuban foreign military aid program included Angola, Somalia, and three other sub-Saharan countries (Guinea, Guinea-Bissau, and Congo), three North African–Middle Eastern countries (Algeria, Syria, and Southern Yemen), and the three countries of Indochina (Vietnam, Cambodia, and Laos). There had been earlier programs in Cameroon and Sierra Leone.[53] In 1976, the military programs in Indochina, though mostly conducted by civic soldiers, had very modest military significance. The program in Syria had been sharply reduced, as Syria fought the Palestinians. Military aid

TABLE 3.2
Cuban Foreign Assistance

Country	Military Aid	Other Forms of Aid	Date Begun	Date Ended[a]
Africa				
Algeria	Rear-guard troops and support in 1963; training for anti-Morocco Saharan guerrillas	None (?)	1963	—
Cameroons	Unknown	Unknown		
Congo	Training and advice; some troops	Student scholarships; training for political and other organizations	1966	—
Ethiopia	Training and advice: troops	Public health personnel; other aid	1977	—
Guinea	Internal security; presidential guard; some troops	Construction of schools and hospitals	late 1960s	—
Sierra Leone	Unknown	Unknown		
Somalia	Training and advice	Training of political cadres; technical assistance for public health and the sugar industry	1972	1977
Tanzania	None	School construction; technical training	early 1970s	—
Africa (ex-Iberian)				
Angola	Troops (max. 20,000); training	All types of social, economic, political assistance	early 1960s	—
Equatorial Guinea	None (?)	Intermediate school teachers	1973	—
Guinea-Bissau	Training and advice; some troops	Personnel in public health, education, economic planning	early 1960s	—
Mozambique	Training and advice; some troops	None (?)	late 1960s	—
São Tomé-Principe	None (?)	Physicians; training in public health, education, fishing, agriculture, cattle raising	1976	—

Indochina				
Cambodia	Training	Medical aid	early 1975	?
Laos	Training	Material gifts; medical brigades; airport construction	early 1960s	—
Vietnam	Training; some antimissile and antiaircraft technicians	Medical brigades, training in public health, hotel and restaurant management; construction; some gifts	early 1960s	—
Latin America				
Chile	Internal security	Reciprocal gifts	1971	1973
Guatemala	None	$10,000 for earthquake relief	1970s	
Guyana	None	Gifts, shipments of cement; construction of fishing port	early 1970s	—
Honduras	None	Medical brigades, construction personnel for earthquake relief	1970s	?
Jamaica	None	Construction for schools, dams, waterworks; personnel training	1975	—
Nicaragua	None	Medical brigades, construction personnel for earthquake relief	1970s	?
Panama	None	Training for labor union leaders	mid-1970s	?
Peru	None	Medical brigades, construction personnel for earthquake relief	1970s	?
Middle East				
South Yemen	Training; troops	Unknown	early 1970s	—
Syria	Rear-guard troops; logistical support; training and advice; combat troops	Training in public health; medical brigades	1973	1975 (?)

a. A question mark in this column indicates that aid has ended but the precise data is unknown; a dash indicates that aid is continuing.

had thus been concentrated in African countries (minus Sierra Leone and Cameroon) plus Southern Yemen. The program was then expanded in new directions. Cuba and Mozambique established diplomatic relations in August 1975. By the beginning of 1976, a small party of several dozen Cuban military advisors had increased their collaboration with Zimbabwan or Rhodesian guerrillas in Mozambique; by August 1976, Cuban advisors were going up to the border with the guerrillas in their attacks on Rhodesian forces. Cuba also opened a large and rapidly growing military program in Ethiopia in the spring of 1977, following Castro's visit in March 1977.[54]

Another direction of the military program in 1976 was renewed support for Algeria. Fidel Castro told the party congress in 1975 that the two countries where regular Cuban troops had been present in substantial numbers prior to the Angolan war, though in rear-guard positions and primarily for symbolic purposes, were Syria and Algeria. The support for Algeria occurred during the 1963 Moroccan-Algerian war, when perhaps one hundred fifty Cuban troops were stationed in Algeria; because the Cuban troops, though expected to defend themselves if attacked, were not intended for actual combat, the military doctrine had not been modified. After the Angolan war, the renewal of Cuban support for Algeria in the conflict with Morocco over the former Spanish Sahara—and Morocco's retaliation by sending troops to support Zaire's government—could have more serious connotations. During the first quarter of 1976, Cuban military trainers worked with Saharan guerrillas in southern Algeria; Prime Minister Castro visited Algeria in March 1976, where he met with the prime minister of the Algerian-sponsored Saharan Arab Democratic Republic, though without according it official recognition.[55]

The functions that can be performed by the foreign military aid program are impressive. Internal security aid includes presidential protection (of President Sekou Touré, for example), investigative work, regular police and fire services, military counterinsurgency operations, and internal and external espionage. Programs for the armed forces include the sending of front-line combat troops, the manning and maintenance of complex military equipment, military logistical support, the training of officers and troops for combat and command roles, and coast guard development. Other services include the development of civilian organizations to support internal security work, the establishment of a civil defense program, and the organization of a political party within the armed forces and internal security forces to ensure the political allegiance of these services.

Cuba has had few foreign aid programs in the Americas; these have little overt emphasis on military missions or aid. Cuban foreign aid programs in the Middle East have emphasized military dimensions; those in Africa and in Indochina have had more mixed characteristics, depending on country and timing. Most Cuban programs, however, have a military dimension because they seemed to be staffed by civic soldiers. Though some Cuban programs have been declining in importance (Indochina, Sierra Leone, Cameroon, Syria), and two were terminated against Cuba's will (Chile and Somalia), others have been expanding in the mid-1970s. Cuba has established close relations with the successor states of the Iberian empires and has devised foreign aid programs to assist even countries, long independent, with which it had not had diplomatic relations for many years. Thus the flexibility of Cuban foreign policy in administering its foreign aid program is quite remarkable.

The principal threat posed by the Cuban foreign aid program derives from its military aspects: the stationing of civic soldiers in so many countries; the training of other armed forces; and the stationing of regular troops overseas, as in Angola or Syria. Declared Cuban foreign policy on the meaning of the Angolan intervention is not entirely reassuring, for it leaves open several possibilities of a replication of that war: to assist allied incumbents in suppressing an internal revolt: to assist allied countries in conventional combat; to assist insurrections in southern and northern Africa; and to assist insurrections generally, provided regular troops are not used. In short, the potential and explicit military features of Cuba's foreign aid program have become the principal threat posed by Cuba to other countries.

Subversion

Cuban subversive policies—so prominent in the 1960s—have become less important in the 1970s. Some efforts at subversion failed, and they have not been repeated on the same scale. Some support for insurgents has succeeded, most spectacularly in Angola, and also in other successor states of the Portuguese empire. In the Americas, according to U.S. government sources, Cuba has provided "indirect support in the form of guerrilla training" to insurgents from Chile and Uruguay, and to some extent from Honduras in the mid-1970s.[56] Cuba has also provided asylum, rest, and recreation to oppositionists from many countries. Its mass media, including the powerful Radio Havana and its book and magazine publishing facilities, provide propaganda outlets to these oppositionists. This support is broadly available for Brazilians, Central Americans, and Puerto Rican independence groups, among others. Cuba has also had training programs for labor union leaders from countries with which its relations vary from warm to nonexistent. For example, thirty-five labor union leaders from Colombia, Ecuador, Peru, and Panama graduated from the Lázaro Peña National Labor Union Leadership School in May 1976.[57] Cuba has also played host to conferences of Latin American Communist parties, some legal in their countries and some not. On the whole, Cuban subversive policies in the Americas are directed only to those countries with whom Cuba has bad relations (Chile, in particular); they are characterized by expressions of hospitality to visiting leftist politicians and by some propaganda assistance of the sort practiced by governments the world over. This declining practice poses no serious problems to most American countries, with the few exceptions noted. Cuban subversion continued more vigorously with quasi governments outside the Americas such as the MPLA in Angola before it came to power. The same may be said for Cuban support for Zimbabwan guerrillas in Mozambique and for Saharan guerrillas in Algeria. Cuba has also provided support to the Palestine Liberation Organization (PLO), welcomed Arafat as a head of state in Cuba, and allowed the PLO to establish a diplomatic mission in Cuba (see chapter 8 of this volume).

A remaining irritant in Cuban relations with other countries is the continued pursuit of military intelligence and connections with revolutionary groups, even at the expense of government policies. For example, Cuban foreign economic agencies and leaders had sought to improve political and economic relations with France during the first half of 1975, cool since 1968. The improvement was interrupted when the French police discovered that Cuban undercover agents had maintained close links with South American, Palestinian, and other terrorist groups operating in Paris—the so-called Carlos affair led to the expulsion of three Cuban diplomats from Paris in July 1975.

A related problem appeared in Cuban-Canadian relations. In 1974 Canada broke through the U.S. embargo on trade with Cuba by subsidiaries of U.S.-based multinational enterprises and in 1975 initiated a small grant aid program in technical assistance and opened a line of credit worth $100 million on "soft" repayment terms. Cuban exports to Canada increased fourfold, to $82 million, from 1966 to 1974. The two countries planned a trade exchange of up to $500 million in 1976-1980. Prime Minister Trudeau visited Cuba in January 1976. Less than a year later, Canada expelled five Cuban diplomats from the Ottawa embassy who were engaged in military intelligence work. The Cuban Foreign Relations Ministry argued that these activities did not interfere with the bilateral relations because Cuba's principal purpose was to recruit personnel in Canada to go to southern Africa. Cuba did not engage in efforts aimed at the Canadian government, but it jeopardized its relations with Canada by exercising such poor restraints on its own undercover activities.[58]

Cuban connections with revolutionary and terrorist groups may be residues of a past era. There is no evidence that Cuba supported the terrorist activities; Cuban goals appear to have been to recruit personnel and to maintain cordial relations with these revolutionary groups in order to gather information. Yet their continued embarrassment of the Cuban government suggests a poor level of policy coordination among the various Cuban government agencies operating overseas. The problem may be not Cuban subversion, but subversive practices and mentalities that linger in a part of the Cuban government's bureaucracies for foreign affairs. If so, the control of subversion by some Cubans overseas is a problem not only for host governments but for the Cuban government, too.

In conclusion, there is much less reason to worry about Cuban subversive activities now than there was during the first decade of revolutionary rule. Such activities are limited principally to the resolution of the final elements of European decolonization in Africa. There is also a focus on Chile and Uruguay. Cuba provides certain kinds of symbolic and very modest material support to some opposition forces (mostly orthodox Communist parties), but this is not very different from the practice of states the world over.

Cuba and the Soviet Union: Military Dimensions

Perception of the Cuban military problem has generally been clouded by fear of the Soviet-Cuban alliance. This formulation suggests that only the Soviet Union matters; it also contributes to an underestimation of what the Cubans do. The Soviet-Cuban alliance presents a problem for U.S. influence and security, yet the evidence is that the Soviet Union has been a moderating influence on Cuban foreign policy over the years, rather than a contributor to added threats.[59] But the Soviet Union had supported the Cuban foreign military aid program, especially in Angola.

Cuba's conduct of the war may have improved its leverage with the USSR by demonstrating that, although the Cuban government may not be exemplary at economic planning, it has an excellent military organization. Thus the political and psychological climate of Soviet-Cuban relations may now be more favorable to Cuba. The Cuban efforts in Angola also allowed a repayment, in political and military currency, for past Soviet assistance to Cuba. This was probably an unstated element in the relationship; it is unlikely that the Soviet Union demanded it in these terms, but both sides probably were conscious of the need for reciprocity in their relationship. Victory in Angola has generally increased Cuba's international political clout. When the Cuban government expresses its solidarity with the government of another country, it has a somewhat different meaning since the Angolan war.

A number of Cuba's foreign aid programs are best understood as joint programs with the Soviet Union, in which the two countries agree to a division of labor. The Soviet Union provides equipment and financial support while Cuba provides personnel to teach recipient countries how to use Soviet assistance and equipment. Angola is the principal example of such programs, receiving aid before, during, and after the war. Especially after the war, aid to Angola has become the responsibility of a consortium of socialist countries because, according to Fidel Castro, "aid to Angola can only be managed through the collaboration of all the socialist countries.[60] The old program in Somalia, and the new one in Ethiopia, have been joint Soviet-Cuban endeavors, as had been the programs in Syria and Indochina. The Latin American foreign aid programs, however, are entirely Cuban, and the programs in a number of the successor states to the Iberian empires have a very strong Cuban initiative and predominance. In Tanzania, substantial Chinese influence has prevented the development of Soviet programs; Cuban input predominates also in the Congo, though not so in Guinea. Cuba may have opened the way for Mozambique-USSR collaboration, and in Algeria the Soviet Union seems to be a moderating force over the Cubans. There is, in short, considerable variation in the importance of Soviet participation in Cuban foreign aid programs, ranging from crucial in Angola, to negligible in other cases.

A relatively minor Soviet-Cuban program has been research on oceanography conducted since 1965 under the auspices of the Cuban Fishing Research

JORGE I. DOMÍNGUEZ

Center, the Cuban Academy of Sciences, and the Soviet Academy of Sciences. Of the 105 articles published between 1965 and 1974, the Soviets participated in 75 percent, the Cubans in 61 percent; 24 percent were exclusively Cuban and 39 percent were exclusively Soviet.[61] Research on the oceans serves the combined interests of the Soviet Union and Cuba; the research output contributes to the practical economic benefit of both countries. Yet is also has modest military implications of two kinds.

The first is the scope of the research. Cuban and Soviet scholars have mapped out the Caribbean and the Gulf of Mexico; their widespread research stations and activities include the entire southern coastline of the United States. While there are many plausible scientific explanations of this research, it also serves the interests of the Soviet and Cuban navies. Because some of these military benefits have been received already, overt military features of continuing research on fishing are few. Although the Cuban navy does not belong to the Scientific-Technological Fishing Council, information useful to the navies may still be derived from this research.[62] Second, the research may have included intelligence gathering, though such activities have not been publicly acknowledged. Apart from research, Soviet and Cuban fishing fleets have collaborated extensively. Some Cuban fishing boats on the high seas are commanded not by Cubans but by Soviet officers and captains.[63] Fishing boats can also be used for gathering intelligence. The principal purposes of ocean research and fishing are probably what they are purported to be, and the purpose of this discussion is not to cast doubt on these activities or on scientific and economic benefits already accrued to Cuba from fishing production and productivity. Nevertheless, these possible military benefits justify some modest concern and monitoring.

Cuba and the Soviet Union have also had more overt military relationships, some of which have been discussed already. The remaining question is the extent and kind of possible Soviet-Cuban strategic collaboration. The best study of the Soviet Union's possible use of Cuba for strategic naval purposes in the 1970s has been prepared by Barry Blechman and Stephanie Levinson.[64] They have shown that the Soviet Union has been making slow qualitative changes in the type of submarine calling at Cuban ports and in the port of call, testing the limits of U.S.-Soviet agreements with regard to the use of Cuba as a Soviet base. The principal effect of this testing—even if it were carried out much further than it has— is political, not military. At present, no part of Cuba serves as an operational base from which the Soviet Union could pose a threat to the United States. The chief effect has been to establish the Soviet Union's political right to patrol the Caribbean.

There are, nevertheless, three modest military aspects of the Soviet Union's strategic use of Cuba. The Soviet Union has now sent Golf II diesel-powered strategic ballistic missile submarines into different Cuban ports, including Havana. Although the United States has placed a special emphasis on preventing nuclear-powered submarines from using Cuba, it is, in fact, more useful to the Soviet Union to be able to utilize Cuba for diesel-powered than for nuclear-powered submarines, because the former can stay on patrol for a shorter period of time. It is not clear how much servicing occurs in Cuba, though refueling and rest and recreation for the crew apparently take place. The net effect has been to increase marginally the time on station for these submarines in the Caribbean. Golf II submarines are among the less sophisticated Soviet strategic submarines; their occasional use of Cuba must be considered of very modest military significance. Second, submarines using Cuba have a faster reaction time than submarines or land missiles located elsewhere. Once again, the military significance is very modest. Third, the North American Air Defense (NORAD) no longer has air defense radars, command and control installations, or weapons in the south central United States. Its capabilities to monitor Cuban activities and to deter Cuba are ordinarily limited to those at Homestead Air Base in southern Florida. The main U.S. defense against a hypothetical attack from Cuba is the U.S. ability to inflict unacceptable damage upon Cuba quickly and decisively from the air and sea, but U.S. forces are no longer poised to invade Cuba.[65] The result of marginally more effective Soviet strategic naval use of Cuba, and of marginally less effective U.S. defenses toward Cuba, is a slight shift in the military relationship in the Caribbean. The nature of the shift should not be overestimated; the principal Soviet-Cuban purpose to achieve the shift may be no more than to assert their joint national sovereignties.

Another aspect of Cuban-Soviet collaboration with possible strategic implications is the nuclear energy program. Some nuclear research had been done in Cuba before the Revolution and, in the mid-1960s, at the University of Havana and in the Ministry of Public Health. New elements of this program began in the late 1960s with a Soviet-Cuban agreement to develop Cuba's nuclear energy capabilities. The Soviet Union gave an atomic reactor, a nuclear physics lab, and a radiochemical isotope lab. The Cuban Institute for Nuclear Physics of the Academy of Sciences was established in January 1969 (before that time, there had been a nuclear physics group in the academy upon Prime Minister Castro's personal initiative). The institute, headed by First Captain Engineer Federico Bell-Iloch, took charge of the atomic reactor; the program for the "use of atomic energy for peaceful purposes" was supervised by Deputy Prime Minister Carlos Rafael Rodríguez. Cuba has had an ambassador accredited to the International Atomic Energy Agency (IAEA). By 1972, the Institute for Nuclear Physics had a staff of 111 persons, divided into 53 university graduates (half of whom had been trained in the USSR), 32 technicians, and 26 support staff. By 1976, there were 120 university graduates, and there were 30 others studying in the Soviet Union.[66]

The National Commission for the Peaceful Utilization of Atomic Energy, created by presidential decree on 5 October 1974, oversees the development of the Cuban nuclear energy program and conducts relations with the Soviet Union, IAEA, and other countries. The first nuclear power plant, under construction near Cienfuegos as part of the 1976–1980 plan, is only scheduled to begin operations in 1981–1985, with a capacity of up to 1000 megawatts. Cuba has a very serious electric power shortage. As of mid-1976, before the more severe economic setback of the decline in the world price of sugar was evident, the plan called for eliminating the electric power shortages in the four western provinces by the end of 1977; there was, however, no foreseeable end to the shortages in the ten central and eastern provinces within the five-year plan.[67]

Details of the Soviet-Cuban nuclear energy program are not part of the public record. However, there is little doubt that Cuba needs to develop energy sources. It has virtually no petroleum[68] or coal deposits and only limited possibilities for hydroelectric power. The use of cane bagasse to produce energy has been economic mainly at the sugar mills, but not elsewhere. It seems likely that, to avoid provoking the United States, the Soviet Union will not facilitate the development of an autonomous Cuban nuclear capability for weapons development. Therefore, the strategic implications of Cuba's embryonic nuclear energy program are limited principally to the need for monitoring. A related issue, of more symbolic than practical significance, is Cuba's refusal to sign treaties to control the use and proliferation of nuclear weapons. Cuban policy was formulated in the early 1960s, and it has remained relatively unchanged. Cuba refused to sign the Nuclear Test Ban Treaty until the United States ceased its hostile actions. Cuba did not adhere to the nonproliferation treaty of 1968 and did not even participate in the negotiations leading to the Treaty of Tlatelolco (1967) prohibiting nuclear weapons in Latin America; it refuses to sign it until the United States agrees to denuclearize the Panama Canal Zone, Puerto Rico, and any U.S. bases in the Caribbean outside the continental mainland, and to return the Guantanamo naval base to Cuba. The Soviet Union refused to sign protocol 2 of the treaty— requiring nuclear powers not to use or threaten to use nuclear weapons against the contracting parties and not to assist them in any way to violate the treaty— because the United States did not adhere fully to protocol 1. The United States signed protocol 2, but introduced important reservations to its signing of protocol 1, which requires countries with territories in the treaty area to exclude nuclear weapons from their possessions. The United States refused to accept the application of protocol 1 to Puerto Rico and the Virgin Islands, though it was willing to accept it with regard to the Panama Canal Zone.[69] Thus the Soviet Union agreed with Cuba. The practical significance of Cuba's nonadherence to these treaties is not military but political: its future adherence will probably be one element in a broad package improving U.S.-Cuban relations.

The military implications of the Cuban-Soviet relationship, narrowly conceived, while not negligible, are rather minor in practice. The principal problem comes from their joint operations overseas as in Angola or in Ethiopia. But there are some military implications from the bilateral oceanographic and fishing research and activities and from the nuclear energy program, including their nonadherence to the Treaty of Tlatelolco. The principal response by other countries is only the continued monitoring of these activities. There is every reason to believe that the principal purposes of the research are scientific, economic, and medical, as stated officially by the Cuban government; there are military benefits but they do not appear to be a primary goal. The Soviet Union's testing of the limits of the 1962 understanding is a more serious matter, though principally for its political implications. These require not only monitoring but a restating and refining of the understanding for the collective security of the Soviet Union, the United States, and Cuba. This redefinition would help to prevent the recurrence of a crisis such as the one in 1970 over Soviet activities in Cienfuegos.

The Cuban Threat?

It has been generally agreed that Cuba does not pose a substantial threat to any other country. In hearings held before the Appropriations Subcommittee of the U.S. House of Representatives, the chairman of the Joint Chiefs of Staff provided a strikingly subdued assessment of Cuba's threat as it might affect the budget for fiscal 1976 (well before Cuba's entry into Angola):

> Some threat to United States security interests is already posed by the regime in Cuba. Soviet naval and air activity in the Caribbean, and an increasing tendency toward confrontation with the United States in several other countries, add to the potential threat. Despite some notable failures in efforts to export revolution through guerrilla warfare, Fidel Castro probably will provide limited support to selected leftist insurgencies in the region. Cuba, in addition, poses a potential threat as a source of supply, training, money and perhaps personnel for subversive and insurgent activities in Panama.[70]

Cuban foreign aid is not included in the CIA's report on *Communist Aid to Less Developed Countries of the Free World, 1975,* published in July 1976, though the report includes foreign aid programs even from minor East European donors. Is the Cuban threat, in fact, at as low a level as it is apparently perceived in Washington?

In the second half of the 1970s, the Cuban armed forces rank among the more impressive military institutions in the world. They have emerged victorious from wars conducted thousands of miles away from the homeland. The Cuban government commits substantial resources to its armed forces; its level of effort exceeds the rest of Latin America and ranks among the world's highest for those countries whose national territorial integrity is no longer directly threatened. Though the standing regular force is not as large as it once was, the personnel at the disposal of the Cuban armed forces, through the mobilization of reserves, is very large and had grown.

Cuban force structure is probably sufficient to deter an invasion of the island, but it is insufficient for most offensive purposes. Cuba lacks a navy capable of launching an offensive well beyond its shores; the force posture of the Cuban air force is primarily defensive; Cuba lacks the ships and aircraft to transport medium and heavy weaponry for its troops on its own to foreign shores. Though Cuba may decide autonomously whether to intervene overseas, and

JORGE I. DOMÍNGUEZ

though it can transport lightly armed troops at great risk and effort by using its civilian airline and shipping fleets, overseas intervention policies cannot be implemented successfully without the consent and participation of the Soviet Union.

The historical bases for discussing the Cuban threat to international order have been two: the strategic military relationship to the Soviet Union, and Cuban support for revolutionary movements in other countries. By the second half of the 1970s, these issues no longer warrant much military concern. The strategic military aspects of the bilateral relationship to the Soviet Union are relatively minor, principally the Soviet testing of the limits of the 1962 understanding. The Soviet Union and Cuba have been able to make some modest military gains by modifying successfully the joint interpretation of the understanding, and the United States has acquiesced; however, the principal purposes of this testing are political—the establishment of fuller political influence in the Caribbean and the erosion of U.S. political influence not only in this area, but also generally in international affairs. Nonstrategic military aspects of the bilateral relationship have declined in importance.

Cuban subversive activities have declined drastically since the first decade of revolutionary rule. Cuba now prefers to deal with governments in power. Its principal remaining targets for subversion are the white-ruled countries of southern Africa and possibly Zaire and the former Spanish Sahara; there is also some subversive effort in the Americas aimed at Chile and Uruguay, and a place for asylum, rest, and recreation, to leftists, Communists, and revolutionaries. These activities are not very different from the contemporary practice of statecraft elsewhere. With the exceptions noted above, the historical dimensions of the Cuban threat are today much less important. They require little more than continued monitoring to make sure that they remain mostly a matter of the past. The only effective way to address these remaining problems is as part of an improvement in bilateral relations between the United States and Cuba. In short, the evaluations of the Cuban threat provided by the U.S. government correctly noted that it was very minor, because those evaluations were based entirely on past history.

There is, however, a new dimension to the Cuban threat, one that has been developing for a number of years. Cuba now has a foreign aid program of substantial scope and domain. The program is government-to-government, low cost, emphasizing the sending of personnel, aiming for long range-goals and not for short-term advantage, linked to internal promotion and reward policies, and highly flexible and quick in its response. As shown above in table 3.2, the program has operated in twenty-six countries on three continents. Several of these were limited to disaster relief assistance. In 1977, Cuban foreign aid programs were active in ten African countries (all, minus Cameroon, Sierra Leone, and Somalia). The military assistance programs in 1977 were limited to Algeria, Guinea, Guinea-Bissau, Congo, Angola, Ethiopia, Mozambique, and Southern Yemen, although there may be some in Equatorial Guinea and São Tomé-

Principe too. Several were a joint effort between Cuba and the Soviet Union. Foreign aid programs have become the principal threat to other governments from the Soviet-Cuban military relationship, that is, the relationship has been multilateralized by its overseas spread.

This new dimension of the Cuban threat should not be exaggerated. Most of the programs have social and economic goals intended to enhance the standard of living of other peoples. They are fully in accord with the Cuban belief in internationalist solidarity. Many of the Cuban foreign military assistance programs are no different from military aid provided by other countries. Most of them have not, in fact, created a real threat to third countries. Concern about the Cuban foreign aid program has three elements. First, the program in Angola blossomed into a full scale intervention based on very broad claims. Second, although the Cuban government has given certain assurances that the Angolan experience will not be repeated, it excluded several categories of actions from such assurances. It is still a possible part of Cuban policy to assist allied incumbents in suppressing an internal revolt, to assist allied countries in conventional combat, to assist insurrections in southern and northern Africa, and to assist insurrections elsewhere provided regular troops are not used. Third, some of the nonmilitary foreign aid programs have been staffed either by personnel just demobilized from the armed forces or, often, by personnel still subject to military command and available for combat (as in Angola). In short, the possible Cuban threat in the late 1970s derives form this concatenation of uncertainties. Are the Angolan and Ethiopian experiences, in fact, replicable? Does Cuba have broader military ambitions? What is the actual military content of apparently civilian foreign aid programs?

The Cuban armed forces suffered institutionally as a result of the Angolan war. Although the war policy probably enjoyed widespread military and civilian support in Cuba, the actual experience of war triggered off some elite and mass civilian resistance against military mobilization of reservists, to a degree unparalleled in the military history of the Revolution. The strain of the war within the armed forces appears to have led to greater than normal troop insubordination (though probably limited to a small minority of troops), refusals to serve in Angola, and more tension between military professionals and military politicians; Communist Youth Union branches within the armed forces performed poorly.

The Cuban government's open-ended interpretation of its military commitment to Angola may tie down a large number of Cuban troops in counterinsurgency activities for some time. The Cuban government has more reason to expect problems after the Angolan war than before, as a result of that experience. The prognosis for the Cuban economy in the last half of the 1970s is much less favorable than it was when the Angolan decisions were made. Thus one implication of the study of the internal characteristics of the Cuban armed forces is that there may be greater caution in committing them again to front-line, large-scale, overseas combat. If so, then the maintenance of a substantial foreign military aid program may be seen more as a surrogate than as a prelude to additional intervention, more as an effort to retain the political and military influence gained from the Angolan war than as a wedge to further adventures. The foreign aid program can be seen as a way to advance both the general aims of internationalist solidarity—a moral principle the Cuban government seeks to uphold—and to improve Cuba's political influence especially in the Third World. Cuba's participation in the Angolan war heightened once again the normative, revolutionary commitments of the Cuban government and its supporters. They have long believed that the revolutionary government survived in part because of the internationalist solidarity of the Soviet Union and other Eastern European countries; so too, they now believe, Cuba should express its solidarity with other revolutionary governments. The joint operation of these programs with the Soviet Union, in turn, can be seen as both a necessity—it buys political insurance against the U.S. and provides transport for military equipment—and a convenience in repaying the Soviets for past and current assistance rendered to Cuba.

This is an optimistic, though not imprudent, view of the consequences for international affairs of the military aspects of Cuban foreign policy. And yet Cuban military support for Ethiopia in its war against Somalia, beginning in 1977, suggests that Cuba may choose to incur all of these costs under specified circumstances—in this instance, assisting an allied Ethiopian government in fighting back the Somali conventional invasion. Cuba may seek to do this to uphold its international commitments, to gain further influence, and to improve even further its relationship with the Soviet Union. There is, then, still a threat from Cuba to other governments; there are serious unanswered questions posed by Cuban policies, institutions, and practices.

The Future of U.S.-Cuban Military Relations

If a moderate scenario of Cuban international behavior could become a reality, then at last a resolution of a number of issues in U.S.-Cuban relations may be possible. Discussions of those issues are beyond the scope of this paper. Yet the principal military issues can be outlined. First, each country will seek assurances that the other will respect its territorial integrity and independence and that actions will be taken to suppress mutual subversion. Thus the United States will need to take more vigorous measures against actions aimed at the Cuban government, including terrorism launched from U.S. soil; the Cuban government will have to refrain from a number of symbolic actions, and certainly from actions beyond symbolic solidarity, with respect to Puerto Rico and other groups within the United States. Second, the United States will seek assurances that the Angolan and Ethiopian war experiences will not be replicated and that the Cuban foreign military assistance program—unilateral or in collaboration with the USSR—remains limited. A related issue will be further assurances that the downward trend in Cuban support for subversive activities will continue. Here may be a paradox. Cuban assistance will make it easier for the governments it supports to establish internal political stability. The defeated groups will often have been supported by the United States. Thus the achievement of internal political stability will run counter to at least some short-term U.S. foreign policy goals in Africa and may lead to international instability (as the Katangan gendarmes' invasion of Zaire already indicates).

Third, both countries—and the USSR will have to be involved too—will seek to define collective security in the Caribbean. This may require a tripartite agreement formalizing the 1962 understanding and its subsequent modifications. A U.S. goal may be to reduce the use of Cuba by the Soviet navy for any purpose, and especially for any strategic purpose, and to ensure Cuban participation in the various treaties seeking to prevent nuclear weapons proliferation. Fourth, Cuba will seek the return of the Guantanamo naval base. The subject of the base is never at the forefront of the Cuban negotiating agenda with the United States, but it is also never omitted from any full statement of the long-term issues at stake. It is included in the Cuban military's international agenda.[71]

The Guantanamo issue will not prevent substantial movement in U.S.-Cuban relations, nor will it prevent some resolution of the first two issues of military importance; but it is likely to stall any resolution of the third military issue of interest to the United States. Cuba and the Soviet Union are not likely to agree to U.S. goals denuclearizing Cuba and ending the Soviet navy's use of Cuban ports so long as a U.S. base remains on Cuban territory; nor is the United States likely to agree to a return of Guantanamo to Cuba without credible assurances that the base will not be used by the Soviet navy for strategic or other purposes. Thus the first two military issues will surface early in any efforts at bilateral reconciliation; indeed it is unlikely that there will be much reconciliation until they are reasonably settled. The last two issues may not emerge for some time, after many other topics have been raised; their resolution may become linked to other tough issues on the bilateral agenda, such as property compensation and most-favored-nation trade treatment. The trade-offs and the outcomes are uncertain.[72]

In a burst of wild optimism, suppose that all four issues are settled. What, then, will be the impact on the Cuban armed forces? Perhaps paradoxically, one cannot tell with certainty. The justification for Cuban military doctrine has explicitly stated that a large military establishment is necessary, even if relations with the United States improve substantially, because the imperialists cannot be trusted. Despite absence of war, it is likely to be argued by the Cuban armed forces, there is still a need for a strong defense capability. Moreover, the justification for the Cuban armed forces has never relied entirely on fear of invasion or of counterrevolution. A moral claim has been made about the value of the military life and about the wisdom of military policies. There will be a debate on the virtues of military training, policies, institutions, and life values in the building of a socialist society. If the armed forces and those who align with them on these questions prevail, then the resolution of many international problems long associated with the Cuban revolution may not necessarily lead to any substantial decline in the weight of the armed forces in Cuba.

NOTES

I wish to thank the Center for International Affairs at Harvard University for providing general support for my research through the Transnational Relations Project funded by the Rockeller Foundation; I am also grateful to the Center for Latin American Studies at the University of Pittsburgh for supporting my research on Cuban foreign military policy through the Project on the Role of Cuba in Hemispheric and World Affairs funded by the U.S. Department of State. A preliminary version of this work was presented at the Conference on the Role of Cuba in World Affairs, held at the Center for Latin American Studies, University of Pittsburgh, November 15-17, 1976. I am grateful to the conference participants for their comments on that version, and particularly to the discussant on my paper, Professor Carol Benglesdorf. The comments of Dr. Dana Sweet, Library of Congress, and of the editors of this volume, Cole Blasier and Carmelo Mesa-Lago, have also been greatly appreciated. These institutions and persons bear no responsibility for my work; indeed, several of them disagree vigorously.

1. See speeches by Fidel Castro and by Carlos Rafael Rodríguez, prime minister and deputy prime minister for foreign affairs, respectively, in *Granma,* April 20, 1976, p. 2; *Granma Weekly Review,* August 29, 1976, p. 7.

2. Jorge I. Domínguez, "Institutionalization and Civil-Military Relations in Cuba," *Cuban Studies* 6 (January 1976), pp. 44-45. There is a reasonable (though not exact) correspondence between estimates of Cuban military expenditures drawn from different sources. U.S. government sources generally underestimate; Cuba's actual military expenditures in the early 1960s were twice those reported by the U.S. Arms Control and Disarmament Agency. In 1972, Cuba's admitted military expenditures were at least 14.4 percent higher than the estimates published by this agency, and in its most recent estimates of the Cuban 1972 military budget the error rises to 25.9 percent. See its *World Military Expenditures and Arms Transfers, 1965-1974* (Washington, D.C.: GPO, 1975), p. 25 (hereafter cited as *USACDA, 1965-1974*).

3. Jorge I. Domínguez, *Cuba: Order and Revolution* (Cambridge, Mass.: Belknap Press of Harvard University Press), chap. 5. The best analysis has been presented by Carmelo Mesa-Lago, *Cuba in the 1970s* (Albuquerque: University of New Mexico Press, 1974), chap. 2. Official U.S. sources have underestimated the recovery of the Cuban economy in the first half of the 1970s, especially 1970-1972, and may thus have underestimated the availability of Cuban resources for overseas combat. U.S. Arms Control and Disarmament Agency, *World Military Expenditures and Arms Trade, 1963-1973* (Washington, D.C.: GPO, 1975), p. 28, hereafter cited as *USACDA, 1963-1973;* and *USACDA, 1965-1974*, p. 25. The Central Intelligence Agency has obscured the Cuban recovery of the early 1970s by noting that growth was negligible between 1968 and 1973; while this is correct, it neglects to mention a sharp decline in the late 1960s and a recovery in the 1970s, continuing through 1974. The CIA acknowledges growth only in 1974. See Central Intelligence Agency, *Cuba: Foreign Trade* (Washington, D.C.: Central Intelligence Agency, 1975), p. 17.

4. *Granma Weekly Review,* December 28, 1975, pp. 5, 8; *Granma,* September 30, 1976, p. 2.

5. *Granma Weekly Review,* January 4, 1976, p. 7.

6. See Domínguez, *Cuba*, chap. 5.

7. *Granma Weekly Review,* May 3, 1970, p. 3; January 4, 1976, p. 7. U.S. government sources have underestimated the degree of Soviet military assistance to Cuba; their estimate of Cuba's

receipts of weaponry are about one-quarter of the value admitted by the Cuban government. U.S. sources also indicate a decline in Cuba's receipt of military weaponry by cost in the early 1970s, when the trend is the opposite. *USACDA, 1963-1973*, p. 70; *USACDA, 1965-1974*, p. 59.

8. *Granma Weekly Review*, January 4, 1976, p. 7.

9. Yuri Gavrikov, "URSS-Cuba: colaboración y solidaridad," *Panorama latinoamericano*, no. 163 (February 15, 1973), p. 5; O. Darusenkov, "Cuba Builds Socialism," *International Affairs*, no. 11 (November, 1975), p. 21; Boris Gorbachev, "Cuba: algunas cuestiones de su integración económica con los países del socialismo," *Panorama latinoamericano*, no. 171 (August 1, 1973), p. 3; Boris Gvozdariov, "URSS-Cuba: unidad de criterios y posiciones," *Panorama latinoamericano*, no. 184 (April 1, 1974), p. 6; *Los Angeles Times*, May 21, 1975, p. 15. For a general discussion of Cuban-Soviet cooperation in the 1960s, see A. D. Bekarevich and N. M. Kujarev, *La Unión Soviética y Cuba: colaboración económica* (Moscow: Nauka, 1973).

10. *USACDA, 1963-1973*, pp. 21-62; *USACDA, 1965-1974*, pp. 19-61.

11. Prime Minister Castro's estimates in *Granma Weekly Review*, December 12, 1971, p. 6; ibid., December 1, 1974, p. 7 See also Osvaldo Dorticós, "El error que no cometeremos jamás es el de no estar alerta," *Cuba socialista*, no. 59 (July 1966), pp. 1, 10-12; *Granma*, April 16, 1973, p. 1; ibid., August 9, 1975, p. 2; ibid., June 8, 1976, p. 4; ibid., November 29, 1976, pp. 5-6; *Granma Weekly Review*, September 28, 1975, p. 7; *Verde olivo* 16, no. 43 (October 27, 1974), 17-18; and International Institute for Strategic Studies, *The Military Balance* (London: International Institute for Strategic Studies) as follows: *1966-67* (1966), p. 11; *1970-71* (1970), p. 76; *1974-75* (1974), p. 65; *1975-76* (1975), p. 64.

12. Domínguez, "Institutionalization," pp. 49-51; Héctor de Arturo and Jorge Blanco, "Primera conferencia del partido en el EJT," *Verde olivo* 17, no. 46 (November 16, 1975), 18; "Acto de fin de zafra del EJT en Matanzas," *Verde olivo* 18, no. 21 (May 23, 1976), 52.

13. *Granma*, March 18, 1975, p. 3; ibid., July 11, 1975, p. 2; *Granma Weekly Review*, December 1, 1974, p. 7; ibid., July 3, 1977, p. 3; and Raúl Castro, "Sabemos que el imperialismo se debilita," *Verdo Olivo* 17, no. 29 (July 20, 1975), 4.

14. Domínguez, "Institutionalization," pp. 42-44; and *Cuba*, chap. 9.

15. John Stanley and Maurice Pearton, *The International Trade in Arms* (New York: Praeger, 1972), p. 216; *Granma Weekly Review*, December 12, 1976, p. 11.

16. International Institute for Strategic Studies, *The Military Balance, 1966-67*, p. 11; and *1970-71*, p. 76; Stockholm International Peace Research Institute, *World Armaments and Disarmament Yearbook, 1973* (Stockholm: Almqvist and Wiksell, 1973), pp. 248-49, 337; T. N. Dupuy and Wendell Blanchard, *The Almanac of World Military Power*, 2d ed. (Dunn Loring, Va.: T. N. Dupuy Associates, 1972), pp. 24-25, and glossary; U.S. Congress, House, Subcommittee on Inter-American Affairs, Committee on Foreign Affairs, "Soviet Activities in Cuba," *Hearings*, 93d Congress (Washington, D.C.: GPO, 1974), p. 56; Gabriel García Márquez, "Colombian Author Writes on Cuba's Angola Intervention," *Washington Post*, January 10, 1976, p. A14; idem., "Castro in the War Room: Tactical Advice to Angola," *Washington Post*, January 11, 1977, p. A11; *Verde olivo* 17, no. 51 (December 19, 1976), 4. See also the more complete version by Gabriel García Márquez, published simultaneously in Mexico as "Cuba en Angola: Operación Carlota," *Proceso*, January 1977, p. 6.

17. Domínguez, "Institutionalization," pp. 46-48; Domínguez, *Cuba*, chap. 9.

18. *Revolución*, January 22, 1965, p. 4; Jorge I. Domínguez, "The Civic Soldier in Cuba," in *Political-Military Systems: A Comparative Analysis*, ed. Catherine Kelleher (Beverly Hills: Sage Publications, 1974), pp. 219-36.

19. Raúl Castro, "Graduación del III Curso de la Escuela Básica Superior 'General Máximo Gómez,' " *Ediciones al orientador revolucionario*, no. 17 (1967), pp. 6-12, 19-21.

20. Ibid., p. 21; and *Granma Weekly Review*, July 30, 1967, p. 5, respectively (italics added).

21. Domínguez, *Cuba*, chaps. 5 and 8.

22. Raúl Castro, "Graduación," p. 22.

23. Jorge I. Domínguez, "Cuba, the United States and Latin America: After Détente," *SAIS Review* 19, no. 1 (1975), 24-25 describes some of these issues.

24. For Cuba's diplomatic range, *Bohemia* 67, no. 23 (June 6, 1975), 83.

25. *Granma Weekly Review*, August 31, 1975, pp. 7-8.

26. Ibid., December 1, 1974, p. 7.

27. *Granma*, July 11, 1975, p. 2.

28. *Granma Weekly Review*, January 4, 1976, pp. 10-11; ibid., January 25, 1976, p. 10; see also ibid., January, 11, 1976, pp. 4-5. On worsening relations with China, see in addition, *Granma*, January 27, 1976, p. 1.

29. *Granma Weekly Review*, January 11, 1976, pp. 2-3; *Granma*, December 25, 1975, p. 1.

30. *Granma Weekly Review*, July 20, 1969, p. 5.

31. Ibid., January 31, 1971, p. 5; *Granma*, July 28, 1977, p. 3.

32. However, U.S. government estimates had been that 90 percent of the aircraft that carried Cubans to Africa were Soviet transports. Drew Middleton, "The Cuban Soldiers in Angola," *New York Times*, March 3, 1976, p. 4; *Granma*, June 8, 1976, p. 4; García Márquez, "Colombian Author," p. A14; García Márquez, "Cuba en Angola," p. 14. For a Cuban acknowledgement on force levels in Angola, see *New York Times*, February 17, 1977, p. 1.

33. Jorge I. Domínguez, "The Cuban Operation in Angola: Costs and Benefits for the Armed Forces," *Cuban Studies* 8, no. 1 (January 1978).

34. Gregory F. Treverton, "Cuba After Angola," mimeo (London: International Institute for Strategic Studies, 1976), pp. 4, 6.

35. *Granma Weekly Review*, August 8, 1976, p. 3.

36. *Granma Weekly Review*, January 11, 1976, pp. 4-5; ibid., February 1, 1976, p. 3; ibid., February 15, 1976, p. 10; June Goodwin, "Cubans in Angola—Army of Occupation," *Christian Science Monitor*, July 8, 1976, p. 6; and García Márquez, "Castro in the War Room," p. A11.

37. *Granma Weekly Review*, August 8, 1976, p. 3; *Granma*, July 30, 1976, p. 1; ibid., December 8, 1976, p. 4; *New York Times*, April 25, 1977, p. 47.

38. Domínguez, "The Civic Soldier"; Domínguez, "Institutionalization"; Domínguez, *Cuba*, chap. 9.

39. *Granma*, June 8, 1976, p. 4; *Granma Weekly Review*, April 3, 1977, p. 1; García Márquez, "Cuba en Angola," pp. 7, 14; Georgie Ann Geyer, "Cuba in Angola: A New Look," *Boston Globe*, June 20, 1976, p. 56.

40. *Granma*, April 20, 1976, p. 2; *Boston Globe*, August 1, 1976, p. A2.

41. *Granma Weekly Review*, April 10, 1977, p. 2; *New York Times*, April 21, 1977, p. A6.

42. "Homenaje a constructores internacionalistas," *Verde olivo* 17, no. 38 (September 21, 1975), 56; ibid., no. 41 (October 12, 1975), 40.

43. *New York Times*, March 21, 1976, p. 7; ibid., May 16, 1976, p. 5.

44. *Granma Weekly Review*, January 4, 1976, p. 7; Robert Shrum, "Party Lines: The Cuban Connection," *New Times*, April 29, 1977, p. 13.

45. *Granma*, July 2, 1966, p. 12; ibid., October 23, 1976, p. 3.

46. *Granma Weekly Review*, September 28, 1975, p. 12; ibid., October 12, 1975, p. 2; ibid., August 8, 1976, p. 3; ibid., September 26, 1976, p. 2; *Granma*, December 6, 1975, p. 4; ibid., December 13, 1975, p. 1; *Bangkok Post*, December 21, 1975, p. 1.

47. *Granma Weekly Review*, October 19, 1975, p. 9; ibid., January 11, 1976, pp. 2, 3; *Granma*, October 14, 1976, p. 3; ibid., October 18, 1976, p. 2; ibid., October 21, 1976, p. 2; ibid., October 23, 1976, p. 3.

48. *Granma*, September 30, 1976, p. 2; García Márquez, "Colombian Author," p. A14.

49. *Granma Weekly Review*, November 4, 1973, p. 7.

50. Ibid., July 30, 1972, p. 4; ibid., September 26, 1976, p. 7; *Granma*, July 16, 1976, p. 5; Brian Crozier, "The Soviet Pressure in Somalia," *Conflict Studies*, no. 54 (February 1975), p. 9.

51. *Granma Weekly Review*, September 16, 1973, p. 6; Crozier, "The Soviet Pressure," p. 9.

52. *Granma Weekly Review*, February 24, 1974, p. 5; *Granma*, October 1, 1976, p. 1; Anne Sinai and Allen Pollack, *The Syrian Arab Republic* (New York: American Association for Peace in the Middle East, 1976), p. 101; see also chapter 8 of this volume.

53. *Granma Weekly Review*, January 11, 1976, pp. 4, 5; Gabriel García Márquez, "Cuba in Africa: Seed Che Planted," *Washington Post*, January 12, 1977, p. A12. For a discussion of Cuban military support for Guinea, most spectacularly in 1970, see chapter 4 of this volume.

54. *Granma Weekly Review*, September 7, 1975, p. 6; ibid., March 27, 1977, p. 4; *Granma*, July 22, 1977, p. 3; *Boston Globe*, March 26, 1976, pp. 1, 40; *New York Times*, August 8, 1976, p. 15; ibid., May 8, 1977, p. 7.

55. *Granma*, March 15, 1976, p. 1; *Boston Globe*, February 15, 1976, p. 49; ibid., March 26, 1976, p. 40; *Granma Weekly Review*, January 11, 1976, pp. 4-5.

56. Committee on Foreign Affairs, "Soviet Activities in Cuba," p. 46.

57. *Granma*, May 12, 1976, p. 3.

58. *Granma Weekly Review*, March 24, 1974, p. 1; ibid., March 31, 1974, p. 11; ibid., May 25, 1975, p. 3; ibid., October 12, 1975, p. 10; *Granma*, March 19, 1975, p. 3; ibid., March 20, 1975, p. 4; ibid., January 26, 1976, p. 7; ibid., January 30, 1976, p. 1; *Le Monde*, January 16, 1975, pp. 1, 4; ibid., July 4, 1975, pp. 1, 24; ibid., July 11, 1975, pp. 1, 8; *Times* (London), July 11, 1975, pp. 1,6; ibid., July 12, 1975, p. 2; *New York Times*, July 20, 1975, p. 13; ibid., January 13, 1977, p. 6.

59. Jorge I. Domínguez, "Taming the Cuban Shrew," *Foreign Policy*, no. 10 (Spring 1973), pp. 94-95, 102-06, 109.

60. *Granma Weekly Review*, August 8, 1976, p. 3.

61. Computed from Domínguez, *Cuba*, Appendix F. The detailed sources are too numerous to present here, but are available on request.

62. See the maps and textual descriptions in the following articles: V. V. Rossov and H. Santana, "Algunas características hidrológicas del mediterráneo americano," *Estudios* 1, no. 1 (November 1966), 47-48, 57; V. M. Nikolaieva and C. Ezpeleta, "Sobre la fauna parasitológica de los peces del Golfo de México," *Estudios* 2, no. 2 (December 1967), 82-83; V. V. Rosov, "Sobre el sistema de corrientes del mediterráneo americano," *Estudios* 2, no. 1 (October 1967); E. V. Smirnov, N. M. Mijailov, and V. V. Rossov, "Algunas características hidroquímicas del mediterráneo americano," *Estudios* 2, no. 1 (October 1967). See also Instituto de Investigaciones Científicas de la Economía Pesquera Marina y de la Oceanografía de Toda la Unión and Centro de Investigaciones Pesqueras de Cuba, *Investigaciones pesqueras soviético-cubanas*, vol. 1 (Moscow: Editorial Pishchevaja Promyshlennost, 1965), esp. V. A. Borodatov, H. Ramís Ramos, and N. E. Salnikov, "Las investigaciones soviético-cubanas de la economía pesquera"; D. V. Bogdanov, "Algunos rasgos de la oceanografía del Golfo de México y del Mar Caribe"; P. Alvarez Pérez, "Trabajos de investigación y búsqueda sobre la plataforma continental de Venezuela"; and G. D. Vasiliev and J. Torin, "Características oceanográficas pesquera y biológica del Golfo de México y del Mar Caribe," p. 266 et passim. See also Jorge González, "El Consejo Científico-Técnico para las investigaciones pesqueras," *Mar y pesca*, no. 114 (March 1975), pp. 44-45.

63. See, for example, Joaquín Jagrenaux, "1970 en la pesca," *Mar y pesca*, no. 51 (December 1969), p. 6; Vicente Cubillas, "El histórico recibimiento del Guasa," *Mar y pesca*, no. 17 (February 1967) pp. 4-9; Alexander Ishkov, "El cuarto producto de Cuba," *Mar y pesca*, no. 100 (January 1974), pp. 14-15; Pedro Morales, "Jornada histórica en el Atlántico sur," *Mar y pesca*, no. 108 (September 1974), p. 7; *Mar y pesca*, special number (December 1975), p. 27; and *Boston Globe*, August 19, 1975, p. 9.

64. See their testimony in Committee on Foreign Affairs, "Soviet Activities in Cuba," pp. 30-33.

65. United States, Congress, House of Representatives, Armed Services Investigating Subcommitee, Committee on Armed Services, "Cuban Plane Incident at New Orleans," *Hearings*, 92d Cong., 1st sess., November–December 1971 (Washington, D.C.: GPO, 1972), pp. 35-37, 41, 57; "The Pentagon's Appraisal of the Latin America Situation," *Inter-American Economic Affairs* 29, no. 2 (Autumn 1975), pp. 91-92, 94.

66. *Cuba Economic News* 3, no. 27 (September 1967), 8; "Inaugurado el Instituto Cubano de Física Nuclear," *Verde olivo* 10, no. 3 (January 19, 1969), 6; *Granma Weekly Review*, August 15, 1971, p. 1; ibid., February 27, 1972, p. 5; ibid., April 4, 1976, p. 4.

67. *Granma Weekly Review,* April 4, 1976, p. 4; *Granma,* June 21, 1976, p. 4; Departamento de Orientación Revolucionaria, Comité Central del Partido Comunista de Cuba, *Directivas para el desarrollo económico y social del país en el quinquenio 1976-1980* (Havana: Instituto Cubano del Libro, 1976), p. 18, recommendation no. 29.

68. See Domínguez, *Cuba,* chap. 5.

69. *Revolución,* October 8, 1963, pp. 1, 4-5; ibid., August 27, 1965, p. 1; Y. Tomilin, "Nuclear-Free Zones: How to Make Them Effective," *International Affairs* (Moscow), no. 8 (1975), p. 69. See also Herbert Goldhamer, *The Foreign Powers in Latin America* (Princeton: Princeton University Press, 1972), pp. 29-31.

70. "The Pentagon's Appraisal," pp. 91-92.

71. See, for example, *Granma Weekly Review,* August 31, 1975, pp. 7-8; ibid., September 28, 1975, p. 7; Frank Mankiewicz and Kirby Jones, *With Fidel* (Chicago: Playboy Press, 1975), p. 139.

72. For a discussion of a speculative package to resolve a broad array of issues, see Jorge I. Domínguez' testimony in U.S., Congress, House of Representatives, Subcommittees on International Trade and Commerce and on International Organizations of the Committee on International Relations, "U.S. Trade Embargo of Cuba," *Hearings,* 94th Cong., 1st sess., May-September 1975 (Washington, D.C.: GPO, 1976), pp. 101-103. For a discussion of recent trends in U.S.-Cuban relations, the state of U.S. public opinion on relations with Cuba, and the bilateral policy agenda between the two countries, see William Watts and Jorge I. Domínguez, *The United States and Cuba: Old Issues and New Directions,* Policy Perspective 1977/1 (Washington, D.C.: Potomac Associates, 1977).

4

NELSON P. VALDÉS

Revolutionary Solidarity in Angola

Cuba's recent African policy raises fascinating and pertinent questions about the nature of the Cuban revolutionary experience. Is the Cuban presence in Angola a logical outcome of the institutionalization of the Cuban Revolution or an aberration? What were the motives and tactics of this policy? Are the Cubans acting on their own accord or are they surrogate soldiers of the USSR? I will touch on these issues, but my main effort will be to explain why Cuba sent troops to Angola. The chapter has been divided into three parts. The first traces the continuity of Cuban revolutionary foreign policy in theory and practice, with particular attention to African liberation movements. In the second part, I briefly discuss Cuba's relations with the liberation forces in the Portuguese colonies and examine in more detail the developments inside Angola and their international context. The concluding part attempts to explain why Cuba sent troops to Angola.

International Revolutionary Solidarity: Departure or Continuity?

Cuban revolutionary commitment to the national liberation struggles of other countries needs serious investigation. There are available some general descriptions of the support Havana has provided to insurgents and revolutionaries in Latin America since 1959. Indeed, there is overwhelming evidence that Cuba has materially backed numerous attempts at establishing revolutionary regimes.[1] Lacking, however, is a thorough investigation of the numerous manifestations of Cuban support to extrahemispheric revolutionary movements and regimes.

Even a summary review of Cuba's foreign policy toward the Third World immediately discloses that international solidarity has been an essential part of revolutionary ideology as well as a consistent revolutionary practice. A brief consideration of this policy will demonstrate that the events in Angola since 1975 are the consistent continuation of policy, rather than a very abrupt departure.

The two leading figures of the Cuban Revolution, Fidel Castro and Ernesto "Ché" Guevara, showed early in their political careers a willingness to identify and participate in the struggles of others for their own emancipation. Ché did so in Bolivia, Guatemala, and then Cuba, as did Fidel in the Confites expedition of 1947 against dictator Rafael Leonidas Trujillo of the Dominican Republic. In 1963, Ché Guevara quoted José Martí on this point: "We must practice true proletarian internationalism, feel any aggression against others as one committed on us; we must feel any affront, any act that goes against the dignity of man,   87 against his happiness anywhere in the world."[2] The ideological dimension of Cuban revolutionary solidarity stemmed from principles deeply rooted in Cuban political history, Marxist-Leninist theory, and the national interest of the country. After all, the survival of the Revolution depended, to a large extent, on breaking the circle of isolation imposed on it by the United States. Hence, to give moral and political assistance to other revolutionary forces in the world was a product of the national revolutionary experience.

Regional isolation, continued subversion by the U.S. Central Intelligence Agency (CIA), and the war in Vietnam dramatically affected the Cuban concept of revolutionary solidarity in international terms. The Cubans developed a coherent and world-oriented conception of their own called "integral coexistence." This principle was spelled out by the then president, Osvaldo Dorticós. Basically, the Cubans held that the struggle of developing countries against colonialism and neocolonialism could not be sacrificed in order to achieve peaceful coexistence between the great powers. Instead, revolutionary countries should demand that the capitalist nations—including the United States—establish peaceful coexistence with (that is, respect the rights of) Third World countries too, and that no aggression against the latter be allowed. Moreover, the demand for peaceful coexistence among all countries clearly implied support for the right of all nations to be free from foreign control.[3]

As the war in Vietnam escalated, the Cubans had no reservations about the meaning of international solidarity. On February 18, 1965, Prime Minister Fidel Castro offered to send volunteers from the Cuban regular armed forces to fight side by side with the Vietnamese. A month later he said: "For us small countries [Vietnam and Cuba], who do not base our strength in millions of men or in atomic power, we are small countries, that realize divisions in the socialist camp weaken us . . . We are not frightened by recent events; rather we are moved to action. We have one position. We are in favor of giving Vietnam all the aid that that country needs. *We are in favor of sending arms and men to Vietnam to help defeat imperialism.* We are in favor of running the risks necessary in order to defend Vietnam."[4]

The Cubans were first in the communist world to make such an offer. Eleven days later, China did the same, with the proviso that Vietnam request volunteers. The Soviet Union followed a day later.[5] The Cuban initiative was revealing not only because it preceded that of the two communist giants and put pressure on them. More important, the island's revolutionary leadership felt compelled to act in a moment of crisis by unfolding a strategy of revolutionary solidarity. Cuban troops did not go to Vietnam only because the National Liberation Front declined the offer.

Such commitment to international solidarity stemmed not just from revolutionary principles or regional political necessity, but from the deep sense of moral outrage and frustration caused by the fight of a small, developing country against the technologically sophisticated machine of the most developed nation in the world. After 1965, the Cuban leadership became more convinced than ever of the need to link up all Third World struggles and battles. In that framework, Ché Guevara went to Africa and attempted to work out a continental strategy with the Afro-Asian Solidarity Organization. The main purpose of the Tricontinental Conference of January 1966 was to promote revolution in the Third World. To that end it created the Organization of Solidarity with the Peoples of Asia, Africa, and Latin America (OSPAAAL) with headquarters in Havana; a Cuban was named secretary general.

On January 3, 1966, President Dorticós outlined the Cuban position. Imperialism, as a world system with an international policy of counterrevolution, had to be fought on a world scale. Moreover, since imperialism used reactionary violence, the people had the right to defend themselves with revolutionary violence. The duty of the people who had already gained independence was to give the necessary aid, in any form required, to the liberation movements in Asia, Africa, and Latin America. This was considered the only true solidarity. The final declaration of the Tricontinental Conference proclaimed the right and duty of all the peoples of Asia, Africa, and Latin America, and of "progressive states and governments of the world" to grant material and moral aid to the peoples who were fighting for their liberation or who were attacked directly or indirectly by imperialism. On this and other occasions Cuba put its commitment to international revolutionary solidarity on the record. The Havana delegation took the following position: "In the face of the imperialistic tactic of protracted wars, the effective answer of the revolutionary movement is to foster wars of liberation in all regions where the conditions exist for that activity. The duty of all progressive countries is to give the corresponding aid unconditionally to those peoples who are engaged in a war of national liberation or who suffer imperialist aggression anywhere in the world."[6]

Throughout 1966 and 1967 the Cubans kept on proclaiming international solidarity, adding that it had to be contingent on revolutionary practice. That is, one could not expect to receive assistance unless the aid was properly used to advance the armed struggle for power.[7] In 1967 they attempted to implement those principles in Latin America by forming the Organization of Latin American Solidarity (OLAS), which held its founding congress in Havana from July 21 to August 10. Again, numerous documents were issued clearly defining all the subtle aspects of international revolutionary solidarity. True, after 1968, Cuban foreign policy was redefined and with it some of the facets of internationalism, but the trend away from adventuristic guerilla plots did not signify a reversal of principles. Fundamental ideological beliefs were left intact; methods for implementing them were changed. Internationalist solidarity continued, but now it was founded on those movements that were already in power, or could succeed in taking power over a short period of time.

Yet, the convictions and daring outlook remained. On May 6, 1972, Fidel Castro, in a speech at Conakry, Guinea, showed Cuba's continuing revolutionary stance. On the last day of his visit Fidel and Sekou Touré declared that "the solidarity of Cuba and Guinea will always be at the service of the revolutionary peoples of the world." A week later, in a visit to Algiers, the prime minister went back to the theme of Vietnam. "For Vietnam we Cubans are ready to do whatever may be necessary. For Vietnam we are ready to fight there with them." During June 1972, on a visit to Poland, Fidel Castro lectured the government about revolutionary internationalism. "We in Cuba, our party, educate our people in the principles of internationalism." True revolutionists should be ready to fulfill their obligations at any time or place.[8]

This view has not been hidden from the world. On September 21, 1974, President Dorticós stressed in a speech that "as before and more than before" the African liberation movement would find "the modest contribution" of Cuba "inspired by the principles of people's international solidarity." The Cuban foreign minister, Raúl Roa, again outlined the country's position, this time at the United Nations. He declared that it was a duty to contribute to the immediate liberation of African nations facing colonial oppression and racism. Further, the Cuban constitution of February 24, 1976, stated in article 12 that Cuba "espouses the principles of proletarian internationalism and of the combative solidarity of the peoples," recognizing that wars of national liberation and "armed resistance to aggression and conquest" were legitimate acts. Finally, it went on to assert that Cuba "considers that its help to those under attack and to the peoples for their liberation constitutes its internationalist right and duty."[9]

From the onset of the Revolution, the Cuban government has shown itself to be, at least verbally, an unflinching and resolute defender of international revolutionary solidarity. The principles have been consistent, even when they have widened the differences between Cuba and other Communist parties or states. One can discern a shift, a reconsideration of what forces should receive aid, but solidarity itself has never diminished as a foundation of foreign policy. Whether that solidarity was translated into material support has depended on the circumstances. Nevertheless, there has been a continued willingness by the revolutionary government to offer effective support in diverse forms (although at times the offers have been declined as in Vietnam in 1965 and in Chile in 1973). How real are these self-proclaimed principles? Should we accept Cuba's assertions as sufficient evidence of adherence to revolutionary convictions? Obviously not. Concrete evidence should be weighed too.

Cuba's involvement in the Angolan conflict has been interpreted as a major departure in its foreign policy. The point is often made that never before has a Latin American revolutionary government committed regular troops outside the western hemisphere. This, however, is incorrect since Cuba had deployed regular military forces in Africa on more than one occasion.

Perhaps the first case was when the new Cuban government, in mid-1960, sent weapons and military advisors to train Algerian guerrillas.[10] Between 1961 and the summer of 1962 many Algerian rebels went to Cuba to rest from wounds suffered in battle or to train for future encounters against French colonial forces.[11] When Algeria became independent in October 1962, relations between the two revolutionary regimes became still closer. In fact, Algeria became the political and military coordinating center from which Cuba dealt with national liberation movements throughout Africa. An undisclosed number of Cuban military, political, and medical advisors flocked to the recently independent state. As early as July 1963, Ché Guevara showed up in Algeria "heading a delegation including military specialists." By September about one thousand guerrillas from Angola, Mozambique, and Namibia received training from Algerians and Cubans in Algeria.

Cuba did not send a significantly large number of military men and weapons to Algeria until the fall of 1963 when, on September 19, a large military mission visited to Algiers.[12] Ten days later a regional revolt in the mountains of Kabylia seriously threatened the stability of the Ahmed Ben Bella regime. To make matters worse, the Moroccan government used this clash to attack the Algerian borders, a portion of which it claimed. A serious clash between the two countries ensued in the first week of October. On October 14 an even larger military mission from Cuba arrived in Algiers. By then the Moroccan forces had advanced twenty-five miles inside Algerian territory.[13] Apparently the Ben Bella government felt sufficiently threatened to proclaim mass mobilization. It is possible that at that juncture it asked the Cubans for assistance. The next day, the Cuban foreign trade minister, Alberto Mora, arrived in Algiers. The terms of any agreement reached between the two governments were not disclosed. Two years later, however, on June 26, 1965, Fidel Castro made reference to those events, claiming that Algeria had "asked us for help, and men and weapons from our country crossed the Atlantic in record time to go to Algeria." He stressed that they were "ready to fight beside Algerian revolutionists."[14] Where did the initiative reside? Did the Algerians ask for help or did the Cubans offer it? The circumstantial evidence suggests the latter. On October 16, 1963, as Ahmed Ben Bella assumed provisional dictatorial powers, Castro and Dorticós sent a telegram to the Algerians offering their "solidarity and support."[15]

On December 22, 1975, Fidel again touched on the Algerian affair by declaring, "Nor is it a secret that at a time of danger for the Republic of Algeria, our men were in Algeria."[16] But he did not disclose the size of the military contingent sent. We know, nevertheless, that the Cubans sent at least three ships, about forty Soviet T-34 tanks, four MiG jet fighters, trucks, and "more than 800 tons of light arms, ammunition and artillery."[17] Apparently the Cuban troops saw no fighting since a truce was reached within a week of their arrival. Relations between the countries remained exceedingly cordial even when the National Liberation Front declared the Communist party illegal. Indeed, the Algerians attempted to build socialism along the "Cuban model," and the Havana leadership followed events in Algeria rather closely.[18] Algeria remained as a coordinating center for its relations with guerrillas throughout Africa until June 19, 1965. On that date Colonel Houari Boumedienne overthrew the government of Ben Bella, and the Cubans, siding with their old ally, called the whole affair a counterrevolutionary coup. Relations between the two countries deteriorated; the Cubans decided to shift their center of operations to the Congo Republic.[19]

By the summer of 1965 the Cuban leadership had decided to foster and support wars of national liberation on the three continents as a way of aiding Vietnam. The Congo Republic became part of that strategy of solidarity. This effort was under the personal direction of Ché Guevara, who organized a group of 125 veterans of the Cuban guerrilla struggle.[20] The idea was to use the Congo (Brazzaville), then ruled by Alphonse Massemba-Debat, as the springboard from which guerrillas were to be launched against the government of Moise Tshombé, then ruling in Leopoldville (now Kinshasa), but representing Katangese interests.[21] Ché's efforts failed, and the Cuban authorities disavowed the enterprise, reducing their aid considerably. Although Cubans participated, it was not presented, nor interpreted, as official national policy. This is the reason why, even today, the Cuban government never mentions these efforts when speaking of official internationalist solidarity. Another reason for the silence, of course, is that no legally constituted government asked the Cubans for aid. Indeed, they backed the insurgent forces of Gaston Soumaliot which attempted to get into power, but failed. Finally, the Cubans did not feel that the rebels were truly serious in their struggle.[22]

The debacle in the Congo late in 1965 did not cause the Cubans to withdraw from the African scene. From then on, however, no regular forces were sent to aid insurgents. Havana opted instead for a more moderate position: to help consolidate revolutionary governments already in power, and to give assistance to African guerrillas without the deployment of regular forces. If some men were assigned to the guerrillas, they were to provide training, rather than engage in actual fighting.

The new Cuban attitude toward Africa was well delineated in relations with the Congo Republic at the new center of Cuban operations in Brazzaville. In June 1965 "several hundred Cuban military personnel" began training the local militia. On July 21, 1965, José Serguera became the first ambassador of Cuba, presenting credentials to Massamba-Debat. By May 1966 there were approximately seven hundred Cuban military advisors in the country working with the Civil Defense Corps (CDC), a military body independent of the army and answering directly to the president. They also created a presidential guard made up solely of three hundred elite Cuban soldiers who had autonomy under the general control of the CDC.[23]

A military revolt which broke out on June 28, 1966, and was led by Captain Marien Ngouabi, chief of the army's paracommando battalion, threatened the good relations between the two countries. The coup apparently was a result of Ngouabi's demotion; some allege that the rebels acted against the Cuban presence. One report notes that the government and ruling party "took refuge in Brazzaville's sports stadium, around which the Cuban-officered presidential guard . . . flung a protective cordon."[24] By all accounts, the Cubans were the key factor in smashing the mutiny. Interestingly, the Cuban government acknowledged the presence of a large number of its regular forces, but said nothing of the role they played in defending Massamba-Debat against Ngouabi.[25] On June 29, 1966, Radio Havana said in an editorial that "the revolutionary government of the Congo, in order to defend the Congolese revolution from external threats and internal conspiracies . . . solicited the cooperation of the revolutionary government of Cuba—due to the experience our country has, [it requested] assistance in organizing and training a militia and some sections of the army. The Cuban government, fulfilling its internationalist obligations, sent weapons and instructors to aid in the military education of the people of the Congo-Brazzaville.''[26]

Later that same year, the Cuban military forces were increased to more than a thousand, but their activities shifted from establishing a popular army to the training of guerrillas fighting against the Portuguese.[27] It became essential to have a low profile inside the Congo, particularly after the president publicly declared that Congolese socialism would be built without Cuban help.[28] The Cubans already had given up the idea of moving their operations to Ghana because it was too remote from the African conflict. Moreover, Kwame Nkrumah had been ousted earlier in the year, and the Cuban embassy had been forced to leave the country in September.[29] Confronted with such dismal prospects, the Cuban government opted for moving its coordinating center to a friendly and stable country. The Republic of Guinea, led by Sekou Touré, fulfilled those conditions, although it too was far from the focus of guerrilla operations, that is, from southern Africa. So the Cubans concentrated on helping rebels fighting against Portuguese colonialism in Guinea-Bissau and Cape Verde, although these two areas were not as important from an economic or strategic perspective as Angola, the Congo, or Mozambique.

Guinea, in fact, was the first African nation to show consistent friendship toward Cuba after 1960. Sekou Touré was the first African dignitary to visit the island, and from 1967 on, the two countries moved unostentatiously closer. Five years later, during May 1972, Fidel Castro visited Guinea and after an unusually long visit declared: ''Our fighters, with the same love with which they have been ready to fight for Cuba, have been ready to fight in support of any revolutionary people. Thus, we will be united in peace, and we will be united in the struggle, and we will be united in combat, and we will be united under any circumstances.''[30] Was this a mere flight of fancy rhetoric? It might have seemed so if one were unaware of the close ties between the two countries. Indeed, Fidel had made a subtle reference to the role played by Cuban regular forces two years earlier. On November 22, 1970, Cuban regular military forces serving in the presidential guard of Sekou Touré fought side by side with Guinean soldiers in Conakry in defense of the president's home against a commando attack launched by Portuguese colonial forces.[31] Although it is not known how many Cubans participated, the Cubans were essential to the defeat of the Portuguese and their hired mercenaries.[32] Over the years Cuba has reaffirmed its moral and material aid to Guinea under any circumstances. Sekou Touré himself, in a speech on March 16, 1976, acknowledged that Cuban regular forces had fought in Guinea.[33]

We know too little about Cuba's military role in Africa, aside from the foregoing information, some hints and subtle remarks. There is precious little hard data. On December 22, 1975, Fidel Castro said, ''It is no secret at all that at

NELSON P. VALDÉS

a time of danger and threats to the Syrian Republic [in October 1973], our men were in Syria.''[34] Israeli intelligence sources have suggested that in late 1973 there were about four thousand Cuban regular troops in Syria as part of an armoured brigade which even took part in the war until May 1974. (See chapter 8 of this volume.) If this is true it means that we know the least about this, Cuba's largest deployment of soldiers outside of the hemisphere before Angola.

This is why at times we must accept, at face value, declarations made by the revolutionary leadership in Cuba. According to Fidel: ''Throughout the revolutionary process, we have conducted a policy of solidarity with the ... governments and revolutionary movements of Africa as soon as the Revolution triumphed. . . . here we sent arms, there we sent men, or military instructors, doctors, builders; now and again we sent builders, doctors, and instructors all together. From the outset, the Revolution has been true to its internationalist policy, giving assistance whenever it could be useful and wherever it was being requested.''[35]

In summary, there seem to be two broad and basic differences on the matter of Cuban assistance to revolutionary forces outside Latin America. These two categories should not be confused. First, there is the material aid given to established, legally recognized governments. Whenever those governments have requested Cuban soldiers, the revolutionary leadership has been willing to supply them. We have called this *legal support,* as in Algeria, the Congo Republic, Guinea, and Syria. There is, however, a key difference in the very nature of this kind of military support. In the case of Algeria and Syria the soldiers were mobilized and sent across the Atlantic in order to confront a pressing military and political crisis. In Algeria they did not see action; in Syria, apparently, they did. Lastly, in the Congo Republic and Guinea the forces were stationed prior to the crisis, and they were willing to act when it came. Hence, we can conclude that there are two major variants in the mobilization of Cuban regular forces to act on extrahemispheric conflict. In the first case they are sent to a particular country, at the request of that country, to fight a pressing foreign threat. In the second case, the troops are already there and agree to a combat role.

Such action, however, ought not to be confused with aiding national liberation movements that are waging guerrilla war and do not yet have control of the government. This type we call *extralegal support.* With the exception of the Congo affair by Ché Guevara, the Cubans have not mobilized regular forces in order to back insurgency with fighting men. Instead, the Cuban government has given war matèriel, training, and allowed individual Cubans to act on their own behalf as instructors of the guerrilla forces. The Cubans, in other words, were willing to acknowledge that their government officially gave money, political support, or training in the island to guerrillas; but Cubans going abroad were acting on their own volition and not as an acknowledged, official act. Such examples abound in Africa. We have already noted the relation between Cuba and Algeria from 1960 to 1962. By the early 1960s, most analysts agree, Cuba furnished aid to the Mozambique Liberation Front (FRELIMO), the African

Party for the Independence of Guinea and Cape Verde (PAIGC) in Guinea-Bissau, the Congolese guerrillas, and revolutionists from Senegal, Malawi, Tanzania, Mali, Morocco, Namibia, Zimbabwe, and Ethiopia.[36]

Thus, to the question whether Cuba has implemented its professed commitment to international revolutionary solidarity, we must answer in the affirmative. Cuba, in theory and practice, has consistently helped revolutionary forces outside Latin America. Cubans have not only talked about it, they have engaged in transnational operations. The Angolan affair is another manifestation of an established policy, but it is complicated by the Cubans' shift from extralegal support of a guerrilla movement, to legal support of that movement after it had seized power and was confronting a foreign invasion. The Cuban involvement in Angola did not export revolution (as Ché tried to do in the Congo); it was massive assistance to a constituted government, similar to, but of far greater magnitude than, the aid given to Algeria, Syria, or Guinea.

The Portuguese Colonies in Africa

The extent and nature of the aid supplied by Cuba to the independence movements fighting against Portuguese colonialism in Africa are not yet known. The available evidence suggests that Cuba established ties with the PAIGC, FRELIMO, and the Popular Movement for the Liberation of Angola (MPLA) in 1961. Cuba initiated its assistance by helping to train men in unconventional warfare after the MPLA and PAIGC opened fronts in their respective countries in 1961. FRELIMO, apparently, obtained the same benefits from 1964 on. By 1961 the three organizations had sent men to Cuba, and in 1962 there were at least fifteen Cuban doctors working for the MPLA in liberated territory.[37]

Of the three organizations, however, the Cubans paid the most attention—at least in their press—to the PAIGC in the 1960s. There were two reasons for this. First, the struggle in Guinea-Bissau had a greater chance of success, since the independence forces were under a united leadership. Second, the Cuban coordinating bureau in Conakry after 1966 was much closer to Portuguese Guinea than to FRELIMO or the MPLA. Finally, the PAIGC already controlled 40 percent of Portuguese Guinea by 1965.[38] Before 1974, Cubans had joined the PAIGC on the battlefield against the Portuguese. At least one Cuban was captured, and apparently many others participated in the struggle.

In 1965, Cuba already considered the MPLA the sole leader of the struggle in Angola, which is why it was the only organization from that country invited to the Tricontinental Conference. At the conference the Cubans stressed the need to give "total aid" to Guinea-Bissau, Angola, and Mozambique. The idea of a coordinated continental struggle against colonialism in Africa, however, had been abandoned that same year. Ché wrote in April 1967, "the social and political evolution of Africa does not lead us to expect a continental revolution."

What actually went on from 1967 to 1970 between these movements and Cuba is unknown. From Havana, throughout 1968 and 1969, OSPAAAL issued numerous calls to support Angola, Mozambique, and Guinea-Bissau. There were frequent reports in the press about their guerrilla operations, and the second highest ranking leader of the PAIGC visited Cuba, but little else is known. Perhaps the 1970 sugar harvest did not allow the Cuban leadership to pay as much attention to Africa. After the summer of 1970, however, all this changed.[39] Sekou Touré's regime had been seriously threatened by a Portuguese attack from Guinea-Bissau. Apparently, Cuba and Guinea now worked much harder on behalf of the MPLA and the PAIGC. Indeed, the Cuban media now reported that Agostinho Neto, leader of the MPLA, already controlled about 60 percent of Angola.

On October 2, 1970, the Cuban delegate to the United Nations said that Cuba would support all efforts to "aid the just struggles of the people of Guinea-Bissau, Angola, Mozambique, Zimbabwe, Namibia, and South Africa." Then on July 14, 1971, the governments of Cuba and Algeria issued a joint communiqué which may have been revealing. It said, in part, "The two delegations analyzed African problems and agreed on the need to step up aid to the movements for liberation in the countries struggling against colonialism."[40]

In May 1972 Fidel Castro made a formal visit to Sekou Touré in Guinea, and did not miss the opportunity of meeting with representatives of PAIGC and the MPLA. Amilcar Cabral, leader of PAIGC, awaited him at the airport.[41] From Guinea, Fidel moved on to Algeria where another joint communiqué was released. The document read, in part, "The fighters of [Guinea-Bissau, Cape Verde, Angola, and Mozambique] have made themselves worthy, through their effort and sacrifices, of the most resolute and efficient aid that the world revolutionary forces can provide." The assistance may have included "volunteers" to fight the Portuguese as well as doctors. They could be found in Guinea-Bissau, Angola, and Cape Verde. It is not clear whether Cubans went at this time to Mozambique, although they had been training Mozambique guerrillas from Tanzania since 1970.[42]

Overall, Cuban policy toward the anti-Portuguese liberation struggles followed very strictly the parameters of what we have defined as extralegal assistance. That is, revolutionists were trained either in Cuba or some friendly African nation (Guinea, Algeria, Tanzania, or the Congo Republic), weapons were provided, as well as financial assistance and political support in international bodies. At times Cuban medical or military personnel were permitted to join such movements, on the understanding that they were volunteers acting for themselves, and not official representatives of the Cuban revolutionary government. That is, extralegal assistance did not entail committing any Cuban institution to the liberation struggle in Africa.

Cuba in Angola

Prelude to Involvement

The Cuban decision to send regular troops to Angola cannot be explained simply by pointing to the continuity of its revolutionary principles, nor to its previous material assistance to national liberation struggles in Africa. Those were necessary but not sufficient factors. It is essential to place the Cuban move in its proper context, showing a set of interacting agents that include the internal situation in Angola, the Portuguese policy in Angola, and the role of the Zairian and South African governments.

In Angola three major political movements—the National Union for the Total Liberation of Angola (UNITA), the National Front for the Liberation of Angola (FNLA), and the MPLA—had fought for independence from Portugal since the 1960s. Each clustered around one of the three largest ethnolinguistic regions of Angola. They had their own territorial base, political structure, and program as well as separate military forces. They all claimed to fight Portuguese colonialism, but competed with one another for hegemony over the struggle.[43] "The result," John A. Marcum states, "was a complex three-way struggle for revolutionary primacy interspersed with fratricidal clashes and suffused with a profound and bitter political rivalry."[44] The problem was further complicated by the world powers since the Peoples' Republic of China backed UNITA, the Soviet Union supported the MPLA and the United States covertly aided the FNLA although it also provided military support to the Portuguese.

On April 25, 1974, the Marcello Caetano dictatorship was brought to an end in Portugal by a military revolt, unleashing a series of events that led to the collapse of Portuguese colonialism. Such an outcome had not been foreseen by U.S. foreign policy experts who felt that whites would continue ruling southern Africa for a long time.[45] What had appeared as an impossibility to the U.S. Security Council analysts now seemed a foregone conclusion. In other words, American foreign policy found itself in serious difficulty in southern Africa.

Meanwhile, the new Portuguese government attempted to establish a truce with the three independence organizations in Angola, but it was not until after a leftist faction within the military in Portugal (the Armed Forces Movement) seized power on September 30, 1974, that fighting ended.[46] At the very moment when negotiations began to find a viable formula for a transition from colony to independent nation-state, Portuguese colonials unleashed a wave of terror inside Angola to avert independence. But the attempt failed.

On January 15, 1975, the representatives of the three groups signed an agreement known as the Alvor Accords. It established a transitional regime that would lead to the proclamation of independence on November 11, 1975. The transitional regime was to be presided over by a Portuguese military officer, while all administrative posts in Angola would be evenly divided among the three contenders. Elections were to be held in October 1975 to decide who would have control. The three separate armies, under the supervision of the Portuguese, were to be unified during the transition.

It was at that point that the ''40 Committee'' of the U.S. National Security Council authorized the use of $300,000 in covert funds for the FNLA. This was justified on the grounds that the Soviet Union and the Portuguese communists had stepped up their shipments of arms to the MPLA in order to help it gain complete power.[47]

The transitional government had its hands full from the outset. Factional fighting broke out in mid-February 1975 in several Angolan cities. To make matters worse, on March 11, rightists within the Portuguese military staged an unsuccessful countercoup. The FNLA, as well as the United States, already feared that the left within the Portuguese government would transfer complete sovereignty to the MPLA. Apparently the FNLA appealed to its foreign ally, the Republic of Zaire, for help. Chinese and Zairian instructors had been training the FNLA forces for several years. Now, on March 13, 1975, Zairian regular troops invaded the oil-rich Cabinda enclave. The FNLA joined the Zaire troops, and on March 23 the MPLA had its first military clash with them.[48] The fighting spread in April.

In a semiofficial version of the Cuban role in Angola at this time Gabriel García Márquez has written that "in May 1975, as the Portuguese were getting ready to pull out of their African colonies, Cuban major Flavio Bravo met Agostinho Neto in Brazzaville, and Neto requested help with shipments of arms and asked about the possibility of further specific aid."[49] At about the same time the FNLA requested more assistance from the United States. On June 18, the Nixon administration approved covert military aid to the FNLA and UNITA amounting to $30 million, to be channeled through Zaire and Zambia. That same month Cuba sent, according to some sources, 230 civilian and military advisors to Angola.

The sending of Cuban advisors to Angola apparently was not opposed by the Portuguese authorities who, at least in name, still had control over the area. Furthermore, the relations between Cuba and the Portuguese government were becoming more friendly. By early June, for example, the military leaders in Portugal claimed they were closely following the Cuban experience.[50] When the Portuguese, instead of pulling troops out, sent more in by mid-June, some interpreted this move as an attempt to help the MPLA further.

When Mozambique became independent, a Cuban delegation headed by Armando Acosta, a Central Committee member and an authority on liberation movements in Africa, held talks with Samora Machel on the Angolan situation. If anything was decided, no news was released.[51] However, since Mozambique at the time coordinated the support given to Angola by former Portuguese colonies, it is more than probable that the Cubans now became a more important part of that overall effort.

By July 9 the Angolan situation had deteriorated into all-out war. In its struggle with UNITA, the MPLA gained the material commitment of the South West Africa People's Organization (SWAPO), expanding even further the number of participants in the Angolan war. On July 11, Francis Meli, secretary general of SWAPO, arrived in Havana. It is possible that through him Cuba received another request for aid. Gabriel García Márquez notes that on July 16, 1975, Cuba received a request for aid from the MPLA.[52] Cuba, however, wanting to avoid alienating or creating difficulties for the Portuguese, invited Portuguese officials to the island to hold discussions on matters of mutual interest. On July

21, 1975, Colonel Otelo Saravia de Carvalho, one of the three members of the Council of the Revolution of Portugal, accompanied by a large delegation, arrived in Havana.[53] He stayed in Cuba for a little over a week. During his stay he expressed his admiration for the Revolution, even saying, "I only wish that something similar could happen in our country."[54] Saravia de Carvalho toured military installations with the chief of the Cuban general staff and Vice-prime minister of the Revolutionary Armed Forces, Commander Senén Casas Reguerio. The latter then flew to Lisbon on July 24, 1975, to meet with other members of the Portuguese government.[55] The nature of the conversations was not disclosed, although Commander Senén Casas, a few months later, had direct command over the Cuban forces in Angola. Significantly, a student of Cuba's military has noted that later in July, Cuba engaged in war exercises "to occupy large areas" using large numbers of troops from several of its army units, including motorized vehicles. One report states that Fidel Castro had asked Colonel Saravia de Carvalho "to arrange Portuguese permission for Cuban aid to Angola."[56]

Such a close relationship between the Cubans and the Portuguese caused considerable apprehension among the anti-MPLA forces. Would the Portuguese and Cubans work together on behalf of the MPLA? The FNLA and UNITA apparently thought so. South Africa also felt threatened by the possibility of an Angolan government aiding liberation movements in Namibia and Azania. The interests of Zaire, South Africa, the FNLA, UNITA, and the United States were the same: to defeat the MPLA.

On August 9, 1975, South African regular forces entered Angola claiming they wanted to protect the Calueque installations supplying electricity to South West Africa. The South African aim, however, was more than defensive. It sought to help UNITA destroy the SWAPO forces, weakening the MPLA while doing away with the revolutionary challenge in Namibia.[57] By August 20 the South Africans had set up two military bases at Cunene, inside Angola. The MPLA issued several communiqués denouncing the situation. The Portuguese Revolutionary Council, confronted with the intervention, dissolved the provisional government in Angola and assumed all administrative powers. Although a reaction to the South African move, the anti-MPLA organizations interpreted the Portuguese decision as clearing the way for Agostinho Neto to assume power.

The Cubans closely followed events in Angola and reported them. On August 27, 1975, *Granma* told its readers that "South African regular troops crossed the Angolan border with the pretext of defending the Ruacana-Calueque hydroelectric complex."[58] And the next day Raul Roa, then foreign affairs minister, declared at a meeting of nonaligned nations in Peru,

The process of decolonization in that country [Angola] has become very alarming. There is evidently a neocolonialist plot on a vast scale aimed at counteracting the liberation movements in southern Africa and setting up dependent governments in a dismembered Angola so the developed capitalist world will continue to receive a constant flow of energy resources from that country, thanks to the control of the transnational companies. The main tool for this is the so-called National Front for the Liberation of Angola, which has the logistical, financial, and military backing of reactionary and neocolonialist African forces. The National Front is also supported by the National Union for the Total Independence of Angola, influenced by South African and European interests. . . . The outcome of this conflict will have a significant bearing on the upsurge or decline of the process of decolonization in Africa. The future of the oppressed and discriminated against peoples of Namibia, Zimbabwe, and South Africa depends, to a large extent, on the outcome of the struggle in Angola. Action by the Non Aligned to safeguard Angola's independence and territorial integrity is imperative and it must be given in whatever manner required.[59]

As events unfolded in Angola, the Cubans held more high-level discussions with the Portuguese government. From August 18 to 24, 1975, Vice-Admiral Antonio Alva Rosa Coutinho visited Cuba and publicly supported the MPLA. Again, no joint communiqué was issued detailing the nature of the talks. In Portugal, Brigadier Pezerat Correia, also a member of the Revolutionary Council, went as far as saying that the FNLA and UNITA "had switched to defending not the interests of their own country on the road to independence but foreign interests." He added, "I think it is time to reappraise their rights." For a significant section of the Portuguese government, the MPLA deserved to have power. Also during August, Major Raul Diaz Arguelles apparently led a civilian Cuban delegation to Luanda, but this was not reported at the time.[60]

The South African intervention in August set loose the forces that eventually resulted in the Cuban expeditionary force. Jorge Domínguez writes that "sometime between August 20 and September 5 of 1975, the Chairman of the Joint Chiefs of Staff, the Chiefs of the three armies, and the Air Force, and other Ministers of the Armed Ministries were relieved of their posts."[61] They began to prepare for "Operation Carlotta." Their plans may have developed to supplement the attempts by the Portuguese to transfer power to the MPLA. This option, however, became less of a possibility due to the strong opposition to it inside Portugal. In fact, the Portuguese government, confronted with many coup attempts in the period, could not take the leading role it had hoped. Cuba, seemingly, moved into that role.

Between October 4 and 11, three Cuban ships arrived in Angola after stopping in the Congo Republic. García Márquez writes that "they docked without anyone's permission—but also without anyone's opposition." Official South African sources have claimed that on October 6 its forces clashed with the MPLA and its Cuban advisors at Norton de Matos. The Cuban government has declared that "in mid-October, at the request of the MPLA, there arrived in Angola a quantity of weapons from Cuba and a number of officers of our armed forces to train the Angolan fighters."[62]

Within two weeks the Cuban contingent had been noticed. On October 19, UNITA told the world press that approximately 750 Cubans had landed near Luanda the previous week to help defend the city against FNLA encirclement. The next day, UNITA claimed that a Cuban force had been seen at Novo Redondo. Radio Lusaka, on October 23, claimed that 1000 Cubans had been transported to Angola from Congolese waters. And on October 28, UNITA charged that some 3000 Cubans were already fighting on behalf of the MPLA.[63]

The number of Cubans in Angola and the nature of their role were both exaggerated by UNITA. But UNITA was accurate about the landings and the fact that the Congo had become a springboard for supplying the MPLA. Earlier, on September 13, 1975, Marien Ngouabi, president of the People's Republic of the Congo, arrived in Havana for a five-day visit.[64] It is quite likely that he discussed the situation in Angola and how best to help the MPLA against South Africa. Ngouabi, of course, was aware of the geopolitical implications for his country if Angola, like Zaire, was dominated by a government unfriendly to his. The Congolese visit was returned by a Cuban delegation going to Brazzaville from October 5 to 8.[65] The Communist party delegation from Cuba, headed by José Llanusa, probably informed the African government of the details of the Cuban enterprise already underway.

The Cubans were not concerned to hide their intentions. On October 10, Ricardo Alarcón, permanent Cuban representative to the United Nations, stated that "in view of the scandalous interference on the part of the imperialists, colonialists, and racists, it is our elementary duty to offer the people of Angola whatever aid is necessary to guarantee the true independence and the full sovereignty of their country."[66]

As Angolan independence moved closer, the level of military activity mounted. There were by mid-October three military fronts. On the northern front serious clashes occurred. The FNLA, trained by Portuguese colonists and South Africans, also had a large contingent of Zairian regular soldiers. In the east, UNITA seriously challenged the MPLA; while in the south the MPLA had made some advances until mid-October. By October 17, the MPLA appeared to be seizing the offensive, except around Luanda where the FNLA had concentrated most of its efforts. On October 23, 1975, however, South Africa openly invaded Angola. The government of Mozambique estimated the strength of the invasion at 10,000 men, with heavy artillery and armed vehicles.[67] Within hours they captured considerable territory. The South African military advances were not new, but now they gained in speed, as shown below:

	Area Captured
July 5	Cunene
August 11	Reinforcements at Cunene
August 20	Two bases at Cunene
October 14	Silva Porto
October 15	Luso

Area Captured (continued)	
October 19	Pereira de Eca
October 20	Rocadas, Negage
October 22	Joao de Almeida
October 24	Sa da Bandeira
October 26	Chibia, Huila, Texeira de Silva
October 27	Caraculo
October 30	Mocamedes, Porto Alexandre, Cubal
November 1	Bahia de Forta
November 2	Benguela Airport
November 4	Benguela, Lobito
November 5	Norton de Matos

The political and military picture changed drastically in favor of the anti-MPLA alliance. Luanda remained encircled. South African forces were 625 miles south of MPLA headquarters by early November, but moving north fast. Zaire's regular forces, meanwhile, invaded Cabinda for the second time. The MPLA had lost most of the southern regions. South Africa had penetrated 350 miles into Angola, moving at a rate of 40 miles per day. On November 3, South African soldiers attacked a training camp at Benguela run by Cuban instructors.[68]

Fidel Castro, in a speech on March 27, 1977, described what ensued:

On November 3, near Benguela, the Angolan students at the military school, beside a group of Cuban instructors, fought, in difficult and disadvantageous conditions, the mechanized troops of the South African racists. That day, November 3, 1975, the first Cubans died beside the MPLA fighters. The situation was difficult but in such a juncture it was necessary to make a decision. Comrade Neto and the MPLA decided and solicited our direct support to face the South African racists, the puppets of imperialism, and the Zairian regular troops.[69]

Now the nature of Cuban assistance to the MPLA was altered. This would be "a major escalation of military assistance not the beginning of it."[70]

Direct Military Involvement

According to the official Cuban version, the cabinet "decided to send its first military unit to Angola"[71] on November 5, 1975. The MPLA already claimed sovereignty, so the Cuban government was able to state that it was aiding an Angolan republic already in existence. The official explanation from Havana is that Cuba went to Angola "at the request of a sovereign government, an independent government, which had the same rights and the same attributes as any other independent sovereign state."[72] This is an exceedingly important point to the Cubans, for it means that their assistance is legal, rather than extralegal; that is, they are aiding an established government instead of interfering in the internal affairs of a country. On November 5, the MPLA may have been a defacto government in Luanda, but it surely was not a government for all of Angola, nor was it a de jure government since the Portuguese had sovereignty—at least nominally—until November 11.

The task of immediately stopping the South African offensive was given to a special fighting battalion of the ministry of the interior. It comprised Cuba's elite forces which, accompanied by antitank platoons, organized a first line of defense with the MPLA. The first contingent, made up of 82 men, left Havana on November 7, at four o'clock in the afternoon, on a special flight of Cubana de Aviación. In order not to raise any suspicions, they travelled in civilian clothes on an old Bristol Britannia BB-219. They carried their own passports and other identifying papers. "But in their briefcases," writes García Márquez, "they carried machine pistols, and in the cargo of the plane, instead of baggage, there was a substantial load of light artillery, small arms, three 75 mm. cannons and three 82 mm. mortars."[73] Altogether 650 men flew to Angola within a week. As Fidel related on June 6, 1976, "A few hours after arriving at Luanda, they marched toward the front."[74] At no point during the whole war did the MPLA confront such an overwhelming situation as on November 7, when the FNLA had forces just nine miles from Luanda. The next day, Guinea-Bissau, Mozambique, Cape Verde, the People's Republic of the Congo, and Guinea formed a coordinating committee to provide whatever the MPLA needed from abroad.

On the night of November 10, Portugal granted independence to the Angolan people. Immediately three different governments were officially formed—by the MPLA in Luanda, the FNLA at Carmona, and UNITA at Huambo. The MPLA held effective control over just 20 percent of Angolan territory. By November 11, 1975, there were close to twelve hundred Cuban military men who had come from Cuba and other parts of Africa.[75] In Havana that night, Jorge Risquet, a member of the Central Committee of the Communist Party of Cuba (PCC) hinted at what was already under way when he said, "Our solidarity toward Angola can be given in any form, including our blood—which we are willing to fuse with that of the Angolan people." In an official communiqué from Havana the party declared that only revolutionary solidarity evidenced by the mobilization of efforts and resources could assure Angolan independence.[76] Indeed, Cubans mobilized all the necessary resources in order to cross the Atlantic as fast as possible.

Apparently, despite all later assertions to the contrary, U.S. intelligence knew of no deployment of regular Cuban troops before November 11. The American secretary of state, Henry Kissinger, on the date of Angolan independence, denounced as a very serious matter the Soviet and Cuban military role in sending weapons and advisors. As the number of planes leaving Cuba increased, however, it became obvious what was going on. From November 7 to December 9, Cuban planes made seventy trips to Angola from Havana by way of Barbados, Guinea-Bissau, and the Congo Republic. On December 9, however, the flights were discontinued. About a week later Barbados no longer permitted the Cubans to refuel there.[77]

Apparently some trial runs by way of Guyana were made beginning on December 24, but this attempt had to be given up because the runway seemed too short and the American gasoline company cut off its supply. Moreover, on December 30, the United States officially protested to Guyana about the landings.[78] At the end of December, the Cubans tried a third route. They flew from Holguín, the easternmost airport in Cuba, to the Azores, and from there to Cape Verde, Guinea-Bissau or Guinea, then to the Congo Republic, and finally Angola. Using the Azores, however, created difficulties for the Portuguese and the rest of Europe. A right-wing secessionist movement became active about the same time in the Azores, receiving much press coverage and friendly comment from the United States. On January 21 the Cubans were informed by the Portuguese authorities that they could not use the Azores any more.[79] Some trial runs were made via Canada on January 28, but two days later the Canadian embassy in Havana informed the Cubans they could not use Gander International Airport on their flights to Africa. The Cuban planes had no other choice but to fly from Holguín to the island of Sal, in Cape Verde, without stopping. García Márquez writes: "It was a high-wire act without a net, for on the way out the planes arrived with fuel for only two more hours of flight and on the way back, because of headwinds, with only one hour's fuel left. But even that circuitous route was changed, to avoid endangering defenseless Cape Verde. Finally, the cabins of the planes were modified to take four supplementary gasoline tanks, which allowed non-stop flights but with 30 fewer passengers from Holguín to Brazzaville."[80]

Fidel Castro confirmed this version of events in general terms on July 26, 1976, declaring that the troops were sent to Angola on merchant ships and passenger airplanes. The Cubans were forced to modify some passenger planes, but if they faced a bottleneck in airlifting Cuban troops to Africa, it was not due to a lack of long-range transport aircraft. United States intelligence estimates that 90 percent of the planes used in the airlift were Soviet-made transports.[81] The Anatov 2 has a range of 550 miles without refueling, but it carries, without difficulty, only 14 persons. The Cubans also had the giant Anatov 24 which can transport at least 50 men at 360 miles per hour for 1800 miles without refueling. With some minor changes, the aircraft can carry up to 100 soldiers for about 2200 miles. Moreover, the Cubans also possessed the Ilushin 14 which can fly 2300 miles nonstop with at least 122 persons aboard. The Ilushin 18D with maximum fuel capacity can cover at least 4000 miles nonstop, and it can refuel in mid-air. It carries more than 140 persons per flight. Finally, Cuba has at least one Ilushin 62 which has a range of 6,400 miles nonstop and can carry 212 persons without alterations.[82] It is possible, of course, that the Cubans used their military transports to transfer equipment while passenger planes were utilized to move the military personnel. However, since most observers have noted that large quantities of equipment were flown from Eastern Europe to Angola, it is doubtful that the Cubans had to use their aircraft to move much equipment.

The Cuban forces reaching Angola in the second week of November were joined by elite forces from Mozambique, Guinea, Guinea-Bissau, and the Congo

Republic. Some Algerian, Yugoslav, and Nigerian advisors may have helped too.[83] Jorge Domínguez has noted that, in addition to the elite troops of the Ministry of the Interior, Cuban troops included artillery, motorized tank, rocketry, air force, and infantry units (see chapter 3 of this volume). Heavy weapons were flown or transported by sea from Eastern Europe via East Germany, Cape Verde, and Conakry. Russian, Bulgarian, and Yugoslav ships unloaded hundreds of tons of equipment including T-34 and T-54 tanks, PT-76 amphibious tanks, MiG-21J jet fighter-bombers (most of which were assembled in Luanda), helicopters, and numerous armored vehicles. A source close to the CIA reported that the Cuban-MPLA forces had at their disposal 120 T-54 and T-34 tanks, 70 Soviet-made BRDM vehicles, numerous multi-barreled rocket launchers, 12 MiG-21s and 10 MiG-17s.[84]

This whole enterprise would have been exceedingly difficult if the Soviet Union had not promptly supplied much logistical support, as the Cubans and Angolans have repeatedly acknowledged. On April 19, 1976, Fidel Castro pointed out that the USSR "provided besieged Angola with basic aid in military equipment and collaborated with our efforts when imperialism had cut off practically all our air routes in Africa." Carlos Rafael Rodríguez added, a few months later, "Cuba and Angola did not have all the technical means for their men to fight the racist South African army," but the USSR changed this. "Without the USSR, imperialism would have defeated the Angolan people."[85]

It took approximately a month for the MPLA, with the assistance of Cuba, the USSR, other Eastern European countries, and numerous progressive African countries to turn the tide. The Cuban reinforcements conducted military operations on several fronts. Of the two main fronts, the FNLA-Zaire forces to the north constituted the most pressing threat because since October 23 they had been less than ten miles from Luanda. Thus, the Cubans concentrated their efforts just to the north of Luanda, where they held the line, and reorganized the MPLA for a counterattack. Since the enemy to the north was less proficient in military skills—compared with the South Africans—it was felt the possibility of rapid success was better. Moreover, the FNLA-Zaire troops could be pinned down, if necessary, by using the Republic of the Congo. Last but not least, the oil-rich Cabinda enclave had to be secured. All of these elements led to the initial concentration on the northern front, resulting in the battle of Quifangondo, on the banks of the Queve river. By December 16, 1975, Zairian forces had retreated from the vicinity of Luanda. On the following day the MPLA-Cuban forces began their counteroffensive in the north.

In mid-December the Cubans concentrated their forces near Quibala to contain the South Africans. The South Africans, who had stopped their offensive on November 23, after taking 1,974 miles in thirty-three days, began pushing north again. In the second week of November they were just seventy miles south of Luanda. Between December 9 and December 18, the Cubans and South Africans clashed in the largest battle of the war, at the Salazar Bridge over the Cuanza River north of Mussende. This was the farthest north the South Africans

NELSON P. VALDÉS

advanced. The main weapons used by the MPLA-Cuban forces were 122 mm. rocket launchers, heavy artillery, and mortars. The South Africans possessed 140 mm. guns, armoured cars, and tanks. Early in the clash the South Africans delivered heavy blows against the revolutionary forces. García Márquez relates: "A South African column had managed to repair a bridge under the cover of the morning mist, and had surprised the Cubans, who were in the midst of a tactical withdrawal." The use of air power, particularly MiG-17s and tanks, however, blocked any further advances by South Africa and UNITA.[86]

If the tide was to be turned, the Cubans felt, they needed experienced troops. The enemy was close; there was no time to train raw recruits. The number of Cuban troops increased rapidly, as published estimates of American and Swedish intelligence show.[87]

November 15, 1975	2,000
November 20, 1975	3,000
November 30, 1975	5,000
January 6, 1976	9,500
February 3, 1976	14,000

The Cuban forces turned the tide. From November to the end of December, the anti-MPLA forces gained no more territory. Militarily, the two opposing camps had stabilized their territorial control. The MPLA, meanwhile, waged a successful political struggle inside and outside Angola which, in the end, isolated the FNLA, UNITA, and South Africa.

One factor working on behalf of the MPLA was the alliance made by UNITA and the FNLA with South Africa. At first all three parties denied it. South Africa, for example, denied its existence on November 18. But on November 27 South Africa appealed to the United States to give more direct aid to the anti-MPLA organizations. South Africa acknowledged officially that it was giving advice and logistical assistance to UNITA and the FNLA. The following day the London *Times* released information showing South African troops operating in southern Angola "with the concurrence and to the satisfaction of Dr. [Jonas] Savimbi." The Organization of African Unity (OAU) immediately denounced both organizations for employing "Africa's arch-racist enemy to fight against fellow Africans in Angola." Moreover, in late November widespread reports indicated that white mercenaries were utilized by UNITA and the FNLA.[88]

African nations now felt compelled to show their support of the MPLA as a way of attacking South African apartheid. South Africa posed a threat to Angolan independence but also could set a most dangerous precedent, for a success in Angola would mean the extension of racist policies into other regions of Africa.[89] A special decolonization committee of the United Nations, which considered the Angolan issue on December 5, denounced the intervention by South Africa. (All efforts by the United States to obtain a resolution denouncing Cuba failed.) Moreover, by December 19 the U.S. Congress successfully blocked covert aid to

Angola. During the congressional session it became evident that the CIA had supplied millions to the anti-MPLA leadership.[90]

South Africa became ever more isolated. And much opinion in the United States opposed creating another Vietnam war. Involvement with South Africa in a continental struggle against all the independent black nations was not appealing. On December 28 the South African forces expressed their willingness to withdraw from Angolan territories. UNITA and the FNLA were weakened when they broke their political-military alliance and declared war on one another at the end of the year.

Thus, as the anti-MPLA forces lost their financial backing from the United States, their military support from South Africa, and their unity of purpose, the MPLA-Cuban offensive gained strength. Cuban military assistance made the difference, but only because the sociopolitical context was propitious. As shown in table 4.1, the MPLA-Cuban forces made dramatic advances in early 1976. On February 21, the South Africans regan to withdraw.

The swift success of the MPLA-Cuban forces took everyone by surprise. By February 22, 1976, the military confrontation, for all practical purposes, was over. Symbolically, that same day, the Portuguese government established diplomatic relations with the People's Republic of Angola.

TABLE 4.1
Major Towns Captured by MPLA-Cuban Forces

	Town	Former Control
December 15, 1975	Caxito	FNLA
December 17, 1975	Ambriz	FNLA
January 5, 1976	Carmona	FNLA (headquarters)
January 9, 1976	Sanza Pombo	FNLA
January 13, 1976	Nova de Seles	UNITA
January 15, 1976	Ambrizete	FNLA
January 21, 1976	Cela	UNITA
January 23, 1976	Porto Amboiva	UNITA
January 26, 1976	Alto Homa	UNITA
February 2, 1976	Lobito	UNITA
February 8, 1976	Sao Antonio de Zaire	FNLA (headquarters)
	Huambo	UNITA (headquarters)
February 9, 1976	Sao Salvador	FNLA
	Benguela	UNITA (railway town)
February 11, 1976	Silva Porto	UNITA (military headquarters)
	Sa da Bandeira, Mocamedes	UNITA, South Africa
February 12, 1976	Benguela Railway	UNITA, FNLA
February 17, 1976	Luso	UNITA (last stronghold)
February 12–25, 1976	Luciar, Mocamedes, Porto, Alexandre, Sa da Bandeira, Joao de Almeida, Chibemba, Serpa Pinto	UNITA, South Africa

All that remained was to get the South African forces out of Angola. On December 28, South Africa made its first offer to take its forces out if Cuba and the USSR reciprocated. The OAU, however, rejected the conditions made by the South Africans.[91] The next month the South Africans moved from central Angola, closer to the border, remaining in nonoperational zones.[92] The retreat occurred three days after a United Nations Special Committee Against Apartheid called for the complete liberation of southern Africa. At the end of the month, the U.N. Security Council unanimously approved a resolution demanding elections in Namibia and condemned the use of South West Africa ''as a base for attacks on neighboring countries.''

In early February the South Africans were just thirty miles north of Namibia. In order to exert further pressure, Angola now threatened to aid the SWAPO guerrillas in Namibia. The London *Times* also reported the desire of Cuban troops to move aggressively against South Africa. On March 2, SWAPO said it was considering offers of aid from Cuba: ''We reserve the right to invite Cubans to Namibia.''[93]

In a visit to Guinea, March 15, 1976, Fidel said: ''If the South African occupation of the Cunene dam results in occupation of a single inch of Angolan territory, if the war spreads to Namibia, and if black Africa organizes a multinational army in order to liquidate every aspect of apartheid from the continent, South Africa will have to bear the responsibility. . . . Nobody can prevent the total liberation of Angola. . . . The countries supporting Angola have *no aggressive intentions* toward other African countries.''[94] Nine days after Angola guaranteed the United Nations that it would not damage the Calueque hydroelectric facilities, on March 27, South Africa retreated further. At the United Nations a resolution was passed urging South Africa to desist from using Namibia as a base of aggression. The Security Council also asked South Africa to pay compensation to Angola for damages. A week later, on April 5, 1976, Angola and South Africa signed a diplomatic agreement. South Africa agreed to remove its forces while Angola promised to guarantee the security of Calueque.[95] Thus, the Cubans' intervention had proven to be a complete success. According to Fidel Castro they had minimal losses: ''Fewer Cuban soldiers were killed in action over four months of fighting in Angola than in three days of fighting at Girón.'' The war was waged on four different fronts, and they reconquered ''almost a million square kilometers.''[96]

Reasons for Cuban Involvement in Angola

One of the most controversial issues in recent discussions of the Cuban Revolution is why Cuban regular troops were sent to Angola. The question of motives is central here because it indicates the nature of the Revolution and the extent of its independence in foreign policy. The Cubans' version is clear and forthright: They went to Angola because they were asked and because they are revolutionaries who know that solidarity recognizes no borders. Whether these assertions should be accepted at face value is open to debate, but we must at least understand the Cubans' position as they themselves explain it. Fidel Castro has addressed this issue in speeches broadcast by Radio Havana:

> Some wonder why we help the Angolans, what interests we have there. They are accustomed to thinking that whenever a country does something, it is in pursuit of oil, of copper, or some other natural resource. No! We are not after material interests, and logically, the imperialists do not understand this, because they are exclusively guided by chauvinist, nationalist, and selfish criteria. We are fulfilling an elementary internationalist duty when we help the Angolan people. (December 19, 1975)

> We want to tell the imperialists that we seek nothing there [in Angola], that we just practice our traditional internationalist policy.... Loyal to its internationalist policy, what the Revolution has been doing since the beginning is to help wherever it can, help whenever it may be useful and moreover—wherever this help is requested. (December 22, 1975)

> We Cubans have helped our Angolan brothers, first because it is a revolutionary principle, because we are internationalists. Second, because our people are an Afro-American people... and [because] today our people are revolutionary, free, internationalist, capable of fulfilling their revolutionary duties. (Conakry, March 16, 1976)

> From Angola we will not take anything, absolutely nothing, because we are not imperialists, we are revolutionists, we are internationalists. Our aid was carried out in fulfillment of a mandate from our principles. The only thing that interests our people... is the advancement of the Angolan revolution... and the total liberation of Africa. (June 6, 1976)

Needless to say, few students of international politics are willing to concede even the remote possibility that international revolutionary solidarity is at the root of the matter, regardless of the public proclamations made in Havana. In other words, subjective principles are not considered an acceptable explanation. Involved in this question of motivation is a major political issue which affects our analysis. If one accepts the Cuban position, one, by definition, sees Cuba as a society based on principles, acting out its convictions in the world arena, without material self-interest, always willing to sacrifice, and without any type of political or economic pressure coming from outside.

The opposite interpretation does not acknowledge the role of principles at all. Instead it sees Cuban foreign policy as one more confirmation that the revolutionary leadership is controlled from the Soviet Union. The Cuban troops in Angola, in other words, were the "surrogate soldiers" of the USSR. General S. Brown of the United States Air Force has written, "through the employment of the surrogate Cuban force in Angola, the Soviet Union recently has been successful in expanding its influence in Africa at a relatively low cost and risk."

The Angolan affair, in other words, shows that Cuba is merely a pawn, a satellite.[97] One analyst said that "the only rational" explanation is that the Cubans were "persuaded" to dispatch troops to Angola by the Kremlin." [98]

It is unlikely that the Cubans have accepted a submissive, client-state relationship in which the USSR plays the dominant and deciding role. Instead, it may be very useful to see the Angolan involvement in a framework already outlined by W. Raymond Duncan. "Based upon the record of past Cuban insistence upon demonstrating its own independence, albeit qualified by the increasing Moscow-Havana ties, it is more likely that Soviet and Cuban interests *converged* in the Angolan situation."[99] This is a central point that needs to be stressed. To have, on a given issue, identical interests does not necessarily mean that one country is subordinated to another. In fact, the coincidence in policy may be due to entirely different reasons. That Cuba and the USSR acted in unison with respect to Angola in no way provides any proof that the Cubans were forced to send troops to Angola by the USSR.

Fidel Castro has addressed himself to this question on more than one occasion. On April 19, 1976, he said: "Cuba made its decision completely on its own responsibility. The USSR ... never requested that a single Cuban be sent to that country. The USSR is extraordinarily respectful and careful in its relations with Cuba. A decision of that nature could only be made by our own party." He repeated the same thought the following year to a Swedish television audience. "A decision of that type could only have been made by our party and by our government. ... This is a question that is so delicate and so serious that no country could possibly ask another country to do that."[100] The public statements by Angolan leaders support the Cuban contention that it was the MPLA that asked Cuba to send troops to Angola.[101]

Numerous other factors must be taken into consideration to explain the Cuban action. But first we must give up the assumption that the foreign policy of Cuba is determined exclusively by the USSR. Cuba's foreign policy has been consistently revolutionary over the years, but not merely because of principles. A revolutionary is an opportunist with principles. A revolutionary foreign policy, by implication, is an assessment of international situations in order to discern the most appropriate moment when specific circumstances (opportunities) can be fully exploited so as to make revolutionary principles and interests a reality. Fidel Castro himself has told us that "if you want to be an accurate observer of reality and not a theoretician passing judgment on the problems of this world from an ivory tower ... you have to understand politics as a principle, one bound by conditions, by reality." Here lies the key to the Cuban involvement in Angola. The interaction of revolutionary principles and objective political conditions produced the context for action.

We must consider three different aspects of this issue: revolutionary tradition; the international context; and the events in Angola proper. Cuba's revolutionary tradition has shown a persistent commitment in theory and practice to international revolutionary solidarity. Internationalism is an integral part of revolutionary experience and ideology. In fact, the Cubans feel that one cannot build a new society if one is not willing to sacrifice on behalf of others. Internationalism, as such, is a function of the revolutionary commitment and convictions of the nation as a whole. This complex belief system ought to be taken seriously because it plays a significant part in the Revolution. There are numerous examples of these beliefs being put into practice. The Cubans have provided legal and extralegal assistance to revolutionary movements and governments in Africa since the 1960s, and their political ties with the MPLA go a long way indeed. Moreover, the Cubans have always been ready to send men abroad if other governments so requested. Angola is exceptional only in the large size of the Cuban force.

The international situation also affected Cuban behavior. As far as the Cubans were concerned, the United States was becoming progressively more isolated and isolationist. Little popular support could be obtained for new military actions abroad. Since 1973 the Third World, following the example of the OPEC (Organization of Petroleum Exporting Countries) nations, challenged the industrialized capitalist nations, particularly the United States. They felt the "correlation of forces" on a world scale were changing to their benefit. The international situation, particularly after Watergate, appeared very favorable. American power appeared to be on the decline, and its political system was in disarray. Moreover, the April 1975 debacle of American power in Vietnam, Laos, and Cambodia left no room for doubt. All these events were interpreted as meaning that if the United States was confronted with a major foreign policy crisis it would not be able to do much about it. The disclosures of CIA "dirty tricks" by congressional hearings further reflected the disunity in the American power structure. The USSR apparently shared this assessment of the international situation and did not feel compelled to dissuade the Cubans from action in Angola. Moreover, the USSR, perceiving a growing radicalization in Africa as Portugal's African colonies became independent, seized an opportunity in 1975 to gain more supporters in the struggle against the United States and China.

Angola's political fluidity and the blatant foreign intervention by South Africa and neocolonial Zaire created the right context for Cuban involvement. Moreover, the Portuguese authorities, who were friendly to Cuba, followed a decolonization policy of not blocking any action from abroad. Cuba did not have to act alone. The MPLA and Cuba enjoyed the logistical, material, and political support of the Soviet Union, Guinea-Bissau, Cape Verde, the People's Republic of the Congo, Guinea, Mozambique, Algeria, Tanzania, the German Democratic Republic, and North Vietnam. The risks, in other words, were shared.

There were also certain incentives. Since 1972 Cuba has paid more attention than ever to the Third World. Cuba identifies with their struggles, and as a result more attention has been paid to Africa. Before 1972, Cuba had diplomatic relations with eight African countries; since that year the number has grown to thirty-one.

NELSON P. VALDÉS

Number of New African Countries Having
Diplomatic Relations with Cuba

1959	2
1960	3
1961	0
1962	2
1963	0
1964	1
1965-1971	0
1972	5
1973	1
1974	11
1975	5
1976	1
Total	31

As more Portuguese colonies became independent, relations among the nations south of the Sahara changed. All of the former Portuguese colonies were now led by radical nationalist movements which, in all cases, identified with the Third World and were committed to fight against neocolonialism. These governments created new pressures for radicalization of other nations in the region. Cuba, of course, wanted to participate and collaborated closely with the new nations toward that end. Cuba's policies had potential in a broader context—that is, a coalition within the Nonaligned Nations Movement had promise since that movement over the long run might encompass all the Third World.

The success of the liberation struggle in Angola, moreover, could alter radically the nature of the regimes in southern Africa. With Angola on the west, controlling the Benguela railways, and Mozambique and Tanzania on the east, the neocolonial government of Zambia faced strangulation. Needless to say the Rhodesian white settler state could not last long. Similarly, Zaire, surrounded by Angola, the People's Republic of the Congo and Tanzania, was also vulnerable. A defeat of South African forces in Angola would definitely give encouragement to the struggles inside Zimbabwe (Rhodesia), Namibia (South West Africa), and Azania (South Africa) itself. With such prospects before them, the makers of U.S. foreign policy would be driven into a corner. The Americans could not afford to back the settler states, thus alienating the majority of the African nations. Moreover, Afro-Americans would oppose the use of regular troops to defend racism in southern Africa. The U.S. authorities, faced with so many contradictions in the aftermath of the Vietnam War, could take decisive action only covertly. Yet covert operations were at the same time under heavy attack in the American Congress and the news media.

South Africa's intervention in Angola provided a twofold incentive to the Cubans. First, it forced the Cubans to act rapidly to defend the MPLA and Cuban advisors already in Angola. Second, it created interesting opportunities. A radical victory over the South Africans would cast a serious doubt on their military capabilities. This could contribute to the black cause in Zimbabwe, Namibia, and Azania. On the other hand, if the conflict went on for a fairly long time, the rest of black America would have felt compelled to fight against South African forces in Angola to check apartheid expansionism. In such a confrontation the Cubans would have played a leading role.

The Cubans had an efficient military force available which could gain field experience. Moreover, the military had been imbued, as part of their political training, with their duty to serve abroad. This orientation, however, should not be equated with militarism, even though the Cuban military has been the best organized and professionally skilled institution of the Revolution. The Cuban forces were a *political* army, and over half of the Cuban soldiers in Angola were reservists, not professional soldiers.[102]

From the Cuban standpoint such involvement would have lasting effects that could be beneficial to the Revolution too. First, it would demonstrate that Cuba could develop a foreign policy in agreement with the USSR, but independent, nevertheless, of Moscow. Second, it would show the Soviets that Cuba could get results in Africa, thus making the USSR more beholden to Cuba.

In conclusion, the Cuban involvement in Angola was responsive to long established revolutionary principles and was a milestone in the long history of assistance to extrahemispheric independence struggles. Not only did the international situation in the mid 1970s seem propitious but the intervention by Zaire and South Africa and the MPLA invitation gave the Cubans legal grounds and the political incentives to send troops. Moreover, their actions had promising ramifications for the revolutionary cause in southern Africa. Angola demonstrates that Cuba's revolutionary foreign policy has been the result of principles which were put into practice when opportunities allowed.

NOTES

1. Needless to say the authors' perspectives have shaped the way they have looked at the phenomena. Thus, some would call such policy "exporting the revolution" while others would interpret it as a means of expressing "revolutionary solidarity." See Richard Gott, *Guerrilla Movements in Latin America* (New York, 1972); William E. Ratliff, *Castroism and Communism in Latin America: The Varieties of Marxist-Leninist Experience* (Stanford: Hoover Institution on War, Revolution and Peace, 1976).

2. Rolando E. Bonachea and Nelson P. Valdés, eds., *Ché: Selected Works of Ernesto Guevara* (Cambridge, Mass.: MIT Press, 1969), p. 10.

3. *El Mundo,* October 17, 1964.

4. *Revolución,* March 14, 1965 (italics added).

5. *El Mundo,* March 26, 1965; ibid., March 27, 1965.

6. *Política Internacional,* January–March 1966, p. 47.

7. *El Mundo,* May 21, 1967.

114

NELSON P. VALDÉS

8. *Bohemia,* July 14, 1972, p. 8; *Horoya* (Conakry), May 8, 1972, p. 1; *Bohemia,* July 14, 1972, p. 13; ibid., p. 25.

9. Radio Havana, September 21, 1974; *Bohemia,* October 18, 1974, p. 41; *Granma Resumen Semanal,* March 7, 1976, p. 3.

10. Houari Boumedienne briefly noted this aid in a Havana speech on April 14, 1974. *Bohemia,* April 26, 1974, pp. 33-36; see also Fidel's speech of May 17, 1972, in *Granma Resumen Semanal,* May 28, 1972, p. 4.

11. *New York Herald Tribune,* March 19, 1962, p. 1; Daniel James, *Ché Guevara: A Biography* (New York: Stein and Day, 1969), p. 158.

12. Maurice Halperin, *The Rise and Decline of Fidel Castro: An Essay in Contemporary History* (Berkeley and Los Angeles: University of California Press, 1972), p. 275; David Ottaway and Marina Ottaway, *Algeria: The Politics of a Socialist Revolution* (Berkeley and Los Angeles: University of California Press, 1970), p. 163; Radio Havana, September 19, 1963.

13. Radio Havana, October 14, 1963; *Middle East Journal* 18, no. 1 (Winter 1964), 79-80.

14. Radio Havana, June 27, 1965.

15. Ibid., October 16, 1963. Cuban doctors in Algeria presented themselves as volunteers to fight against the Moroccans the same day.

16. *First Congress of the Communist Party of Cuba* (Havana, 1976), p. 305.

17. Ottaway, *Algeria,* p. 166; "La revolución argelina avanza y triunfa," *Cuba Socialista,* November 1963, pp. 176-84.

18. See the following articles in *Cuba Socialista:* "La independencia nacional de Argelia," April 1962, pp. 111-14; "La victoria del pueblo de Argelia," August 1962, pp. 109-11; "La proscripción del Partido Comunista de Argelia," January 1963, pp. 106-10; "El Primer Congreso del Frente de Liberación Nacional de Argelia," June 1964, pp. 117-23; "El Islam y los problemas del socialismo en Argelia," September 1964, pp. 94-99; Albert Paul Lentin, "La reconstrucción del FLN y la lucha por el socialismo en Argelia," February 1965, pp. 63-73.

19. Relations between both countries were normalized after September 1965 when the Cubans were satisfied with the revolutionary character of the new regime. *Africa Report,* November 1965, p. 33.

20. James, *Ché,* p. 158.

21. The Cubans supported Prime Minister Patrice Lumumba in 1960-1961 against Joseph Mobutu and Moise Tshombé. Richard Gott, "Their Men From Havana," *Guardian* (London), February 22, 1967; M. Crawford Young, "Rebellion in the Congo," in *Protest and Power in Black Africa,* ed. Robert I. Rotberg and Ali A. Mazrui (New York: Oxford University Press, 1970), p. 992.

22. A. Zapata stated in the Cuban Communist party paper: "We wish to stress our readiness to stand side by side" with Zairian revolutionists but on one condition: that they put into practice their revolutionary views. See "To Defend Lumumba," *Granma Weekly Review,* February 23, 1969, p. 12. On March 12, 1966, the prime minister of Zaire accused Cuba of sending "specialists on guerrilla warfare to train rebels in the northern part of the country." *Africa Report,* May 1966, p. 33.

23. *Yearbook on International Communist Affairs* (Stanford: Hoover Institution on War, Revolution and Peace, 1967), p. 209; *Africa Report,* October 1965, p. 41; Wolfgang Berner, "Intervention by Cubans in Africa and Arabia," *Aussenpolitik,* July–September 1976, pp. 325-31; René Gauze, *The Politics of Congo-Brazzaville* (Stanford: Hoover Institution Press, 1973), p. 225.

24. *Africa Report,* October 1966, p. 32.

25. The relations between these two men and Cuba is, to say the least, disconcerting. When Ngouabi succeeded in ousting Massamba-Debat, the Cubans shifted their alliance and supported the winner. Ngouabi was assassinated in March 1977. Massamba-Debat was executed for planning the murder.

26. *Granma,* July 5, 1966, editorial.

27. *New York Times,* October 21, 1966; *Africa Report,* December 1966, p. 23.

28. Agence Congolaise d'Information, January 10, 1967.

29. "El golpe militar en Ghana," *Cuba Socialista*, April 1966, pp. 184-88; *Ghanian Times*, November 1966, p. 38; Orlando Contreras, "El golpe de Ghana," *Juventud Rebelde*, March 1, 1966, p. 3.

30. *Bohemia*, July 14, 1972, p. 8.

31. "Rechaza Guinea segundo ataque de mercenarios," *Juventud Rebelde*, November 24, 1970, p. 7; Margarita Dobert, "Who Invaded Guinea?" *Africa Report*, March 1971, pp. 16-18.

32. Statement made by Sekou Touré, Jr., to the author. See also Fulvio Fuentes, "La batalla de Conakry," *Bohemia*, February 11, 1972, pp. 58-69; R. Casals, "Sensational Disclosures by Two Spies of the CIA in Guinea," *Granma Weekly Review*, September 26, 1971, p. 12; Virgilio Calvo, "Activities of the Fifth Column in Guinea Exposed," ibid., October 10, 1971, p. 2; and reference made by Fidel Castro on May 9, 1972, in *Granma Resumen Semanal*, May 21, 1972, p. 2.

33. Colin Legum, ed., *Africa Contemporary Record* (London), 1972-1973, p. B621; Ciro Perez, "Guinea, presencia cubana," *Bohemia*, May 5, 1972, p. 31; *Prensa Latina*, November 25, 1970; *Granma Weekly Review*, March 28, 1976, p. 2.

34. *First Congress*, p. 305.

35. Ibid., pp. 300-01.

36. On Cuban aid to guerrillas fighting Portuguese colonialism see: *Africa Report*, April 1966, p. 5; ibid., December 1966, p. 23; ibid., May 1970, p. 14; Legum, *Africa Contemporary Record*, 1974, p. B548; "Un gran abrazo para mi pueblo," *Bohemia*, September 20, 1974, pp. 62-63; speech by Amilcar Cabral, May 6, 1972, in Conakry, Guinea. For Zaire, see James, *Ché*, p. 195; on Senegal, *Africa Report*, August 1965, p. 31; on Malawi, *Africa Report*, March 1967, p. 27; on Mali and Morocco, *Yearbook on International Communist Affairs*, 1971; on Tanzania, William Redman Duggan and John R. Civille, *Tanzania and Nyerere; A Study of Ujamaa and Nationhood* (New York: Orbis Books, 1976), p. 79; on Namibia, Radio Havana, October 5, 1976; on Ethiopia, *New York Times*, March 3, 1967.

37. Speech by Julius Nyerere, September 21, 1974; *Africa Report*, May 1970, p. 14; *New York Times*, November 22, 1967; *Est et Quest* (Paris), October 1, 1976; *Internationales Africaforum* (Munich), no. 3 (1969), pp. 202-09; John Marcum, *The Angolan Revolution: The Anatomy of an Explosion, 1950-1962*, (Cambridge, Mass.: MIT Press, 1969), I, 261.

38. "Amilcar Cabral: una bandera y un compromiso para todos los revolucionarios," *Granma Resumen Semanal*, February 11, 1973, p. 7; "Un gran abrazo para mi pueblo," *Bohemia*, September 20, 1974, pp. 62-63; Richard Gibson, *African Liberation Movements* (London: Oxford University Press, 1972), pp. 257-61.

39. A. R. Wilkenson, *Insurgency in Rhodesia, 1957-1973*, Adelphi Paper no. 100 (London, 1973), pp. 25, 47.

40. *Granma Weekly Review*, July 25, 1971, p. 12.

41. *Granma*, September 16, 1973, p. 4.

42. *Granma Resumen Semanal*, May 28, 1972, p. 4; letter from Cuban U.N. mission to Kurt Waldheim, January 23, 1976; *Bohemia*, January 30, 1976, p. 51; *Granma Resumen Semanal*, October 21, 1973, p. 10; speech by Sekou Touré, Conakry, on March 16, 1976 (reported by Radio Havana, March 17, 1976); Wilkenson, *Insurgency*, pp. 25, 47.

43. Eduardo de Sousa Ferreira, *Portuguese Colonialism* (Paris: UNESCO, 1974); Basil Davidson, *In the Eye of the Storm: Angola's People* (London: Longman, 1972); Colin Legum, "National Liberation in Southern Africa," *Problems of Communism*, January-February, 1975.

44. John Marcum, "The Anguish of Angola: On Becoming Independent in the Last Quarter of the Twentieth Century," *Issue: A Quarterly Journal of Opinion* 5, no. 4 (Winter 1975), 3-4.

45. *The Kissinger Study on Southern Africa* (Nottingham: Spokesman Books, 1975); and President Richard M. Nixon's Foreign Policy Report to the U.S. Congress, February 25, 1971.

46. A faction led by the Maoist Daniel Chippenda attempted to continue the guerrilla war; he broke with the MPLA taking with him his army of 2,000.

47. Neil C. Livingstone and Manfred Von Nordheim, "The United States Congress and the

Angolan Crisis," *Strategic Review,* Spring 1977, p. 37; U.S. Congress, Senate, Committee on Foreign Relations, Subcommittee on African Affairs, *Hearings on U.S. Involvement in Civil War in Angola,* 94th Cong., 2d sess. (Washington, D.C.: GPO, 1976), p. 9.

48. Radio Luanda, March 25, 1975.

49. Gabriel García Márquez places the meeting in May. See "Operation Carlotta: Cuba's Role in Angolan Victory," *Cuba Update* (New York), April 1977, p. 1.

50. Carlos Rafáel Rodríguez says Cuba sent 230, but Fidel has given the figure at 250. David Binder, "Cuba Says Africans' Vote Won't Affect Angolan Aid," *New York Times,* January 12, 1976; *Facts on File,* February 21, 1976, p. 138; *Corriere della Sera* (Milan), January 15, 1976; *Granma,* June 2, 1975.

51. Radio Havana, June 25, 1975; ibid., June 27, 1975. The other members of the delegation were Carlos Codelo, advisor to the Central Committee, and Oscar Oramas, head of the African Section of the Ministry of Foreign Relations, and presently Cuban ambassador to Angola.

52. Radio Havana, July 11, 1975; García Márquez, "Operation Carlotta," p. 2.

53. Radio Havana, July 28, 1975; Lisbon Radio Clube Portugues, July 30, 1975.

54. Lisbon Domestic Service, July 28, 1975; O Seculo (Lisbon), July 28, 1975.

55. Lisbon Domestic Service, July 24, 1975.

56. Jorge I. Domínguez, "The Cuban Armed Forces and International Order," duplicated, November 15-17, 1976, p. 43; García Márquez, "Operation Carlotta," p. 2.

57. Statement by the South African prime minister, March 21, 1976; letter from the government of Portugal to the secretary general of the United Nations, March 26, 1976; "The Angolan War," *South African Panorama,* March 1977, p. 6.

58. Paul Jorge Texeira, "Angola: la segunda guerra de liberación," *Bohemia,* September 12, 1975, p. 69.

59. Radio Havana, August 30, 1975; *Granma Weekly Review,* September 7, 1975, pp. 8-9.

60. Radio Havana broadcasts, August 20-24, 1975; *Granma Weekly Review,* September 7, 1975, p. 1; *Expresso* (Lisbon), August 23, 1975, p. 15; García Márquez, "Operation Carlotta," p. 1.

61. "Cuban Armed Forces," p. 45. See also chapter 3 of this volume.

62. García Márquez, "Operation Carlotta," p. 2; "The Angolan War," p. 6; Radio Havana, March 27, 1977.

63. AFP (Paris), October 19, 1975; Radio Lusaka, October 20, 1975; ibid., October 23, 1975; *Latin* (Buenos Aires), October 28, 1975.

64. "Bienvenido compañero Ngouabi," *Bohemia,* September 19, 1975, pp. 50-55.

65. Radio Havana, October 8, 1975.

66. *Granma Weekly Review,* October 26, 1975, p. 12.

67. Radio Luanda, October 15, 1975; ibid., October 18, 1975; Radio Lourenco Marquez, October 24, 1975.

68. Radio Lourenco Marquez, October 23, 1975; *Diario de Lisboa,* October 24, 1975; *U.N. Chronicle,* March 1976, p. 8; AFP, October 24, 1975; *Expresso,* October 25, 1975, p. 13; Fidel Castro's speech of April 19, 1976.

69. *Granma Weekly Review,* March 28, 1976, p. 3.

70. Letter of Professor John A. Marcum to the author, September 21, 1977.

71. *Granma Weekly Review,* March 28, 1976, p. 3.

72. *U.N. Chronicle,* April 1976, p. 64; Radio Luanda, November 5, 1975.

73. Gabriel García Márquez, "Operation Carlotta," p. 4.

74. Fidel Castro, speech of June 6, 1976.

75. "Independence and Civil War: Angola," *Africa Research Bulletin,* November 1-30, 1975, pp. 3819-20; *Diario las Americas* (Miami), November 14, 1975, p. 1.

76. Radio Havana, November 11, 1975.

77. *Diario las Americas,* November 12, 1975, p. 1; ibid., March 5, 1976; *Miami Herald,* December 17, 1975.

78. Don Bohning, "No Cuban Troops Stationed in Guyana, Minister Says," *Miami Herald,*

May 19, 1976, p. 12a; *Excelsior* (Mexico), December 30, 1975, p. 2a; "Cuban Planes Refueled in Guyana," *Miami Herald,* March 10, 1976, p. 10.

79. *New York Times,* January 24, 1976, p. 10.

80. *Washington Post,* January 31, 1976, p. 5.

81. Radio Havana, July 26, 1976; Drew Middleton, "The Cuban Soldier in Angola," *New York Times,* March 3, 1976.

82. On Cuba's aircraft see: *Jane's All the World's Aircraft,* 1976–1977; David W. Wragg, *A Dictionary of Aviation* (London: Osprey, 1973); International Institute for Strategic Studies, *The Military Balance* (London, 1975–1976); *Almanac of World Military Power,* (New York: R. R. Bowker, 1977).

83. Information provided by the nephew of Sekou Touré to the author. See also *Diario las Americas,* November 14, 1975, pp. 1, 23; statement by Luis Cabral on Radio Havana, October 14, 1976; Cuban-Angolan Joint Communiqué from Havana, July 29, 1976; Cuban-Congolese Joint Communiqué from Brazzaville, June 7, 1976; statement by Angolan prime minister in Moscow, TASS, May 25, 1976.

84. *Est et Ouest,* October 1, 1976, pp. 14–19; *Washington Post,* November 15, 1975; *Congressional Record,* April 7, 1977, pp. S5816–18.

85. Radio Havana, April 20, 1976; *Bohemia,* August 27, 1976, pp. 60–65.

86. "Operation Carlotta," p. 7; *Granma Weekly Review,* May 2, 1976.

87. See *New York Times, Washington Post, Le Monde,* and *Excelsior* (Mexico) for the dates given in the table.

88. *Pravda* (Moscow), November 30, 1975.

89. *Daily News* (Tanzania), December 6, 1975.

90. Livingstone and Von Nordheim, "The United States Congress."

91. *Excelsior,* December 31, 1975, p. 3.

92. *New York Times,* January 26, 1976, p. 1.

93. *Times* (London), March 2, 1976.

94. Radio Havana, March 16, 1976.

95. "Not Rhodesia Again?" *Economist* (London), March 27, 1976, p. 12.

96. *Granma Weekly Review,* May 2, 1976.

97. "Current JCS Theater Appraisals," *Commanders Digest,* March 17, 1977, p. 15. This has been the official U.S. government view as represented by Henry Kissinger, Patrick Moynihan, Professor Leon Gouré from the University of Miami, or Dr. Ramon L. Bonachea. See *Hearings,* p. 90; *New York Times,* December 15, 1975, p. 30. The Chinese government has taken basically the same stance.

98. George Volsky, in *Current History,* February 1976, p. 71.

99. W. Raymond Duncan, "Cuba: National Communism in the Global Setting," *International Journal* (Canada), Winter 1976, p. 71. Emphasis added.

100. *Direct from Cuba,* January 15, 1977.

101. Don Oberdofer, "Cuban Hands and Arms Across the Sea," *Guardian* (London), February 29, 1976; David Binder, "Cubans Say Africans' Vote Won't Affect Angolan Aid," *New York Times,* January 12, 1976; Radio Ethiopia, January 15, 1976, interview with Agostinho Neto; TASS (Moscow), January 17, 1976; *Times* (London), January 19, 1976, statement of Julius Nyerere; Agostinho Neto's speech in Conakry on March 16, 1976; *Miami Herald,* April 30, 1976, p. 5a; *New York Times,* May 16, 1976, report of Neto's speech; *Granma,* May 24, 1976, report of Elisio de Figuereido's speech at the United Nations; speech by Neto on July 26, 1976 in Havana; Cuban-Angolan Joint Communiqué of July 29, 1976, issued in Havana; *Journal do Angola,* December 5, 1976, pp. 1, 5.

102. *Direct from Cuba* (Havana), January 15, 1977.

5

AUSTIN LINSLEY

U.S.-Cuban Relations:
The Role of Puerto Rico

The mid-1970s are often characterized as a period of rapprochement in U.S.-Cuban relations. There are, however, a number of serious obstacles to be overcome before relations between the two countries can be fully normalized. One of the major impediments is Cuba's involvement with the Puerto Rican Socialist Party (PSP) and her sponsorship of the Puerto Rican independence movement in such international organizations as the United Nations and the Movement of Non-Aligned Countries. An indication of the importance attached to this issue is the reaction it has evoked from the U.S. government. In December 1975, President Ford said: "I want to be on record as forcefully as I can say, the action of the Cuban government is an attempt to get Puerto Rico free and clear of the United States and the action of the Cuban government to involve itself in a military way in Angola ends as far as I am concerned any efforts at all to have friendlier relations with Cuba."[1] Six months later, in Puerto Rico, Ford again commented on Cuban support for the Puerto Rican independence movement: "Those who might be inclined to interfere in our freely determined relations should know that such an act will be considered as an intervention in the domestic affairs of Puerto Rico and the United States; it will be an unfriendly act which will be resisted by appropriate means."[2]

President Ford's final act with respect to Puerto Rico came in the closing weeks of his administration. He announced on December 31, 1976, that he would recommend to Congress that Puerto Rico be admitted as the fifty-first state. Following the announcement a White House aid said that it was meant in part to convey to the Cuban government the intensity of U.S. commitment to its interests in the Caribbean.[3] But President-elect Jimmy Carter reacted negatively to the Ford statehood proposal: "Until the Puerto Rican people themselves express a preference for statehood . . . the Congress should not take the initiative." He further noted that a recent public opinion poll showed the majority of the Puerto Rican people were in favor of maintaining the island's commonwealth status.[4] This reaction, however, was the product of a number of factors other than lack of concern over Cuban interference with the interests of the United States in the Caribbean. In May 1977, President Carter remarked at a press conference that the question of Cuban involvement with Puerto Rico was one of the three major issues hampering attempts to normalize relations with the Cuban government.[5]   119

AUSTIN LINSLEY

This chapter will examine (1) the Cuban position on the question of Puerto Rican independence, (2) the impact of Cuban activities on internal Puerto Rican politics, and (3) the role Puerto Rico has played and will play in U.S.-Cuban relations.

The Cuban Position

In order to understand Cuba's motive for supporting Puerto Rican independence, one must first appreciate the ambiguity in the relationship between the United States and Puerto Rico. Culturally and economically the relationship is fairly straightforward. Puerto Rico is a Spanish-speaking, Hispanic-Caribbean culture totally integrated into and dependent upon the economic system of an English-speaking, Anglo-European culture, the United States. The political relationship between the island and the mainland has evolved as a continuous effort to provide an institutional setting in which Puerto Rico can be integrated into the U.S. economy but retain its cultural autonomy.

Since 1898, when Puerto Rico was ceded to the United States by Spain, there have been two phases in the political relationship between the island and the mainland. From 1898 to 1952 Puerto Rico was a territory of the United States, and its local government was considered an agency of the federal government.[6] The second phase began on July 25, 1952, when the Commonwealth of Puerto Rico was proclaimed, following the passage by Congress of the Puerto Rican Federal Relations Act and its approval by referendum in Puerto Rico by a majority of 387,016 (75.6 percent) to 119,169 (23.5 percent).[7] Commonwealth status has been interpreted by the Supreme Court as in between statehood and territorial status. The island government has the quasisovereignty of a state government but is subordinate to the federal government while lacking voting representation in either the House of Representatives or the Senate.[8] In addition, while Puerto Rico participates in the nominating conventions of both the Republican and Democratic parties, residents of Puerto Rico cannot vote for either president or vice-president of the United States. The exclusion of 3 million citizens from participating in national elections is justified on the grounds that Puerto Rico is not subject to federal taxation and there is no precedent for "representation without taxation."

Puerto Rico's commonwealth relationship with the United States is characterized by (1) common citizenship, (2) common defense, (3) common currency, and (4) common market. The rapid industrial development that took place between 1952 and 1972 was stimulated by the free movement of labor, capital, and goods and services between the island and the mainland and the absence of federal income taxes in Puerto Rico.

Despite the economic advantages of commonwealth status, there has been a continuing debate on the island over its relationship with the United States.[9] Since 1973, with the internal collapse of the Puerto Rican economy (GNP in fiscal year 1973–1974 declined 2.6 percent and in 1974–1975 another 2.4 per-

cent), the status debate has become increasingly intense.[10] Two factors compli-
cate the issue. First, any significant change in political status is likely to cause
even greater economic problems on the island. Second, if Puerto Rico becomes
independent, U.S. economic and military interests on the island might be
threatened. Private investment from the United States in Puerto Rico is reported
to be about $12 billion.[11] In addition, it is often argued that the U.S. naval base at
Roosevelt Roads is crucial to the security of the Caribbean.

The U.S. government has consistently maintained that the political status of
Puerto Rico is an issue of domestic concern only to the United States and Puerto
Rico. Since the early 1970s, however, the United Nations, specifically the De-
colonization Committee, has been considering the "colonial case of Puerto
Rico." This consideration is based primarily on two points. First, the U.S.
Supreme Court has ruled that Puerto Rico belongs to, but is not a part of, the
United States.[12] Second, in 1960 the U.N. General Assembly passed resolution
1514 (XV) expanding the scope of consideration of colonialism by the United
Nations. It reads, in part, "In those territories which are in trust and not autonomous, and in all other countries which have not won their independence, immediate measures should be taken to transfer all power to the people."[13] The
argument made by Cuba and other Third World members of the Decolonization
Committee is that the Supreme Court's definition is a clear statement of a colonial relationship and that the 1960 resolution requires the United Nations to take
immediate measures to eliminate this vestige of late-nineteenth-century colonialism.

The United States, of course, holds that Puerto Rico's status is an expression of the will of the Puerto Rican people. This position has, however, come
under increasingly heavy attack. Until 1977 only the relatively small number of
supporters of independence had denounced commonwealth status as a facade for
colonialism. But in the wake of the 1976 election, won by the New Progressive
Party (NPP), a party closely associated with support for statehood, advocates of
Puerto Rican statehood have announced their intention to testify before the Decolonization Committee that Puerto Rico is a colony of the United States. Their
strategy is to force the status question into a dichotomy between statehood and
independence. They are confident that, given only those two choices, statehood
would be the overwhelming choice of the Puerto Rican people.[14] Even the former
governor, Rafael Hernández Colón, leader of the Popular Democratic Party
(PDP), the party most closely associated with commonwealth status, has admitted that it is increasingly difficult to argue that Puerto Rico is not a colony.[15]

Basically, the Puerto Rican "problem" can be summarized by the following
four points: (1) the Puerto Rican economy is dependent upon a peculiar political
relationship with the United States; (2) that relationship is similar to, and has
evolved from, a classical nineteenth-century colonial situation; (3) the current
tone of international public opinion is in large part set by newly independent
countries that are radically anticolonial; and (4) while the United States would
like to present itself as an anticolonial power, any change in its relationship with

Puerto Rico is severely constrained by seventy-eight years of political and economic integration.

The Impact of Cuban Activities

Puerto Rico and Cuba share a common cultural and historical legacy. Cuban support for Puerto Rican independence dates back to the early nineteenth century when the causes of Cuban and Puerto Rican independence from Spain were so closely connected that they were practically indistinguishable. The most important contemporary difference between the two islands is the relationship each maintains with the United States.

Since the Revolution, Cuba has actively sponsored Puerto Rican independence in two international forums, the United Nations and the Movement of Non-Aligned Countries. Cuba has played two roles in the activities of the independence movement. First, she has introduced or sponsored a number of resolutions in both organizations in support of Puerto Rican independence. Second, the Cuban delegation has been a conduit for transmitting information and documents from supporters of independence on the island to the United Nations. The PSP has held permanent observer status in the Movement of Non-Aligned Countries for a number of years and is thus able to represent itself in that organization.

Consideration of Puerto Rico's political status at the United Nations is nearly as old as the organization itself. When the United Nations was formed, Puerto Rico was considered a nonautonomous territory under the administration of the United States. Following the proclamation of the Puerto Rican Commonwealth in 1952, the United States maintained that the island was no longer a dependent territory, and on November 27, 1953, the General Assembly approved resolution 748 (XIII) which removed Puerto Rico from the list of non-self-governing territories. This has been the basis of the U.S. claim, up to the present, that consideration of Puerto Rico's political status is not within the jurisdiction of the United Nations. Since the passage of resolution 1514 (XV), the U.N. debate has revolved around the question of whether the resolution applies to Puerto Rico. Interestingly, the first attempt to make the connection did not come from the United Nations, but rather from the Movement of Non-Aligned Countries. In the final declaration of the Second Conference of Heads of States or Governments of Non-Aligned Countries (Cairo, 1964) the attention of the United Nations was drawn to the case of Puerto Rican colonialism in light of the 1960 resolution.[16]

The year after the Cairo conference, Cuba's minister of foreign affairs asked that the question of Puerto Rico be placed on the agenda of the Decolonization Committee. The United States protested, arguing that because of the General Assembly's resolution of 1953, any discussion of Puerto Rico was outside the competence of the committee. Although the Cuban proposal was given some attention, it was finally dropped, and from 1967 to 1971 Puerto Rico's political status was not discussed at the United Nations.

The next phase in the international controversy over Puerto Rico began in 1971 and peaked in 1975. During this period the Cuban government played a central role in coordinating activities in a number of areas.

On August 17, 1971, Cuba's permanent representative to the United Nations, Ricardo Alarcón Quesada, requested that the "colonial case of Puerto Rico" be included on the agenda of the twenty-sixth session of the General Assembly.[17] This request was rejected by the General Assembly, but in 1972 Alarcón Quesada was successful in getting the Decolonization Committee to consider the issue. As in 1965, the United States protested the proposal, but due to a shift in the membership of the committee it was unable to counter the Cuban initiative. Between 1971 and 1972 the United States, the United Kingdom, and Poland had been replaced by China, Czechoslovakia, and Indonesia.[18]

On August 18, 1972, the Decolonization Committee passed a resolution introduced by Iraq recognizing "the inalienable right of the people of Puerto Rico to self-determination and independence in accordance with General Assembly resolution 1514 (XV) of 14 December 1960."[19] The vote was twelve to zero, with ten abstentions.

It appears that the influence of the United States on the committee has continued to decrease. Between 1972 and 1973, Ecuador and Madagascar were replaced by Australia, Chile, and the Congo. Ecuador had consistently voted against and Madagascar with the United States. While Australia has generally supported positions consistent with U.S. interests, Chile and the Congo were closely associated with Cuba. The only major changes on the committee since 1973 came with the Chilean coup of September 1973 (which shifted Chile to the U.S. side) and the replacement of Venezuela by Cuba in 1975.[20]

In 1973 the Decolonization Committee continued its consideration of the Puerto Rican question. Although Cuba was not officially a member of the committee at this time, the Cuban representative was invited to participate in the committee's deliberations. And on August 22, 1973, the committee voted to hear statements from the PSP and the Puerto Rican Independence Party (PIP). Eight days later, on August 30, it adopted a resolution introduced by the representatives of the Congo and the Syrian Arab Republic, and supported by Iraq and Mali, which reaffirmed the 1972 resolution and decided to keep the Puerto Rican question under continuous review.[21]

The Puerto Rican question received more attention from the non-aligned countries in 1973 as well. At the Fourth Conference of Heads of State or Government of Non-Aligned Countries held in Algiers from September 5 through September 9, 1973, a resolution on Puerto Rico was passed. Taking note of the August 30 resolution of the Decolonization Committee, the conference called on the General Assembly to approve the committee's report and then went on to make recommendations for further action in the committee itself. The final paragraph of the resolution "calls on the United Nations Committee on Colonization and other official bodies to step up and expand measures which could help the Puerto Rican people gain complete sovereignty and independence and re-cover its heritage."[22] At this conference the PSP was granted permanent observer status in the organization.

During 1974 groups within the United States were active and a number of *independentistas* spoke at the United Nations, but there was no specific de-velopment in the independence position. In 1975, however, international concern over the issue peaked. On December 18, 1974, Cuba had been elected to the Decolonization Committee. In March 1975, at the meeting of the Coordinating Bureau of the Non-Aligned Countries held in Havana, a statement was issued which urged "the United Nations to recognize the Puerto Rican National Libera-tion Movement as the legitimate representative of its people and [asked] that the Committee of 24 [the Decolonization Committee] study seriously and positively the proposal of sending a mission to visit the aforementioned territory under colonial domination."[23] This statement formed the core of a resolution on Puerto Rico later submitted to the Decolonization Committee by Cuba.

Immediately following the meeting of the Coordinating Bureau, it was announced that the World Peace Council would sponsor an International Confer-ence of Solidarity with the Independence of Puerto Rico. The conference opened in Havana in the first week of September 1975 and seems to have been timed to coincide with Cuba's Puerto Rican initiative at the United Nations. On August 15, 1975, Cuba introduced a resolution to the Decolonization Committee, based on the statement of the Coordinating Bureau, calling for recognition of the independence movement as representing the legitimate aspirations of the Puerto Rican people. The Cubans had intended to include a recommendation that the PSP be given permanent observer status at the United Nations (similar to the status of the Palestinian Liberation Organization) but were dissuaded from this action by their allies on the committee.[24] Had the Cuban proposal been adopted by the Decolonization Committee it would have come up for ratification in the General Assembly soon after the meeting of the Solidarity Conference in Havana. As it turned out, the Decolonization Committee voted eleven to nine with two abstentions (China did not participate and Ethiopia was absent) to postpone further consideration of Puerto Rico until 1976.[25]

While the Solidarity Conference may have been the single most important public expression of Cuban support for Puerto Rican independence, it must not be taken as a statement of unconditional support. A number of statements by Cuban officials at the time indicate that Cuba's position and behavior on the Puerto Rican question are full of conditions. First, immediately following the preparatory meeting for the conference, held in Havana in March 1975, its presiding officer, Juan Marinello, president of the Cuban World Peace Council and a member of the Central Committee of the Communist Party of Cuba, made the following statement:

> If we take it that the case of Puerto Rico has entered a new phase linked
> to an international situation which in many aspects is favorable to it, it

is our duty therefore to bring about the broadest possible solidarity, a real true solidarity aimed at the real and immediate liberation of the Puerto Rican nation. However, every demonstration of good will, will be welcomed with joy because it will form part of the task we are engaged in.[26]

Two comments can be made about this statement. First, Cuban support for Puerto Rican independence is linked to international considerations. Second, Marinello seems to be suggesting that the issue is negotiable.

The second statement with respect to the Solidarity Conference comes from Carlos Rafael Rodríguez. According to a report by Abraham Lowenthal at a conference at the University of Pittsburgh in 1976, Rodríguez told him in an interview that the Cuban government had not particularly wanted to host the Solidarity Conference. Unfortunately Rodríguez provided Lowenthal no further explanation. It seems reasonable to suspect that the Cubans may have been concerned about turning Puerto Rican independence into a narrowly defined issue identified too closely with the Cuban government. Had this identification been made it might have unnecessarily limited the international base of support for Puerto Rican independence and restricted Cuba's maneuverability on the issue. This interpretation is strengthened by the statement of Cuban President Osvaldo Dorticós in the closing speech of the conference. "In some official and semi-official declarations there has been an attempt to show the Puerto Rican problem and Cuban solidarity as a significant impediment to U.S.-Cuban relations. The Cuban Revolutionary Government cannot accept involvement in the Puerto Rican cause and our unyielding duty of solidarity with it as a controversial bilateral issue between the United States and Cuba."[27]

What do these three statements tell us about Cuba's position on the question of Puerto Rican independence? First, Cuban solidarity with the cause is "unyielding." Second, the form in which this moral solidarity is translated into material and political support is determined by international considerations. Third, the Cuban leadership sees no reason why the Puerto Rico problem should be an issue in U.S.-Cuban relations.

In 1976 the Puerto Rican debate cooled considerably. The Decolonization Committee again voted to postpone consideration of the issue, this time until 1977. In addition, at the Fifth Conference of Heads of State or Government of Non-Aligned Countries, held in Colombo, Sri Lanka, August 16–19, 1976, the Cubans were unsuccessful in having their statement on Puerto Rico included in the political declaration of the conference. The Cubans proposed a resolution that would have recognized the Puerto Rican "National Liberation Movement as the sole legitimate representative of the Puerto Rican People."[28] It should be remembered that this is no more than the Coordinating Bureau of the organization had called for in its political declaration issued in Havana in 1975. However, the final document of the Sri Lanka meeting only asked the "United Nations Special Committee on Decolonization to recommend to the General Assembly effective measures for the implementation in respect to Puerto Rico of its resolution 1514 (XV)."[29]

In August 1977, the Decolonization Committee took up the Puerto Rican question. It appeared that internal Puerto Rican political considerations were going to be more important in deciding the issue in the committee than international politics. However, the United States was able once again to have the issue tabled.

Internal Politics

The closest connection between the Cuban government and Puerto Rican politics is through the PSP. This group, formerly the Pro-Independence Movement, has maintained a close relationship with the Cuban government since the early 1960s. It has a permanent delegation in Havana, and in 1966 its chief representative, Narciso Rabell Martinez, was named to the permanent secretariat of the Organization of Solidarity with the Peoples of Asia, Africa, and Latin America.[30] The PSP has participated in almost every international conference sponsored by the Cuban government, and there is a constant flow of PSP members between Puerto Rico and Cuba. In June 1977, Juan Mari Bras, secretary general of the party, was in Havana to confer with Fidel Castro. At this time, he said that Cuba was still the leading champion of Puerto Rican independence in the international arena.[31] Both the statement and the meeting are important because they came in the wake of speculation that Cuba was cutting back its support for the PSP because of its miserable showing in the November 1976 elections, less than 1 percent of the vote.[32]

The most controversial question with respect to Cuban involvement in Puerto Rico is whether there is any connection between the Cuban government and Puerto Rican terrorists. A number of attempts have been made to establish this connection, but the controversy to date consists only of allegations and denials. One attempt was made by the Senate Judiciary Committee's Subcommittee to Investigate the Administration of the Internal Security Act and other Internal Security Laws. An unidentified witness testifying before the subcommittee cited the numerous statements by the PSP approving of terrorist activities. David Martin, the subcommittee's senior analyst, asked the witness, "Is there any evidence of direct ties between the Armed Commandos and the Puerto Rican Socialist Party, other than the statement from PSP leaders?" The answer he received was, "Well, I don't have any hard evidence in that direction. . . ."[33]

Had a connection between the PSP and terrorists been established, it would have been impossible to believe that the Cubans were not involved. But as yet the connection has not been made authoritatively. In fact, in 1972, the Cuban delegation at the United Nations transmitted a document from the PSP to the Decolonization Committee accusing the Commonwealth government of attempting "to establish on the basis of false, fabricated evidence an organic connection between PSP-MPA and CAL [Commandos Armados de Liberación]. For that reason it offered Alberto Gonzalez-Fernandez, a former militant of the PSP a salary of $1,500 a month, in addition to dropping various court cases (non-political) which were pending against him in return for his services as a false witness against various national leaders of our party. Similar offers have been made to a number of other compatriots.''[34] Without taking a position on the validity of this statement, one can still get a good idea of the importance of the issue.

Another attempt to establish Cuban involvement in Puerto Rican terrorism came from a former Puerto Rican governor, Rafael Hernández Colón. In Washington, D.C., in 1976, the governor said, "Cuba is training and aiding terrorists to overthrow the government of the island commonwealth." In response to his comments, the *New York Times* quoted a "high ranking Ford Administration official" as saying: "We have no evidence of the Cubans doing any muscle work in Puerto Rico. Their support is confined to providing free vacations for the leaders.''[35]

And according to Fidel Castro, in his interview with the American journalist, Barbara Walters, "Nobody can accuse Cuba of having fomented violence; nobody can accuse Cuba of having taken part in violent actions in Puerto Rico or fomenting violence in Puerto Rico. We give the Puerto Ricans political and moral support. We'd be fakers if we didn't.''[36]

In the absence of evidence, one can only speculate about whether the Cubans are supporting Puerto Rican terrorists. There are a number of reasons for rejecting the possibility; two are especially significant. First, the Cubans have been quite successful in recent years in their diplomatic activities in Latin America, many of which are incompatible with guerrilla operations. The Cubans would have much to lose by rekindling animosities on this issue by supporting armed revolutionaries in Puerto Rico. Second, and most importantly, it would be inconsistent with a Cuban desire to establish economic ties with the United States.

Future Prospects

Puerto Rico holds an interesting position in the complex relationship between the United States and Cuba. Cuban behavior with respect to Puerto Rico can only be understood as the product of two seemingly contradictory goals. The first is an ideological and historical commitment to Puerto Rican independence. The second is a very real and practical need for improved political and, especially, economic relations with the United States. In pursuing these two goals it appears that she has attempted to keep her support for Puerto Rican independence primarily within the context of international organization. The crucial point is that the Cuban government has very adroitly kept itself insulated from direct involvement in Puerto Rico and has attempted to predicate its moral and political support on international considerations.

At the height of her activities in support of Puerto Rican independence, Cuba was also at odds with the United States over her operations in Angola. In addition, the Puerto Rican economy had collapsed, and internal support for the independence movement appeared to be growing. These are two aspects of the "international situation" referred to by Marinello in the statement quoted above. In early 1977, the international situation changed. In response to apparently auspicious conditions, the PSP participated for the first time in the Commonwealth elections of 1976. The party's candidate for governor, Juan Mari Bras, received only 10,487 votes (0.75 percent) of the total. The PIP candidate, Ruben Berríos, received 76,810 votes (5.46 percent), giving the independence movement a total of 87,297 votes (6.21 percent).[37] This dismal support for Puerto Rican independence coincided with an easing of tensions between the United States and Cuba over Cuban involvement in Africa. The Carter administration was no longer demanding the complete withdrawal of Cuban troops from Africa as a prerequisite to normalization of relations. President Carter had asked for the "decrease" of Cuban involvement and stated that more important than the presence of Cuban troops was the "attitude" of the Cuban government.[38]

One can imagine a scenario in which Cuba, recognizing an altered international situation, tacitly agrees to "lighten up" on the issue of Puerto Rican independence in response to economic or technological concessions from the United States. This prospect is strengthened by the new strategy of the statehood advocates in supporting the move to have Puerto Rico declared a colony, forcing the assimilation of the island. Furthermore, a "high ranking State Department official" was quoted on July 8, 1977, as saying, "We don't expect Castro to back off from his commitment to Puerto Rican independence, but we do expect him to tone down his rhetoric."[39] The major weakness of this view could be the growing interest of the Decolonization Committee in the Puerto Rican question.[40] While Cuba has been the major force on the committee supporting Puerto Rican independence, she by no means has been in complete control of the issue. Should there be a surge of interest in Puerto Rican independence, the Cubans might have no alternative but to ride the wave, a wave they have been instrumental in creating.

In looking to the future of relations between the United States, Puerto Rico, and Cuba, one rather simple statement both summarizes the most likely future and points toward the most important area of research: The future of Puerto Rico will most likely be determined by conditions on the island itself. The policies of both Cuba and the United States should develop in response to these conditions.

NOTES

1. *New York Times,* December 1, 1975, p. 1.
2. Ibid., June 27, 1976, p. 1.
3. Ibid., January 1, 1977, p. 1.
4. Ibid., January 2, 1977, pp. 1, 44.

5. "The President's remarks to a question and answer session with publishers, editors, and broadcasters, May 20, 1977," *Weekly Compilation of Presidential Documents* (Washington, D.C.: GPO, 1977), p. 768.

6. On the question of Puerto Rico's status see, for instance, Office of the Commonwealth of Puerto Rico, *Documents on the Constitutional History of Puerto Rico* (Washington, D.C.: Hennage Lithograph Co., 1964); and Surendra Bhana, *The United States and the Development of the Puerto Rican Status Question* (Lawrence: University of Kansas Press, 1975).

7. These figures come from "Puerto Rico: Basic Political, Social and Economic Data," mimeo (Washington, D.C.: Office of the Commonwealth of Puerto Rico, 1976).

8. See "Cases on the Political Status of Puerto Rico," in *Documents*, pp. 217–331.

9. See Rita Maldonado, "The Economic Costs and Benefits of Puerto Rico's Political Status," *Southern Economic Journal* 41 (Summer 1974), 267–88.

10. *Wall Street Journal*, March 9, 1976, p. 20.

11. This figure was used by Arthur Kinoy, a professor at Rutgers University Law School, in testimony before the House Subcommittee on Territorial and Insular Affairs on February 10, 1976. A mimeographed copy of the testimony has been circulated by the Puerto Rican Solidarity Committee.

12. *Documents*, p. 3.

13. "Resolution 1514 (XV), Declaration on the granting of independence to colonial countries and peoples," U.N. General Assembly Official Records, 15th Session, 1961, Supplement No. 16a (A/4684), pp. 66–67.

14. *Washington Post*, January 11, 1977, p. 5; and *New York Times*, August 21, 1977, p. 7.

15. *Washington Post*, January 11, 1977, p. 15.

16. Laura Menes de Albizu Campos, the widow of Pedro Albizu Campos, Puerto Rico's most famous contemporary *independentista*, provides an interesting link between Cuba, the Puerto Rican Independence Movement, the United Nations, and the Movement of Non-Aligned Countries. After her husband's death she was granted Cuban citizenship and subsequently became a member of Cuba's mission to the United Nations. It has been reported that she was instrumental in bringing about the resolution on Puerto Rico at the Cairo conference. See U.S., Congress, Senate, Subcommittee to Investigate the Administration of the Internal Security Act and Other Internal Security Laws of the Committee on the Judiciary, *Communist Threat to the United States Through the Caribbean (Violence in Puerto Rico), Hearings*, 90th Cong., 2d sess., November 27, 1968, pp. 1368, 1373.

17. U.N. Documents, August 17, 1971 (A/8441).

18. For summary of the membership of the committee from 1962 to 1974, see U.S., Congress, Senate, Subcommittee to Investigate the Administration of the Internal Security Act and Other Internal Security Laws of the Committee on the Judiciary, *Terroristic Activity: The Cuban Connection in Puerto Rico; Castro's Hand in Puerto Rican and U.S. Terrorism, Hearings*, 94th Cong., 1st sess., July 30, 1975, pp. 423–36.

19. U.N. Documents, August 26, 1972 (A/AC.109/PV.942).

20. U.N. General Assembly Official Records, 30th Session, 1977, Supplement No. 23 (A/10023/Rev. 1), p. 9.

21. U.N. Documents, August 16, 1973 (A/AC.109/PV.938); ibid., August 23, 1973 (A/AC.109/PV.942); U.N. General Assembly Official Records, 28th Session, 1974, Supplement No. 23, (A/9023/Rev. 1).

22. *Documents of the Gatherings of Non-Aligned Countries 1961–1973* (Belgrade: Secretariat for Information of the Federal Executive Council, 1973), p. 37.

23. "Final Declaration of the 3rd Ministerial Meeting of the Coordinating Bureau of Non-Aligned Countries," *Granma Weekly Review*, March 30, 1975, p. 8.

24. *New York Times*, August 16, 1975, p. 22.

25. "Terroristic Activity," p. 422.

26. *Granma Weekly Review*, April 31, 1975, p. 8.

27. The entire text of the speech is translated and reprinted in "Terroristic Activity," pp. 475–81.

28. Working paper of the Cuban delegation to the Fifth Conference of Heads of State or Government of Non-Aligned Countries, Colombo, Sri Lanka, 1976.

29. The documents of the conference are reprinted in *International Affairs* (Belgrade) 27 (653–654): 18–43. The quotation on Puerto Rico is found on p. 27.

30. "Terroristic Activity," p. 340.

31. *Granma Weekly Review,* June 19, 1977, p. 10.

32. Election results released by the Office of the Commissioner of the Commonwealth of Puerto Rico.

33. "Terroristic Activity," p. 328.

34. The letter is reprinted in "Terroristic Activity," pp. 373–76.

35. *New York Times,* May 20, 1976, p. 11.

36. *Granma Weekly Review,* July 24, 1977, p. 3.

37. Election results released by the Office of the Commissioner of the Commonwealth of Puerto Rico.

38. "The President's remarks in a question and answer session with a group of publishers, editors, and broadcasters on April 16, 1977," *Weekly Compilation of Presidential Documents* (Washington, D.C.: GPO, 1977), p. 554.

39. Richard Schroder, "Puerto Rican Status Debate," *Editorial Research Reports,* July 8, 1977, p. 523.

40. See *New York Times,* August 21, 1977, p. 7.

6

RONALD E. JONES

Cuba and the English-speaking Caribbean

The end of Cuba's isolation in the hemisphere is nowhere more obvious than in its relations with the English-speaking nations of the Caribbean. The four largest of these former English colonies—Barbados, Guyana, Jamaica, and Trinidad and Tobago—established relations with Cuba by joint action in December 1972, well before the Organization of American States (OAS) voted to lift its ban on such relations. Subsequent diplomatic activity has generated substantial interest and, in some quarters, concern. One journalist sees a "grand design" for a "Marxist axis" running across the Caribbean. Another observer describes Cuban relations with the Caribbean nations as Cuban "penetration" and "expansionism." Yet another "Cuba watcher" sees Fidel Castro forcing a choice between the "East" and the "West" in the Caribbean. His conclusion is that "we [the West] are losing."[1] This chapter will first discuss the context of diplomatic relations in the Caribbean region. Second, Cuba's relations with each of the four nations will be described and compared. Finally, Cuba's more extensive ties with Jamaica and Guyana will be interpreted in the light of the domestic and foreign policies of the three countries.

The Caribbean Context

In the early 1970s the Cuban government began what appeared to be a diplomatic and press offensive aimed at reestablishing relations with many of its neighbors in the hemisphere. Peru and Panama, for example, were the target of numerous positive references in the Cuban press prior to the resumption of relations.[2] Favorable statements about the four Caribbean nations were, however, absent. In this case the public overtures came from three of the four governments: explicit statements by Forbes Burnham of Guyana and Michael Manley of Jamaica, hints by Eric Williams of Trinidad and Tobago, and an invitation, the first since 1959, to participate in the Caribbean Recreational Arts Festival held in Guyana.[3]

The position of the four governments on the Cuban question was established at the Seventh Conference of the Heads of Government of the Caribbean in Port of Spain, Trinidad, on October 15, 1972: "The independent English speaking states of the Caribbean, exercising their sovereign right to maintain relations with any sovereign nation and in keeping with their determination to promote regional solidarity and obtain significant and total economic cooperation among all Caribbean nations, will work toward the rapid establishment of relations with Cuba, be they economic, political or both. In order to bring this about, the independent English speaking states of the Caribbean will work together on the basis of measures agreed upon.''[4] The joint decision, agreed upon and announced at a multilateral forum, is in contrast to the unilateral decisions by other governments in the Americas to reopen relations with Cuba. However, this initiative by the Caribbean governments need not have come as a surprise. Rapprochement with Cuba was a natural outgrowth of their domestic and foreign policies.

Recognition of Cuba was, first of all, an extension of their established policy that favors regional integration and a common front toward the developed world as a means of promoting economic growth in each nation. Prior to October 1972 several attempts at regional integration and cooperation, including the West Indies Federation and the Caribbean Free Trade Association, were made. A third major effort, the Caribbean Common Market, was in the early stages of development as well. In the later efforts a break with the policy of including only the English-speaking nations in these schemes led to the consideration of Haiti, Surinam, the Dominican Republic, Venezuela, and Colombia as associated parties under various arrangements.[5] Forbes Burnham, speaking in 1970 on the topic of regional unity, urged his audience to go beyond the mere consideration of the nation-state or a narrowly defined conception of cooperation: ''In this world the larger the group, the better and we cannot be satisfied with the group excellence of one territory. I think we ought to consider the group excellence of a larger body within the region.'' Manley had urged the same tactic in dealing with developed nations—''the third world desperately needs the strength that can come from regional economic groups''—and suggested that level of economic development might be a better basis for cooperation than ideology or system of government.[6]

Second, establishing relations with Cuba was part of a broader pattern of expanding relations with socialist countries and the nonaligned world. Guyana had become very active in the Movement of Non-Aligned Nations, had opened relations with the People's Republic of China, and had also conducted preliminary talks with the German Democratic Republic and the Soviet Union.[7] Trinidad and Tobago had since the early sixties established relations with such diverse nations as Yugoslavia, Iran, Ethopia, Nigeria, Lebanon, and India.[8] That Jamaica, which had never severed its pre-1959 consular-level relations with Cuba, should move toward full diplomatic ties after Manley's election in February 1972 is not unusual given the Jamaican prime minister's views on regional cooperation.

A third purpose for establishing relations with Cuba was to enable certain of these Caribbean governments to undermine left opposition at home. While some observers have viewed the decision by the Williams government in this light,[9] the best case for such an argument can be made regarding Guyana. Forbes Burnham's government is not without serious opposition. Cheddi Jagan, a Marxist, three times a prime minister of Guyana, and a long-time friend of Fidel Castro, still commands the respect and support of approximately one-third of the Guyanese population. Despite his successes in returning some measure of political and economic stability to Guyana, Burnham has been unable to placate this force. His critics have pointed to his extremely generous settlements with nationalized foreign interests, his resistance to controversial Black Power figures teaching at the University of Guyana (despite his frequently professed support for such movements), and his lack of progressive domestic policies as evidence that his more radical nationalist policies are, in fact, motivated less by principle than by sheer opportunism and the desire to undercut Jagan.[10] Regardless of whether one views Burnham as the devoted radical nationalist he would prefer or as the Machiavellian personality his critics see, the possible political benefits derived from the establishment of relations with Cuba should not be overlooked.

The Cuban government welcomed the four governments' decision and moved promptly to establish ties. Castro hailed this "challenge to imperialism," indicating "that the English speaking nations of the Caribbean did not acquire the bad habit—as did the Latin American governments—of being dreadfully afraid of Yankee imperialism."[11] Moreover, the action of the Caribbean governments was complementary to dramatic changes in Cuban foreign policy objectives. Since 1970 the thrust of Cuban policy has shifted from the support of revolutionary movements to efforts to end Cuban isolation in the hemisphere, including cooperation with conventional governments. The desire to further legitimize the Cuban regime in the eyes of the world in a partial explanation for this shift.

Another advantage is the opportunity for Cuba to acquire some of the raw materials and manufactured goods needed for economic growth: petroleum, automotive products, machines, and advanced technology (see chapter 9 of this volume).

However, the potential for more Cuban trade with the British Caribbean nations appears limited. The economies of the four nations in question are competitive and not complementary. The bulk of their foreign earnings is provided by exports of sugar, bauxite, aluminum, rice, bananas, and petroleum.[12] Only the last is of interest to Cuba.

Cuba is now heavily dependent for petroleum on the Soviet Union, which supplies approximately 98 percent of its energy needs. A supplemental source of petroleum would mean not only lower transportation costs and quicker deliveries, but reduced reliance on, and greater leverage with, the Soviet Union. The strengthening of Cuban ties to Third World suppliers could increase solidarity among those nations. The oil strike off Trinidad and the prospect of others off Guyana have been seen as a possible advantage in Cuban ties to the Caribbean nations.[13] No agreements between these nations have yet been announced, however, and Cuban relations with Trinidad and Tobago are not encouraging in this respect.

One post-1970 objective of Cuban foreign policy is the acquisition of "vanguard technology" from the West.[14] Obviously the United States, not the Caribbean nations, can best supply such technology. Equally obvious is the fact that

RONALD E. JONES

present U.S. policy toward Cuba does not allow for the transfer of technology in sufficient quantity to satisfy Cuban needs. The existence of diplomatic relations between Cuba and a growing number of Latin American nations not only renders the U.S. position increasingly anachronistic, but adds to the pressure for a change in that policy. One instance of indirect pressure was the pointed statement by Eric Williams that U.S. policy toward Cuba "does not have a leg to stand on." In another more dramatic instance during the Tlateloco Conference, with Secretary of State Kissinger in attendance, Dudley Thompson, the Jamaican foreign minister, stated simply and bluntly that "to ignore Cuba is sheer stone age stupidity." Later Prime Minister Manley revealed that he had been a source of direct pressure on the United States in his self-appointed role as a go-between in discussions with Castro and Kissinger regarding methods to restore normal relations between their respective governments.[15]

Cuban ties to the British Caribbean nations serve to further another Cuban foreign policy objective as well—that of pursuing "selective confrontation with imperialism." This policy allows the Cubans to take advantage of the trend toward common action by Third World nations and at the same time avoid the appearance of violent and uncompromising opposition to the policy of the United States.[16] One element of this tactic is the Cuban support for producer associations along the line of the Organization of Petroleum Exporting Countries (OPEC) and, more relevant to the Caribbean, the International Bauxite Association (IBA). Jamaica and Guyana belong to this latter group, and the Castro government has on many occasions praised the efforts of the association and its individual members to recapture control of their natural resources.[17] A second element is Cuban support for multinational groupings that exclude the United States and pursue policies that are directly or indirectly opposed to the United States. Cuban participation in, and support of, joint Caribbean economic schemes should be seen primarily as a political move motivated by the policy of "selective confrontation" and not as an effort to gain immediate economic benefits. The economies of the Caribbean nations are too similar and their populations too small to provide a strong incentive for economic integration; the economic advantages of participation in specific ventures such as the Caribbean Multinational Shipping Enterprise (NAMUCAR), are likewise not that great (see the discussion in chapter 14 of this volume).

In sum, a combination of forces created a situation in which the foreign policy objectives of Cuba and the other Caribbean governments complemented each other. The result was the establishment of relations between Cuba and the four nations in December 1972.

The Development of Bilateral Relations

Although the decision to seek full diplomatic ties with Cuba was made collectively by the four Caribbean nations, a uniform relationship between Cuba and each nation has not developed. Instead, the nations form a continuum with Barbados having the weakest ties and Jamaica the strongest.

In June 1972 the Peruvian government urged the OAS to normalize relations with Cuba. The resolution failed by a vote of thirteen to seven. Two of the seven voting in favor of the resolution were Jamaica and Trinidad and Tobago. Three nations abstained—one was Barbados. Thus while the other former British colonies that are members of the OAS were taking a stand favoring a larger role for Cuba in the hemisphere, the government of Barbados, just four months prior to the joint decision by the Caribbean heads of state, was hesitant to do so.

The reluctance of Barbados was evident even on the very day relations with Cuba officially opened. The joint communiqués issued by Cuba and each of the four nations on December 8, 1972, are revealing. Three of them—those issued by Cuba and Guyana, Jamaica, and Trinidad and Tobago—referred to the Cuban government as the "Revolutionary Government of Cuba." The communiqué issued by Cuba and Barbados referred simply to the "Government of Cuba."[18] It is unlikely that the deletion was an oversight or a typographical error. A more plausible argument is that it indicates a coolness on the part of the government of Barbados toward the government of Cuba.

This coolness is suggested in other ways as well. While the heads of state of Guyana, Jamaica, and Trinidad and Tobago have all visited Cuba, there has been no such visit by their counterpart in Barbados. In fact, there has been no reported visit of any official of ministerial level from Barbados since immediately before relations were established in November 1972. At that time the deputy minister of foreign relations visited Cuba and advocated closer ties between the two countries.[19] However, closer relations have been slow to develop. In fact, it could be argued that relations between the two nations have become more distant— especially in light of Cuba's participation in Angola. In late December 1975 and early January 1976 a delegation from the Popular Movement for the Liberation of Angola (MPLA) visited the Caribbean area in an attempt to secure support. Not only did the government of Barbados refuse to support the MPLA but it attempted to obstruct Cuban assistance by refusing to allow Cuban aircraft to refuel in Barbados en route to Africa and referred to Cuban troops in Angola as meddling in the internal affairs of that country.[20]

Cuban-Barbadian cooperation on technical and economic matters can be treated very briefly. According to Cuban reports, such cooperation consists of a regularly scheduled air link between Havana and Bridgetown, established in 1973, and limited exchanges of agricultural technicians, a practice which apparently existed before 1972.[21]

In certain respects Cuban relations with Trinidad and Tobago are on firmer grounds than those with Barbados. The joint communiqué issued at the end of Prime Minister Williams's visit to Cuba said, in part, that "both Governments will examine ways and means to develop closer bilateral relations" and indicated that the two governments had agreed to take the steps necessary to establish closer collaboration on technical projects.[22] In August 1975 a joint group of technicians explored areas of possible cooperation in industrial development, food production, physical infrastructure, and sugar products, but no further progress in these areas has been reported.[23] In matters of foreign policy the positions of Cuba and Trinidad and Tobago show greater similarity than those of Cuba and Barbados. Unlike Barbados the Trinidad and Tobago representative to the OAS voted in support of the June 1972 resolution for the normalization of relations with Cuba, and Williams had reportedly dropped hints earlier that bilateral relations with Cuba were being considered. He has long been identified with Caribbean integration and was the first Caribbean leader to seek extensive ties with nations of Africa and Asia. His administration, while rejecting demands for complete nationalization of oil concerns in his country, has established, through taxing policies and majority ownership, a progressively larger role for the government of Trinidad in the control of its natural resources. The Cuban government has indicated support of these actions on several occasions.[24]

Despite these areas of agreement, tension does exist between Cuba and Trinidad and Tobago on other points. While concern over Cuban involvement in Caribbean Black Power movements does not appear to be as strong as it was in 1970, Cuban ties to the Soviet Union are still viewed with displeasure. Prime Minister Williams has written rather critically of Cuba for "turn[ing] its back on the Caribbean in preference for the Communist Bloc." More recently the Cuban involvement in Angola prompted a spokesman for the foreign ministry of Trinidad to say, "If Cuba wanted [growing ties with the Caribbean] to continue, then the Angolan involvement should have been stopped before it got started."[25] This generally moderate foreign policy, activist but decidedly nonrevolutionary, probably accounts for the difference between Williams's reception in Cuba and that of his Jamaican and Guyanese counterparts. The latter two, Manley and Burnham, were awarded the José Martí National Order, established "for heads of state and government and leaders of political parties and movements who have distinguished themselves for their international solidarity with the struggle against imperialism, colonialism and neo-colonialism and for their friendship with the Socialist Revolution of Cuba." Prime Minister Williams was instead awarded an honorary degree in history.[26]

The strength of Cuban ties to Guyana is derived from, and reflected in, matters of foreign policy. Since declaring itself a cooperative republic in 1970, Guyana has followed a policy with marked nationalist overtones. Its active participation in the Conference of Non-Aligned Nations has led Eric Williams to describe Guyana as the nation that has taken the most dramatic steps in associating the Caribbean with the rest of the Third World.[27] The Cuban Council of Ministers singled our Burnham's role in these policies when awarding him the José Martí National Order in 1975. The Guyanese government has also succeeded in gaining control over foreign investment by nationalizing virtually all the foreign holdings in the economy. Cuban participation in Angola received support from the Guyanan government in several ways. The Guyanese representative to the United Nations cosponsored a resolution submitted to the Security Council that condemned South African intervention but made no mention of the presence of Cuban troops. More importantly, Guyana also permitted Cuban aircraft en route to Africa to refuel in Guyana despite strong U.S. protest.[28]

Exchanges between Cuba and Guyana that fall under the general heading of commercial relations or technical assistance are more advanced than those between either Cuba and Barbados or Cuba and Trinidad and Tobago. Cuba has purchased from Guyana 10,000 tons of rice and unknown quantities of railroad ties, lumber, and railway cars.[29] Cuba has exported cement products, which Cuba itself imports, to Guyana.[30] Technical assistance agreements relating to sharing sugar technology have been signed, and Cuba is training a small number of Guyanese pilots through its civilian air carrier, Aviación de Cuba.[31] The Cuban government is also involved in a program to assist in the development of a Guyanese fishing industry. In December 1976 there were reportedly one hundred Cuban fishermen in Guyana, and fifty-six Guyanese fishermen had previously received training in Cuba.[32]

Of the four Caribbean nations under consideration it is Jamaica which has developed the closest ties with Cuba. This conclusion is based on an assessment of the similarity of Cuban and Jamaican foreign policy and the expressions of mutual support for these positions, the extent of commercial relations between the two countries, and the range of technical assistance provided the Jamaican government by Cuba.

Before his election in February 1972, Prime Minister Michael Manley stressed the need to build closer bonds with the Third World and indicated that he would seek to establish relations with Cuba.[33] Since that time the foreign policies of Jamaica and Cuba have shown numerous points of agreement. Manley has been an active member of the Conference of Non-Aligned Nations and in September 1973 flew to the Algiers conference with Castro and Burnham. Excerpts of his speech in Conakry were reprinted in the Cuban newspaper *Granma* along with those of Castro. Manley's position regarding Third World unity parallels that of the Cuban government and is best expressed in the following statement: "Since *every* Third World country is faced with the same dilemma in its dealings with the metropolitan world, it follows that the Third World countries need to develop a *unified* response to their problems."[34]

One of the main aspects of this "unified response" concerns greater control of natural resources. In Jamaica this means greater control over bauxite; Jamaica is the second largest producer of bauxite in the world. In June 1972 the first indications of Manley's position regarding bauxite were seen in the decision of Jamaica and Surinam to study the possibility of developing a common bauxite policy. Manley's policy was termed "cautious" at first, but by 1974 the government had taken the position that further bauxite developments were to ensure Jamaican dominance over foreign capital and had acquired majority ownership in the biggest part of the industry. The Cuban position regarding the Jamaican effort is clear. According to the joint Cuban-Jamaican communiqué issued in July 1975: "The Cuban side reaffirmed its support for the measures adopted by the Government of Jamaica to achieve economic and social development and to obtain greater control over the enterprises which exploit the natural resources of the country."[35]

The question of Cuban involvement in Angola, a point that had created controversy in Cuba's relations with the governments of Barbados and Trinidad and Tobago, has proved to be another strong point of unity with the Manley government. Jamaican support was made quite clear when Manley said: "We regard Cuban assistance to Angola as honorable and in the best interests of all those who care for African freedom."[36]

Commercial relations between Cuba and Jamaica, while not substantial enough to provide significant assistance to the Cuban economy, have been steadily increasing. In early October 1972, Keble Munn, the Jamaican minister of agriculture, indicated that Jamaica wished to establish ties with Cuba in order to gain a market for light manufacturers and to benefit from Cuba's "advanced" cattle-rearing technology.[37] Since that time Jamaica has sold a number of products to Cuba including 1,000 metric tons of sulphuric acid and unspecified quantities of beer, welding rods, aluminum products, and barrels and has signed agreements to provide Cuba with plastic conduit worth $360,000. Cuban trade with Jamaica, which totaled only a little more than $150,000 in 1975 might be considerably augmented as a result of talks conducted in the summer of 1976. The discussions, termed "well advanced" by Cuban Trade Commissioner Abdo Soto, were seen as possibly providing Jamaica with export orders totaling $5 million.[38]

The number and range of cooperative agreements between Jamaica and Cuba deserve special attention as well. In July 1975 it was announced that delegations from the two governments had reached "specific decisions for collaboration in the field of fisheries, sugar byproducts industries, agriculture, tourism and foreign trade, including aluminum products." In November an agreement that established mutual aid in a number of public health sectors was signed in Jamaica. Other agreements have been signed in matters of construction, and talks have been carried out in the areas of transportation and communication.[39] These agreements and discussions have led to sizable exchanges of personnel and a number of joint projects in a variety of areas. In February 1976, Dudley Thompson, the Jamaican Minister of External Affairs indicated that approximately 80 Cuban technicians were present in Jamaica—21 assisting in the building of micro-dams, 9 directing the construction of prefabricated housing, and 50 preparing to erect a factory for the manufacture of a school. By August the number had risen to 277, and they were engaged in medical projects in addition to those identified by Thompson. As of July 1977, some Cuban technicians were still present in Jamaica; however, they apparently never neared the 600 that Thompson saw as a possible figure.[40] The number of Jamaicans working in Cuba was also substantial. In July 1975, Fidel Castro noted the presence of 33 Jamaicans who were learning "the principles, techniques and methods of construction" and another "brigade of 141 young Jamaicans who came to Camaguay for a year, cooperating in the plans for the province's development and learning all about the Girón system of construction." In October 1976 it was reported that another brigade of Jamaicans left for Cuba to receive training in the building trades. At that time it was reported that 180 Jamaicans were then studying construction in Cuba. Other reports indicated that under technical agreements signed in 1975, 300 Jamaicans were to take part in the exchanges.[41]

The most interesting aspect of Cuban relations with Jamaica concerns the nature of the assistance provided. Unlike reported Cuban assistance to Guyana, which consists entirely of exchanges of technical personnel and information and the training of Guyanese technicians, much of the Cuban assistance to Jamaica has been highly visible, widely publicized, and aimed directly at problems faced by lower income groups in Jamaica. The construction of the José Martí secondary school in Spanish Town by a joint Cuban-Jamaican work force and Cuba's assignment of doctors to the Jamaican health service are two examples. The most striking instance of such direct efforts to promote social welfare is the Cuban sale of condensed milk to Jamaica. On April 11, 1975, Prime Minister Manley announced that Cuba had agreed to sell Jamaica 120,000 cases of LaCrema, a high quality condensed milk which Cuba itself must ration. The milk was to be sold at about half the price of comparable Jamaican brands and was to be made available to lower income groups through special government retail shops. The milk added a rather significant increment, just under 10 percent, to the Jamaican supply.[42] The importance of this addition is understood when one realizes that, according to the 1973 estimate, 50 percent of Jamaican children suffered from malnutrition due to a shortage of moderately priced foodstuffs.[43] Thus the Cubans made available to Jamaica a high quality, low priced foodstuff in relatively significant quantities. Furthermore, the product, which is easily distinguished from its Jamaican counterparts by its Spanish brand name, is available only to lower income groups through government sources. Manley emphasized the significance of this action, increased the visibility and publicity accorded it, and strengthened the Cuban-Jamaican link at a press conference in April 1975. With the Cuban ambassador to Jamaica and the Cuban trade commissioner present, Manley thanked Castro and his government for their generosity, referring to the sale as "another example of solidarity among Third World nations."[44]

Guyana and Jamaica

From the previous discussion it is clear that Cuban relations with Jamaica have progressed further than Cuban ties to the other three Caribbean nations. That Cuban ties to Barbados and to Trinidad and Tobago are rather modest does not seem surprising as neither of these two governments strives to present a radical image. However, that Cuban-Jamaican cooperation is greater than Cuban-Guyanese cooperation creates a question, since in many respects Guyana and Jamaica seem to pursue similar policies. The differences reflect an evaluation by the Cuban government of the different internal political situation in each country.[45]

Forbes Burnham took office in 1964, replacing Cheddi Jagan, a Marxist and close ally of Castro. From 1964 to 1970 the Burnham government followed very moderate policies: encouraging foreign investment, cooling relations with Cuba, and following a capitalist model of economic development. In 1969 the government began to encounter growing unrest and increased pressure from the left which was, and still is, led by Jagan and his significant support. In 1970 Burnham declared Guyana to be a "Cooperative Republic" and began to nationalize foreign enterprises. He became more active in Third World forums and enunciated a more nationalistic foreign policy. However, his domestic policy, despite the nationalizations, has still been characterized as moderate, as shown by his generous settlements with the nationalized industries.

Manley, on the other hand, does not have such a checkered past. He urged closer ties to Third World nations, including Cuba, before his election in 1972 and urged them to unite against the industrialized nations. His economic policies have been consistently reformist and have featured such programs as reclamation of unused lands, increased wage scales for unskilled workers, an increased minimum wage, and housing assistance. In short, while the history and political economy of the Manley period remains to be written, there seems to be a consensus among observers that Manley, unlike Burnham, shows no indications of sheer opportunism in his politics.[46]

Thus two major differences between Jamaica and Guyana are readily apparent. First, the Burnham government has lacked the consistency of the Manley government, and as a result it is frequently characterized as primarily opportunistic rather than leftist. Second, the Manley government is a leftist (although not Marxist) government, while in Guyana a long-time Marxist, Jagan, still commands a large following and offers an alternative to Burnham.

If these characterizations are accurate, then it is reasonable to suppose that the Cuban government, while willing to have diplomatic relations with governments of various ideological leanings, seeks, like any other government, to furnish assistance where it will provide the greatest returns. It is in Cuba's interest to strengthen Manley's position by offering quantitatively more and qualitatively different assistance to Jamaica than to Guyana. The projects undertaken in Jamaica are highly visible and concrete actions aimed at bettering conditions for Jamaicans, especially the low income groups, and thereby increasing support for the Manley government. In Guyana, support to the Burnham government might well be assistance to a government which could, given its past history, change its policies and move in a direction less acceptable to Cuba. Furthermore, such assistance would in this case serve to strengthen the government at the expense of a more reliable leftist group that is still of no little significance in the nation and is led, moreover, by a Castro ally.

Cuban statements evaluating the two governments support this interpretation. These include the joint communiqués issued by Cuba and Guyana and Cuba and Jamaica and the speeches of Castro during the visits of Burnham and Manley. In praising the government of Guyana, Cuba has dealt almost exclusively with foreign policy. Castro's only references to Burnham's domestic policy came seemingly as a brief afterthought in a statement regarding the control of natural resources: the Guyanese government "are also making a great effort in the fields of education and public health, and are fully determined to carry out a policy of recovery of natural resources and of development of their country." In the joint communiqué, the Cubans refer twice to domestic policies of the Guyanese government as policies of economic independence. This is in contrast to Cuba's own policies which are those of economic development. Finally, the Burnham government has consistently been characterized as following a "progressive course" and taking "nationalistic and progressive stands."[47] Such statements suggest that a distinction is made in characterizing specific and limited policies of governments as opposed to evaluating them overall. The distinction was apparent in the Declaration of the Conference of Communist Parties of Latin America and the Caribbean in June 1975. One of the signatories to the declaration was a representative of the People's Progressive Party of Guyana, the party of Cheddi Jagan and the opposition to Burnham. This document has two references to Guyana. In one section, describing the "revolutionary outbursts" of the early 1950s, and including references to the Bolivian Revolution and the Arbenz government in Guatemala, the following statement appears: "In the British Colonies of the Caribbean a new upsurge of the democratic movement took place in the post-war period, which saw its greatest success in Guyana in April, 1953, with the overwhelming electoral victory of the People's Progressive Party." In a later section dealing with the response of the United States and associated powers to the Cuban Revolution, the declaration states that "the imperialists helped overthrow Goulart in Brazil and the Government of the People's Progressive Party in Guyana in 1964—which had refused to go along with their attacks on Cuba."[48] What makes these statements significant is that while Jagan's party is lauded for having led the "greatest success" of the postwar period, the present government of Forbes Burnham, which came to power in 1964, is linked to imperialist machinations. These two statements and the absence of any vindicating statement suggests that the Cuban government has serious reservations about the Burnham government.

Cuban references to Jamaica are of a different nature. Fidel Castro's personal references are far more enthusiastic: "Our esteem for Comrade Michael Manley stems not only from his friendly attitude toward our country but also from recognition of his extraordinary efforts on behalf of his people." Not only are references more enthusiastic but more approving as well. Where Guyana's efforts to obtain economic independence were only noted, the Cubans speak highly of the Jamaican government for "introducing important changes in internal policy aimed at aiding the economic, social and cultural construction of the country." The Cuba-Jamaica joint communiqué referred not to economic independence but rather to "the measures adopted by the Government of Jamaica to achieve economic and social *development*" (emphasis added). As for a general characterization of the Jamaican policies, Castro summed it up as follows: "In a nutshell, we like the Government of Jamaica because we believe it is a progressive government." [49]

In short, it does not seem unreasonable to suggest that Cuban-Jamaican relations have progressed further than Cuban-Guyanese relations due to a different Cuban evaluation of the two administrations in question.

Future Prospects

The intensity of Cuba's relations with these four governments is not likely to change in the near future. Forecasting the future of Cuban relations with Barbados is difficult in the sense that there is so little intercourse on which to base a prediction, and simple because both governments seem to prefer to keep it that way. The administration of Errol Barrow, the prime minister from 1972 to 1976, showed no great enthusiasm for the establishment of relations with Cuba and later was displeased with the Cuban assistance to the MPLA. Barrow's successor, J. M. G. Tom Adams, has shown no more interest in closer ties to Cuba. As for the Cuban side, Barbados, with a population of roughly 240,000 and a per capita gross national product of less than $1,000, is too small to provide an attractive market for Cuban exports, has no strategic resource Cuba needs, and commands no special position in regional or Third World politics. In short, Barbados will most likely remain on the periphery of Cuban interests.

Trinidad and Tobago's petroleum resources would seem to make closer ties to its government attractive to Cuba, but several factors inhibit vastly improved relations. First, Cuba and Trinidad are competing for expanded influence in the Caribbean: Cuba by offering technical assistance and association with the Revolution and Castro's prestige, and Trinidad by monetary assistance.[50] There is also the clash of personalities between Castro and Williams, both men of sizable ego, for leadership in the Caribbean. In view of these obstacles, Cuban relations with Trinidad and Tobago will remain "correct" with neither party making unusual efforts to woo the other.

Cuban relations with Guyana are likely to continue to be ambivalent. The Cubans will have no problem supporting the foreign policy of the Burnham government and will continue to applaud Guyanese participation in such organizations as the Movement of Non-Aligned Nations and the International Bauxite Association. The Cubans will also continue to support the Guyanese position toward control of natural resources. However, due to the presence of Jagan and his continued strength, the Cubans will avoid a close identification with the Burnham government; Castro, himself, will especially avoid any such link. The Cubans will treat the Burnham government as one worthy of selective support but, as implied by the Declaration of the Communist Parties of Latin America and the Caribbean, will continue to prefer Jagan and the People's Progressive Party.

Cuba's relations with Jamaica have received considerable attention, especially from journalists. Unfortunately, most of the coverage has generated more heat than light. The basis for Cuban-Jamaican ties is not a "Cubanization" of Jamaica but rather an effort to overcome their insularity and to use multilateral cooperation as a central means for dealing with industrialized powers. Cuba will continue to provide technical assistance in numerous areas and to support the Manley government. Cuba will also, unlike its policy in Guyana, continue to identify the Revolution with the Manley government and its efforts to bring a life to the Jamaican masses. For its part the Manley government will support Cuba in international and regional forums under its general policy of promoting unity and cooperation among Third World nations. The Jamaican government will maintain closer and more active ties to the Cuban government than the other three governments.

In short, there appears to be no "grand design" of a "Marxist axis" stretching from Cuba to Jamaica to Guyana. Cuba has ceased its support for guerrilla movements in the hemisphere, and there is no immediate prospect of a Marxist regime in either Jamaica or Guyana. Guyana's Marxist party is in opposition, and the Burnham administration has a firm grip on the electoral machinery if not the electorate. Manley, for all his expressed admiration of the Cuban Revolution and Castro, has on several occasions indicated his disagreement with Cuba's eradication of the private sector and the establishment of one party rule, common features of a Marxist regime.[51] Fears or dreams of a "Marxist axis" are equally unfounded.

What is happening, however, is that the trends toward closer ties and greater cooperation among Third World nations is being repeated in the Caribbean. The bases for these developments are the shared needs of developing countries, not ideology. For the present, Cuba's ties with these four governments should be recognized for what they are—a natural outgrowth of recent global trends and not a concerted effort at ideological or political subversion.

NOTES

1. Arnaud de Borchgrave, "Cuba's Role in Jamaica," *Newsweek,* February 28, 1971, pp. 37–38; Richard C. Schroeder, "Cuban Expansionism," *Editorial Research Reports* 1, no. 19 (May 20, 1977), 375–91; Comment attributed to Jaime Suchlicki, *Wall Street Journal,* May 17, 1976, p. 1.

2. See Carmelo Mesa-Lago, *Cuba in the 1970s* (Albuquerque: University of New Mexico Press, 1974), pp. 109–15.

3. *Granma Weekly Review,* December 24, 1972, p. 11; *Latin America* (London), October 20, 1972, p. 329; *Granma Weekly Review,* December 24, 1972, p. 11.

4. *Granma Weekly Review,* October 22, 1972, p. 3.

5. Eric Williams, "The Foreign Policy of the Caribbean States," *Roundtable,* no. 249 (January 1973), pp. 82–84.

6. L. F. S. Burnham, "Statements and Speeches," *Guyana Journal* 1–4 (September 1970), 123; Michael Manley, "Overcoming Insularity in Jamaica," *Foreign Affairs* 49, no. 1 (October 1970), 100–01.

7. *Latin America,* April 28, 1972, p. 135.

8. Williams, "Foreign Policy," pp. 85–86.

9. *Latin America,* October 20, 1972, p. 329.

10. See *Latin America,* October 18, 1974, pp. 324–26; Cheddi Jagan, "Political Flexibility,

Ideological Implacability," *World Marxist Review* 18 (December 1975), 55–61; Cheddi Jagan, *The West on Trial* (New York: International Publishers, 1966); and Walter Rodney, "Contemporary Political Trends in the English-Speaking Caribbean," *Black Scholar* 7, no. 1 (September 1975), 15–22.

11. *Granma Weekly Review*, April 20, 1974, p. 4.

12. *Granma Weekly Review*, December 24, 1972, p. 11.

13. *Latin America*, September 7, 1973, p. 281.

14. Edward Gonzalez and David Ronfeldt, *Post-Revolutionary Cuba* (Santa Monica: The Rand Corporation, 1975), pp. 51–52, 58–61.

15. Williams, "Foreign Policy," pp. 84–85; *Latin American Index* (Washington, D.C.) 2, no. 4 (February 16–28, 1974), 15; *New York Times*, November 21, 1976, p. 15.

16. Gonzalez and Ronfeldt, *Post-Revolutionary Cuba*, pp. 51–52, 61–66.

17. See, for example, *Granma Weekly Review*, April 20, 1975, p. 6; ibid., July 20, 1975, p. 6; ibid., July 11, 1976, p. 6.

18. *Granma Weekly Review*, December 24, 1972, p. 11.

19. Ibid.

20. *Latin America*, January 9, 1976, p. 16.

21. *Granma Weekly Review*, December 24, 1972, p. 12; *Caribbean Monthly Bulletin* (Rio Piedras, Puerto Rico) 9, no. 5–6 (June 1975), 11.

22. *Granma Weekly Review*, July 6, 1975, p. 12.

23. Havana Domestic Service, August 9, 1975, reported in U.S. Foreign Broadcast Information Service, *Daily Report for Latin America*, August 11, 1975, p. Q1.

24. Williams, "Foreign Policy," pp. 77–88; *Latin American Report* (San Francisco) 3, no. 9 (April 1975), 3; *Granma Weekly Review*, July 6, 1975, p. 12.

25. Williams, "Foreign Policy," pp. 86–87; *Christian Science Monitor*, January 2, 1976, p. 26.

26. *Granma Weekly Review*, April 20, 1975, p. 3; ibid., June 29, 1975, p. 1.

27. Williams, "Foreign Policy," p. 85.

28. *Granma Weekly Review*, April 20, 1975, p. 3; *Latin American Economic Report* (London), February 27, 1976, p. 35; *New York Times*, April 2, 1976, p. 2; *Latin America*, January 9, 1976, p. 16.

29. *Granma Weekly Review*, April 20, 1976, p. 4; ibid., June 18, 1975, p. 11; *Sunday Gleaner* (Kingston, Jamaica, June 6, 1975, p. 11, reported in *Daily Report for Latin America*, June 12, 1975, p. S2.

30. *Granma Weekly Review*, June 18, 1975, p. 11.

31. *Advocate News* (Bridgetown), November 6, 1976, p. 3, reported in *Daily Report for Latin America*, November 12, 1976, p. V1; *Washington Post*, March 10, 1976, p. 17.

32. Havana Domestic Service, December 7, 1976, reported in *Daily Report for Latin America*, December 8, 1976, p. Q5; *Guardian* (Port of Spain, Trinidad), February 8, 1975, p. 2, reported in ibid., February 13, 1975, p. S3.

33. *Latin America*, October 20, 1972, p. 329.

34. *Granma Weekly Review*, September 16, 1973, p. 4; Michael Manley, *The Politics of Change* (London: Andre Deutsch, 1974), p. 128 (emphasis added).

35. *Latin America*, June 9, 1972, p. 179; ibid., January 5, 1973, pp. 7–8; ibid., June 7, 1974, p. 176; *Granma Weekly Review*, July 20, 1975, p. 6.

36. *Wall Street Journal*, March 22, 1976, p. 6.

37. *Latin America*, October 6, 1972, p. 320.

38. *Caribbean Monthly Bulletin* (Rio Piedras, Puerto Rico) 9, no. 8 (August 1975), 2; ibid., 10, no. 8–9 (August 1976), 29; *Advocate News*, July 19, 1976, p. 5, reported in *Daily Report for Latin America*, July 23, 1976, p. S1.

39. *Granma Weekly Review*, July 6, 1975, p. 12; ibid., November 30, 1975, p. 3; Havana Domestic Service, March 28, 1975, reported in *Daily Report for Latin America*, March 31, 1975, p. S1; ibid., January 17, 1975, reported January 20, 1975, p. Q2; ibid., March 19, 1975, reported March 21, 1975, p. Q1.

40. *Daily Gleaner*, February 20, 1976, p. 1, reported in *Daily Report for Latin America*, February 25, 1976, p. S1; *Latin American Report*, August 1976, p. 4; *Wall Street Journal*, March 22, 1976, p. 6.

41. *Granma Weekly Review*, July 20, 1975, p. 4; *Daily Gleaner*, October 21, 1976, p. 12, reported in *Daily Report for Latin America*, October 27, 1976, p. S2; *Caribbean Monthly Bulletin* 10, no. 8-9 (August-September 1976), 29.

42. *Daily Gleaner*, April 12, 1975, p. 1, reported in *Daily Report for Latin America*, April 16, 1975, p. S1.

43. *New York Times*, May 9, 1973, p. 5.

44. *Caribbean Monthly Bulletin* 10, no. 4 (April 1976), p. 13; *Latin American Index* 3, no. 8 (April 16-30, 1975), p. 31.

45. The following description is drawn from many sources, including B.A.N. Collins, "The End of a Colony," *Political Quarterly* 36, no. 4 (1965), 406-16; Ernst Halperin, "Racism and Communism in British Guinea," *Journal of Inter-American Studies* 7, no. 1 (January 1965), 95-134; Embert Henricks, "New Directions for Republican Guyana," *The World Today* 27, no. 1 (January 1971), 33-39; Ralph B. Premdas, "Guyana: Communal Conflict, Socialism and Political Reconciliation," *Inter-American Economic Affairs* 14 (Spring 1977), 63-83.

46. For Jamaica the description is based primarily on journalistic sources and Anthony Payne, "From Michael with Love: The Nature of Socialism in Jamaica," *Journal of Commonwealth and Comparative Politics* 14 (1976), 83-100.

47. *Granma Weekly Review*, April 20, 1975, pp. 4, 6, 3.

48. *Latin America in the Struggle Against Imperialism*, Declaration of the Conference of Communist Parties of Latin America and the Caribbean (New York: International Publishers, 1975), pp. 33-34, 15, 20-21.

49. *Granma Weekly Review*, July 30, 1975, pp. 2, 4, 6.

50. In June 1976 the Williams government provided the beleaguered Jamaican economy with short term relief through a loan of $77 million. See *Latin American Report* 4, no. 24 (December 1976), 93-95. The significance of this loan to Trinidad and Tobago's own financial position should not be overlooked. Eric Williams has stated that the loan constituted 11 percent of Trinidad and Tobago's external assets. *Caribbean Monthly Bulletin* 11, no. 4-5 (April-May 1977), 12.

51. See the interview conducted with Prime Minister Manley in the *Sunday Gleaner*, August 3, 1975, p. 9, and reprinted, in part, in *Daily Report for Latin America*, August 8, 1975, p. S1.

7

ROZITA LEVI

Cuba and the Nonaligned Movement

Cuba's relations with Latin America, the Soviet Union, and the United States are well known, but much less attention has been paid to the active role she has played in the nonaligned movement. Cuba is the only Latin American country which has participated, as a full member, in all the conferences of heads of state or government summit meetings of the nonaligned countries, ministerial meetings, meetings of the Coordinating Bureau, and in the work of other bodies of the movement.

The nonaligned movement has been important to Cuba partly because of Cuba's long isolation in the Western Hemisphere, imposed upon her after the Revolution of 1959. But more important are the political and economic interests that Cuba shares with many of the nonaligned countries. Cuba's role in the nonaligned movement may be analyzed in three periods, the first lasting through the mid-1960s, the second beginning in 1968, and the third beginning in the mid-1970s and lasting up to the present time.

The first period was characterized by Cuba's attempt to withstand U.S. pressure, protecting her security and her choice of internal political organization. In this effort Cuba relied heavily on the Soviet Union. After the missile crisis of 1962, however, when Cuba believed the USSR conceded to U.S. pressures, Cuba gave less emphasis to her relations with the Soviet Union and, instead, gave increased emphasis to establishing closer ties with the nonaligned countries then emerging as an important independent force in international relations.

Cuba's interest in the nonaligned movement was not surprising. First, its basic principles, such as the strengthening of national independence by struggling against dependence—economic, political, and cultural—and its emphasis on economic and social development and the reduction of the gap between developed and developing countries, corresponded to Cuba's own foreign policy aims. The nonaligned countries also stood for freedom of choice of internal political structures, noninterference with internal affairs, equality of states, and so on, principles essential to Cuba's survival and undisturbed development.

The Belgrade Declaration of the nonaligned countries of 1961 stated in article 13:

> (a) All nations have the right of unity, determination and independence by virtue of which right they can determine their political status and freely pursue their economic, social and cultural development without intimidation or hindrance.

(b) All peoples may for their own ends freely dispose of their natural wealth and resources without prejudice to any obligations arising out of international economic cooperation, based upon the principle of mutual benefit and International Law. In no case may a people be deprived of its own means of subsistence.

The participating countries believe that the right of Cuba, as that of any other nation to freely choose their political and social systems in accordance with their own conditions, needs and possibilities, should be respected.[1]

Moreover, the nonaligned countries not only pronounced themselves against foreign military bases in general (in articles 11 and 12 of the declaration) but made explicit references to the abolition of the U.S. base on Cuban territory at Guantanamo, thus fully supporting the Cuban position. The subject was also on the agenda of the second summit conference of the nonaligned countries in Cairo in 1964. On that occasion, Osvaldo Dorticós Torrado addressed the conference on the subject:

The final Declaration of the Belgrade Conference recognized that the United States military base in Guantanamo, in Cuba, to whose existence the Government and people of my country are manifestly opposed, diminished our sovereignty and territorial integrity. It is opportune to point out that due to force, this military base in Cuba is still existing today. It is illegitimately usurping a part of our national territory and from that base provocations against our country are continuously carried out. . . . That is why it is an indispensable duty for me to ask this Conference, striving to maintain a continuity in the principles postulated in Belgrade, to reaffirm in its final declarations the request included in the document of the First Conference and urges the government of the United States to withdraw its military base in Cuba. . . . It is also time that the United Nations takes up resolutely the problem of foreign military bases and it would be a fruitful contribution to the cause of peace if this gathering could make such a request during the course of the next General Assembly of the United Nations.[2]

As a result of Dorticós's appeal, the Cairo program for peace and international cooperation provided for the following:

The Conference considers that the maintenance at Guantanamo (Cuba) of a military base of the United States of America, in defiance of the will of the Government and the people of Cuba and in defiance of the propositions embodied in the Declaration of the Belgrade Conference, constitutes a violation of Cuba's sovereignty and territorial integrity.

Noting that the Cuban Government expresses its readiness to settle its dispute over the base of Guantanamo with the United States on an equal footing, the Conference urges the United States Government to negotiate the evacuation of the base with the Cuban Government.[3]

The Cairo program also gave strong support to Cuba's demand that the commercial and economic blockade imposed upon Cuba be lifted: "The Conference, considering that foreign pressure and intervention to impose changes in the political, economic, and social system chosen by a country are contrary to the principles of international law and peaceful co-existence, requests the Government of the United States of America to lift the commercial and economic blockade applied against Cuba."[4]

Clearly, Cuba's active participation in the nonaligned movement was very beneficial to her. First, Cuba enjoyed the nonaligned countries' strong support on a number of essential internal and foreign policy questions. Second, her links to the nonaligned countries tended to soften the image of Cuba, as seen in the West, as a "Soviet tool" in Latin America. Her relations with the Soviet Union, while still strong and important to her, could be viewed in a wider framework.

The second period began after 1968, when the support and understanding Cuba expressed for the Warsaw Pact countries' action in Czechoslovakia drew the countries closer together. Before 1968 the Cuban-Soviet relationship was very close in the economic sphere, but Cuban-Soviet political ties could be characterized at that time as cordial but not exceptionally close. After 1968, Cuban foreign policy involved a strong political and ideological alliance with the Soviet Union. But this did not mean the abandonment of her activities within the nonaligned movement; Cuba continued to play a very active role, fully subscribing to the nonaligned countries' foreign policy aims such as the strengthening of world peace and security—disarmament, the reduction of international tensions, the transcendence of block alignment, the elimination of local conflicts, the creation of zones of peace and cooperation, peaceful settlement of disputes, and the strengthening of the United Nations.

These principles were the major issues discussed at the third summit conference of nonaligned countries in Lusaka in 1970. Thereafter, Cuba tried hard to bring the nonaligned movement closer to the Soviet Union, justifying this position on the grounds that the principles on which nonaligned countries based their policies were much closer to the Soviet Union than to the western countries. At the fourth nonaligned summit in Algiers in 1973, Prime Minister Castro not only stressed Cuba's close relations with the Soviet Union but insisted on the establishment of similar relationships with the other nonaligned countries:

> The theory of "two imperialisms," one headed by the United States and the other allegedly by the Soviet Union, encouraged by the theoreticians of capitalism, has been echoed at times deliberately and at others through the ignorance of history and the realities of the present-day world, by leaders and spokesmen of nonaligned countries. . . . In certain political and economic documents drafted for this Conference we've seen that current come to the fore in one way or another, with different

shadings. The Government of Cuba will always oppose that current in all circumstances.... How can the Soviet Union be labeled imperialistic? Where are its monopoly corporations? Where is its participation in the multinational companies? What factories, what mines, what oil fields does it own in the underdeveloped world? What worker is exploited in any country of Asia, Africa, and Latin America by Soviet capital?...

Any attempt to pit the nonaligned countries against the socialist camp is profoundly counterrevolutionary and benefits only imperialist interests. Inventing a false enemy can have only one aim, to evade the real enemy.[5]

Cuba's efforts to persuade nonaligned countries to align themselves with the socialist countries continued after the Algiers conference. At Cuba's suggestion it was discussed at a meeting of the Coordinating Bureau of the nonaligned countries in Havana in March 1975.[6]

During the second period, in addition to leaning toward the Soviet Union, Cuba sought to establish relations with more Latin American countries and with other developed countries all over the world. Its effort to expand its diplomatic and trade ties in Latin America went forward in spite of the de jure embargo by the Organization of American States (OAS). By moderating her stand on the armed struggle and accepting the "many-roads-to-socialism" approach, by stressing the similarity of the problems of underdevelopment in Latin America, and by emphasizing Latin America's common interests, Cuba's posture coincided more harmoniously with the tides of nationalism in Latin America. Symbolizing the end to Cuba's isolation and the new trends in her foreign policy, Prime Minister Castro began to travel outside the island in the 1970s, visiting South American countries in December 1971 and later making a trip to Africa, Eastern Europe, and the Soviet Union.

The growing ties of various Latin American countries with Cuba coincided with an increased interest on their part in the nonaligned movement. Like Cuba earlier, the leaders of these countries recognized that the nonaligned movement provided the best framework for the struggle for the solution of numerous political and economic problems. As one of the nations that had spoken out most decisively on these problems, particularly the economic ones, Cuba appeared to be a natural ally. Meanwhile, at the Georgetown ministerial meeting in 1972 and at the Algiers summit conference in 1973, Cuba was playing a very active role in the formulation of the conferences' conclusions about the most important economic questions facing the developing world. In 1974, Cuba, together with Mexico and Venezuela, initiated a proposal for the creation of the Latin American Economic System (SELA).

Cuba's efforts at this time to retain strong ties with the Soviet Union on the one hand, while opening relations with more Latin American countries on the other, were not really contradictory. Cuba's reliance on the Soviet Union was not, for example, so much a question of choice for Cuba as a means of survival. Therefore, Cuba's rapprochement with Latin American countries served to counteract her reliance on the USSR. More important, Cuba's emergence from isolation was related to her interest in becoming a leader of the Latin American modernization process. Castro and other Cuban revolutionary leaders had always believed that Cuba's experiences in struggling against poverty and underdevelopment were relevant, in fact mandatory, lessons for her Latin American neighbors.

These trends tended to be reconfirmed in the third period, which began in the mid-1970s. Cuba's policy emphasis was, however, changed in two respects. First, Cuba's insistence on extremely close relations with nonaligned countries and the Soviet Union was toned down. This development did not signal any cooling off in Cuba's relations with the Soviet Union but simply meant that she would place first emphasis on their bilateral rather than on their multilateral aspects. Second, Cuba gave new impetus to her efforts to become a leading force in Latin America and world affairs generally, particularly with regard to national liberation movements. Thus, at the Colombo Conference, Cuba spoke out strongly against interference in the internal policy of some English-speaking Caribbean countries which she characterized as "destabilization" efforts. Cuba also came out very strongly in support of the aspirations for independence of Angola, Belize, and Puerto Rico.

The sixth conference of heads of state or government of the nonaligned countries is scheduled to convene in Cuba in 1979. The selection of Cuba as the site is recognition of the increasing importance of Latin American countries in the nonaligned movement as well as of Cuba's position of leadership. Thus, new opportunities are opened up for Cuba in Latin America, her natural community.

In the future, Cuba may play a more important role in the nonaligned movement than she has in the past. It also appears likely that Cuba may be prepared to reach accommodations with the United States in order to create a better climate for her assuming a role of leadership in Latin America. Her relationship with the Soviet Union will continue to be important, depending on the extent to which Cuba is able to find relief from her economic difficulties elsewhere.

NOTES

1. *Medjunarodna politika* (Belgrade) 15, no. 348 (October 5, 1964), 8–12 (italics added).
2. *Medjunarodna politika* 15, no. 350 (November 5, 1964), 60–61.
3. Ibid., pp. 85–87.
4. Henry M. Christianman, ed., *Neither East nor West* (New York, 1973), pp. 128–29.
5. *Medjunarodna politika* 24, no. 563 (September 20, 1973), 16–17.
6. Materials published in *Medjunarodna politika* 26, nos. 600–12.

8

YORAM SHAPIRA

Cuba and the Arab-Israeli Conflict

The Cuban presence in the Middle East, as in Angola, raises questions about Cuba's role in areas distant from Latin America. In particular, how does involvement there serve the interests of the Cuban revolutionary government?

Castro's policies toward Israel and toward the Israeli-Arab conflict diverged from those of the Soviet Union until 1973, serving as a symbol of Cuba's autonomy in foreign policy. Since 1973, however, Cuban policies have tended to parallel those of the Soviet Union. Moreover, the appearance of Cuban military forces in significant numbers in Syria in 1974 was a further link with the USSR. More recent developments, however, have introduced new complications in Cuba's relations with the Middle East and the United States and may also have had an impact on the treatment of the Jewish community in Cuba.

From the Sierra Maestra to the Algiers Conference of 1973

The history of Cuban-Israeli relations is dotted with many peculiar episodes and contradictions. Initially, the Castro government was friendly toward Israel. When Raúl Castro rushed to visit Egyptian President Nasser early in 1960, Israeli visitors to Cuba could still report good will and sympathetic coverage of Israeli issues in the government-controlled press.[1] A little-known episode that attests to Castro's early favorable attitude toward the Jewish state was Cuban emigration to Israel in 1961. Jews leaving for Israel received preferential treatment and were permitted to take out personal property and valuables. The Cuban national airline flew several hundred emigrants to Israel in several flights, and the Cuban government did not attempt to levy charges on the emigrants.[2] Furthermore, while the politically endorsed attitude toward nationals leaving the country was contemptuous (branding them *gusanos,* or worms), Jews leaving for Israel were classified officially as *repatriados* (the repatriated).[3] When Israel's president, I. Ben-Zvi, died in 1963, an official three-day national mourning period was declared in Cuba.[4]

The revolutionary elite's initial attitudes toward Israel are illuminated by I. Silber, an ex-leader of the Cuban branch of Hashomer Hatzair (a Zionist socialist pioneering youth movement) who left Cuba for Israel in 1949. He was a university classmate of Fidel Castro's and revisited Cuba in the early 1960s, maintaining contacts with some prominent Fidelistas. According to his testimony, attitudes among the original Fidelistas (both in the July 26 and the Sierra Maestra   153 groups), as well as among leaders of other non-Marxist revolutionary elements (the Directorio Estudiantil Revolucionario), were far more pro-Israel than those adopted by veterans of the PSP (Partido Socialista Popular), the pre-1959, Moscow-oriented "orthodox" Communist party of Cuba. The views on Israel of Fabio Grobart, a Polish Jew and founding father and ideologue of the PSP, are not known, but Carlos Rafael Rodríguez, another member of the PSP, took an early interest in Israel.[5] In 1963, Silber still corresponded with Rodríguez concerning the establishment of a Cuban counterpart to the newly organized Israel-Cuban Friendship Committee, an idea which Rodríguez received warmly.[6] The only Jewish member of the first cabinet of the revolutionary government was Enrique Oltuski, who served as minister of communications. He was not in the elite's inner circle, so his position could have had little influence on Cuba's policies toward Israel.

Israel's initial diplomatic objectives in postrevolutionary Cuba—maintaining and strengthening relations—were consistent with Israel's policy of striving to cultivate ties with radical and neutralist regimes in an effort to mitigate their potential or actual pro-Arab tendencies. It was also hoped that Cuba might serve as a link with other radical movements. Additional consideration was given to Cuban influence in leftist circles in Latin America.

To attain these objectives, the Israelis sought to offer technical assistance and promote visits of Cuban personalities and trainees to Israel.[7] The first Israeli representative to Cuba, a chargé d'affaires, arrived in Havana in November 1959. This indicated the increased importance attached to ties with Cuba. The first Cuban minister resident in Israel was appointed by Batista in 1958 and served there for several months.

The turning point in Cuba's initially cordial relations with Israel came after Mikoyan's visit to Havana in February 1960. The resulting closer relations between Cuba and the USSR, growing links with other members of the socialist camp, and the desire for Arab support on various international issues determined the basic Cuban stance on the Middle East. This position was influenced primarily by considerations outside Cuban-Israeli bilateral relations and was largely impervious to subsequent Israeli goodwill efforts.

For her part, Israel's options for major initiatives vis-à-vis Cuba were severely circumscribed by the worsening relations between Cuba and the United States. While Israel was definitely interested in maintaining normal ties with Cuba, it became equally clear that Israel was unwilling to challenge its North American benefactor by, for example, significantly expanding commercial ties or providing large-scale technical assistance to Castro.

Thus, these intervening influences reinforced each other in limiting interaction between the two nations. Of the initial optimistic Israeli intentions, very little materialized. The sole visit of a Cuban of importance took place in early 1960, when José Pardo Llada, the senior radio commentator and chief of the radio and television corporation, FIEL, visited Israel over the objections of the Cuban foreign ministry. He returned impressed with what he saw, but soon defected to Mexico. Trade links and technical assistance remained extremely modest and were played down by both parties.

Cuba, in her attempt to achieve a position of leadership in the world "revolutionary camp" and among radical leftist forces, initiated and hosted various international conferences which were often the scene of verbal attacks on Israel. Usually, however, explanations were subsequently offered to Israel; and Cuba, despite Soviet pressures, did not sever diplomatic ties with Israel until the Algiers conference of nonaligned nations in 1973.

The Tricontinental Conference of Solidarity of Peoples, held in Havana on January 3–12, 1966, and attended by delegates from African, Asian, and Latin American liberation movements, was a forum for the anti-Israel stand of Latin America's radical left. Spurred on by Arab delegations, the conference adopted an extreme anti-Israel resolution which condemned the Zionist movement and the presence of Israel "in occupied territory." Zionism was termed "an imperialist movement by nature," whose methods are "racist and fascist." The conference advocated combating Zionist infiltration and penetration, and called for the cancellation of all treaties with Israel, an immediate break of all political relations, total economic and cultural ostracism of Israel, and the expulsion of Israel from all international organizations. Furthermore, it expressed full support for the Palestine Liberation Organization in its "war of liberation."[8] Significantly, some delegations did not subscribe to these extreme positions and either abstained or were absent from the session. Among these were the delegations of Uruguay, Argentina, Chile, and the Soviet Union.

Subsequently, too, high Cuban officials made it clear to Shlomo Levav, Israel's minister in Cuba, that the Cuban government did not consider itself responsible for resolutions adopted at the Tricontinental Conference and was not committed to them. They stressed that the conference's participants were representatives of political parties and organizations, not governments. It should also be noted that Cuban publications containing the text of the Tricontinental Conference often omitted the resolution adopted against Zionism and the state of Israel.[9]

The conference of the Organization of Latin American Solidarity (OLAS), held in Havana in August 1967, also reflected the tensions of the Arab-Israeli conflict. Here again, Cuba's independent posture within the Communist camp was described in a speech by Fidel Castro at the close of the conference. He began by condemning "Israeli aggression and U.S. imperialism." However, he also replied to the attacks leveled at Cuba—mainly by pro-Moscow Latin American Communist parties—for its refusal to sever diplomatic relations with Israel after the Six-Day War, as did all other Communist countries except Rumania. He said; "Neither did our country break off relations with Albania when a great number of countries from the socialist camp did."[10]

Castro elaborated on his reasons in an interview with K. S. Karol, correspondent for the British *New Statesman* and the French *Nouvel Observateur*. He said that although Cuba condemned Israel unequivocally, she did not question

YORAM SHAPIRA

Israel's right to exist. When asked why Cuba did not break off relations with Israel, he replied: "We have responded to them that the socialist countries never upheld the principle of breaking relations with those who commit aggression. Had that been the case, they would have broken relations a long time ago with the American aggressors in Vietnam."[11]

According to Karol, Castro was also critical of the conduct of Arab countries before and after the 1967 war. Referring to Arab propaganda on the eve of the war, Castro stated that true revolutionaries would never threaten a whole country with extermination. He also claimed that the United States was the "real instigator" of the war and added that for Cuba the lesson of the Middle East crisis was clear: Nobody can save a country if that country is unable to save itself.[12]

At the International Cultural Congress in Havana in January 1968, Arab delegates threatened the congress's unity by insisting on a joint condemnation of American and Zionist imperialism. Non-Arab delegates did not agree completely with the strong, anti-Israeli resolution, and the Cubans had to mobilize Vietnamese and North Korean delegates to calm tempers and remove the Middle Eastern topic from the agenda.[13]

Nevertheless, the Cuban mass media have systematically presented a pro-Arab, pro-Palestinian view. Middle Eastern news published in the major daily *Granma* comes from Arab sources. The verbal support given to the Arabs before 1973 was reflected in the frequent coverage of pro-Arab announcements, often in the form of joint communiqués issued after visits by Arab delegates to Cuba, and vice versa.[14] Furthermore, an anti-Israeli clause would occasionally be introduced into joint declarations which concluded Fidel Castro's visits to countries having no direct interest in the Middle East conflict.[15] Editorials siding unconditionally with the Palestinian cause were printed.[16] Cuba also became a lobbyist on behalf of the radical Arab regimes, parleying with delegations of the "progressive" Latin American nations at the United Nations when such support was called for.[17]

Long before the Cubans decided to side actively with the Arabs, they provided moral support to the militant Palestinian organizations by means of propaganda. This support was initially a reflection of Cuban ideology and a commitment to the Palestinians, who had been accepted as *guerrilleros* and members of the world "guerrilla fraternity."[18] However, the legitimation of the terrorist organizations as a national liberation movement meant not only that the Cubans were taking a stand in the Palestinian-Israeli conflict, but also that the Cubans were identifying with the "progressive" Arabs against the "reactionary" Arabs.[19] The official Cuban press has long considered what it calls the "Palestinian Revolution" to be part of the Arab liberation movement in the Middle East.[20]

Evidence of concrete, rather than verbal, Cuban support for the Palestinian organizations is meager during the 1960s. There are reports thereafter that a FATAH delegation visited Havana in July 1970, that Cubans have been involved in training Palestinian guerrillas, and that Cubans have been involved in "combat operations" in the area.[21]

Bilateral relations between Cuba and Israel continued during the 1960s and early 1970s. The first and only postrevolutionary Cuban minister in Israel was Ricardo Subirana y Lobo, a Jew and veteran Zionist who had provided aid to Fidel Castro during the difficult days of the anti-Batista struggle.[22] Yet, of the seventeen Latin American nations maintaining resident diplomatic representation in Israel, only Cuba did not elevate hers to the rank of embassy.

Both governments maintained a low profile. Trade, totaling less than $2 million in both directions at its peak in 1959, was never significant. Figures on trade with Cuba are missing from official Israeli records since 1965, although small transactions are known to have taken place through third parties. Agricultural experts from Israeli *kibbutzim,* as well as Israeli scientific personnel, visited Cuba unofficially. Castro, through Subirana y Lobo, a trained chemist, was kept well informed about scientific developments in Israel. When a new idea was considered applicable to Cuban needs, Castro did not hesitate to invite Israeli experts to inform the Cubans concerned. D. Goldberg, of the Hebrew University's Faculty of Agriculture at Rehovot, was invited to instruct Cubans on new irrigation techniques and other agricultural matters. Israeli experts also helped the Cubans improve their inland lake fisheries by introducing a new species of carp to the island.[23]

At the fourth summit conference of nonaligned nations in Algiers in September 1973, Castro suddenly announced his decision to sever diplomatic relations with Israel. Foreign Ministry officials in Jerusalem were not the only ones caught by surprise; the Cuban minister in Israel also expressed astonishment.[24] Israeli observers explained Castro's unexpected move as a spontaneous attempt to placate the Arabs, particularly Libya's Qadaffi, who had been denying the legitimacy of Castro's attending a "nonaligned" conference.[25] The official Cuban rationale, as explained by the government organ *Granma,* was that the diplomatic break was in accordance with Cuba's condemnation of Israel's "imperialistic aggression" and her refusal to evacuate occupied Arab lands. The move, said *Granma,* was in response to the demands and sentiments of the nations represented at the Algiers conference.[26]

This maintenance of diplomatic relations with Israel had been a valuable asset to Cuba. It enabled Castro to demonstrate his autonomy vis-à-vis the Soviet Union without straining the good relations he maintained with the "progressive" Arab regimes. Once Castro became more docile and conformist in his relations with the Kremlin—a tendency that increased after 1968—it became more difficult for him to maintain relations with Israel.

Although semiofficial anti-Zionism had already surfaced in Cuba in the mid-1960s, Castro did not fully develop his attacks until the Algiers conference in late 1973. Since then, stepped up anti-Israel pronouncements and virulent anti-Zionist declarations have become Cuba's major means of mobilizing Arab support in international organizations and Third World forums.[27] Occasionally, pro-Palestinian pronouncements even go beyond the Soviet stance, which does not deny Israel's right to exist.[28]

The high honors conferred on visiting Palestine Liberation Organization (PLO) functionaries, the composition of the Cuban party receiving them at the airport, the access granted them to top Cuban officials, the Playa Giron (Bay of Pigs) national order bestowed upon Yassir Arafat by President Osvaldo Dorticós, and the unusual press coverage given to Arafat's Cuba-initiated visit all demonstrate Castro's desire for Arab support for his foreign policy objectives.[29] These tactics have already reaped handsome diplomatic dividends for the Cubans, particularly in obtaining firm Arab backing for legitimating Cuban membership in Third World and nonaligned forums, and it has strengthened Castro's efforts to support the Soviet Union in nonaligned conferences.[30]

Cuba's activities in the United Nations with respect to Israel passed through three distinct stages. Starting in 1959, and more clearly after 1960, the Cuban voting record on Israel-related issues in the General Assembly has been consistently pro-Arab, a departure from the pattern characterizing the last Batista administration.[31] Nevertheless, anti-Israel expressions in the UN were relatively mild until mid-1967. The second stage began in the aftermath of the June 1967 war, when Cuba for the first time initiated an anti-Israel draft resolution of its own, thus competing with the pro-Arab draft resolutions sponsored by the Soviet Union, Yugoslavia, and Albania. Cuba's verbal attacks on Israel from the General Assembly's podium also became more frequent thereafter. The third stage was reached in late 1973, when Israel became a central issue in Cuba's "anti-imperialist" campaign.

The Cuban Jewish Community

The Jewish community in Cuba, once organized, dynamic, and viable, numbered some twelve thousand on the eve of the Revolution. By 1975, it had dwindled to a mere fourteen hundred. The community has a substantial number of old people (about 30 percent over sixty), and many of the younger generation are Jewish in little more than name. In the absence of rabbis, the community lacks proper religious leadership. The purpose of this chapter, however, is not to examine the causes of the decline but to determine whether the Cuban government's policy toward Israel has affected the treatment of the local Jewish community.

For most of the period since 1959, Cuba's harsh stand on the Middle East conflict and her ideological allegiances have not noticeably affected her behavior toward the local Jewish community, behavior which could be described as "correct." Castro's authorization of the import of Passover products has enabled Cuban Jews to observe the rituals of Pesach properly and to maintain a link with world Jewry. This arrangement, which has been operating for more than fourteen years now, has been regarded as an act of benevolence, earning

Castro sympathetic press reactions abroad as well as the gratitude of the World Jewish Congress.[32]

A visitor to Cuba in 1975 reported that despite its anti-Israel policy, the government was not restricting the normal life of Cuban Jews, and he noted no change in the attitude of the authorities toward the Jewish community. In mid-1975, all five synagogues in Havana and one in Santiago were still functioning. The synagogues were even partially supported by rents the government paid for the use of the auditoria. The daily afternoon Hebrew school (Escuela Albert Einstein) had an enrollment of about forty. The pupils attending the school were bused daily from their homes and given lunch at the school at government expense. Most strikingly, the Zionist Federation in Cuba continued to function openly and actively. Formal permission was granted both in 1974 and 1975 to hold large public celebrations to commemorate Israel's independence day.[33] Castro's lenient policy toward the Jewish community may have been aimed at pleasing liberal and intellectual circles in Western Europe and North America.

Recent moves suggest that the situation is deteriorating, succumbing to the political weight of Cuba's Middle East posture. In mid-1976, visitors returning from Cuba reported the withdrawal of government support for the afternoon Hebrew classes at the Albert Einstein School. Another ominous sign is that the building of the Zionist Center now also houses the office of the Palestine Liberation Organization. Other bureaucratic actions also testify to a tougher policy toward the Jewish community.[34]

Not surprisingly, the Jewish community in Cuba is too small, weak, and dependent to play a meaningful role as a pro-Israel pressure group, as are Jewish communities in most, if not all, the East European Communist countries.

The Rationale Behind Cuba's Involvement

After the October 1973 war the Cubans began to lend more than verbal support to the Arab and Palestinian causes. The Cuban presence in the area had previously been limited to Cuban military personnel assisting the Republic of Southern Yemen.[35] In April 1974 a Cuban military presence in Syria was reported in the press. Later that year, Cubans were also reported on the Island of Perim, which controls the entrance to the Red Sea.[36] Cuban military presence in the Middle East signaled closer coordination of Castro's policy not only with the Arabs, but also, more significantly, with the Soviet Union. Until early 1977 the Soviet and Third World connections were the two major factors shaping Castro's Middle East policy, both pulling in an anti-Israel direction.

Deployment of Cuban regulars in the Middle East should be viewed within the context of Cuba's overall foreign policy objectives and state interests. As of late 1976, Cuban military involvement, ranging from "advisory" functions to combat assignments, was reported in ten foreign countries: eight in Africa and two in the Middle East (Syria and South Yemen).[37]

One of the cardinal goals of Castro's foreign policy, with the possible exception of the years 1967 and 1968, has been to secure and maintain Soviet political and economic support for the Cuban revolutionary regime. During the 1960s, Castro's tactics involved domestic radicalization and attempts to capitalize on Cuba's prestige in revolutionary movements in Latin America and elsewhere in order to extract concessions from the Soviet Union. Important developments in the world, in Latin America, and in Cuba in the latter part of the 1960s caused fundamental changes in Cuba's foreign policy.[38]

Differences with the Soviets had to be thrashed out, and the results crippled Cuba's claim to an autonomous foreign policy. The post-1968 redefinition of the "terms of dependence" on her Soviet patron and the need for a continuing and increased flow of Soviet assistance required that Cuba remain an important strategic and political asset for the Soviet Union, thereby justifying the massive allocation of economic and other aid.

Thus, Cuba continued to provide important services for the Soviets. Her "technicians" and troops were dispatched to remote areas which seemed unrelated to Cuban national interest. In South Yemen, as in the Congo (Brazzaville) and Tanzania, Cubans helped the Soviets fend off or preempt Chinese influence. And, in some highly charged situations in Angola and Syria, the Cuban presence appeared to support Soviet political objectives.

Cuban support of Soviet interests has also been reflected in official pronouncements concerning the Middle East. In his lengthy opening speech delivered to delegates of the first congress of the Communist Party of Cuba (PCC) on December 17, 1975, Castro inserted a brief, though revealing, note. When referring to actions of "the United States, through the Zionist State of Israel" in "that decisive part of the world," Castro expressed his primary concern as to how these "threaten the southern flank of the Soviet Union." Only then came the customary paean to the Arab countries deprived of their occupied territories and to the frustrated national aspirations of the "Palestinian people."[39]

The other Cuban objectives to be reached by military involvement in the Middle East and Africa have been related to its Third World political tactics. Taking active part in conflicts involving Third World nations engaged in struggles against "imperialism" or its "lackeys" (terms used by the Cubans in reference to both the Middle Eastern and Angolan situations) has bolstered Castro's claim for a position of leadership among the nonaligned. Such a claim is all the more important because it disguises the harsh reality of dependence. The apparent dichotomy of "pro-Soviet nonalignment" has been worked out also through the PCC first congress resolutions on foreign policy. There, Cuba is presented as the link between the nonaligned and the Soviet bloc.[40]

Concomitantly, Cuban military expeditions revitalize a sagging revolutionary image. The abandonment of active support for Latin American guerrilla movements, the shift to legitimate bilateral contacts with a growing number of Latin American governments, and the rapprochement with the Soviet Union considerably tarnished Cuba's initial image of revolutionary dynamism. But now, through military involvement overseas, Cuba has returned to the center of the world stage as an activist revolutionary vanguard faithful to its radical commitments.

Developments in 1977

The year 1977 was a time of renewed momentum and further expansion of Cuban involvement within the Middle East proper as well as in the region's immediate, and strategically vital, East African vicinity. The main focus of this activity was the geopolitically pivotal area of the Horn of Africa, controlling the southern approaches of the Red Sea. Several interrelated developments converged in early 1977 to create great political flux in the region. With France planning to grant independence to Djibouti in mid-1977; with tension between Ethiopia and Somalia mounting; and with relations between Addis Ababa and Washington deteriorating—hectic diplomatic and military activity by the global powers (with the initiative clearly in Soviet hands) as well as by rival regional actors was set in motion in an attempt to affect the strategic balance in the area. The March 1977 African tour of Premier Fidel Castro was part of this multiple maneuvering. It started, after a brief stopover in Algiers, with a ten-day visit to Libya, which had drawn closer to the Soviet Union after the falling out between Egypt's President Sadat and the Russians.

Several facts surrounding Fidel's Libyan visit are noteworthy. One is the haste with which the trip was arranged. In early February, Libya's ambassador to Paris arrived in Havana with a message from Qaddafi. On February 25, Fidel's envoy reached Tripoli and on the twenty-eighth Castro's visit was announced. In addition to the unusual duration of the visit, its timing was also revealing. Fidel was the guest star during the inauguration of a Libyan variety of "people's power," which was signified by a symbolic change of the name of the country to the People's Socialist Arab Al-Yamahiria (masses' state) of Libya. More important yet were the international-regional connotations of the visit: It interfered with the Arab-African solidarity conference being hosted at that time by Egypt, and it followed by a few days an important inter-Arab political move, namely, the meeting of presidents Sadat, Assad, and Numeiri in Khartoum. The Syrian movement toward closing ranks with two "avowed enemies" of Libya, and Libya's conspicuous absence from the Arab-African conference in Cairo, accentuated Libya's isolation. That sentiment, no doubt, prompted Castro's public reassurance to his hosts that "the efforts made by the imperialists to isolate Libya don't matter! ... Libya is not isolated nor will it be."[41] A subtle criticism of Syria was further reflected in a clause addressing the situation in Lebanon, contained in the joint communiqué issued at the conclusion of the visit. It denounced "any foreign intervention" in the Lebanese crisis, an unmistakable allusion to Syria's role, particularly its attempt to keep the Palestinian organizations at bay.[42]

Concerning Cuba's stand on the fighting in Lebanon, it should be noted that while close liaison with Palestinian organizations has continued (for

YORAM SHAPIRA

example, the January 1977 visit of Nayef Hawatmeh, head of the Democratic Front for the Liberation of Palestine, to Havana[43]), the Cubans have carefully refrained from any initiative that would affect the already delicate Soviet-Syrian relations, strained by Assad's moves to control the Palestinian militants as well as by his seemingly improving relations with the U.S.

After paying a short visit to the People's Democratic Republic of Yemen, his veteran outpost in the Red Sea area, Castro went to Somalia, until that time Moscow's closest ally in black Africa. His next, and surprising, stopover was Ethiopia, with whose leaders he conferred in what has been widely interpreted as a Soviet-inspired effort to mediate between Ethiopia and Somalia. Evidently the mediation attempt failed, but consequently the U.S. military presence in Ethiopia (bases, a military assistance program) was rapidly phased out, and the Soviet Union stepped in, still managing to maintain its influence with its older East African client. Later, after full scale hostilities between Ethiopia and Somalia had erupted in mid-July, low profile presence of Cuban military instructors and medical personnel in Ethiopia was reported.[44]

Cuban diplomatic and military involvement (the latter initially in an advisory capacity) in support of the Soviet diplomatic offensive in East Africa and the Red Sea area has obviously been appended to great power rivalry over influence in a volatile region that controls a major world maritime route and much of the Middle East oil traffic. It has also directly concerned the states of the Red Sea littoral. The Arab countries' intense interest in the issue has been aroused primarily by security and political considerations related to their conflict with Israel, and by their desire to prove their value to the United States by countering Soviet advances in the area. After being dormant for some time, this interest was reactivated due largely to the developments cited above. It came to the fore in two consecutive Arab summit meetings held in late February and late March 1977. The first (mentioned above) took place in Khartoum and was attended by the leaders of Egypt, Syria, and Sudan, enjoying the blessing of Saudi Arabia. It was followed by a meeting in Taizz of North and South Yemen, Sudan, and Somalia, to coordinate activities in the Red Sea "in the face of Israeli aggression."[45] A major objective of the Arab trust has been the conversion of the Red Sea into an "Arab lake." This could be achieved by enlisting the cooperation of newly independent Djibouti, which indicated an early interest in joining the Arab League,[46] and by assisting the Moslem Eritrean secessionist movement in its drive for independence. If such a scheme succeeded, Ethiopia might become a land-locked country, losing not only its Red Sea ports of Massawa and Assab, but a substantial portion of its national territory as well. For Israel, Arab control of the Red Sea would mean a constant threat to its trade with Africa and Asia, and, more significant at the present, to oil supplies imported mainly via Eilat, Israel's Red Sea port. Such a position would give the Arabs extra leverage in any negotiations for a Middle East settlement, as well as in a case of actual hostilities. It should be recalled that two of the four Arab-Israeli wars were triggered by attempts to block shipping bound for Eilat. Consequently, the continued territorial integrity of Ethiopia, the only other non-Moslem state on the Red Sea, has long been considered by Israel to be of vital importance to its national security.

The intersection of multiple rivalries and the convergence of distinct national interests gave rise to an unforeseen juxtaposition of forces. Momentarily at least, the desire to assist Ethiopia in its present plight has created unlikely partners. While Israel, although deeply concerned about Soviet aims, hopes to see Ethiopia prevail (and as some sources suggest is actually assisting it[47]), the Arabs, including client states of the Soviet Union like Syria and Iraq, have been actively helping Somalia, the irridentist "Western Somali Liberation Front," and apparently the Eritrean separatists.[48] That is, all the Arabs except Libya. Libya, the most vocally intransigent of Israel's foes, because of its feud with Sudan and Egypt, exercises leverage politics through aid to Ethiopia which, in turn, has been embroiled in a territorial, ethnic, and religious conflict of its own with the Sudanese. The USSR, along with it Caribbean helper, has been trying to provide simultaneous support for old and new allies who are now bitterly fighting each other. Its goal is to further expand Soviet influence and become the dominant foreign power in the area.

While these developments, on the whole, reiterate established patterns of Cuban activity, led and coordinated by the Soviets, they also reveal a fledgeling incongruence between pro-Soviet and Third World politicking (tercermundismo). There is little doubt that with the 1977 involvements, the makers of Cuban foreign policy have been realizing, probably for the first time in recent years, that some of their newest ventures in the region are, diplomatically, far less productive than others, and that Soviet and Third World priorities may not always coincide. Viewed politically and diplomatically, rather than militarily, a rough distinction can be drawn. In the category of more successful involvements are the Cuban assistance to the Syrians following the 1973 October War and the unwavering support for the militant Palestinian organizations against Israel. Pertaining thematically, although not geographically, to this cluster are the involvements in Angola and in the Rhodesian question. The common denominator of the episodes in this group, accounting for their positive diplomatic and propagandistic impact on Third World governments, is that they rested on a wide consensus uniting either the Arab world or most of the black African countries.

Taking an active part in other regional conflicts, however, proved more costly for tercermundismo. To this second category belong involvements such as Cuba's siding with Algeria and the Polisario against Morocco and Mauritania in the four-sided struggle over the former Spanish Sahara; her deepening association with Libya in clear defiance of Egypt,[49] Sudan, and even Chad; and Castro's reported assistance to Ethiopia in that country's struggle against Somalia and internal separatist pulls. The common feature of the conflicts in this group is that they represent struggles that are not as obviously "anti-imperialist" or "progressive" as those in the first category, primarily because they have involved Third World nations on both sides of the warring camps.

The growing number of Cuban entanglements in conflicts of the second type indicates a widening gap between tercermundismo and pro-Moscow politicking. It also attests to Cuba's readiness to pay the diplomatic price incurred by antagonizing a number of Arab and African nations and to give clear priority to considerations related to Cuban-Soviet relations.

NOTES

This is an expanded version of a paper presented at the international conference on The Role of Cuba in World Affairs held at the University of Pittsburgh, November 15-17, 1976.

1. *Haaretz,* February 26, 1960; "Impression from a Visit to Cuba," *Davar,* November 4, 1960.

2. Interview with the organizer of the 1961 Cuban Jewish emigration to Israel, Israel, February 1976.

3. See also Gertrude Miller, "The Cuban Connection," *Jerusalem Post,* September 14, 1973.

4. This provoked Ben Bella into canceling Castro's proposed state visit to Algeria. Latin American Jewish Congress, *Information Bulletin* (Buenos Aires) (hereafter cited as *OJI*), no. 186 (September 12, 1973).

5. Fabio Grobart, who worked behind the scenes during most of his career, was publicly honored by the assignment of nominating Fidel Castro as first secretary of the Communist party at its first congress in 1975. Furthermore, Fidel warmly praised Grobart during a speech at a mass rally at the closing of the congress, mentioning his historic role and referring to him as "a tailor by trade, Polish by birth and citizen of the world, like all Communists." *Granma Weekly Review*, January 11, 1976, p. 7.

Carlos Rafael Rodríguez is a leading member of the Cuban political elite, a close confidant of Fidel Castro's, and one of five persons holding positions both in the PCC's Politburo and the Secretariat. His sympathies toward Israel developed through his contacts with Hashomer Hatzair in the late 1940s.

6. Interview with I. Silber, Israel, 1976.

7. Interview with an Israeli diplomat serving in Cuba during the period under discussion, Jerusalem, September 1976.

8. For the text of the draft resolution, see *Israel un tema para la izquierda,* 2d ed., rev. (Buenos Aires: Editorial Nueva Sión, 1968), pp. 218-19.

9. *Israel un tema,* p. 290.

10. Quoted from the official Cuban government translation in *Latin American Radicalism,* ed. Irving Louis Horowitz, Josue de Castro, and John Garassi (New York: Vintage Books, 1969), p. 565.

11. *Israel un tema,* p. 291.

12. Ibid.

13. K. S. Karol, *Guerrillas in Power* (London: Jonathan Cape, 1971), p. 400. See also Andrew Salkey, *Havana Journal* (London: Penguin Books, 1971), p. 208.

14. See, for example, the Syrian-Cuban communiqué issued while a Cuban delegation, headed by Armando Hart, visited Syria, July 1968, *Granma,* July 29, 1968.

15. See the joint communiqué issued during a visit by Castro to Guinea, *Granma,* May 14, 1972.

16. See the editorial by A. Zapata, *Granma*, June 5, 1969, on the second anniversary of the Six-Day War. His closing sentence reads: "As long as the voice of the Palestinian combatants—carried in the fire of their AK-10s, bazookas and mortars—is not heeded and respected, there will be no solution in the Middle East." The armed forces journal was never far behind in its virulent anti-Israel stance; see "Barbarie de los ocupantes," *Verde Olivo* 13, no. 12, March 21, 1971.

17. See "Sadat Convenes Defence Council to Discuss US Aid to Israel," *Haaretz,* November 22, 1970.

18. For Cuban commentators, the Jewish prestate underground organizations, such as the Hagana and what they label "Stern," were merely "paramilitary and terrorist organizations dividing their activities between sabotaging the British occupation forces in Palestine and harassing the Arab population." See *Bohemia,* November 15, 1968, p. 84.

19. The Cuban ideological perception of the Palestinian armed movement is well presented in "Olor a polvora," by Carlos Lechuga, in *Bohemia,* March 8, 1968.

20. See R. Casals, "El pueblo palestino no se rendirá ni se someterá a los designos del imperialismo yankui y el sionismo," *Granma,* September 18, 1972.

21. Robert Peters, in *Frankfurter Allgemeine Zeitung,* quoted in *OJI,* no. 232, (September 13, 1974).

22. Miller, "Cuban Connection." This has been corroborated in several interviews conducted by the author.

23. *El Mundo* (Cuba), July 3, 1968.

24. Joseph Harif and Dan Arkin in *Maariv,* September 10, 1973.

25. Harif, in *Maariv.* Another Israeli nongovernment source, familiar with Cuban affairs, expressed the belief that the motivation was economic, but this has not been substantiated. See *OJI,* no. 186 (September 12, 1973).

26. *Granma,* as quoted in *Maariv,* September 12, 1973.

27. See, for instance, Tony Fernandez, "Zionism: A Form of Racism and Racial Discrimination," *Granma,* November 17, 1975. It ends with the statement: "Zionism is an enemy of social progress and mankind in general." Later, in an issue listing the important world events of 1975, *Granma* did not neglect to mention the anti-Zionist U.N. General Assembly resolution (*Granma Weekly Review,* January 18, 1976).

28. See reference to "the racist structure of the Israeli Zionist regime that is occupying Palestine," *Granma Weekly Review,* January 18, 1976, p. 11. In his speech at the General Assembly, Cuba's ambassador to the U.N. referred to "the full exercise by the Palestinian people of their inalienable right to self-determination, independence and sovereignty over their usurped territory." Quoted in *Granma Weekly Review,* October 27, 1975.

29. See *Granma Weekly Review,* November 24, 1974, and December 1, 1974.

30. As reflected conspicuously by the constant Cuban effort to use that arena to denounce the concept that there are "two imperialisms" (that is, of the United States and the Soviet Union).

31. J. Barromi and C. Feldman, "Latin American Voting on Israeli Issues in the U.N. General Assembly, 1947–1968," *Jewish Social Studies,* 36, no. 2 (April 1974), 142–65.

32. On Castro's attitude toward the Jewish community, see Miller, "Cuban Connection," and Paul Jacobs, in *Maariv,* May 14, 1973.

33. Based on a report concerning the Jewish community of Cuba prepared by a functionary of a non-Cuban Jewish organization (name withheld) who visited Havana in 1975.

34. Report of a visitor, name withheld, made available to the author.

35. Israeli Broadcasting Commission (Hebrew News), March 10, 1973; *Maariv,* April 18, 1973.

36. *Washington Post,* as quoted in *Maariv,* October 14, 1974.

37. As to the exact size and nature of the Cuban units deployed in Syria, there are several versions. An Israeli government source, quoted in late December 1975, maintained that a Cuban armored brigade that had been stationed in Syria for two years was apparently sent to Angola some time in 1975. This contingent of four thousand men was airlifted to Syria shortly after the 1973 October war and took part in the "war of attrition" that lasted until May 1974. See *Haaretz,* December 24, 1975. This information was rectified later by "informed Israeli sources" who maintained that all Cuban troops were pulled out of Syria except for "some advisers." According to this version, however, the Cuban unit was an infantry brigade with mechanized elements; it arrived in Syria in 1974, did not take part in any fighting, and left the same year. Still, the Cubans were the only non-Arab force of that size in Syria. See *Jerusalem Post,* February 18, 1976. On February 24, Defence Minister S. Peres told the Israeli Knesset that the Cuban force in Syria, consisting of soldiers

manning a tank brigade, returned home after being stationed on the Golan Heights front for about a year and a half (*Jerusalem Post*, February 2, 1976). Another version was given by *Time*, February 23, 1976 (armored brigade, two commando battalions, and MiG pilots). According to *Time*, these forces were still in Syria at the time of the report. *U.S. News & World Report* (December 8, 1975) reported much smaller numbers.

38. For an in-depth analysis of internal and external developments and their impact on Cuba's foreign policy and relations with the Soviet Union during the 1960s, see three articles by Edward Gonzalez: "Castro's Revolution, Cuban Communist Appeals, and the Soviet Response," *World Politics* 21 (October 1968), 39–68; "Castro: The Limits of Charisma," *Problems of Communism* 19 (July–August 1970), 12–24; and "A Comparison of Soviet and Cuban Approaches to Latin America," *Studies in Comparative Communism* 5 (Spring 1972), 21–35.

39. *Granma Weekly Review* (English version), January 4, 1976, p. 10.

40. "Resolution of the First Congress of the Communist Party of Cuba on Foreign Policy," *Granma Weekly Review*, January 25, 1976, p. 10.

41. Speech delivered by Fidel Castro on March 9 in Tripoli. *Granma Weekly Review*, March 20, 1977.

42. Libyan-Cuban joint communiqué. *Granma Weekly Review*, March 20, 1977.

43. *Granma Weekly Review*, January 16, 1977.

44. *Newsweek*, August 29, 1977. The numbers of Cubans cited by this source are 110 medical personnel and 50 military advisors training the militia.

45. *Haaretz*, March 24, 1977.

46. *Haaretz*, June 29, 1977.

47. See "Israelis, Out of Favor in Africa, Still Find Home in Ethiopia," *Washington Post*, October 1, 1977.

48. See David Ottaway, "Moscow Finding it Hard to Satisfy Both Ethiopia, Somalia." *Washington Post*, September 27, 1977; and the statement of the leader of the Western Somali Liberation Front cited in *Newsweek*, August 29, 1977. In an interview published by *Granma*, Ethiopia's Mengistu Haile Mariam claimed: "The Sudanese Government supports the so-called Eritrean Liberation Front—which was set up some time ago—and provides it with offices, medical supplies and weapons." *Granma Weekly Review*, March 27, 1977.

49. The Egyptian press claimed that Cubans were fighting alongside the Libyans during the July 1977 border clash with Egypt. *Haaretz*, July 31, 1977.

II CUBA'S ECONOMIC ROLE IN WORLD AFFAIRS

9

CARMELO MESA-LAGO

The Economy and International Economic Relations

This chapter will examine in detail the current and planned capacity of the Cuban economy as well as the island's ongoing international economic relations as bases for analysis and prediction of Cuba's economic performance and changes in her foreign trade during the rest of the decade. The chapter is divided into two sections. The first considers the past, current, and future capacity of the Cuban economy. The crucial question here is whether Cuba, after the dramatic reorganization of its economy in the early 1970s, is capable of generating a sufficient surplus to both honor past export commitments and expand exports in the near future. The second section analyzes the structure of Cuba's foreign commerce in the 1960s and 1970s—volume of trade, composition of exports and imports, trade partners. This information in turn permits an analysis of: the actual degree of Cuban dependency on the USSR and other socialist countries; possibilities for Cuba's changing that dependency in the future; and (if that shift is possible) which market economies could be potential trade partners. This chapter provides a basis for the following one which explores the possibilities and economic effects of U.S.-Cuban rapprochement.

The Capacity of the Cuban Economy: Past, Present, and Future

In the tradition of the "dismal science," the story of Cuban economic performance in the decade of the 1960s is, in general, a dreary one. The radical transformation of both the domestic economic structure and international economic relations, the numerous changes in economic policy and development strategy (for example, the initial neglect of the sugar industry and the later imposition of grandiose sugar output targets, or the attempt to apply mechanistically the Soviet model of planning and economic organization followed by an enchantment with the Sino-Guevarist dream of the "New Man"), the embargo imposed upon the island, and the crucial errors of the policy makers resulted in a virulent combination.[1]

Table 9.1, a compilation of official Cuban statistics published during the last six years, gives an overall view of trends in economic growth. The table, however, presents four serious problems for an accurate analysis. (1) Cuba uses the Soviet methodology for national accounts, which makes comparisons with 169

CARMELO MESA-LAGO

TABLE 9.1
Indicators of Economic Growth in Cuba, 1962–1975
(in constant 1965 prices for 1962–1966; in current prices for 1967–1975)

	Global Social Product		Gross Material Product		Industrial Product	
	Million pesos	Growth rate	Million pesos	Growth rate	Million pesos	Growth rate
1962[a]	6,082.1	—	3,698.2	—	2,746.2	—
1963	6,013.2	− 1.1%	3,736.7	1.0%	2,700.7	− 1.7%
1964	6,454.5	7.3	4,076.4	9.0	2,813.5	4.2
1965	6,770.9	4.9	4,137.5	1.5	2,913.0	3.5
1966	6,709.3	− 1.0	3,985.5	− 3.7	2,858.5	− 1.9
1967	7,211.6	—	4,082.8	—	3,185.1	—
1968	7,330.9	1.6	4,376.5	7.2	3,129.9	− 1.8
1969	7,236.1	− 1.3	4,180.6	− 4.5	3,178.0	1.5
1970	8,356.5	15.4	4,203.9	0.6	4,000.3	25.9
1971	8,966.5	7.3	4,821.8	14.7	4,177.0	4.4
1972	10,417.9	16.2	6,041.2	25.3	4,458.3	6.7
1973	11,921.8	14.4	6,712.3	11.1	4,988.3	11.9
1974	13,423.5	12.5	7,414.1	10.5	5,393.1	8.1
1975	15,047.7[b]	12.1[b]	—	—	6,007.9	11.4
Average 1962–69		1.7		1.8		0.6
Per capita[c]		− 0.4		− 0.3		− 1.5
Average 1970–75		13.0		12.4		11.4
Per capita[c]		11.3		10.7		9.7

Sources: República de Cuba, Junta Central de Planificación, Dirección Central de Estadística, BE Boletín Estadístico 1966 (Havana, 1969), p. 20; idem., BE Boletín Estadístico 1971 (Havana, 1973), pp. 44–45; idem., Anuario Estadístico de Cuba 1972 (Havana, 1974), pp. 30–31; idem., Anuario Estadístico de Cuba 1973 (Havana, 1975), p. 35; idem., Anuario Estadístico de Cuba 1974 (Havana, n.d.), p. 35 and "Fe de erratas"; Economía y Desarrollo, no. 32 (November–December 1975), pp. 193, 197; and Comité Estatal de Estadística, La economía cubana, 1975 (Havana, n.d.), I-3.
   a. The year 1962 was a year of severe recession, probably the trough in the period 1959–1975. In his report to the first congress of the Communist Party of Cuba, Castro gave the average annual rate of GSP growth in 1961–1965 as 1.9 percent. We know that 1961 was a good economic year; assuming a moderate rate of growth of 4.5 percent for that year, the decline in 1962 may be estimated at −8 percent.
   b. Excludes commerce.
   c. The average annual rate of population growth was 2.1 percent in 1962–1969 and 1.7 percent in 1970–1975.

the Western concept of gross national product (GNP) extremely difficult. The Cuban gross material product (GMP) is smaller than the western GNP because it excludes the value of transportation, communication, and commerce and of services not directly connected to production. On the other hand, the Cuban global social product (GSP) includes the value of transportation, communications, and commerce but excludes the value of services such as education, health, housing, public administration, and personal services. GSP is therefore larger than GMP, but usually it is also larger than GNP because of considerable duplicate counting in the GSP aggregation process.[2] (2) The table omits the period of steady economic growth from 1959 to 1961 and starts with the recessive years 1962–1963. Hence growth rates in the table are related to a trough instead of to a normal starting year. (3) Figures for 1962–1966 are given in constant prices—hence deflated—while figures for 1967–1975 are in current prices and thus affected by inflation. (4) Data for 1970–1975, published in 1975–1977, were not linked to the previous historical series and their form of presentation was somewhat modified. Questions arise as to whether some of these data are in current or constant prices.

According to the table, in 1962–1969 and in absolute terms, GSP increased at an annual average rate of 1.7 percent, GMP at 1.8 percent, and the industrial product (IP) at 0.6 percent. In per capita terms, GSP and GMP declined at an average yearly rate of 0.3 to 0.4 percent, and IP declined at 1.5 percent. If the whole series had been calculated in constant prices (available only for 1962–1966), the rates would have been considerably lower: in terms of GSP per capita, possibly −0.9 percent in 1962–1969.[3]

In 1970 the Cubans had a record sugar harvest which according to table 9.1 gave a significant boost to GSP. However, official information from Cuba reported a sharp decline in the nonsugar output and a general dislocation of the economy reflected in table 9.1 by an almost stagnant GMP. These were some of the main factors that caused the Cuban government to return, in the first half of the 1970s, to the conventional Soviet model of economic organization: Technocrats took over from idealists, central planning was reintroduced, cybernetics began to be applied to planning and management, material incentives were revived and rapidly expanded, emphasis was placed on increasing both capital efficiency and labor productivity, and a more rational sugar policy was designed with targets that could be achieved realistically without depleting resources of other sectors of the economy. The Soviets helped also by raising the price paid for Cuba's two main exports (sugar and nickel), deferring for thirteen years the payment of the Cuban debt accrued to them in 1960–1972, and granting additional credits and trade subsidies in 1973–1975.[4] These positive changes were enhanced by an unexpected cornucopia: The price of sugar in the international market increased sixteenfold, from 4 cents per pound in 1970 to a record-breaking 65.5 cents in November 1974. Western credit was generously open to Cuba, thus facilitating imports and giving additional impetus to the boom.

As a result of these improvements, in the first half of the 1970s the Cuban economy performed very well. According to table 9.1, average yearly rates of growth in 1970–1975, in absolute terms, were 13.0 percent in GSP, 12.4 percent in GMP, and 11.4 percent in IP. In per capita terms (favored by a slowdown in population growth), rates were 11.3 percent in GSP, 10.7 in GMP, and 9.7 in IP. These figures are in current prices; the Junta Central de Planificación (JUCEPLAN) has recently released figures, probably at constant prices, which show GSP absolute rates at 10.1 percent and per capita rates at 8.4 percent for the same

CARMELO MESA-LAGO

period.[5] Trying to avoid the problems discussed above (but creating probably as many new problems), U.S. intelligence sources have converted Cuban figures for 1970–1975 into the equivalent of real GNP, calculating absolute rates of only 2.7 percent and per capita rates of 0.6 percent.[6] All in all, the Cuban rates of 1970–1975 probably constitute a record in the Revolution's history (growth rates in 1910–1920, during another sugar boom, were higher) and rank among the highest in Latin America during these years.[7]

Tables 9.2 and 9.3 show the magnitude and fluctuations in output of Cuba's most important agricultural and industrial products, both for export and domestic consumption, in 1957–1975. In agriculture, the production of sugar, tobacco, and citrus fruits is fundamental to foreign trade. Average annual sugar production

TABLE 9.2
Physical Output of Selected Agricultural Products in Cuba, 1957–1975[a]
(in thousand metric tons)

	Sugar	Tobacco	Citrus Fruits	Rice[b]	Yucca	Malanga	Eggs[c]	Coffee
1957	5,742	42	111	261	186	91	275	44
1958	5,863	51	70	253	213	226	315	30
1959	6,039	36	70	326	224	240	341	48
1960	5,943	45	73	323	255	257	430	42
1961	6,876	58	91	207	155	77	580	48
1962	4,882	52	117	207	162	60	660	52
1963	3,882	48	110	204	90	45	750	35
1964	4,474	44	119	124	73	43	830	32
1965	6,156	43	116	50	62	47	920	24
1966	4,537	52	160	68	93	71	1,019	33
1967	6,236	45	144	94	49	42	1,178	34
1968	5,164	46	165	95	53	43	1,205	29
1969	4,459	36	155	177	37	35	1,289	32
1970	8,538	32	164	291	22	12	1,426	20
1971	5,925	25	124	286	27	14	1,509	26
1972	4,325	40	162	239	65	26	1,532	25
1973	5,253	44	176	237	73	20	1,598	21
1974	5,925	45	176	309	70	26	1,688	29
1975	6,200	43	199	338	83	32	1,770	—

Sources: Carmelo Mesa-Lago, ed., Revolutionary Change in Cuba (Pittsburgh: University of Pittsburgh Press, 1971), pp. 288–89; updated with República de Cuba, Junta Central de Planificación, Dirección Central de Estadística, BE Boletín Estadístico 1968 (Havana, 1970); idem., BE Boletín Estadístico 1970 (Havana, 1971), BE 1971, Anuario 1972, Anuario 1973, Anuario 1974; Banco Nacional de Cuba, Desarrollo y perspectivas de la economía cubana (Havana, 1975); and La economía cubana, 1975.
a. Since approximately 1963, figures for various products (sugar is an exception) refer to acopio on both state and private farms, excluding farmers' consumption, and a small amount of barter and sales.
b. Milled rice as reported by JUCEPLAN. Another series published by the Banco Nacional reports paddy or unmilled rice, hence its figures are considerably higher.
c. Million units. Probably total production. Another series (acopio) shows smaller figures. Still a third series (not defined) shows higher figures.

in 1959–1975 was 5.5 million tons, fluctuating between 3.9 million tons in 1963 and 8.5 million tons in 1970. There is a very low possibility of repeating a harvest similar to that of 1970 in the second half of the 1970s. Nevertheless, the current five-year plan (1976–1980) calls for an increase of sugar output to reach from 8.0 to 8.7 million tons by 1980 through the following improvements: expansion in the cultivated and irrigated area of sugar cane, the replanting of all sugar-cane areas with higher yielding seed, augmented use of fertilizers and pesticides, significant advances in mechanization of the harvest (60 percent of cutting and 100 percent of lifting the cane), modernization and construction of sugar mills, modernization of refineries and railroad transportation, and an increase in qualified personnel.[8] In view of recent performance, a more realistic target for 1980 is probably 7.5 million tons, providing that most planned improvements materialize.

Poor crops were not the only problem that the sugar industry faced in the 1960s: Low prices in the international market were the other side of the coin. The combination of the two variables worked against the Cubans; whenever they had a good crop, prices were low and, conversely, when prices were high, they had a poor crop. Thus, the harvests of 1959, 1961, 1965, and 1967 yielded above 6 million tons but international market prices were from 2 to 3 cents per pound, and most of the 1970 crop of 8.5 million tons was sold at 4 cents per pound. In 1963, the price was 8 cents per pound, but the sugar harvest reached only 3.9 million tons. (The two variables are, of course, interrelated to a good extent. Cuba was the largest world exporter of sugar in this period; thus a substantial decline in its sugar output reduced the world supply and pushed prices upward.)[9]

In the first half of the 1970s a series of factors combined to favor Cuba. World demand for sugar increased, sugar harvests in the United States declined, Cuba's output and export of sugar remained stagnant and at a low level, and world inflation reached unparalleled heights. The net result was a phenomenal increase in the price of sugar from 4 cents (annual average) in 1970 to 5 cents in 1971, 7 cents in 1972, 10 cents in 1973, and 30 cents in 1974. Cuba could not take full advantage of the escalation in international market prices because more than half (3.2 million tons) of its 1974 sugar crop was committed for export to socialist countries at a price set at 11 cents per pound by the 1972 agreements. In August 1974, however, the USSR increased the price paid for Cuban sugar to about 20 cents per pound, perhaps retroactively.[10] This loss of 10 cents per pound for Cuba was partly compensated by the lower prices of oil charged by the USSR to the island. Eastern Europe and China paid even less for Cuban sugar (probably an average of 17 cents per pound) with a loss to the Cubans of 13 cents a pound. The rest of the crop (more than 2 million tons) was sold to Japan and the West at international market prices.

As a result of a slowdown in the growth of world demand for sugar, a significant increase in the sugar-cane and sugar-beet supply, and the expanded output and consumption of sugar substitutes, the international market price of sugar fell in 1975 to an average of 24 cents per pound, 14 cents by the end of the

CARMELO MESA-LAGO

year.[11] The Cuban sugar crop of 1975 was 6.2 million tons; thus the Cubans could still sell more than 2 million tons to the international market at a very good price. In 1976, the sugar crop declined to an estimated 6 million tons and the price of sugar went down further to 8 cents per pound. Although this price was still more than twice the average price paid in the 1960s, spiraling inflation and increasing production costs considerably reduced both sugar revenue and profits. The USSR again came to the rescue of Cuba, agreeing to pay 30 cents per pound of sugar in 1976-1980 and to buy 200,000 tons more a year at that price in that period.[12] Other socialist countries began to pay prices above the world market price but below the Soviet subsidized price. In 1977, the sugar crop was affected by insufficient rainfall during the growing season and by heavy rainfall at the start of the harvest. Estimated crop output fluctuates between 4.5 and 6.2 million tons, while the world market price had declined to about 7 cents per pound.[13]

The combination of small sugar crops, plummeting sugar prices, and skyrocketing prices of imports and fuel deeply affected the Cuban economy in 1976-1977. Castro claimed that the price of 7 cents per pound was below production cost and similar—in purchasing power—to the depressed price of sugar during the Great Depression. As a result, Castro said, the goals of the five-year plan were negatively affected and restrictions had to be imposed, such as curtailment of imports and reduction of food rations. And yet he stated that an "anti-sugar attitude" will not be allowed, that his country will "stick to sugar" and avoid cleaning sugar-cane land to plant other crops because of the comparative advantages of sugar.[14] (Another factor that may have hurt the economy in this period was the heavy drain on scarce Cuban resources imposed by the operations in Angola. Troops, weapons, and equipment were transported mainly by sea, using part of the merchant marine[15] and probably the fishing fleet, which had a negative impact on fishing output and the movement of foreign trade. Although the USSR provided the weapons and may have subsidized other operations, Cuba had to send thousands of technicians and skilled workers to Angola—even truck drivers—which aggravated the shortage of qualified personnel in the island and created serious bottlenecks in production.)[16]

The previous discussion illustrates the degree to which the Cuban economy is intertwined with the performance of sugar in the international market. A forecast of Cuba's future economic performance, therefore, needs to be based on an analysis of negative and positive factors that may affect sugar prices. On the negative side, there is a substantial rise in the world supply of sugar resulting from steady increases in the production of sugar cane and beet and the development of sugar substitutes. Combined with high sugar stocks and sluggish demand, this has provoked the declining price trend. World production has steadily risen from 74 million tons in 1972 to 88 million tons in 1977, an 8 percent jump over 1976. Leading producers have either increased their output in 1977 or plan to do so by 1980: The USSR produced between 7 and 8 million tons and plans to reach 11 million tons and 96 percent self-sufficiency; Cuba probably produced 6 million tons and plans to reach 8 to 8.7 million tons;[17] Brazil has steadily increased its output to more than 7 million tons and plans to continue this rising trend. Production of a sugar substitute, fructose derived from corn, began in 1974. It has steadily increased to almost one million tons in 1977 and is expected to reach almost 2 million tons by 1980.[18] Record sugar prices in 1973–1974 resulted in a decline in world demand in 1975, while declining prices in 1975–1977 generated a weak recuperation of demand in 1976 (below the 1974 peak) and a slight increase in 1977. World stocks of sugar have jumped from a low of 19.6 percent of total output in 1974 to an estimated 29.4 percent in 1977. This has been the result of excess supply over demand combined with stockpiling by exporters and speculators hoping for higher prices. Based on these trends the gloomy forecast calls for a further dip of sugar prices in the near future.

On the positive side, the current low sugar price, if truly below production costs, should eventually force cuts in output, a decline in supply, and a subsequent increase in price; in addition, a cartel of producers, a new international sugar agreement, and/or the reinstitution of U.S. import quotas may push prices up. Sugar producers claim that although current sugar prices are twice as high as 1950–1960 prices, in terms of purchasing power they are substantially lower. Furthermore, they argue, production costs are almost twice what they were, due to the phenomenal jump in the price of certain inputs such as oil and machinery. The expectation is that sugar prices have already gone below any acceptable minimum and that prices will increase and stabilize at 9 to 12 cents in 1978–1980.[19] A Latin American and Caribbean Sugar Exporting Group (GEPLACEA) was established in 1974 with the goal of creating a cartel to fix a minimum price for sugar. No significant progress has been achieved so far due to the reluctance of large producers such as Brazil and the Dominican Republic.[20] Attempts to revive the International Sugar Agreement (ISA) both in 1973 and the spring of 1977 failed. The spring 1977 meeting broke up due to the disagreement between producer and consumer countries on three issues: the level and financing of stocks, the level of minimum and maximum prices, and the assignment of export quotas. But in October 1977 a new meeting, held in Geneva, agreed on a minimum sugar price of 11 cents per pound and a maximum price of 20 cents.[21] Since imported sugar was being sold in the United States below domestic sugar producing costs, the U.S. government first considered establishing an import tax and finally decided, in 1977, to subsidize domestic producers setting the internal price at 13.5 cents.[22] The import quota system, dismissed in 1974, is now being reconsidered and, if adopted, will help to stabilize sugar prices.

Production of two other agricultural goods important to Cuba's exports is uneven. As table 9.2 shows, tobacco output reached a record high in 1961 but gradually declined to less than one-half in 1971, a year in which it was reported that 40 percent of the tobacco crop was lost due to drought. The 1972–1974 harvests showed strong recuperation, possibly aided by good weather and the use of a new higher yielding variety of tobacco. The Cubans had claimed that the 1961 record would be repeated in 1975 but apparently there was a slight decline in output in that year. Production of citrus fruits increased steadily to 1966 when the output was more than double that of 1958-1959; in the following seven years production was stagnant, but new records were set by the harvests of both 1973 and 1975.

Production of agricultural products for domestic consumption had a rather poor performance with few exceptions. Rice, a staple in the Cuban diet, declined in 1961-1963 and dipped further in 1964-1965 due to the conversion of rice fields into sugar plantations. The Cubans then alleged that they could earn much more cultivating sugar and trading it for rice from China; the 1966 quarrel with China, however, resulted in a reduction of rice imports, and rice fields were again expanded. There was a steady increase in production in 1966-1970 followed by a decline in 1971-1973 and a recuperation in 1974-1975 that reached the level of 1959-1960. But drought affected output in 1976. Domestic production of rice satisfies half the consumption needs, the other half was imported mostly from China at least until 1975. Production of tubers (yucca, malanga), another important staple in the Cuban diet, peaked in 1960 but declined until 1970 with a slight recuperation therafter; output in 1975 was 33 percent (yucca) and 12 percent (malanga) of the 1960 levels. Production of coffee reached its apex in 1962 and declined thereafter. Due to severe drought, coffee output in 1975-1976 reached a record low, about one-third of the 1962 mark. Large amounts of coffee imported in 1973-1975 could not be imported in 1976 due to high prices, hence a further cut in the coffee ration took place. The only major agricultural product that has had an excellent performance is eggs, with a steady increase throughout the Revolution: production in 1975 was more than five-and-a-half times higher than in 1958.

Table 9.3 shows the performance of selected industrial products. The main exports are nickel and fish. Both are capital-intensive, dynamic sectors, with modern equipment; their significance in exports has slowly increased. Cuba is the third largest exporter of nickel in the world, the fifth largest producer, and has the fourth largest reserves of this metal. The nickel industry suffered a serious blow in 1960-1961 due to the exodus of U.S. and Cuban technicians, problems with spare parts, and the lack of Soviet know-how in the advanced technology of the American plants. But by 1963, these problems had been overcome and the prerevolutionary output level recuperated; production increased thereafter, stabilizing at about 36,000 metric tons in 1968-1975, about twice the output of 1958. The Soviet Union and the Council for Mutual Economic Assistance (COMECON) established credit for $600 million for Cuba to expand nickel facilities and increase production by 60,000 metric tons by 1980, for a total output close to 100,000 tons, probably too ambitious a goal. In 1972, the USSR increased the price paid for a ton of Cuban nickel to $5,450, while the market price was $3,500 per ton. (For 1976-1980, the Soviet price was set at $6,000 a ton, while the international market price in 1976 was about $4,000 a ton.)[23] Fish and shellfish are possibly the most successful economic venture of Revolutionary Cuba. Output steadily increased, reaching 165,000 metric tons in 1974, eight

TABLE 9.3
Physical Output of Selected Industrial Products in Cuba, 1957–1975

	Nickel (thousand metric tons)	Fish (thousand metric tons)	Electricity (million kwh)	Cement (thousand metric tons)	Beer (thousand hectolitres)	Cigarettes (millions)	Cigars (millions)	Refrigerators (units)
1957	20	22	2,357	673	1,292	9,803	—	—
1958	18	22	2,589	736	1,232	10,197	628	—
1959	18	27	2,806	673	1,557	11,434	591	—
1960	13	31	2,981	813	—	—	—	—
1961	15	30	3,030	871	1,394	13,611	—	—
1962	17	35	2,998	779	927	14,400	—	—
1963	20	36	3,057	812	891	15,346	369	—
1964	23	36	3,250	806	1,036	16,015	615	1,093
1965	28	40	3,387	801	993	16,462	657	11,871
1966	27	43	3,625	750	1,088	18,455	623	1,711
1967	32	63	4,068	835	1,360	19,627	727	730
1968	37	65	4,162	780	784	21,756	724	19
1969	35	80	4,366	679	659	25,145	422	2,080
1970	37	106	4,888	742	1,001	19,806	364	5,481
1971	36	126	5,021	1,088	1,308	10,246	277	20,168
1972	37	140	5,265	1,474	1,665	11,218	327	30,097
1973	35	150	5,703	1,757	1,851	14,971	353	40,220
1974	34	165	6,016	1,814	1,808	14,531	378	42,001
1975	37	144	6,583	2,083	—	—	—	50,000

Sources: Mesa-Lago, *Revolutionary Change in Cuba,* pp. 288–89; *BE 1968, BE 1970, BE 1971; Anuario 1972, Anuario 1973, Anuario 1974;* Banco Nacional de Cuba, *Desarrollo y perspectivas; La economía cubana,* 1975. Electricity data for 1957–1964 are from United Nations, *Statistical Yearbook,* and for 1965–1974 from *Anuario 1973* and *Anuario 1974.* Data for 1968–1969 are estimated by the author based on projections of electricity self-generated in the sugar industry plus data from all other sectors.

CARMELO MESA-LAGO

times the prerevolutionary level. Surprisingly, output declined in 1975, for the first time in the Revolution, to 144,000 tons, setting production back to the 1972 level. This may be one of the negative consequences of the Angola intervention, since part of the fishing fleet was probably diverted as military transport.[24] The goal for fish output in 1980 is 350,000 metric tons; a more realistic goal would be 250,000 tons.

The output of manufactured goods for domestic consumption has been uneven but much better than agricultural output. Once again, the most modern, concentrated, capital-intensive lines of production are the ones that have had the best performance. Electricity output steadily climbed, with the exception of 1962, and in 1975 was 2.5 times higher than the prerevolutionary level. The goal for 1980 is 9 billion kilowatt hours, a little too high in view of the 1963–1975 trend. Cigarettes also had a good performance with the 1969 output being more than twice the prerevolutionary level. However, there has been a slump in 1970–1974. Production of cigars (still mostly handmade) declined in the early 1960s, recuperated to a record level in 1967, and then sharply declined, with production in 1971 being one-third of that in 1967. The sharp fall in tobacco leaf output obviously affected both cigarette and cigar production after 1969–1970. The production of many manufactured goods was badly hurt, first in the early 1960s by nationalization, inefficiency, and the embargo, then in the late 1960s by the gigantic mobilizations and obsession with sugar typical of the Revolutionary Offensive; but production recovered in the 1970s. Cement production peaked in 1961, became stagnant in the middle years, and dipped sharply in 1969, but recovered in the 1970s and by 1975 had increased threefold over 1957–1958. The goal for 1980 is 4 million tons, also a little too high in view of the 1971–1975 trend. Beer output reached its height in 1959, suffered ups and downs throughout the 1960s but without recovering the 1959 level; after a trough in 1969, production steadily increased and, by 1973, was approximately 20 percent above the 1959 peak. Cuba began producing refrigerators late in 1964 but, after a good performance in 1965, output declined with a trough in 1968; there was a recuperation thereafter with 1975 output being more than four times that of 1965.

Planned changes in economic organization in 1977–1980 are certain to have an impact on growth. According to the five-year plan and recent statements of the leadership, a new Economic Management System (EMS) cast in the Soviet mold will be gradually implemented in Cuba during this period: in 1977, a national accounting system, the national budget, and purchase-and-sale relations among enterprises; in 1978, a new system of prices, taxation, and of banking, credit, and interest, as well as a pilot plan in selected enterprises which will operate with increased independence, be based on self-financing, use profit as a major indicator of managerial performance, and create an economic incentive fund; and in 1978–1980, the pilot plan will extend to all enterprises, hence completing the EMS.[25] These changes should prove beneficial in the long run because they will improve efficiency and productivity and provide better incentives to management and labor. In the short run, however, a major reform like this will probably create confusion, resistance, and slowdown, hence the potential impact of the EMS in 1978–1980 may well be negative.

In summary, the Cuban economy rapidly recovered in the first half of the 1970s probably reaching a record height in 1975. This was caused, in part, by better organization and management of the economy and a more balanced development policy, trends which are likely to continue in the rest of the decade. The big push, however, was generated by an external factor, the phenomenal increase in sugar prices. The stable production of nickel, combined with high prices and the steady increase in fish output, also helped the economy. Conversely, the output of citrus fruits was only fair and that of tobacco was extremely poor; but these two products currently have relatively small importance in the economy. Output of products for domestic consumption steadily increased or recuperated after a slump in the most modern sectors (eggs, fish, electricity, cement, beer, refrigerators), one exception being cigarettes. Most agricultural products (and traditional manufactured products such as cigars) had a poor performance, although a few showed signs of recuperation in the early 1970s.

In 1976–1977 there was a serious slowdown and possibly a decline in economic growth mainly due to the dramatic dip of sugar prices in the international market. (Another negative factor may have been the cost of the Angola operation.) Although the USSR is paying Cuba four times the current international market sugar price, which is still twice as high as in the 1960s, inflation and rising costs of both sugar production and imports (including oil) have probably offset those gains.

The possibility of replicating in 1978–1980 the high growth rates of the 1970s is very unlikely. The easiest organizational measures for rationalizing the economy were used up in the first half of the 1970s, while the new Economic Management System, to be gradually implemented in 1977–1980, may initially have a negative impact on growth. The main factor determining the path of economic growth in the rest of the decade, however, will be international sugar prices: If they continue to decline, Cuba's absolute growth rate may be 4 percent or below; if prices stabilize at 8 cents the growth rate may be about 5 percent; and if there are price increases from 9 to 12 cents, the growth rate may fluctuate between 6 and 8 percent.

In the agricultural sector, increases should occur in industrial crops if planned improvements materialize (sugar, tobacco) and in a few products in the modern sector (eggs, citrus fruits), but most of the traditional crops will be stagnant or show modest increases (tubers, coffee). A better performance should take place in the industrial sector with major increases in fishing, electricity, nickel, cement, and domestic appliances, although below the planned targets of the five-year plan. In any case, Cuba's output of most foodstuffs and manufactured items will be insufficient to satisfy domestic demand. The country's capacity to maintain and expand imports of the needed goods will basically depend on the outcome and value of the sugar sector.

CARMELO MESA-LAGO

Cuba's International Economic Relations: Past, Present, and Future

In the 1960s, and particularly since the end of that decade, economic collaboration between capitalist firms and multinational corporations (mostly dominated by U.S. capital) and the socialist countries of Eastern Europe has been expanding.[26] This collaboration assumes three basic forms, each one involving increasing degrees of interrelation and length of association. First is the one-time selling of licenses, machinery, equipment, and industrial plants. In the last fifteen years some 1,700 licenses alone have been purchased from Western firms by Eastern Europe. Second is "industrial cooperation"—longer lasting, joint undertakings in research and development, expertise, investment, production, construction projects, training of specialists, and marketing. Some 1,500 agreements of this nature have been signed with Yugoslavia, Hungary, Poland, Czechoslovakia, Rumania, and Bulgaria. Third are the "joint ventures"— ongoing, jointly-owned enterprises in which the two sides pool assets (with the socialist partner holding a majority), share risks and profits proportionally, and join in management on an equal basis. Legislation in the socialist country guarantees that the foreign partner will not be expropriated, that net profits after taxes can be repatriated, and that assets can also be repatriated after the termination of the venture. Some eighty-two of these joint ventures have been established in Yugoslavia, Rumania, and Hungary. Economic collaboration is normally in industrial fields: motor vehicles, electrical engineers, electronics (now including computers), metal-working machinery, chemicals, construction machinery, mining equipment, shipbuilding, food processing, and household appliances. Motives for the collaboration from the capitalist side include new markets and relatively good investment and payoff; from the socialist side, acquisition of up-to-date technology, expertise, foreign capital, and better accessibility to capitalist markets.

So far Cuba has had little economic collaboration with the capitalist world aside from the first type, that is, buying of machinery, transportation equipment, and industrial plants. This has mainly been the result of the fifteen-year embargo imposed upon the island but is probably also a reaction to prerevolutionary economic domination by the United States. It is symptomatic that although since 1961 Cuba has received substantial credit, capital goods, and technical aid from the USSR, these two countries do not have any "joint venture," which is now common within Eastern Europe. (The only case of a Cuban-Soviet enterprise is fishing: Fleets of both countries fish together and probably share their profits.)

With the opening to the nonsocialist world, Cuba, however, seems to be moving into the second type of economic relation, industrial cooperation. As we will see later, the Cuban government is asking several multinationals (most of them are foreign based and have agreements with Eastern Europe—Dunlop-Pirelli, Massey-Ferguson, Mitsubishi, Volkswagen) to submit tenders in order to build industrial plants in Cuba, possibly including the training of personnel and future supply of spare parts and technical services.

Concerning the third type of economic relationship, Cuban Deputy Prime Minister Carlos Rafael Rodríguez stated in Canada, in the fall of 1975, as head of a large trade mission, that his country was not yet ready for joint ventures with foreign firms on Cuban soil. At that time, however, Cuba was involved in some sort of joint tourism venture with Club Méditerranée. In April 1977, high Cuban officials told a group of visiting businessmen from Minnesota that joint ventures were possible in tourism, nickel, food, citrus processing, auto parts, pulp and paper.[27] In June, another Cuban official told *Business International* that although there were no agreements at the time, joint ventures with international corporations could be formed if Cuban planners concluded that they were desirable.[28] In his television interview with Barbara Walters, shown in the United States in June 1977, Castro was asked if he would accept U.S. investment in Cuba and if so how. He seemed surprised by the question and denied that the investment issue had been discussed during the visit of the Minnesota businessmen, but he said, "when the time came to tackle the matter of foreign investment in our country, we would have to analyze, from a practical point of view and without dogmatism, what was good for our country and what wasn't and then we act accordingly."[29]

Currently Cuba's international economic relations are basically centered on trade, and the country is heavily dependent on foreign trade. As table 9.4 shows, Cuba's average trade volume for 1962–1974 in relation to GMP was 42 percent,

TABLE 9.4
Importance of Foreign Trade to the
Cuban Economy, 1962–1974

	Exports as % of GMP	Imports as % of GMP	Total trade as % of GMP
1962	14.1	20.5	34.6
1963	14.6	23.2	37.8
1964	17.5	25.0	42.5
1965	16.7	20.9	37.6
1966	14.9	23.2	38.1
1967	17.3	24.4	42.7
1968	14.9	25.2	40.1
1969	16.0	29.2	45.2
1970	24.9	31.2	56.2
1971	17.8	28.7	46.6
1972	12.7	19.7	32.4
1973	17.2	21.8	39.0
1974	30.0	30.0	60.0
Average 1962–74	17.7	24.8	42.5

Sources: Tables 9.1 and 9.5.

CARMELO MESA-LAGO

with dependency on imports considerably higher than on exports. In general, the trend is of increasing dependency.

Table 9.5 gives a general picture of Cuba's foreign trade both at the eve of and during the first seventeen years of the Revolution. Until 1962, the value of Cuban exports was roughly similar to that of imports, although the volume of total transactions declined somewhat. Beginning in that year and until 1973, however, exports either declined or were stagnant (with the exception of 1970) while imports increased. The main reasons behind the decreasing exports were the decline in sugar output and the low prices of sugar in the international market. The incremental growth of imports was related to the step-up in importing capital and intermediate goods to meet the expanding demand of an increasing population compounded with stagnant or declining domestic output of many consumer goods which forced the importation of basic foodstuffs and selected manufactures. As a result of these trends, trade deficits climbed steadily, reaching records of a half-billion pesos in 1969 and 1971. The huge sugar crop of 1970, although

TABLE 9.5
Foreign Trade of Cuba, 1957–1975
(in million pesos)

	Exports (f.o.b.)	Imports (c.i.f.)	Total Transactions	Trade Balance
1957	807.7	772.9	1,580.6	+ 34.8
1958	733.5	771.1	1,510.6	− 37.6
1959	636.0	674.8	1,310.8	− 38.8
1960	608.3	579.9	1,188.2	+ 28.4
1961	626.4	638.7	1,265.1	− 12.3
1962	522.3	759.3	1,281.6	−237.0
1963	545.1	867.3	1,412.4	−322.2
1964	714.3	1,018.8	1,733.1	−304.5
1965	690.6	866.2	1,556.8	−175.6
1966	597.8	925.5	1,523.3	−327.7
1967	705.0	999.1	1,704.1	−294.1
1968	651.4	1,102.3	1,753.7	−450.9
1969	666.7	1,221.7	1,888.4	−555.0
1970	1,049.5	1,311.0	2,360.5	−261.5
1971	861.2	1,386.6	2,247.8	−525.4
1972	770.9	1,189.8	1,960.7	−418.9
1973	1,153.0	1,467.0	2,620.0	−314.0
1974	2,222.2	2,225.9	4,448.1	− 3.7
1975	2,948.0	3,207.0	6,155.0	−259.0

Sources: for 1957–1958, Carmelo Mesa-Lago, "Availability and Reliability of Statistics in Socialist Cuba," *Latin American Research Review* 4, no. 2 (Summer 1969), table 5; for 1957–1974, *BE 1966*, pp. 124–33, *BE 1968*, pp. 148– 65, *BE 1970*, pp. 188–209, *BE 1971*, pp. 214–63, *Anuario 1972*, pp. 192–232, *Anuario 1973*, p. 189, and *Anuario 1974*, p. 184; for 1975, United Nations, *Monthly Bulletin of Statistics*, May 1977, p. 118.

boosting exports to a record one billion pesos, was accompanied by an even higher augmentation of imports, thus provoking a deficit. The increase in sugar prices in 1973 resulted in new records in both exports and imports. In 1974 the value of exports went up to a new record of 2.2 billion pesos (the equivalent of the value of exports for almost four average years in the 1960s). Imports also rose to a record of 2.2 billion pesos with the trade deficit dramatically reduced to 3.7 million (the lowest throughout the Revolution except for the surplus year of 1960).[30]

In spite of the decline of sugar prices in the international market, in 1975 the value of exports increased to almost 3 billion pesos but the value of imports increased even more (both setting new records) and a deficit of 259 million pesos resulted.[31] High export figures in 1975 may have been caused by the higher prices paid for Cuban sugar by the USSR and Eastern Europe, plus sugar sales to the West in 1975 signed by the end of 1974 at the record prices then prevailing in the international market. Preliminary estimates for 1976, when the full impact of the dip in sugar prices was felt, indicate a sharp decline in exports (2,417 million pesos) and a significant but less dramatic fall in the value of imports (2,892 million pesos) resulting in an acute increase in the trade deficit (475 million pesos).[32]

The grave problem of declining value of sugar exports and increasing trade deficits was compounded by Cuban orders to market economies for hundreds of millions of dollars worth of machinery, equipment, and manufactures extended before the turn in the economy was apparent. In 1973-1975 Cuba had received $3.5 billion in credit from the West (see table 10.2), and although only part of it had been used by 1976, the debt service on obligations was estimated to cost from $300 to $400 million a year. In the fall of 1976, facing a sharp drop in foreign reserves and determined not to default but maintain a good reputation with the banking community, Cuba's Ministry of Foreign Trade began to ask several Western suppliers (Argentina, Japan, Canada, Spain) to postpone delivery of imports already contracted for and to accept delayed payments of a total sum over $1 billion.[33] As Castro put it: "For us, the principle of meeting our international financial obligations comes before the acquisition of merchandise and industrial plants."[34] This decision nevertheless involved a substantial economic loss for the Cubans (most sellers requested payment of interest, insurance, and warehouse fees for stockpiled goods), considerable irritation for the debtors, and a negative image for other potential trade partners.

Cuba's cumulative trade balance for 1959-1975 registers a deficit of 4.3 billion pesos, most of it resulting from trade with the USSR and financed with Soviet loans or credits. Currently, the Cuban debt to the USSR is above 5 billion pesos, but repayment will not start until 1986 (except for 300 million pesos granted in 1973-1975 and scheduled for repayment beginning in 1976).[35] This will give the island a ten-year break to put its economic house in order. In addition, although Cuba has used part of the $3.5 billion credit received from the West, it is mostly still unexpended and can be used during the next ten years. In

TABLE 9.6
Percentage Distribution of Cuban Trade, 1959–1974

Country[a]	1959	1960	1961	1962	1963	1964	1965	1966
Socialist								
USSR	1.0	15.5	44.8	49.4	44.2	39.5	48.2	52.2
China[b]	0.0	3.6	14.2	14.0	11.6	11.0	14.3	11.4
Czechoslovakia	n	0.7	3.7	5.8	6.6	4.6	5.2	5.4
E. Germany	0.0	0.4	2.6	4.1	5.4	3.2	3.4	4.4
Bulgaria	0.0	0.1	1.1	1.7	1.0	1.5	2.4	3.1
Poland	n	1.2	3.3	3.2	3.3	1.7	0.8	1.4
Others[c]	n	0.2	0.3	0.5	0.6	1.0	0.9	0.5
Rumania	0.0	n	0.7	1.6	1.0	0.5	0.3	0.2
Hungary	0.0	0.1	0.8	1.8	1.7	0.9	0.6	0.6
Yugoslavia	n	n	0.6	0.4	0.3	0.6	0.7	1.0
Total	1.1	21.8	72.0	82.5	75.8	64.3	76.8	80.2
Nonsocialist								
Japan	2.6	2.1	2.9	2.8	1.9	5.2	1.6	1.3
Others[d]	12.7	9.3	7.3	5.3	3.8	5.0	4.0	1.0
Spain	1.1	1.8	1.0	0.8	2.6	6.2	5.2	7.1
U.K.	2.7	2.5	2.2	1.8	2.4	3.7	4.1	2.4
France	1.6	1.7	0.7	0.2	0.6	1.3	1.9	1.5
Canada	1.8	2.0	3.2	1.2	1.8	2.6	1.3	0.7
Italy	0.7	0.7	0.4	0.2	0.9	1.6	0.7	1.5
W. Germany	2.8	2.7	2.1	1.1	0.9	1.1	0.4	0.4
Morocco	1.0	1.0	0.9	1.5	2.9	4.5	1.3	1.4
Holland	2.0	1.8	1.4	0.4	1.2	1.6	0.7	0.9
Egypt	n	1.0	1.4	1.5	1.9	1.8	1.2	0.8
Sweden	0.4	0.3	0.2	0.1	0.7	0.8	0.4	0.5
USA	68.7	50.5	4.1	0.4	2.5	n	n	n
Belgium	0.9	0.9	0.4	0.2	0.3	0.4	0.4	0.3
Total	98.9	78.3	28.2	17.5	24.2	35.7	23.2	19.8

Sources: for 1959, *BE 1970,* p. 188; for 1960–1967, *BE 1971,* pp. 216–19; for 1968–1972, *Anuario 1972,* pp. 196–97; for 1973, *Anuario 1973,* pp. 189–91; and for 1974, *Anuario 1974,* pp. 186–89.
Note: n indicates negligible.
a. Summation of individual countries may not equal totals because of rounding.
b. Years 1961–1966 have been directly reported by Cuba. Remaining years have been estimated by the author based on Cuban data and CIA estimates.
c. Includes Mongolia and unspecified other socialist countries (probably - Albania, Democratic Republic of Vietnam, and Democratic Republic of Korea).
d. Includes Latin America, Africa, Asia, and the remainder of Western Europe.

1977–1985, therefore, Cuba should try to balance its foreign trade and generate a trade surplus. Ideally, the island should be carefully searching in the future for

1967	1968	1969	1970	1971	1972	1973	1974	Average 1961–1974
55.6	54.8	47.6	51.7	46.0	47.9	49.3	41.3	48.0
8.9	7.9	7.6	6.3	6.5	6.3	6.8	5.4	9.4
4.5	4.6	3.8	3.4	3.4	3.5	2.9	2.5	4.3
5.1	4.3	4.3	4.2	5.0	3.8	3.4	3.5	4.0
2.6	2.6	2.8	2.2	2.5	2.8	3.1	2.7	2.3
0.8	0.6	0.6	0.4	0.4	0.4	0.6	0.5	1.3
1.3	1.3	1.7	1.4	2.0	1.4	0.9	1.3	1.1
0.1	1.0	2.3	1.5	1.2	1.0	0.9	1.0	1.0
0.5	0.4	0.5	0.4	0.9	0.8	0.6	0.7	0.8
0.6	0.5	0.4	n	0.4	0.4	0.2	0.5	0.5
80.0	78.0	71.4	71.5	68.2	68.3	68.7	59.2	72.6
1.6	2.9	4.0	6.0	7.1	9.3	10.1	12.4	4.9
1.8	1.7	2.5	3.8	6.0	8.4	5.1	6.9	4.5
3.6	3.5	4.7	3.3	3.1	2.8	3.2	5.3	3.7
2.4	2.6	4.3	3.3	3.5	2.8	3.2	2.9	3.0
3.3	4.7	3.2	3.1	3.1	1.3	1.3	1.5	2.0
0.8	0.8	1.1	1.6	1.7	1.5	2.0	3.9	1.7
2.1	2.9	2.5	2.9	2.8	1.3	1.5	1.7	1.6
0.8	0.8	1.7	1.5	0.9	1.4	1.7	2.5	1.2
1.0	0.8	1.2	0.6	0.8	0.3	0.3	0.3	1.2
1.1	1.7	1.5	1.5	1.0	0.4	1.0	1.1	1.1
0.8	0.6	0.6	0.2	0.4	0.3	0.1	n	0.8
0.4	0.4	1.0	0.5	1.0	1.1	1.0	1.5	0.7
n	n	0.0	n	n	n	0.0	0.0	0.5
0.1	0.3	0.3	0.2	0.4	0.5	0.8	0.7	0.4
20.0	22.0	28.6	28.5	31.8	31.7	31.3	40.8	27.4

markets where it could get the highest price for its exports and pay the lowest price for its imports. The question is, in view of the limitations discussed above, how much real flexibility Cuba will have in choosing trade partners.

As table 9.6 shows, in 1959 almost 69 percent of Cuban total trade was with the United States. As a result of the conflicts of 1960-1961, the elimination of the U.S. sugar quota to Cuba, and the imposition of the U.S. embargo in 1962, U.S. trade with Cuba was reduced to a negligible proportion in 1962. (In 1963 there was a slight increase in trade resulting from the U.S. exporting of goods to Cuba in exchange for the prisoners taken during the Bay of Pigs' invasion. In 1971-1975 the United States, mostly through health organizations, sent close to

CARMELO MESA-LAGO

$20 million to Cuba in bulk gift parcels and medicines, but this accounted for only 0.1 percent of Cuba's trade volume.)[36]

The largest and most industrialized socialist countries rapidly substituted for U.S. trade, absorbing an average of 73 percent of Cuban total transactions in 1961-1974. Within the socialist camp, the USSR was the main trade partner taking an average of 48 percent of Cuban trade. The other socialist trade partners in that period were: China (an average of 9 percent), Czechoslovakia and East Germany (above 4 percent each), Bulgaria (2 percent), Poland, Rumania, and Hungary (about 1 percent each), and Yugoslavia (half of one percent). As table 9.7 indicates, trade with socialist countries has ended in a deficit in the majority of cases, particularly with those countries that have the largest share of Cuban trade. The cumulative trade balance in 1959-1974, in millions of pesos, was as follows: USSR (−3,526), China (−178), Rumania (−25), East Germany and Hungary (−16), Poland (+5), Yugoslavia (+25), Czechoslovakia (+44), and Bulgaria (+67).

The remainder of Cuban foreign trade in 1961-1974 (an average of 27 percent of total transactions) was with nonsocialist countries, mostly in Europe and all industrialized (see table 9.6). Japan took an average of 5 percent; Spain 4 percent; United Kingdom 3 percent; France, Italy and Canada 2 percent each; West Germany, Holland and Sweden 1 percent each; and Belgium half of one percent. There was a small amount of trade with a few African countries like Morocco and Egypt (one percent each) and Algeria, Iraq, and Syria (1 percent combined). Trade with nonsocialist countries (with the notable exception of Japan, Spain, and Morocco) has also been at a deficit. The cumulative trade balance in 1959-1974, in millions of pesos, was as follows: United Kingdom (−344), France (−330), West Germany (−328), Canada (−189), Italy (−188), Holland (−75), Belgium (−70), Sweden (−28), Morocco (+153), Spain (+158), and Japan (+689). In 1974, Cuba's total trade with Latin America was 1.8 percent with the largest shares going to Argentina (1.2 percent) and Mexico (0.3 percent).[37]

Trade with nonsocialist countries was at a low level in 1962-1968 due to the combination of a poor Cuban surplus to trade with the West and the embargo imposed by the United States and the Organization of American States (OAS). Since 1969, however, trade with nonsocialist countries other than the United States rose steadily, reaching a record 41 percent in 1974 (compared to 30 percent in 1959). Japan took the largest share of this expanding trade and has, since 1971, become Cuba's second most important trade partner, increasing its total trade share from 4 percent in 1969 to 12 percent in 1974. At the same time, trade with socialist countries reached a record low of 59 percent in 1974 (41 percent with the USSR and 18 percent with other socialist countries). Estimates for 1975 suggest a continuation of the previous trend; Cuban sources indicate a trade distribution of 52 percent with socialist countries (40 percent with the USSR) and 48 percent with nonsocialist countries.[38]

Table 9.8 can be used as an indicator of the increasing overtures of Cuban foreign policy, a good deal of which is centered on economic issues. From January-February 1974 to January 1975 four of the total of seven visiting dignitaries were from socialist nations, two from prosocialist African nations, one from a socialist Middle East emerging nation, and none from the West. In the second year (February 1975 to January 1976), out of a total of eleven visitors, only two were from socialist nations, two from African nations (one pro-Western and another prosocialist), and seven from the West. Many of the visits resulted in economic and trade agreements. In 1975, ten ministers of foreign trade of market economies visited Cuba, some from countries that had previously participated in the embargo.

Cuba's increasing independence in foreign trade and economic relations during 1971-1975 may, however, be reversed during the second half of the 1970s due to the decline in sugar prices in the international market and the 1976-1980 Cuban-Soviet economic agreements. Thus U.S. estimates of Cuba's trade distribution for 1976 suggest that the previous trend has indeed been dramatically reversed with from 68 to 71 percent of trade going to socialist countries (56 to 58 percent to the USSR) and only 29 to 32 percent to nonsocialist countries. [39]

When Cuba had a high-priced commodity to trade in 1974-1975, the island chose to expand trade mostly with industrialized, nonsocialist countries. Early in 1976, a high Cuban official in the Ministry of Foreign Trade told *Business Latin America* that a desirable distribution of future Cuban trade should be: 40 percent with socialist countries, 30 percent with the United States, and 30 percent with other market economies. One year later, however, facing declining sugar prices, the Cuban director of commercial policy for North America told the group of Minnesota businessmen that Cuba's trade breakdown would stay roughly as it is today (60-40 percent) in favor of socialist countries and that U.S. firms would have to carve their share from the nonsocialist 40 percent. [40]

The five-year Cuban-Soviet agreements signed in 1976 on trade (February 6) and economic-technical cooperation (April 14) indicate a future increase in Cuba's dependency on the USSR. Carlos Rafael Rodríguez ranked such agreements as the most important in the history of relations between the two countries and announced that the level of Cuban-Soviet economic cooperation will be 2.5 times greater in 1976-1980 than in 1971-1975 (the level of trade will be two times greater). [41] If the anticipated heavy subsidy of Cuban sugar materializes in 1976-1980 and the price of Soviet oil continues below the price charged by the Organization of Petroleum Exporting Countries (OPEC), it will be disadvantageous for Cuba to shift her trade to nonsocialist countries (see chapter 13 of this volume).

In spite of the radical transformation of Cuba's society and ownership in fifteen years of Revolution, the structure of its economy and foreign trade remains basically unchanged: the island is still a monoculture economy depending

CARMELO MESA-LAGO

TABLE 9.7
Cuba's Balance of Trade, 1959–1974 (in millions of pesos)

Country[a]	1959	1960	1961	1962	1963	1964	1965	19
Socialist								
USSR	+12.9	+23.3	+41.1	−189.5	−297.1	−135.0	−105.9	−2
China[b]	n	+22.2	+ 3.0	− 0.8	− 18.1	− 27.9	− 22.9	+
Rumania	0.0	+ 0.1	− 6.1	− 7.1	− 0.1	− 7.7	− 3.4	−
Hungary	0.0	− 0.8	− 6.8	− 2.8	n	− 14.4	− 6.2	−
E. Germany	0.0	− 3.5	−13.3	− 1.5	+ 3.5	− 21.4	+ 3.4	−
Poland	n	+ 5.3	+ 6.5	− 3.9	− 10.8	− 13.4	− 4.2	+
Yugoslavia	n	+ 0.3	− 2.0	+ 2.9	− 1.0	+ 2.8	+ 0.7	−
Czechoslovakia	+ 0.1	− 5.5	− 3.7	− 0.4	− 16.8	− 49.3	+ 9.7	+
Bulgaria	n	− 1.0	− 2.5	+ 3.3	+ 4.1	+ 3.3	+ 4.8	−
Others[c]	+ 0.7	+ 1.0	+ 0.7	− 0.9	− 0.8	− 5.9	+ 1.9	−
Total	+13.7	+41.3	+16.9	−201.1	−337.1	−269.0	−122.1	−2
Nonsocialist								
U.K.	−17.9	−12.4	− 2.6	− 0.1	+ 12.2	− 11.7	− 37.6	−
France	− 3.4	− 2.4	− 5.5	− 0.3	− 3.4	− 15.7	− 8.9	−
W. Germany	− 8.5	− 8.0	− 5.6	− 13.7	− 11.4	− 17.8	− 4.6	−
Italy	− 6.4	− 8.4	− 3.4	− 2.1	+ 11.3	+ 14.2	+ 2.4	−
Canada	− 2.6	− 8.6	−31.1	− 9.1	+ 3.7	− 39.2	− 10.3	−
Holland	+ 8.4	n	− 7.5	− 2.0	+ 0.3	− 22.5	− 2.5	−
Belgium	− 4.9	− 6.3	− 4.1	− 1.9	− 0.5	− 3.7	− 5.0	−
Sweden	− 0.4	− 1.5	− 1.5	− 1.0	+ 1.5	− 8.0	+ 1.8	−
Others[d]	−31.5	−22.3	+ 6.8	− 37.1	− 5.6	− 23.4	+ 1.0	+
USA	−17.0	+36.9	+ 4.1	+ 3.4	− 35.5	n	n	
Egypt	n	+ 5.6	− 5.8	+ 0.3	+ 4.0	+ 1.2	− 3.9	−
Morocco	+12.8	+11.7	+ 9.1	+ 5.2	+ 13.5	+ 52.7	+ 9.9	+
Spain	− 2.2	− 2.9	+ 1.7	+ 7.4	+ 9.1	+ 29.0	− 12.9	−
Japan	+21.0	+ 5.7	+16.1	+ 14.8	+ 15.8	+ 9.4	+ 17.1	+
Total	−52.6	−12.9	−29.3	− 36.2	+ 15.0	− 35.5	− 53.5	−
Grand total	−38.9	+28.4	−12.3	−237.0	−322.2	−305.5	−175.5	−

Sources: for 1959, BE 1970, p. 188; for 1960–1967, BE 1971, pp. 216–19; for 1968–1972, An 1972, pp. 196–97; for 1973, Anuario 1973, pp. 189–91; for 1974, Anuario 1974, pp. 186–89.
Note: n indicates negligible.
a. Summation of individual countries may not equal total because of rounding.
b. Years 1961–1966 have been directly reported by Cuba. Remaining years have been estim by the author based on Cuban data and CIA estimates.
c. Includes Mongolia and other socialist countries (probably Albania, Democratic Repub Vietnam, and Democratic Republic of Korea).
d. Includes Latin America, Africa, Asia, and the remainder of Western Europe.

upon sugar as the fundamental source of exports and foreign exchange. As table 9.9 shows, 78 percent of Cuban exports in 1957–1958 were sugar and sugar by-products; in 1959–1974 the proportion of sugar to total exports averaged 81 percent. At the same time tobacco, which used to be Cuba's second major export, has slipped down from 6 to about 3 percent of total exports. Conversely,

1967	1968	1969	1970	1971	1972	1973	1974	Cumulative 1959-1974
215.9	−382.2	−436.0	−161.5	−427.1	−490.3	−301.3	−214.5	−3526.3
6.0	− 16.3	− 16.0	− 6.8	− 12.0	− 28.0	− 27.0	− 34.2	− 178.2
0.1	− 0.8	− 24.6	− 10.1	+ 2.2	+ 1.3	+ 7.8	+ 25.4	− 25.3
0.8	+ 1.0	+ 1.9	− 1.4	+ 3.7	+ 0.6	+ 2.3	+ 11.7	− 16.2
13.9	− 3.0	− 5.2	− 1.2	− 14.4	+ 2.2	+ 7.2	+ 51.0	− 15.7
0.1	+ 2.7	+ 2.8	+ 2.1	+ 4.3	+ 4.2	+ 2.5	+ 3.0	+ 4.8
2.8	− 0.4	+ 1.6	− 1.0	+ 7.1	+ 7.1	n	+ 11.4	+ 24.8
5.1	+ 2.2	+ 15.0	+ 19.0	+ 13.5	+ 8.5	+ 7.4	+ 29.2	+ 44.1
3.8	+ 4.2	+ 1.1	+ 5.5	+ 6.3	− 7.2	+ 21.8	+ 25.6	+ 64.5
0.2	+ 1.3	+ 1.0	+ 7.0	+ 10.5	+ 8.3	+ 21.8	+ 20.3	+ 67.0
217.0	−391.3	−458.4	−148.4	−405.7	−493.2	−257.6	− 71.0	−3556.7
16.4	− 17.5	− 52.0	− 39.6	− 44.1	− 31.2	− 21.0	− 39.4	− 344.4
25.4	− 51.4	− 32.5	− 46.8	− 57.3	− 10.8	− 18.1	− 44.4	− 329.6
11.5	− 8.8	− 29.0	− 32.8	− 14.8	− 20.2	− 34.6	−101.5	− 327.9
25.3	− 33.1	− 25.2	− 42.1	− 45.5	+ 1.6	− 0.6	− 17.6	− 188.8
4.4	− 4.5	− 6.5	− 19.1	− 16.1	− 7.6	− 18.5	− 12.4	− 188.0
10.6	+ 10.7	+ 16.3	− 6.7	− 10.1	+ 3.5	− 13.8	− 29.8	− 75.6
3.1	+ 0.8	+ 0.8	− 1.5	− 2.6	− 2.8	− 6.2	− 26.6	− 69.8
1.0	+ 1.8	− 18.3	− 1.7	− 10.8	− 2.6	+ 1.8	+ 12.0	− 28.5
2.9	+ 1.8	+ 0.1	− 7.1	+ 27.8	+ 21.8	+ 27.8	+ 10.6	− 24.3
n	n	n	n	n	n	0.0	0.0	− 8.1
1.8	+ 0.4	+ 0.9	+ 0.7	− 1.0	+ 1.7	− 0.6	n	− 0.4
6.3	− 0.5	+ 4.1	+ 2.1	+ 10.9	+ 2.6	+ 7.0	− 0.9	+ 153.1
4.2	+ 20.8	− 6.8	+ 3.7	+ 2.8	+ 24.6	+ 8.3	+113.9	+ 158.5
9.0	+ 19.6	+ 57.2	+ 74.7	+ 39.6	+ 91.2	+ 85.0	+203.3	+ 689.3
77.1	− 59.9	− 90.9	−116.2	−121.2	+ .71.8	+ 17.8	+ 67.2	− 584.4
294.1	−451.1	−549.4	−264.7	−527.0	−421.7	−239.8	− 3.7	−4142.2

nickel has risen from third to the second major export, climbing from 6 to about 14 percent of total exports. A new export generated by the Revolution is fish, which now constitutes 3 percent of exports. The rest of exports are mainly fruits and rum.

The pattern of Cuban imports has changed somewhat more than the pattern of its exports, as a careful analysis of table 9.10 will illustrate. (The years 1960-1962 are missing from the table because of lack of data. There are also problems of comparison between the year 1959 and the rest of the series.) A first inspection of the table shows that the proportion of most imports remains basically unchanged—foodstuffs, raw materials, fuel, chemicals, and machinery-transportation (except for 1967-1971). Significant differences appear when some

CARMELO MESA-LAGO

TABLE 9.8
Visits of Principal Foreign Dignitaries to Cuba, January 1974 to January 1976

	Post	Nation	Date
Leonid Brezhnev	First secretary of party	USSR	Jan.–Feb. 1974
Erich Honecker	First secretary of party	East Germany	March 1974
Pham Van Dong	Prime minister	Vietnam	March 1974
Houari Boumedienne	President	Algeria	April 1974
Julius K. Nyerere	President	Tanzania	Sept. 1974
Yassir Arafat	Chairman	Palestine (PLO)	Nov. 1974
Edward Gierek	First secretary of party	Poland	Jan. 1975
Forbes Burnham	Prime minister	Guyana	April 1975
Kenneth D. Kaunda	President	Zambia	April 1975
Eric Williams	Prime minister	Trinidad & Tobago	June 1975
Olof Palme	Prime minister	Sweden	June 1975
Michael Manley	Prime minister	Jamaica	July 1975
Luis Echeverría	President	Mexico	Aug. 1975
Marien Ngouabi	President	Congo	Sept. 1975
Janos Kadar	First secretary of party	Hungary	Dec. 1975
Todor Zhivkov	First secretary of party	Bulgaria	Dec. 1975
Omar Torrijos	President	Panama	Jan. 1976
Pierre Trudeau	Prime minister	Canada	Jan. 1976

Sources: Granma and Granma Weekly Review, 1974–1976.

of these categories are disaggregated, for example, in 1959 most transportation imports were passenger cars, now they are trucks, ships, and so on. A substantial proportion of machinery imports is in tractors and other agricultural equipment. The most evident shift, however, is in imports of manufactured products which is twice as large in 1959 as in 1963–1974. On the other hand, the category of "others" is almost insignificant in 1959 but increases to an average of 24 percent in 1963–1974. It is suspicious that this category has not been disaggregated in the series in spite of the fact that it is one of the three most important. One possibility is that strategic goods such as weapons are included in "others," and yet both Cuba and the USSR have asserted that Soviet-made weaponry supplied to Cuba (1.5 billion pesos in 1962–1971) has been free of charge. Another interpretation is that part of "others" may be manufactured products.

In any event table 9.10 shows that the percentage of manufactures out of total imports significantly declined in 1967–1971 although there seems to be an upward turn in 1972–1974. This downward and upward trend is also observed in another category of consumer goods, that of food and fats: decline in 1968–1970, recuperation in 1971–1974. Conversely, importation of machinery and transportation dramatically increased in 1967–1971, regressing in 1972 to the 1959 level. The explanation of these trends is to be found in the idealistic, mobilization philosophy of Sino-Guevarism which was in vogue in 1967–1970. At that time Cuba emphasized capital accumulation by sacrificing consumption; in other words, bread and butter were cut in order to buy more capital equipment. With

TABLE 9.9
Percentage Distribution of Cuban Exports by Product,
1957–1974

	Sugar	Tobacco	Minerals	Other[a]	Total
1957	78	6	6	10	100
1958	78	7	3	11	100
1959	77	9	2	12	100
1960	80	10	1	9	100
1961	85	6	6	3	100
1962	83	5	7	5	100
1963	87	4	6	3	100
1964	88	4	5	3	100
1965	86	5	6	3	100
1966	85	4	7	4	100
1967	86	4	8	2	100
1968	77	6	12	5	100
1969	76	6	13	5	100
1970	77	3	17	3	100
1971	76	4	16	4	100
1972	74	5	15	6	100
1973	75	5	14	6	100
1974[b]	87	3	6	4	100

Sources: for 1957–1958, Mesa-Lago, "Availability and Reliability of Statistics," table 5: for 1959–1974, BE 1966, pp. 124–33, BE 1968, pp. 150–51, BE 1971, pp. 222–23, Anuario 1973, p. 186, Anuario 1974, p. 181.
a. Mainly fish, shellfish, fruits, and rum.
b. Preliminary estimates.

the return to a less frugal, more realistic policy in the 1970s, with emphasis on material incentives, the trend has been reversed: The proportion of consumer goods out of total imports is now increasing while that of machinery is declining. The table also shows a significant increase in importation of fuel in 1972 that probably continued in 1973–1975, although, due to Soviet-subsidized prices, Cuba has not been affected by skyrocketing oil prices as have other non-oil-producing countries.

In summary, the combination of tables 9.6, 9.9, and 9.10 proves that trade is fundamentally with industrialized nations, both socialist and nonsocialist, to which Cuba exports a few raw materials (sugar, nickel, tobacco, fish, fruits, rum) in exchange for capital and intermediate goods, foodstuffs, manufactures, and fuel. It is obvious that the possibilities of Cuban trade with developing countries, unless they are oil exporters, are slim because such countries are usually exporters of raw materials and importers of capital and intermediate goods as well as manufactures. With the exception of Venezuela, the Latin American countries with which Cuba can trade (Argentina, Mexico, Peru, Colombia, Costa Rica, Panama, British Caribbean) do not need Cuba's principal export because they are sugar exporters themselves. Chile is an exception, and in

CARMELO MESA-LAGO

TABLE 9.10
Percentage Distribution of Cuban Imports by Product, 1959 and 1963–1974

	Food & Fats	Raw Minerals	Fuel & Minerals	Chem-icals	Manu-factures	Machinery & Transportation	Other[a]	Total
1959	27	4	9	9	31	19	1	100
1963	24	3	9	6	15	14	29	100
1964	24	4	9	6	15	14	28	100
1965	24	3	10	4	17	15	27	100
1966	23	4	10	7	16	14	26	100
1967	24	5	9	9	11	24	18	100
1968	21	5	8	9	10	27	20	100
1969	19	4	9	6	10	31	21	100
1970	20	4	9	6	10	28	23	100
1971	23	5	9	4	10	28	21	100
1972	25	4	12	5	12	19	23	100
1973	24	4	11	5	12	21	23	100
1974	25	4	9	4	13	21	24	100

Sources: Tables 9.1 and 9.5.
Note: Years 1960–1962 are omitted due to lack of data.
a. Not disaggregated in the original source.

1971–1973, when Allende's socialist coalition was in power, that country imported a substantial amount of Cuban sugar in exchange for Chilean beans, garlic, and other minor products. This trade ended in a deficit for Cuba, and its main objective was political not economic: to support the second socialist country in the hemisphere and to erode the hemispheric embargo of Cuba.

The cases of Mexico and Argentina are more relevant, because these countries, together with Brazil, are the most industrialized in Latin America. In 1960–1967, trade with Mexico, the only Latin American country with which Cuba then had trade and diplomatic relations, was at low levels (2 to 6 million pesos). Mexico exported beans, rice, garlic, corn, coffee, spare parts, and other goods to Cuba in exchange for some nickel, films, and canvas; this exchange resulted in a large deficit for Cuba. After the Tlatelolco incidents of 1968, trade dipped to an insignificant amount. Now Mexico is trying to export manufactures to Cuba, transportation equipment, steel, sugar-mill equipment, and possibly some oil, mostly in exchange for Cuban nickel; obviously this exchange is also going to end in a deficit for Cuba. A similar situation has occurred with Argentina, which in 1973 opened a significant credit line to Cuba for the purchase of transportation equipment. This move was politically and economically important for Cuba because it challenged the embargo and, for the first time, facilitated the acquisition of transportation equipment made by U.S. subsidiaries in the Western Hemisphere. But Argentina does not need sugar and imports little nickel, so once again, its trade has to end in a deficit for Cuba. Brazil is another possible trade partner as has been recently acknowledged by Fidel Castro and Carlos Rafael

Rodríguez. Brazilian manufacturers of cars, trucks and tractors, are aware of the growth in Argentinian-Cuban trade in spite of political differences and are exerting pressure upon the government to open the dialogue. The mutual interests between Brazil and Cuba (they are the largest sugar producers in Latin America) have brought them together in some multinational organizations. Cuba has praised Brazilian recognition of Angola despite U.S. opposition and is watching other conflicts between the two countries over nuclear energy and human rights. Castro has stated that trade between Brazil and Cuba can take place regardless of different social systems and has offered to help Brazil in expanding its market with socialist and nonaligned nations.[42] But once again, Brazil is a major sugar producer and there is little that Cuba can offer in exchange for manufactures. (For the current state of Cuban diplomatic and trade relations with Latin America, see table 9.11.)

The success of Cuban trade with the industrialized market economies of North America (Canada), Europe (Spain, France, England, West Germany, Italy), and Asia (Japan) has been based on the advantage of exchanging mutually needed production surpluses. Cuba has traded sugar (and to a lesser extent nickel, tobacco, fish) for oil, transportation equipment (ships, trucks, locomotives, planes, buses, cars, port machinery), agricultural goods (tractors, irrigation equipment, harvesters, fertilizer plants), steel, chemical and pharmaceutical products, electrical appliances, electronic equipment, building materials, and foodstuffs (wheat, corn, fats, dairy products, beans). The United States can

TABLE 9.11
Cuban Relations with Latin American and Caribbean
Nations, 1977

Diplomatic and Trade Relations	Some Trade and Contacts	No Relations
Argentina	Dominican Republic	Bolivia [b]
Bahamas	Ecuador	Brazil
Barbados	Honduras	Chile [b]
Colombia		El Salvador
Costa Rica [a]		Haiti
Guyana		Guatemala
Jamaica		Nicaragua [b]
Mexico		Paraguay [b]
Panama		Uruguay [b]
Peru		
Trinidad-Tobago		
Venezuela		

Sources: Granma and Latin America, 1973–1977.
a. In February 1977, Costa Rica and Cuba agreed to renew diplomatic relations at the consular level.
b. Strongest mutual rejection.

CARMELO MESA-LAGO

certainly supply most of these products to Cuba and is a consumer of all products that Cuba exports.

Although it is in Cuba's interest to expand its trade with nonsocialist countries in the future, the feasibility of this expansion—at least in the short run—is linked to the performance of sugar in the international market. Unless there is a healthy recuperation in international sugar prices, Cuban-Soviet economic relations will either continue at current high levels or increase during the rest of the decade. The short-run possibility of a powerful nonsocialist country (or group of countries) substituting for the USSR in subsidizing the Cuban economy is slim at best. The United States could perform such a role, but first the process of normalization of relations between the two countries would have to be completed and this may take several years. Chapter 10 discusses the economic aspect of that process and its potential effects for both countries.

NOTES

Drafts of this and the following chapter were presented at the Council on Foreign Relations, Current Issue Review Group on Cuba, New York, April 17, 1975; at the State Department, Colloquium on Cuba, Washington, D.C., May 22, 1975; and at the International Conference, "The Role of Cuba in World Affairs," University of Pittsburgh, November 17, 1976. I gratefully acknowledge the comments of the participants at these meetings as well as the valuable help given by my research assistant Steven Reed in computing some tables and tracing obscure data, and the materials and comments contributed by Linda A. Bernstein, Jorge I. Domínguez, and Lawrence H. Theriot.

Most statistical data used in this and the following chapter come from official Cuban publications, mainly from the complete collection of statistical bulletins and yearbooks that I have gathered at the University of Pittsburgh since 1967. In terms of scope, detail, continuity, and accuracy, foreign trade statistics are probably the best in the collection. Output data are not as good but have showed a substantial improvement in the last decade. The worst data are global, macroeconomic indicators, due to the excessive aggregation, poor continuity, and lack of precise information on the methodology of Cuba's national accounts. Additional sources of data have been reports from various U.S. government agencies as well as articles by Cuban and Soviet specialists.

1. For details see Carmelo Mesa-Lago, ed., *Revolutionary Change in Cuba* (Pittsburgh: University of Pittsburgh Press, 1971), part II; and Archibald Ritter, *The Economic Development of Revolutionary Cuba: Strategy and Performance* (New York: Praeger, 1974).

2. Because of Marxist ideology, socialist countries only compute gross output of goods and material services in their material product system (MPS), thus excluding nonmaterial services. See United Nations, *Yearbook of National Account Statistics 1973* (New York, 1975), I, xxix–xxxiii. For a discussion of measurement difficulties and upward biases in the MPS see Robert W. Campbell, *Soviet Economic Power* (Boston: Houghton-Mifflin, 1966), pp. 112–26; and Richard L. Carson, *Comparative Economic Systems* (New York: Macmillan, 1973), pp. 218–24.

3. Castro has given an average annual rate of GSP growth, probably at constant prices, of 3.9 percent for 1966–1970 (Fidel Castro, "Main Report Presented to the First Congress of the Communist Party of Cuba," *Granma Weekly Review*, December 28, 1975, p. 5). Using figures from table 9.1 (including 1967) a higher rate of 4.4 percent is calculated for the same period, the difference of +0.5 percent possibly being the annual rate of inflation. Other figures, however, suggest a much

higher rate of inflation, thus real GNP declined by 9.3 percent in 1967 but if using inflated current prices increased by 1.1 percent. (For original sources see Mesa-Lago, *Revolutionary Change*, p.331.)

4. See Carmelo Mesa-Lago, *Cuba in the 1970s: Pragmatism and Institutionalization* (Albuquerque: University of New Mexico Press, 1974), chap. 2.

5. Comité Estatal de Estadística, *La economía cubana, 1975* (n.p., n.d.), I-3. Other annual rates of "economic growth," probably at constant prices, released by top Cuban leaders are considerably smaller than those in table 9.1: 2.5 and 5 percent in 1971; and 9 and 10 percent in 1972 (for original sources see Mesa-Lago, *Cuba in the 1970s,* pp. 52–54). A Soviet scholar has published Cuban rates of growth, possibly in constant prices, which are also smaller than those in the table: 6.7 percent for 1973 and 7 percent for 1974 (Vladimir Bondarchuk, "La economía cubana en vísperas del I Congreso del Partido Comunista de Cuba," *América Latina* [Moscow], no. 4 [1975], p. 14). For the period 1970–1974, the National Bank of Cuba has given an annual average growth rate of 8.6 percent of GMP in constant prices, also smaller than that in table 9.1 (Banco Nacional de Cuba, *Desarrollo y perspectivas de la economía cubana* [Havana: 1975], p. 22; see also "Cuba económica," *Economía y Desarrollo,* no. 32 [November–December, 1975], pp. 193–94). In an addendum to the 1974 statistical yearbook it is said that the whole 1971–1975 series will be revised in the *Anuario 1975.*

6. Central Intelligence Agency, *The Cuban Economy: A Statistical Review, 1968–1976,* ER76-10708 (Washington, D.C., December 1976), p. 2. The CIA series of Cuban real GNP were estimated as follows: (1) an index of physical output was developed for 1957–1975 using Cuban data; (2) since there were no prices available for most of the revolutionary period, 1957 price weights were used; (3) the value of services was estimated using, again, 1957 prices; other gross estimates were developed for construction and military services. In addition to the problems involved in the estimates, the CIA index probably seriously underestimated growth by using 1957 prices.

7. The glowing recuperation of the Cuban economy has been exaggerated by spurious comparisons of prominent Americans but nonspecialists that have recently visited the island. For instance, Pat M. Holt, Chief of Staff of the Senate Foreign Relations Committee, has quoted the figure of 10,380 million pesos as the Cuban GNP for 1973 (in constant 1965 prices). Converting this figure into $15,888 million, he has arrived at a per capita figure of $1,587 and from this reached the controversial conclusion that Cuba has "the highest GNP *per capita* in Latin America with the exception of Venezuela where everything is distorted by oil." See *Cuba: A Staff Report Prepared for the Use of the Committee on Foreign Relations, United States Senate* (Washington, D.C.: G.P.O., 1974), p. 2. Holt's figure must refer to GSP which, as mentioned, is usually larger than GNP because of duplicate counting. Furthermore, he used a conversion ratio of 1 peso for $1.45 when the Cuban official rate of exchange in 1973 was 1 peso to $1.20. Even if the correct Cuban exchange rate had been used, it was inappropriate to compare the resulting Cuban GSP figure in dollars with GNP figures from Latin American countries which are normally estimated in dollars using exchange rates set by the international market.

8. Based on Ivan Petushkov, "Desarrollo integral de la industria azucarera de Cuba," *América Latina,* no. 1 (1975), pp. 38–41; and Comité Central del PCC, Departamento de Orientación Revolucionaria, *Directivas para el desarrollo económico y social del país en el quinquenio 1976–1980: Tesis y resolución* (Havana, 1976), p. 16. See also Linda A. Bernstein, "Cuba's Agriculture, led by Sugar, Shows Improvement in Key Crops," *Foreign Agriculture* 12, no. 21 (May 27, 1974), 16; and "Cuba," *The Agricultural Situation in the Western Hemisphere,* Foreign Agricultural Economic Report, no. 103, April 1975, p. 7. These two reports, published by the U.S. Department of Agriculture, for the first time in the last decade, acknowledged improvements in Cuban agriculture.

9. In the 1960s Cuba was the third largest world sugar producer, the USSR and United States being respectively the first and second producers. In the early 1970s Cuba fell to fourth place behind Brazil, which moved to second place surpassing the United States and approximating the USSR. If these trends continue, Brazil will become the world's largest sugar producer by the end of the decade. However, due to its larger population and domestic consumption, Brazil exported only about one-third of Cuban sugar exports in 1975.

10. It was not until 1975 that the Russians and the Cubans publicly referred to the 1974 increase in sugar prices and then without specifying the magnitude of the increase. See N. Gladkov, "URSS-Cuba, colaboración amistosa," *Panorama Latinoamericano* (Moscow), no. 201 (May 1975), p. 20; and Osvaldo Dorticós, "Speech at the Main Ceremony for the 25th Anniversary of the National Bank of Cuba," *Granma Weekly Review*, November 9, 1975, p. 7. The U.S. Department of Agriculture estimated, in April 1975, the increase in sugar price paid by the Soviets at 20 cents per pound and suggested that it could have been paid retroactively (Linda A. Bernstein, "Cuba's Trade Horizons Widen as Diplomatic Ties Expand," *Foreign Agriculture* 13, no. 17 [April 28, 1975], 4). According to the National Bank of Cuba, the USSR paid 12.02 cents (in U.S. dollars, F.O.B.), per pound of Cuban sugar in 1973 and 19.64 cents in 1974. See Banco Nacional de Cuba, *Desarrollo y perspectivas*, p. 32.

11. For an historical series of sugar prices see chapter 13 of this volume.

12. Banco Nacional de Cuba, *Desarrollo y perspectivas*, p. 32.

13. Estimates of the 1977 Cuban sugar harvest (in million tons) are: 4.5 (*Business Latin America*), 5.7 (U.S. Department of Agriculture), 5.8 (F. O. Licht), and 5.7 to 6.2 (*Latin America Commodities Report*). Fidel Castro has said that, in spite of the 1977 crop difficulties, output would come close to the goal, possibly above 6 million tons. See "Speech at the Closing of the 5th Congress of ANAP," *Granma Weekly Review*, May 29, 1977, p. 4. Also Marcelo Fernández Font, ibid., May 1, 1977, p. 10.

14. Fidel Castro, "Speech at the Main Rally to Celebrate the 16th Anniversary of the CDRs," *Granma Weekly Review*, October 10, 1976, pp. 2–5. See also Raul Castro, "Speech at the 20th Anniversary of the Revolutionary Armed Forces," ibid., December 12, 1976, p. 12. Details on the 1976-1977 economic decline will not be available until the end of the 1970s, because of the two-year delay in publishing statistical data.

15. See Fernando Morais, "Quatro horas de entrevista com Fidel Castro," *Veja*, July 13, 1977, p. 44; and Fidel Castro, "Speech Given in the Ceremony to Celebrate the 23rd Anniversary of the Attack on the Moncada Garrison," *Granma Weekly Review*, August 8, 1976, p. 4.

16. Information on the negative economic impact of the Angola operation is kept strictly secret by the Cuban government for military and political reasons. However, foreign diplomats and journalists in Havana have leaked some details. See the articles by James Nelson Goodsell, "Cubans Still in Angola—But Most are Civilians?" *Christian Science Monitor*, April 12, 1977; and "Cuban Revolution Loses Some of its Early Sizzle," ibid., April 20, 1977.

17. The USSR sugar targets for 1980 (11 million tons and 96 percent self-sufficiency) are quite ambitious when compared with the poor performance of 1970–1976; after a record crop of 9.6 million tons in 1968, output declined to 7-8 million tons to supply only 72–86 percent of domestic needs. Cuban targets for 1980 (8–8.7 million tons) are also too optimistic compared with an average output of 5.6 million tons in 1971–1976. But assuming that the Soviet and Cuban targets are fulfilled, what would they do with so much sugar? In more realistic terms, either Soviet and Cuban planners do not expect their targets to be reached or they will have to modify sugar plans in one or both countries. See Linda A. Bernstein, "USSR Apparently Planning on Self-sufficiency in Sugar Production in 1980," U.S. Department of Agriculture, Economic Research Service, December 8, 1976.

18. When prices of sugar (sucrose derived from cane and beet) reached a peak in 1973-1974, the production of HFCS (high-fructose corn syrup) became profitable. HFCS is 33 percent sweeter than sucrose but has a different flavor. It is expected to capture 20 percent of the U.S. market by 1980. See David C. Garlow, "Corn Syrup: Basin Sugar's Tough Competitor," *Caribbean Basin Economic Survey* 3, no. 2 (April –May 1977), 10–11; and "Foreign Sugar Suppliers Face Gloomy Future," *Times of the Americas*, March 2, 1977, pp. 1, 3.

19. The low estimate is from Kim Badenhop, "El mercado del azúcar," *Visión*, June 17, 1977, pp. 44–47. The high estimate is from Edward V. Jesse and Glenn A. Zepp, *Sugar Policy Options for the United States*, Agricultural Economic Report No. 351 (Washington, D.C.: U.S. Department of Agriculture, February 1977). Sugar brokers have been forecasting a sharp increase in sugar prices, promising profits with a minimum price of 13 cents per pound. See as an example First Commodity

Corporation of Boston, "A Special Report from the President's Office: Sugar," Boston, Winter 1977.

20. See chapter 14 in this volume. GEPLACEA has met in Argentina and Mexico (1974), the Dominican Republic and Peru (1975), Colombia (1976), and Havana (1977). Former President Dorticós ("Speech at the Main Ceremony," p. 7) has stated that Cuba's efforts to stabilize sugar prices "at profitable levels" do not aim at a confrontation with importing nations but at a dialogue on equal footing.

21. See the *Times* (London), October 6, 1977, p. 7.

22. See Jesse and Zepp, *Sugar Policy Options*.

23. Marcelo Fernández Font, *Granma Weekly Review*, March 14, 1976, p. 5.

24. The Cubans ascribed the 13 percent decline in 1975 output to malfunctions of fishing ships and refrigeration equipment; most of these, however, are new, and there were no previous reports of malfunctions. See *Direct from Cuba*, no. 169, May 15, 1977.

25. "Congress of the Party Resolution on Economic Management and Planning System," *Granma Weekly Review*, January 11, 1976, pp. 10-11; "Política Económica," *Plataforma Programática del Partido Comunista de Cuba* (Havana: Departamento de Orientación Revolucionaria del C.C. del P.C.C., 1976), pp. 61-74; and Raul Castro, "Speech at the Inauguration of Three Courses at the National School of Management," *Granma Weekly Review*, March 14, 1976, p. 2. See also chapter 15 in this volume.

26. The following information is a summary of the excellent article by Jozef Wilczynski, "Multinational Corporations and East-West Economic Co-operation," *Journal of World Trade Law* (London) 9, no. 3 (May–June 1975), 266-86.

27. Jerry Flint, "Cubans Admit their Economy is in Serious Trouble," *New York Times*, April 25, 1977; and John Virtue, "U.S. Investments are Needed by Cuba," *Miami Herald*, May 1, 1977.

28. "Letter from Havana I: How Cubans View Prospects of U.S. Trade," *Business Latin America*, June 30, 1977, p. 202.

29. Barbara Walters, "An Interview with Fidel," *Granma Weekly Review*, July 17, 1977, pp. 2-3. This is the full version of the four-hour interview although some sensitive sections of the televised interview were omitted. The transcript of the program is available as "Fidel Castro Speaks," ABC TV, June 9, 1977.

30. Both Cuban and U.S. government agencies prepared too optimistic preliminary estimates of the Cuban trade balance in 1974 which showed record surpluses as compared with the deficit of $3.7 million eventually released by the Cubans. By the end of 1974, the National Bank of Cuba estimated the trade balance of that year at $440 million (resulting from exports of $2,680 millions and imports of $2,240 millions) but by the end of 1975 the estimated surplus had been reduced to $14 million (exports of $2,224 millions and imports of $2,210 millions). See Banco Nacional de Cuba, *Statement of Condition* (Havana, December 31, 1974), and *Desarrollo y perspectivas*, p. 30. In June 1975, the U.S. Department of Commerce gave as the 1974 trade surplus the figure of $495 million resulting from estimated imports of $2,250 million and exports of $2,745 million ("Statement for the Record . . .Before the Subcommittee on International Trade and Commerce of the House International Relations Committee," Washington, D.C., June 11, 1975, Table 5). In the following month, the CIA published an "Unclassified Reference Aid" with its own estimates, reducing the surplus to $295 million, as a result of estimated higher imports of $2,450 million (Central Intelligence Agency, *Intelligence Handbook Cuba: Foreign Trade*, A [ER] 75-69, July 1975, p. 5). In the revised document finally published by the Department of Commerce, its initial figures were substituted by the CIA figures, except for total transactions which remained erroneously unchanged (*United States Commercial Relations with Cuba: A Survey*, prepared by Lawrence H. Theriot et al. [Washington, D.C.: GPO, 1975], p. 41).

31. Dorticós ("Speech at the Main Ceremony," p. 7) had reported a record trade surplus of 295 million pesos in the first three quarters of 1975, which spurred a wave of unfounded optimism. The value of Cuban exports is heavily concentrated in the first three quarters of the year when the sugar crop is exported, while imports are more evenly spread throughout the year.

CARMELO MESA-LAGO

32. CIA, *The Cuban Economy*, p. 7.

33. "Latin America Suffers from Sugar Price Fall," *Latin America Economic Report*, September 24, 1976, pp. 146–47; ibid., October 8, 1976, p. 1; "Cuban Economic Setback Threatens to Reduce Gains from any U.S. Opening," *Business Latin America*, February 2, 1977, pp. 33–34; and *Latin American Times*, March 30, 1977.

34. Fidel Castro, "Speech at the Solemn Session to Set Up the National Assembly of People's Power," *Granma Weekly Review*, December 12, 1976, pp. 2–3.

35. The year 1986 will be critical for Cuba because at that time the bulk of her debt with USSR will mature. If relations between the two countries are as good in 1986 as now, the USSR may postpone the debt again or agree to commute it. If Cuba's relations with the USSR have cooled off and a workable and safe relationship has been developed with the United States, Cuba might default on her debt.

36. *United States Commercial Relations With Cuba*, p. 20.

37. República de Cuba, Junta Central de Planificación, Dirección Central de Estadística, *Anuario Estadístico de Cuba 1974* (Havana: JUCEPLAN, n.d.), pp. 188–89.

38. Marcelo Fernández Font, *Granma Weekly Review*, March 14, 1976, p. 5.

39. Estimates in "Statement of Arthur T. Downey Deputy Assistant Secretary for East-West Trade Before the Subcommittee on International Trade and Commerce of the House International Relations Committee," Washington, D.C., July 22, 1976, table 2; and CIA, *The Cuban Economy*, p. 7.

40. "Letter from Havana," p. 202; and "U.S. Business Trip to Havana Shows Keen Interest in Trade on Both Sides," *Business Latin America,* May 4, 1977, p. 137.

41. It should be noted nevertheless, that the two most important projects to be financed by the USSR in Cuba—a metallurgical complex and an atomic power plant—are not to be completed until 1981–1985. See Estefanía Seoane, "Cuba-USSR: Fraternal Cooperation," *Foreign Trade* (Moscow), no. 8 (1976), pp. 12–14; and *Granma Weekly Review*, April 25, 1976, p. 9.

42. Morais, "Quatro horas," pp. 38–46; and "Brazilians Study Possible Trade Openings with Cuba," *Times of the Americas*, December 8, 1976, p. 2.

10

CARMELO MESA-LAGO

The Economics of U.S.-Cuban Rapprochement

From late 1974 to the end of 1975, there was a trend toward U.S.-Cuban rapprochement highlighted by direct negotiations between the two countries and the U.S. decision partly to lift the Cuban embargo for subsidiary firms abroad. The trend was interrupted in late 1975 by several events: Cuba's support of both the Popular Movement for the Liberation of Angola (MPLA) and the independent movement in Puerto Rico; the U.S. presidential campaign; the bombing of a Cuban airlines plane; and Fidel Castro's subsequent repudiation of the U.S.-Cuban antihijacking agreement. The inauguration of President Carter reopened the door to rapprochement with initial statements from both sides in early 1977 favoring negotiations. The United States subsequently suspended reconnaissance flights over Cuba, removed the prohibition on U.S. citizens traveling to Cuba and authorized them to spend money there, and granted visas to selected Cuban technicians to travel to the United States. In return the Cubans allowed a U.S. volleyball team to play in Havana, enabled groups of tourists and businessmen to visit, and released a dozen U.S. prisoners. In the spring of 1976, direct U.S.-Cuban negotiations were renewed in New York and Havana and eventually resulted in an agreement on fishing boundaries and rights and the exchange of "interest sections" representing each country. In the summer, however, the situation seemed to have reached an impasse. The Cubans demanded a total lifting of the U.S. embargo, and the Americans requested that the next step come from Havana. There also seemed to be a growing realization by both sides that the path for full normalization of relations would be long. In 1978, Cuba's intervention in the Ethiopian-Somali War induced a new freeze with Washington.

It is assumed for this discussion that, in spite of temporary slowdowns and setbacks, the trend toward normalization of relations between the two countries will continue and a resumption of economic ties will eventually take place. The chapter anticipates and explores the economic issues that might be of key significance in U.S.-Cuban rapprochement during the second half of the 1970s. As an economist, I have selected for discussion the field in which my background and training can contribute most to a better understanding of rapprochement between the two nations. This does not mean, however, that the economic aspect is necessarily the most important in that process. Humanistic issues such as freedom of political prisoners, the liberalization and democratization of the Cuban

199

regime, and a freer entry to and exit from the island certainly have first priority in my mind, and I truly hope that rapprochement will have a positive impact on them.

The chapter is divided into four sections. The first reviews the main products and services which could be involved in a U.S.-Cuban economic relationship. The second section discusses potential economic advantages and disadvantages for both sides. The third section analyzes obstacles to, and restrictions on, the resumption of an economic relationship. The fourth section evaluates the economic strength of both parties in the negotiations, identifies areas of relatively easy agreement and those difficult for consensus, and suggests what the U.S. attitude should be on lifting the embargo.

The Subject of the U.S.-Cuban Economic Relationship

Although the previous chapter showed that the Cubans are prepared to consider joint ventures with and investment from the United States, economic relations will probably be focused, at first, on trade. It is significant that both sides have compiled lists of what they would like to trade.[1] The basic products that Cuba can sell to the United States are sugar, nickel, fish, tobacco, citrus fruits, and rum; the basic service is tourism.

Cuba should have, in the rest of the decade, enough sugar—apart from long-run trade commitments—to satisfy most U.S. import needs. In the early 1970s, a rough average of 60 percent of Cuba's sugar exports went to the USSR and other socialist countries, 20 percent to Japan, and 20 percent to market economies, mostly Western Europe and Canada.[2] Sugar exports committed to the socialist countries are difficult to shift to market economies, because such commitments have been taken into account in the 1976–1980 economic plans of those countries and are included in long-run trade agreements. In addition, current prices paid for Cuban sugar by the USSR are about four times the international market price, which makes shifts in sales to market economies even more difficult.

Cuba is facing, however, a sluggish demand for sugar from China and traditional nonsocialist buyers. Due to political conflicts, exports of Cuban sugar to China fell from a yearly average of 319,000 tons in 1972–1974 to 90,000 tons in 1975. The Cuban-Chinese protocol for 1976 scheduled exports of 170,000 tons, but in view of the escalating conflict between the two countries, it is doubtful that this level of exports did materialize.[3] In 1975, Cuba hoped to sign a five-year agreement with Japan to sell a total of 2.5 million tons of sugar, but in 1976 she signed a four-year agreement to sell only 1 million tons: 100,000 in 1977 and 300,000 annually in 1978–1980.[4] Sugar sales to Spain averaged 345,000 tons in 1974–1975, but the 1976 record crop in Spain brought a reduction to 120,000 tons and an agreement for only 90,000 tons in 1978.[5] In trade agreements recently signed by Cuba with Western European countries, sugar probably has been included as an exportable Cuban product to be potentially exchanged for imports coming from those countries; the chances are, however, that Cuba is not bound to sell specific amounts of sugar, providing that she pays her debts from other sources.

Assuming export commitments to socialist countries of 3.5 to 4 million tons annually and stagnant sugar harvests for the rest of the 1970s, from 2 to 2.5 million tons of Cuban sugar should be available for the world market. If Cuban sugar harvests increase to reach 7.5 million tons in 1980, then the amount available will be about 4 million tons. However, if sugar prices in the international market continue low, Cuba may try to sell more sugar to the USSR and other socialist countries to take advantage of the subsidized prices that the latter are currently paying.[6]

What are the possibilities that the United States will return to the sugar quota system with Cuba? Under the U.S. Sugar Act of 1961, the Cuban quota was fixed at 50 percent of U.S. sugar imports and reduced, in 1971, to 24 percent of such imports. The quota, however, was suspended (until the time of reestablishment of trade with Cuba) and temporarily prorated to the Dominican Republic, Mexico, Brazil, Peru, and other minor producers. For a while it was speculated that if the United States were to reestablish trade with Cuba, the reassignment of its sugar quota to other Latin American countries would create if not a legal problem at least a diplomatic one. This preoccupation seemed to end in 1974 when the Sugar Act expired and with it the quota system. In 1975-1977 the United States continued buying sugar from its customary suppliers but competed, in terms of prices, with other buyers in the world market. There are now talks in the United States on the conveniences of returning to the quota system. When direct trade between the United States and Cuba is reestablished, Cuba should logically resume her sugar sales either through competitive prices or the quota system. In any event, in terms of freight costs, Cuban sugar would be cheaper to the United States than sugar imported from more distant suppliers such as the Philippines, Brazil, and Peru.

In nickel production, Cuba's planned expansion to 100,000 tons by 1980 may not be realized, but total output of sinter and oxide (of nickel and cobalt) should increase substantially. In the early 1970s, the bulk of nickel exports went to Western Europe with only a small fraction committed to the USSR and Eastern Europe. Currently the United States has to import about 90 percent of its raw nickel and Cuba should be able to supply about half of the U.S. needs.[7]

The steady increase of fish and shellfish output (fresh, frozen, and canned) should enable Cuba eventually to export a significant amount of these products to the United States. Cuban exports have gone mostly to Western Europe (France, Holland, Italy, Spain), Canada, and Japan; nothing to Eastern Europe, except a small fraction to East Germany.

The production of cigars has declined, but exports (helped by domestic rationing) have jumped 75 percent between 1970 and 1972. Almost one-half of Cuban cigar exports go to Spain and about one-third to the rest of Western Europe and Canada; only 14 percent is committed to Eastern Europe. The former

CARMELO MESA-LAGO

U.S. market for Cuban cigars is currently taken by imported cigars from the Caribbean, Central America, and the Canary Islands as well as by the expansion of domestic production. (Exiled Cuban cigar manufacturers, now residing in the United States, Spain, and Latin America, have developed successful cigar factories and won lawsuits in the United States to use the famous old brand names.) Still, the taste for and status of real Havana cigars continues in the United States, although limited to a minority.[8]

Practically all rum manufactured in Cuba for export goes to the USSR and Eastern Europe. Representatives of old Cuban brands like Bacardi successfully filed suit to ban the Cuban government from use of their labels in the world market. Such brands are now produced with the same quality in Puerto Rico, Mexico, Brazil, and Spain. Trade possibilities for this product are, therefore, small. The same is true of citrus fruits. Cuba has current commitments to export all its citrus to the USSR and Eastern Europe; in the United States, Cuban citrus would have to compete with Florida and California producers.[9]

After sugar, the most important commodity that Cuba can offer to the United States is natural beauty: unspoiled beaches, spectacular valleys, tropical forests, fishing spots, and wonderful climate. Prior to the Revolution, tourism was called "the second sugar harvest"; some 300,000 tourists annually visited the island. Interest in Cuba's historical past (preserved in some colonial cities like Trinidad) and curiosity about the dramatic changes that have occurred on the island under socialism are potent magnets for the American tourist. The island has been traditionally known for its music and folklore, to which a first-rate modern ballet company has recently been added; some of the old and internationally famous nightclubs, like the Tropicana, are still open.

Cubatour, the state tourist agency, is expanding its facilities for domestic use. Eighteen hotels were under construction in the fall of 1975, some at the unique Varadero beach, a one-and-a-half hour drive from Havana. The target is to open sixty-two new hotels by 1980.[10] The Cuban domestic tourist season—especially at the beach resorts—is during the summer; thus tourist facilities are practically empty in late fall, all winter, and early spring, when the country's climate is most attractive to northerners. Aware of this luxurious waste, the Cubans are beginning to fill their resorts with foreign tourists. In 1974, 15,000 tourists from Canada, Western and Eastern Europe visited the island; the number increased to 50,000 in 1975, and to 60,000 in 1976 (two-thirds of whom were Canadians). The current five-year plan projects 300,000 tourists in 1980.[11] Tours to Cuba are currently advertised in Canadian, Mexican, and Venezuelan newspapers with prices ("all included") for a week's vacation ranging from $300 to $600. Both Canada and Jamaica are giving technical aid to Cuba in planning tourism and training personnel; obviously, the United States could play an important role in assisting the reemerging Cuban tourist industry. At the end of 1975 the Paris-based Club Méditerranée, with one million members and sixty-eight vacation resorts in twenty-two countries, completed construction of a new 200-bed club in Cuba for Canadians and Europeans at the Bacuranao beach. A second club is being planned for Americans. Scheduled for opening in 1977, it will be made up of "villas" with a 600-bed capacity.[12] This is possibly Cuba's first "joint venture" with a foreign firm.

Cuba could earn $45 million annually if 100,000 American tourists visited the island. In early 1977, nineteen U.S. travel agents went to Cuba to negotiate tours for American tourists. The lifting of the prohibition against U.S. citizens visiting the island in March 1977 allowed a cruise liner, the *Daphne*, carrying 320 American tourists to touch in Havana harbor in May for the first time in sixteen years. This resulted in a flourishing of tour agencies including the Cuban Travel Bureau (a subsidiary of Orbitair International) which opened in New York as the first U.S. travel agency officially to represent Cubatour.[13]

In spite of these dramatic changes, U.S. tourism is not expected to reach massive proportions in the near future. On the Cuban side, old fears, actual security reasons, the danger of economic dependence on foreigners, and the effect that wealthy Americans may have on the frugal Cubans are reasons to control the tourist inflow. And yet, when asked in 1977 by a French journalist about these potential "risks," Castro verified that tourists would be allowed into Cuba: Even if they succeed in "corrupting an infinitesimal part of the population," this evil would be compensated for by showing Cuba's revolutionary accomplishments to the tourists.[14] On the U.S. side, the type of tourist that was attracted in the 1950s by gambling casinos, fancy prostitution, and other spurious incentives will not have anything to do in Cuba. But even the puritan tourist will not be able to travel direct to Cuba because the U.S. Treasury Department only permits American tour operators to sell tickets or charter flights on foreign carriers that have service to Cuba from points outside the United States.[15] Finally, a solution would have to be found by both nations to the problem of Cuban exiles who want to go back to the island as tourists or to visit relatives. Interestingly, Fidel Castro first said that exiles will not be allowed to return under any circumstances. Later, however, Blas Roca, an old Communist and head of the Constitutional Commission, declared that those exiles who had not taken part in any activity against Cuba would be allowed to return.[16] In spite of this, Cubatour has warned U.S. tour operators that Cuban-born people, even if naturalized U.S. citizens, will not be allowed into Cuba. When the *Daphne* visited Havana, four Cuban exiles were not allowed to disembark initially, although authorization was granted by Cuban customs at the last minute. This double standard actually helps the terrorist activities of a minority of exiles who bombed a travel agency in Miami, provoking the cancellation of the service scheduled by Mackey International Airlines between Fort Lauderdale and Havana, as well as successive trips of the *Daphne* in 1977–1978.[17]

What can the United States supply to Cuba? Above all, the Cubans want technology, and they know it cannot be developed domestically and hence has to be imported. In private conversations with U.S. businessmen, politicians, and journalists, Cuban officials have hinted that their effort to import Soviet technology has not been very successful.[18] The top Cuban economic official, Carlos

Rafael Rodríguez, has publicly stated that the socialist camp does not have a whole range of technology which is only available from the West.[19] There is significant evidence that the Cubans distrust the Soviet technological capacity to deliver on their promises to fulfill some of the pivotal goals of Cuba's 1976–1980 plan. For instance, the initial agreement to expand the island's nickel industry was signed with the USSR in 1975. Almost two years later nothing had materialized, and at the seventy-ninth meeting of the Executive Committee of Council for Mutual Economic Assistance (COMECON), held in Havana, it was announced that COMECON would be the one to help Cuba in this plan, following the program used in Mongolia! A future protocol to be signed would include a plan to study, for one-and-a-half years, the construction of new nickel plants.[20] Hence actual construction would start, at the earliest, in 1979, and the goal to increase nickel output by 60,000 tons by 1980 is highly improbable. The Cubans have also expressed some disappointment with Western European technology and seem to have come to the realization that the best solution for them rests in U.S. technology.[21] Castro has candidly proclaimed that ''the United States is the most advanced country in the world in technology and science; Cuba could benefit from everything America has.''[22] High Cuban trade officials have consistently expressed their admiration for American technology to U.S. businessmen visiting the island.

In 1972–1974 about one-fourth of Cuban imports were of capital and intermediate goods, primarily transportation equipment: trucks, cars, buses, merchant and fishing vessels, port equipment, locomotives and railway equipment, and aircraft. Another significant portion consisted of agricultural and industrial machinery: sugar-cane harvesting equipment and tractors; auto tire, fertilizer, textile, cement, nickel, and electricity plants; and road-building equipment. A substantial amount of U.S.-made spare parts were also imported through triangular trade. Finally there were chemicals, pharmaceutical products, and fertilizers. The main supplier of these goods was the USSR; with Western Europe (Italy, Spain, France, United Kingdom, West Germany) and Eastern Europe (Czechoslovakia, East Germany, Bulgaria) as secondary sources.[23] Certainly the United States can supply all these goods to Cuba.

Since the late 1960s, there has been a significant development of electronic data processing and computer science in Cuba. Some seventy computers were installed in 1969–1973. Western Europe (France, Italy, and Great Britain) has supplied most computer equipment, trained the personnel, and helped the Cubans produce their own small computers. Cuba has not yet imported any computer hardware manufactured in Eastern Europe because of the notorious lag in computer technology between the socialist camp and the West. It is logical to assume that if the Cubans had had the option, they would have bought U.S. computers, which are more technologically advanced than those from Western Europe.[24] In fact the Cubans have tried to buy IBM computer equipment through a Canadian subsidiary but without success. Computer science is being applied in Cuba to solve management problems, in systems analysis, operational research, simulation, and linear programming. Currently Cuba is developing a teleprocessing network to link minicomputers to the data generated by work centers; they face serious difficulties in the field of software. Finally, the Cubans are rapidly developing informational science and trying to apply it in solving everyday problems. Most technical aid in the application of electronic data processing to management, labor, and so forth, has come from the USSR (250 fellowships have recently been granted by the USSR to the Cubans). Canada, however, is increasingly involved in projects to improve technological fields in Cuba. The United States could be a major source of equipment, technical aid, and training in the field of cybernetics in Cuba.

Manufactures, although at lower levels than in the 1950s, still represent 12 percent of Cuban imports. Tires, textiles, sheet steel, and electric appliances are among the most important manufactured goods imported by Cuba. Major suppliers are the USSR, Japan, and, increasingly, France. Here lies another area for potential U.S. exports to Cuba.

Crude oil, fuel oil, and gasoline made up about 10 percent of Cuban imports in 1972–1974 with the USSR supplying 98 percent of Cuba's oil needs.[25] The price of oil is subsidized by the Soviets: it was $3.66 per barrel prior to the energy crisis and $5.66 per barrel, one-half the price charged by the Organization of Petroleum Exporting Countries (OPEC) in 1975 (see chapter 13). To keep up with Cuba's oil needs, the USSR has to maintain an expensive oil flotilla; it is said that one Soviet oil tanker arrives in a Cuban port every two days. Transportation costs are paid by Cuba.[26] It would be to the advantage of both countries if an oil producer in the Western Hemisphere such as Venezuela or Mexico would agree to supply Cuba. Apparently Mexico has already sent oil to Cuba through Bermuda-based Joc Oil (related to the same company with headquarters in New York) while the USSR has made a similar quantity available to Joc Oil in the Mediterranean.[27] According to a Soviet-Venezuelan communiqué signed during Carlos Andrés Pérez's visit to Moscow in November 1976, Venezuelan oil could be shipped to Cuba in return for Soviet deliveries of equivalent amounts to Venezuelan clients in Western Europe.[28] The major obstacle is that Cuban refineries may have to be remodified again to process Western crude instead of Soviet crude. Also, it is unlikely that Mexico and Venezuela will get involved in such an operation until U.S.-Cuban relations are normalized. Finally, the USSR, through the Institute of Energy of Leningrad, began in late 1974 to plan a nuclear-powered electric plant with two reactors (900 megawatts) in Cienfuegos, Las Villas Province. However, the 1976–1980 Cuban-Soviet economic cooperation agreement specified that a first reactor—a standard Soviet model with a generating capacity of 440 megawatts—will not be completed until 1981–1985. In mid-1977, Castro stated that the first nuclear plant will begin to operate in 1983 or 1984, the second in 1985, and that all future sources of energy will be nuclear.[29] U.S.-Cuban rapprochement could ease Cuba's energy problem by facilitating triangular arrangements with Venezuela, Mexico, or Ecuador, and, perhaps, providing technical aid for the remodification of former U.S. oil refineries on the island.

The major component of Cuban imports is still foodstuffs (about one-fourth of total imports in 1972-1974): wheat and flour, rice, corn, dried beans, lard and vegetable oil, beef, and dairy products. In the 1950s these products were almost totally supplied by the United States; now the USSR, China and, increasingly, Canada, Argentina, France, and Holland are the suppliers. Because of its climate, Cuba cannot grow some cereals and does not grow wheat because it would not be economical. In 1962-1963, Cuba imported practically all her wheat and flour from the USSR, but, in the fall of 1963, the USSR signed a grain contract with Canada stipulating that 250,000 tons of wheat and 750,000 tons of flour would be diverted to Cuba but transported in Soviet vessels. By 1966 the amount of Canadian wheat going to Cuba had increased by 70 percent and, due to poor Soviet crops, by 1974, Canada was taking care of all Cuban demands for this grain (726,000 tons).[30] Cuba is one of the largest per capita rice consumers in the hemisphere. From 1961 to 1966 China supplied less than 135,000 metric tons of rice annually to Cuba (highest imports were 250,000 metric tons in 1965) but thereafter imports of this product declined. In 1975, probably due to the Cuban-Chinese confrontation over Angola, rice imports from China fell dramatically to 40,000 tons. To partly fill the vacuum, Cuba (with Soviet financing) imported 45,000 tons of rice from Argentina, Colombia, Guyana, and Venezuela plus an unspecified amount from Spain. The USSR, a net importer of rice, agreed to supply Cuba with an unspecified amount of rice during 1976-1980 presumably to be purchased from Western sources on Soviet account.[31] In the fall of 1975, U.S. Congressman John Breaux of Louisiana visited Cuba and began negotiations with Cuban trade officials to sell part of the 1975 U.S. bumper rice crop, but the talks failed because of the trade embargo.[32] In the 1976 protocol, China promised only 60,000 tons of rice to Cuba, hence corn was substituted for part of the monthly rice ration. The USSR supplied Cuba with corn until recently; in 1974 Argentina exported 250,000 tons of corn to Cuba, and the amount increased in 1975-1976. Senator James Abourezk, who visited Cuba in August 1975, reported a conversation in which Fidel Castro showed interest in buying 500,000 tons of corn from the United States as feed grain for Cuban livestock.[33] The USSR is still Cuba's main supplier of lard (70,000 tons were imported by Cuba in 1973), vegetable oil (60,000 tons), and cotton (18,000 tons). Dried beans are supplied by the USSR, Chile (in 1971-1973), and Mexico for a total of 80,000 tons in 1973. Canada has supplied Cuba with a large number of cattle and significant amounts of milk. The United States could also become a major exporter of these agricultural products to Cuba. It has been estimated that Cuba could meet her 1980 meat production target by doubling the level of current livestock feed imports with close, cheap, high quality U.S. feeds.[34] According to a U.S. grain businessman, the cost of soybean imports could be reduced by 30 percent if Cuba bought this grain from the United States instead of Europe; large savings could also be made on rice, beans, and wheat.[35]

There are a myriad of other U.S. products which could find an attractive market in Cuba. For example, Cuba provides free textbooks to millions of students at all educational levels. Currently Cuba does not respect most international copyright conventions and simply copies, translates, and publishes U.S. technical and educational materials. But as Cuba increases its relations with the West, the island has signed agreements for the translation and publication of books with Mexico's two major publishing houses as well as with Argentina and Spain. U.S.-Cuban rapprochement could result in significant royalties for U.S. authors and publishers.

Economic Advantages and Disadvantages of U.S.-Cuban Economic Relations

The mutual gains from resumption of economic relations between the United States and Cuba will not, in general, be spectacular, and yet both countries could benefit at little or no cost. Cuba would benefit more than the United States. A major political advantage of normalizing relations for Cuba, which should also generate a significant economic gain, would be the U.S. recognition of the island's status quo; this should reduce the real and imagined threat to Cuba's national security and allow, in the long run, a transfer of expenditures from defense activities into economic and social development.

The island's major economic gain probably will be in freight savings. Currently, almost 85 percent of Cuban trade is with the USSR, Eastern Europe, Japan, and China; shifting part of that trade to the United States would reduce shipping distances from about six thousand miles (USSR) or nine thousand miles (Japan) to one hundred miles (United States). In terms of travel time, the reduction would be from voyages of twenty to ninety days to voyages of two to three days. (Besides savings in freight, Cuba would ameliorate problems such as lack of sufficient warehouses and port facilities, rotation of ships, and payments for delays in ports due to concentration of ships and spoilage of perishable goods.)[36] Prime Minister Castro has acknowledged freight savings as one of the main benefits of U.S.-Cuban trade.[37] To reduce somewhat the cost of transportation, Cuba has developed in the last fifteen years what is now the fourth largest merchant fleet in Latin America. Table 10.1 shows that total tonnage of the Cuban international merchant fleet increased almost ten times from 1958 to 1975. The goal of the current five-year plan is to double the tonnage by 1980. Orders for construction of ships for the Cuban fleet have been placed with ten countries, and Poland is giving assistance to Cuba in the construction of her own shipyards.[38] Nevertheless, due to Cuba's dependence on foreign trade—the value of exports and imports combined represented 46 percent of Cuba's gross material product (GMP) in 1970-1974—and the great distances that its ships have to

CARMELO MESA-LAGO

TABLE 10.1
Capacity of Cuba's International Merchant Fleet, 1958–1975

	Number of Ships	Tonnage (thousand metric tons)	Percentage of Foreign Trade Carried		
			Cuban Ships	Rented Ships	Others
1958	14	58.0	—	—	—
1960	19	76.9	—	—	—
1965	32	186.8	4	15	81
1970	47	367.2	6	13	81
1972	46	415.5	8	10	82
1974	50	493.6	8	15	77
1975	52	544.5	—	—	—

Source: Raul González Tapia and José González Cobas, "Cuba: Desarrollo de la marina mercante," Economía y Desarrollo, no. 37 (September–October 1976), pp. 127–28.
Note: Coastal vessels are excluded from the figures.

travel, the merchant fleet carried only 8 percent of the island's foreign trade in 1974. Another 15 percent was carried in rented ships, 75 percent of them from socialist countries, and 77 percent in ships of other countries. Even if the planned goal for expansion of the Cuban fleet materializes, by 1980 its ships should be carrying no more than 20 percent of the nation's trade. (Actually the percentage should be considerably smaller because, in the above calculation, the expansion in the volume of Cuban trade has not been taken into account. We have data on the value of trade but not on physical volume.) If Cuban trade would shift significantly to the United States, Cuba's merchant fleet could handle 3.5 times the freight it handled in 1974.[39]

The resumption of trade with the United States would also enable Cuba to save by buying spare parts directly instead of through intermediaries. Most Cuban industrial equipment is still U.S.-made (sugar mills, nickel complexes, electricity plants, cigarette factories), and buying spare parts through triangular trade to keep this equipment running has increased their price by 20 to 30 percent.[40] Cuba may also be able to save by buying goods more cheaply from the United States than from the USSR. One of Cuba's trade problems has been the difficulty in ascertaining the overall terms of trade with the USSR. Since 80 percent of the island's transactions with the Soviets are through barter trade, and since Cuba has not been able to assess the real costs of most Soviet imports at world market, competitive prices, it is almost impossible to determine if the island has been making a profit or a loss. Another advantage for Cuba would be the larger assortment of goods, more advanced technology, and faster supply that the United States may offer in agricultural machinery, electronics, and transportation equipment. In the long run, Cuba could benefit also (as have Yugoslavia and Poland) from remittances of former Cubans living in the United States to relatives on the island. Perhaps the most significant benefit for Cuba would be to reduce somewhat its dependence upon the USSR, to further diversify sellers and buyers.

One major economic disadvantage of the resumption of trade with the United States (or an increase of trade with any other country except for the USSR) concerns the current significant gap between the international market price of sugar and the subsidized price paid to Cuba by the Soviets. The question is whether or not Cuba will have the option to increase sugar exports to the USSR or will have to sell her uncommitted sugar to the world market. In the latter case, the United States will be as good a buyer as any other country.

There are other potential disadvantages, these of a political and social nature. First there is the ever present fear that economic ties to the Colossus of the North may recreate the prerevolutionary dependency relationship. This is difficult to envisage since Cuba would be largely controlling the degree of economic association with the United States and would certainly not cut its ties to socialist countries. The Cubans are also concerned with the effect that U.S. consumerism and values might have on their frugal society but, as noted above, they seem willing to take that risk.

One potential economic disadvantage for Cuba might arise from the lack of credit obtainable from the United States. In 1961–1976 Cuba received Soviet subsidies and credits for a cumulative aid total of $8.2 billion (see table 2.2). The bulk of this aid (56 percent) was made up of credits to cover trade deficits between the USSR and Cuba, with subsidies in the price of sugar being the second most important (30 percent). It is difficult to think that the United States would subsidize the Cuban economy as the Soviets have apparently been doing during the last sixteen years. The Soviet Union is trying to reduce that subsidy to the minimum; both the Cubans and the Russians have pointed out that the increasing efficiency and better planning and management of the island economy are key steps in maximizing Soviet aid. The Soviet-Cuban economic agreements of 1972 were probably designed to give Cuba a thirteen-year period to put the economy into shape. Thus the USSR deferred the debt accrued in 1960–1975 (both principal and interest) until 1986 and extended the amortization period until 2011.[41] Both parties probably are hoping that through the economic plans of 1976–1980 and 1981–1985 Cuba will consolidate her economy and generate a surplus in her foreign trade in order to eliminate the Soviet subsidy and start repaying the Soviet aid received in the 1960s and 1970s.

In the meantime, Cuba's economic boom of 1973–1975 generated $3.7 billion in credit from industrialized, nonsocialist countries, although only a small part had been used by 1977 (see table 10.2). Some of the credits, as in Argentina and Canada, are to buy goods produced by U.S. subsidiaries. The lenders apparently believed that Cuba had the capacity to repay such credits, practiced sound, conservative policies, and showed an excellent record of repaying promptly and without trouble.[42] Her most common method of financing imports was by a letter

CARMELO MESA-LAGO

TABLE 10.2
Trade Credits Extended to Cuba by Nonsocialist Countries, August 1973–August 1975

	Amount (million U.S. $)	Main Exports
Argentina	1,200	Cars and other transportation equipment, grain-processing plants, irrigation equipment
Spain	900	Ships, cement factory, transportation equipment
Great Britain	580	Trucks, buses, airport and communications equipment, fertilizer plant
Euromarkets	383[a]	Transportation equipment
France	350	Transportation equipment, fertilizer plant
Canada	155	Oil tankers, locomotives, buses and trucks, canning plants, pharmaceuticals, pulp and paper, cattle
Japan	94	Textile and food processing machinery, electric generators, commercial refrigerators
Sweden	28	Ships, printing press, health and electronic equipment
Mexico	20[b]	Corrugated steel, sugar mill equipment, data processing and transportation equipment
Total	3,710	

Sources: Granma, Granma Weekly Review, Latin American Economic Report, and Wall Street Journal, 1973–1976.
Note: We lack information on whether other deals concluded or in progress between Cuba and industralized market economies were made on a cash basis or through credit: (1) Japan's sales of $200 million including spinning and weaving, thermal power, and fertilizer plants, as well as transportation equipment; (2) Italy's sale of a fish cannery; (3) West Germany's negotiations to construct a Volkswagen assembly plant; and (4) Spain's negotiations to construct a Pegaso factory of truck engines for $700 million.
a. Increased to $517 million by mid-1976.
b. May have increased to $80 million in 1975–1976.

of credit extended by the central bank to the supplier, with payment to be effected through the supplier's local bank at the time the merchandise was shipped. In some cases, however, the operations was financed by the state or government-operated bank in the supplier's country, such as Japan's Export-Import Bank and Canada's Export Development Bank. (Argentinian and Mexican sales were partly financed also by their respective state banks.) Finally, Cuba also obtained loans from the international money market (usually in deutsche marks) to finance her imports. The last two techniques proved to be safer for suppliers than the first one. The credits are about equally divided between medium term (to be repaid in five years) and long term (to be repaid in ten years), with interest rates fixed at competitive market rates.

Until the end of 1976, the consensus among Western suppliers was that Cuba would not contract an import for which it had not already budgeted payment. But that opinion and the island's credit rating suffered a severe blow when in 1976–1977 Cuba suspended and cancelled a significant number of contracted imports from Argentina, Canada, Japan, and Spain (see chapter 9). Most potential sellers will not produce any goods for Cuba now unless they have an irrevocable letter of credit guaranteed by a commercial or state bank in their own country as well as by the Cuban central bank.[43]

Any assessment of Cuba's future credit rating has to take into account the current level and relative burden of the external debt and the island's capacity to repay it. Cuba's cumulative debt with the USSR was estimated at $4.5 billion by 1975 without considering military and technical assistance.[44] If this assistance is taken into account, and the debt with other socialist and nonsocialist countries is added, Cuba's total debt in 1975 should have been at least $6.5 billion. If the 1961–1976 trend in Soviet aid to Cuba continues (an annual average rate of increase of 15 percent) and Cuba uses most credit granted by nonsocialist countries, the island's total debt by 1980 should be twice what it was in 1975. It should be recalled, however, that repayment of the bulk of the debt with the Soviets will not start until 1986.

According to table 10.3, in absolute figures, Cuba's public external debt in 1975 was the third largest in Latin America, surpassed only by those of Brazil and Mexico. If per capita figures are used, however, Cuba's debt was the heaviest, four times that of Brazil and three times that of Mexico. The debt repayment capacity of a given country can be measured by comparing that country's debt with its gross national product (GNP), and its debt service payments with its exports. Since figures for Cuba's GNP and debt service payment are not available, we have to use global social product (GSP) for Cuba and the relationship between the total debt and exports for all countries. According to the Interamerican Development Bank, the debt/GNP proportion in 1975 for the largest countries in the region (Argentina, Brazil, Colombia, Chile, Mexico, Peru) was 18 percent, and the proportion for the rest was 26 percent; but the debt/GSP proportion for Cuba was 36 percent.[45] According to table 10.3, Cuba's debt/export proportion in the same year was the fifth largest in Latin America despite the record high value of exports caused by booming sugar prices. (If the comparison had been made in 1976 when sugar prices had declined, the debt/export proportion of Cuba would have risen to 222 percent.)[46] In conclusion, Cuba's public debt is the heaviest and one of the most difficult to repay in Latin America. Obviously, Cuba will have to put forth a colossal effort in the future to repay this debt and maintain a high level of imports.

When U.S.-Cuban direct trade resumes, both Cuban foreign trade officials and a good number of American corporations will be interested in making deals on credit. Before opening any credit lines, both U.S. private banks and the Export-Import Bank should carefully evaluate any changes in Cuba's credit ratings, recent honoring of import commitments, and future capacity to repay. Unless such conditions have markedly improved, U.S. business should request an irrevocable letter of credit guaranteed by the Cuban central bank and confirmed by a local bank or should ask the operation to be financed by the Export-Import Bank.

The advantages accruing to the United States from resumption of economic relations with Cuba would probably be more political than economic: normaliza-

CARMELO MESA-LAGO

tion of relations with a neighboring country, and improved image and credibility in Latin America and the Third World. Another political advantage would be the potential influence that the United States could exert upon Cuba, as Castro has candidly stated: "When economic ties are established between two countries, any government that is really concerned about its people, takes those economic ties and interests into account, and, in one way or another, these ties and interests have a certain bearing on the attitudes taken by governments."[47]

Economically, purchases of Cuban products (sugar, nickel, cigars, fish) by the United States will save on transportation, and the island offers a potential annual market for U.S. exports estimated from $600 million (by Arthur T. Downey, deputy assistant secretary of the U.S. Department of Commerce) to $750 million (by Orville L. Freeman, president of Business International). Cuba's

TABLE 10.3
Public External Debt of Cuba and Latin America and the Caribbean, 1975

	Debt (million U.S. $)	Population (thousands)	Exports (million U.S. $)	Debt ($ per capita)	Debt/Exports (percent)
Argentina	4,925	25,384	3,581	194	137
Barbados	44	245	227	180	19
Bolivia	1,214	5,410	476	244	255
Brazil	18,159	109,730	9,626	165	188
Chile	4,400	10,253	1,534	429	287
Colombia	2,988	25,890	2,098	115	142
Costa Rica	691	1,994	596	347	116
Cuba	6,500	9,481	3,304	685	198
Dominican Republic	710	5,118	1,003	139	71
Ecuador	754	7,090	1,073	106	70
El Salvador	376	4,108	572	92	66
Guatemala	288	6,082	792	47	36
Guyana	362	791	372	458	97
Haiti	133	5,888	94	23	141
Honduras	440	3,037	328	145	134
Jamaica	813	2,029	1,112	401	73
Mexico	13,480	59,204	6,134	228	219
Nicaragua	782	2,318	447	337	175
Panama	861	1,676	849	514	101
Paraguay	369	2,647	210	139	176
Peru	3,466	15,689	1,751	221	198
Trinidad & Tobago	213	1,009	1,931	211	11
Uruguay	1,023	3,111	497	329	206
Venezuela	1,578	12,213	9,405	129	17

Sources: Debt and exports (except for Cuba) from Banco Interamericano de Desarrollo, *El endeudamiento externo de América Latina: Situación actual y perspectivas* (Washington, D.C.: BID-Departamento de Desarrollo Económico y Social, 1977). Population from Comisión Económica de América Latina, *Notas sobre la economía y el desarrollo de América Latina*, no. 232 (January 1977), p 1. Cuban debt from discussion in the text and exports from table 9.5 of previous chapter; both figures converted into dollars at rate of $1.21 for one dollar.

current five-year plan involves an investment of 12 billion pesos, largely in industrial, agricultural, and transportation equipment. Out of 4 billion projected for industrial investment, 3 billion are allocated for external supply and, although by the end of 1975, 60 percent of this was already contracted, more than one billion pesos was still uncommitted.[48] The Cubans had told Senator George McGovern in 1975 that a good share of that equipment could be purchased from the United States.[49] Two years later, with the shift in sugar prices and trade, the Cubans became more cautious. Thus in 1977 the director of trade for Western Europe and North America told a group of U.S. businessmen that lifting the embargo would not result in an immediate jump in U.S.-Cuban trade because current trade partners could not be replaced immediately and planned trade commitments had to be honored. The United States could, however, make a significant dent in trade with Cuba in 1978–1980, and the medium-range possibilities are the doubling of U.S.-Cuban prerevolutionary trade, that is, to more than $2 billion.[50]

If we were to determine the potential advantage of U.S. trade with Cuba by the interest shown recently by U.S. firms and multinational corporations, the answer would be quite positive. Prior to 1975 only U.S. subsidiaries abroad (in Argentina, Canada, Mexico) publicly expressed willingness to trade with Cuba. In 1975 when the possibility of lifting the embargo became a real one, both U.S. and foreign-based firms began to show significant interest. In March, *Industry Week* published an article supporting trade with Cuba in order to sell spare parts and agricultural and transportation equipment. In May, 200 corporations represented by the Council for the Americas as well as the Association of American Chambers of Commerce in Latin America called for an end to trade restrictions.[51] Before the partial lifting of the U.S. embargo was announced, Assistant Secretary of State William D. Rogers informed the House of Representatives that the State Department had received requests from more than one hundred firms about trade prospects with Cuba. Some of these firms announced that they were ready to do business with Cuba (Monsanto, Rohm & Haas, Hercules, Smith & Kline); others were doing research on the Cuban market (Dow Chemical, Union Carbide, RCA, DuPont, Thyl). Even some firms which formerly had businesses in Cuba and were nationalized (Coca Cola, Goodyear, Goodrich, Firestone) welcomed the opening of the Cuban market.[52] Transportation companies were active in anticipation of the renewal of economic relations with Cuba. Delta Airlines requested permission from the Civil Aeronautics Board to fly to Cuba. South Florida ports (Palm Beach, Port Everglades), railroads (Florida East Coast Railways), and shipping lines (West India and Tropical Shipping) began to study the situation and some to expand their facilities to receive Cuban trade.[53] When the U.S. embargo was lifted for subsidiaries abroad, many U.S.-based firms complained that this discriminated against them. From September 1, 1975, to December 31, 1976, the Treasury Department issued 319 licenses to U.S. subsidiaries and other foreign firms to sell goods to Cuba for a total value of $345 million. The goods included autos, trucks, tractors, locomotives, electric motors,

CARMELO MESA-LAGO

textile machinery, paper-converting machinery, construction machinery, electronics, pharmaceuticals and drugs, herbicides, and so on.[54]

The opening of trade with Cuba has resulted in a dramatic expansion of information about the island within the corporate world. Business International has sent representatives to Cuba, reports regularly on Cuban news in the newsletter *Business Latin America,* has published a sort of trade manual on how to do business with the island (which sells for $150), and organized in Havana, in the fall of 1977, a meeting of Cuban trade officials and U.S. corporate executives. The American Management Association has conducted seminars in New York, in 1976 and 1977, on U.S.-Cuban trade to which more than one hundred firms have sent representatives (registration fee of $250). Probably the most successful operation is the firm Alamar Associates, organized by Kirby Jones, which has taken representatives from about fifty corporations to Cuba for visits of two to five days (at a cost of $2,000); it also publishes the monthly newsletter *Cuba Business Report* with current economic information from the island.

One disadvantage for the United States which might result from resumption of economic relations with Cuba would be linked to the sensitive issue of compensation for nationalized property. The United States claims that, according to international law, the expropriated have a right to adequate compensation. Aside from the legal question, there is a most significant political and economic issue here: The risk of setting a dangerous precedent for Latin America and other countries with heavy American investment is substantial.

Pending Obstacles and Restrictions

The two crucial issues which the United States and Cuba will have to face first are closely interrelated: from the Cuban side, lifting of the U.S. embargo; from the U.S. side, compensation for property nationalized by the Cubans. The Cuban embargo (called by the Cubans the "U.S. blockade") technically began in early 1962, unilaterally imposed by the United States as a response to Cuban collectivization of property belonging to U.S. citizens and corporations. The embargo is made up of a series of legal measures which: (1) banned all trade (exports and imports) with Cuba except for humanitarian reasons; (2) prescribed the approval of the U.S. Department of Commerce for exports or reexports to Cuba of commodities originating in the United States—this included U.S. subsidiaries abroad and even non-U.S. firms which engaged in triangular trade of U.S. goods with Cuba; (3) restricted the landing in U.S. ports of foreign vessels trading with Cuba; and (4) required an authorization from the U.S. Treasury for the few imports allowed from Cuba, such as books and journals needed for research.[55]

In 1964, the Organization of American States (OAS) approved, by a two-thirds majority, the imposition of the embargo hemispherically. Eventually all Latin American nations, except Mexico, abided by the OAS rule. (Canada, not being a member of the OAS, never joined the embargo.) The United States used economic and political pressure to enforce the embargo in other parts of the world, particularly in Western Europe. At the beginning, therefore, the embargo was effective as an economic tool and caused serious disruption in Cuba. By the mid-1960s, however, Cuba had been able to shift her trade to the socialist countries, from which she received considerable military aid as well as credit. Nonsocialist countries like Spain and Japan resisted U.S. pressure and engaged in trade with Cuba. At the end of the 1960s, two Latin American nations (Chile and Peru) ignored the OAS rule and resumed trade (even if at a very low level) with Cuba, while Canada increased its trade substantially. Vessels increasingly ignored the boycott and began to touch in Cuban ports while Latin American airlines (from Panama, Peru, the British Caribbean) joined Mexican, Spanish, and Canadian airlines flying to Cuba. The gradual erosion of the embargo was accelerated in 1973 when Argentina reestablished trade relations with Cuba, and U.S. subsidiaries in Argentina requested and obtained authorization from the U.S. Department of Commerce to export manufactured goods to Cuba. Similar requests from U.S. subsidiaries in Canada and Mexico ensued. In the meantime, Western European and Japanese trade with Cuba gained momentum. All these events made the embargo ineffective, a fact partly acknowledged by the U.S. Department of Commerce, which in 1975 stated: "the adverse effect of the embargo on Cuba has lessened."[56]

The first serious attempt within the OAS to lift the embargo occurred in Quito, Ecuador, in November 1974. Although a majority of Latin American countries voted in favor of the motion (the United States abstaining), it failed because the required two-thirds majority was not reached. Colombia and Venezuela then ignored the rule and reestablished diplomatic and trade relations with Cuba. A subsequent OAS meeting, held in Costa Rica in July 1975, considered a modified motion to solve the impasse and obtained sixteen votes in favor (now including the United States), two abstentions (Brazil and Nicaragua), and three against (Chile, Paraguay, and Uruguay). Technically the OAS did not end the embargo; such an action would have required ratification by the legislature of each member country, and this might have taken as long as two years. The solution was to allow each country, in accordance with its national policy and interests, to normalize and conduct relations with Cuba at the level and in the form that it deemed advisable.[57]

Based on the above decision, the U.S. Department of State announced on August 21, 1975, a partial lifting of the embargo including three steps: (1) permitting trade transactions between U.S. subsidiaries and Cuba for foreign-made goods when these subsidiaries are operating in countries where local law or policy favors trade with Cuba—a license is still required from the Department of Commerce for each transaction; (2) revoking the suspension of U.S. aid (credit, food) to countries that trade with Cuba or allow their ships and aircraft to carry goods to and from Cuba—in mid-1975, in spite of the erosion of the embargo,

200 carriers were on the U.S. blacklist; and (3) readiness to modify regulations that deny refueling rights in the United States to third-country ships engaged in Cuban trade.[58]

In an interview granted to foreign journalists in Havana, just after the announcement of these measures, Cuban Prime Minister Fidel Castro saluted the gestures as "positive steps" which had been received "with satisfaction." But he added: "In essence, the blockade remains in effect. . . . We are ready and willing to negotiate with the United States in a sincere and responsible manner but we don't want to negotiate with a dagger pointed at our throat." Asked by a *New York Times* journalist, James Reston, whether there could not be talks at all unless the United States completely lifted the embargo, Castro answered: "I think there can be negotiations over how to negotiate [but] in order for there to be serious, responsible, [detailed] and just negotiations . . . the blockade, in its essential points must be lifted. This doesn't mean that we are opposed to contacts. It doesn't even rule out some talks."[59]

In the spring of 1977, the U.S. Senate Foreign Relations Committee voted in favor of a resolution presented by George McGovern to partially lift the embargo against Cuba by permitting the latter to purchase medical supplies, food, and agricultural products in the United States but keeping the embargo on Cuban imports. Fidel Castro, however, rejected this approach as discriminatory against Cuba, saying that Cuba will not buy any U.S. products if not allowed to sell to the United States. He again requested the total lifting of the embargo but indicated that he would accept a partial lifting in both directions, such as allowing free trade of agricultural products between the two countries.[60]

In any event, the lifting of the remaining aspects of the U.S. embargo (direct trade with Cuba; sales to Cuba by U.S. subsidiaries of goods originating in the United States, and so on) will require substantial preparation and discussion not only between the United States and Cuba but also within the United States. As long as claims from U.S. owners of property nationalized by the Cuban government are outstanding, normal banking and shipping relationships cannot be restored, since Cuban assets in the United States might be subject to attachment. This means that imports of Cuban sugar or nickel, for example, could be seized to pay outstanding claims. Furthermore, there is legislation that prevents trade until the U.S. president determines that Cuba has taken appropriate steps to settle the outstanding claims.[61]

To compound this problem, Cuban exports to the United States would be subject to very high, "discriminatory" tariff treatment until "most-favored-nation" and "nondiscriminatory" tariff status is granted to the island. Under the provisions of the Trade Act of 1974, in order to get the most-favored-nation privilege (and receive trade credits from the Export-Import Bank), Cuba will have to meet two conditions: freedom of emigration, and signing of a bilateral trade agreement with the United States.[62] Freedom of emigration is a difficult condition for socialist countries to meet, as the tragic case of Soviet Jews exemplifies. Although on paper Cuba does not place stringent restrictions on emigration, in practice, freedom of exit, which was always precarious, became more curtailed in 1973 when the U.S.-Cuban airlift was stopped by Cuba. The signing of a bilateral trade agreement with the United States is not a condition easy to fulfill either, although successful U.S. agreements with Rumania and Poland are good examples of how much can be accomplished in this area.[63] Freedom of emigration and bilateral trade agreements, important as they are, probably will not be subject to negotiation until a basic understanding is reached in the crucial issue of compensation.

Estimates on the value of U.S. property nationalized by Cuba, mostly in 1959–1960, varies according to the source. The Cubans have calculated 800 to 900 million pesos, based on the declared tax value of U.S. property in late 1960, the time of the big nationalization wave; the U.S. Department of Commerce estimated $956 million in 1961; and the U.S. Foreign Claims Settlement Commission (FCSC) quoted a figure close to $2 billion in 1972. The FCSC reviewed 8,816 claims totaling $3,346 million; of these, 5,911 claims equaling $1,780 million were recognized and 1,195 claims were denied. The sum of recognized claims has increased substantially because 6 percent annual interest has been added for sixteen years. The resulting total claims against Cuba exceed the combined value of expropriations by all socialist countries, excluding In- dochina.[64] Since there have not been funds in the United States to compensate for the claims recognized by the FCSC, claimants have only been granted the right to request payment in the event that compensation is arranged with Cuba. Neverthe- less, a good number of large claimants have already benefited, at least partially, from tax write-offs of their losses. And yet a company could realize only 50 percent of the actual value of the loss, assuming a 50 percent tax rate. Moreover, such tax write-offs could be taken only against the book value of the lost assets, which was extremely low for many companies. Finally, many small claimants have not been able to take advantage of tax write-offs. In case a lump sum for compensation is paid by Cuba, that sum would have to be prorated among all claimants regardless of whether they benefited from tax write-offs or not. Small claimants, therefore, will probably suffer the most from a compensation settle- ment. In late 1975, fifty companies with claims totaling $762 million formed a Joint Corporate Committee on Cuban Claims and requested that claims be settled prior to lifting the trade embargo against Cuba.[65]

What are the probabilities of Cuba paying "adequate" compensation and how can that adequacy be defined? Several socialist countries have agreed to pay compensation for nationalized U.S. property, the percentage actually paid vary- ing from 3 to 90 percent of the total claim.[66] In 1967, Cuba paid compensation to Switzerland and France, and although these countries apparently were satisfied with the settlement, the value of claims involved was small. More substantial sums are claimed by Spanish citizens and firms, and conversations about a possible settlement began, in 1975, between Spain and Cuba.

Cuban expropriation laws of 1960 included a clause to compensate for nationalized U.S. property through a percentage of sugar sales to the United

States applicable above a given minimum of such sales. (Because of the preceding U.S. cut of the Cuban sugar quota, the possibility of compensation was theoretically postponed until sugar sales were resumed at 1959–1960 levels.) Using this clause, a Cuban scholar has calculated that if Cuba's sugar crops remain at 5.5 million tons in the 1970s, the Cuban government would accept payment of $315 million in compensation (35 percent of its own estimate), and if the United States agrees to buy 10 percent of Cuban sugar output annually, compensation would be paid in a period of from six to twenty-six years according to sugar prices in the international market (fluctuating from 5 to 20 cents per pound).[67]

It should be pointed out, however, that the Cubans have on occasion taken a rather negative attitude on compensation. They have alleged, for instance, that Americans should not expect to receive better treatment than Cuban nationals have. Cuban proprietors who either left the island or stayed and became involved in counterrevolutionary activities did not receive any compensation at all, while those who stayed and complied with the revolutionary norms were entitled only to meager monthly payments for a given period of time. Another argument, recently stressed, is that the U.S. embargo and activities against the Revolution have provoked considerable economic losses which would require payment of U.S. compensation three or four times higher than the U.S. claim in compensation for nationalized property.[68]

The above arguments are probably intended to strengthen one of Cuba's important bargaining positions and to reduce the amount of compensation to what is affordable by Cuba and acceptable to the United States. An American scholar who interviewed Deputy Prime Minister of Foreign Affairs Carlos Rafael Rodríguez in mid-1975 and mid-1976 reached the conclusion that Cuba is prepared to arrive at a realistic settlement. This would involve recognition of the principle of compensation, a potential agreement on a final balance favorable to the United States, and a net transfer of funds from Cuba to the U.S. government which would act as trustee for the expropriated firms and individuals.[69] In the secret U.S.-Cuban talks held in 1974–1975, William D. Rogers, then assistant secretary of state for inter-American affairs, discussed compensation of property in a lump sum settlement before taking up diplomatic ties as opposed to resuming ties and then discussing claims.[70] Another approach, one that the Cubans apparently are taking, is to settle individually with claimant companies that are willing to do business with Cuba again. One company, for instance, has offered to forego compensation for its expropriated Cuban factory in return for permission to reequip and supply it.[71]

Some Final Considerations

From what has been said above, it is obvious that the path to full normalization of relations between the United States and Cuba is lengthy, intricate, and laborious. In spite of dramatic advances in rapprochement made in 1976–1977,

The Economics of U.S.-Cuban Rapprochement

Cuban intervention in the Horn of Africa has created new tensions.

In negotiations with Cuba, the United States is in the stronger economic position: it can supply the technology that Cuba so badly needs and that could help substantially to reduce the island's sugar monoculture (by expanding nickel production, for example); it can sell practically all the goods that Cuba needs at a competitive price and deliver them from a very short distance, thus helping to cut Cuba's freight costs and the value of her imports, as well as to triple the present capacity of the island's merchant marine; it can send hundreds of thousands of tourists, generating the second largest source of revenue and foreign exchange for Cuba; and it can extend credits—with the proper precautions—to finance trade and technological transfer to the island. The United States can also wait longer than Cuba for the reestablishment of ties without suffering economically.

On the other side, Cuba is enduring a depressed international sugar market, a somewhat damaged credit rating with important nonsocialist suppliers because of the suspension of imports in 1976–1977, and the economic side effects of the Angola operation. These problems have affected the five-year plan that is crucial for putting the Cuban economy on the right track and enabling it to start repaying the Soviet debt in 1986. The situation is compounded by the heightened expectations of Cubans in the first half of the 1970s and the thorough economic and managerial reorganization that is being implemented during the second half of the decade. Cuba is obviously interested in taking advantage of the propitious political climate and openness in Washington in order to legitimize the Revolution and collect the benefits of a natural economic relationship with the United States. Resolving the feud should also allow Cuba, in the long run, to transfer current defense expenditures into socioeconomic development and to diversify her foreign markets, thus reducing her economic dependence on the USSR. In this renewed relationship, Cuba should not be unduly concerned about a resurrection of her past economic dependence on the United States since the island will largely control the extent of her economic ties with the United States. Cuba has more to lose economically from a stalemate in the negotiations. To avoid that she may possibly be willing to make some nondemeaning concessions, but the Cuban leadership will not yield (at least publicly), on political issues that are considered a matter of principle for the Revolution.

The economic leverage that the United States enjoys in the negotiations with Cuba should be sternly and shrewdly used to bargain in areas in which a successful outcome is feasible. Cuba will eventually agree to some sort of compensation for U.S. nationalized property and probably defer—if the negotiations are conducted in private and with respect for her sovereignty—by freeing some political prisoners and relaxing exit from and entry to the island. The terrain of Cuba's foreign policy is much more dangerous: perhaps a mutually acceptable compromise can be worked out, under strict secrecy, on the Western Hemisphere (for example, Puerto Rico) and even Africa, but the United States must refrain from publicly imposing conditions on Cuba that would cause her to lose face in the Third World.

CARMELO MESA-LAGO

Finally, should the embargo be lifted first by the United States to further the negotiations? The embargo is practically ineffective today and its removal will not weaken the United States; besides, the United States would have plenty of positive economic leverage to use with Cuba. On the other hand, in spite of their rhetorical proclamations that the lifting of the embargo is a precondition to serious talks, the Cubans have indeed entered into delicate negotiations with the United States and reached agreements on fishing boundaries and the exchange of interest sections. There are possibilities of reaching additional agreements on antihijacking, visitation rights, and other issues. Hence the United States can pursue the current strategy and see how far it will lead; if a true deadlock is reached, the United States should be prepared to break it by lifting the embargo, at least partially, but in reciprocal terms (that is, in one trade area but both for exports and imports). Another possibility is that with interest sections installed in both countries, permanent and secret negotiations may produce a basic understanding on the key issues, and then the United States could lift the embargo as a public concession to Cuba.

The fact that both Carter and Castro have stated that full normalization of relations is not foreseeable even in the medium range has been taken by some Americans as an indication of a cooling off or freezing of the trend. Conversely, it could be interpreted as a healthy sign that both countries are beginning to understand the complexity of the process and are prepared to enter into a long period of tough negotiations with a spirit of equality, mutual respect, and patience. The agreement on the Panama Canal, after several years of difficult bargaining, is a model of what the U.S.-Cuban talks will be. If the U.S.-Panamanian negotiations appeared lengthy and complex, we have to expect an even more difficult process in achieving concurrence between two neighboring countries that have been split by almost two decades of bitter, bloody, and vicious confrontation.

NOTES

In addition to the acknowledgements in the previous chapter, I want to express my appreciation for the comments and information related to this chapter from Mary Manzoli, Eduardo Masferrer, Robert S. Walters, and Rosemary Werrett.

1. The few available analyses of the U.S.-Cuban trade potential prepared by or delivered at U.S. federal agencies take negative or skeptical viewpoints. See as an example of the former view, Eric N. Baklanoff, "Statement on Proposal for Resumption of Trade Relations Between the United States and Cuba," International Trade and Commerce Subcommittee, International Relations Committee, U.S. House of Representatives, August 21, 1975. The U.S. Department of Commerce (*United States Commercial Relations with Cuba: A Survey* [Washington, D.C.: GPO, 1975]) makes a thorough analysis of the complex situation taking a cautiously skeptical stand. Nevertheless, the publication of reports on Cuban trade, both by the Commerce Department and the CIA, in *Intelligence Handbook Cuba: Foreign Trade,* A(ER) 75-69, July 1975, is revealing, particularly if one

considers that both reports insert a list of Cuban trading enterprises including their addresses. Not surprisingly, the U.S. business community has more interest in, and takes a brighter view of, the economic opportunities that the Cuban market offers. See, as an example, Business International Corporation, *Cuba at the Turning Point: How the Economy Works, Changes in the Offing, New Opportunities for MNCs* (New York: Business International Corporation, 1977). From the Cuban side, the Minister of Foreign Trade Marcelo Fernández has candidly listed Cuban priorities in imports from and exports to the United States. See "Official Lists U.S. Goods Cuba Wants if 17-Year Trade Embargo is Lifted," *Miami Herald*, March 5, 1977.

2. República de Cuba, Junta Central de Planificación, Dirección Central de Estadística, *Anuario Estadístico de Cuba, 1972* (Havana, 1974), pp. 214–17. Subsequent data in the text on the destination of Cuban exports come from this source.

3. Based on information provided by Linda A. Bernstein, U.S. Department of Agriculture. On the Cuban-Chinese conflict see the following editorials: "In Fulfillment of Internationalist Duty," *Granma Weekly Review*, February 8, 1976, p. 12; "It is Evident to Revolutionaries," ibid., February 15, 1976, p. 1; "A Page of Ignominy," ibid., April 11, 1976, p. 2; "Escalation in Infamy," ibid., July 18, 1976, p. 1; and Castro's personal attacks in ibid., March 7, 1976, p. 6; September 26, 1976, p. 7; December 12, 1976, pp. 2–3; May 22, 1977, p. 3; and July 24, 1977, p. 3.

4. Norman Pearlstine, "Japan Finds a Ready Market in Cuba," *Wall Street Journal*, October 27, 1975, p. 6; and *Granma*, July 2, 1976.

5. Linda A. Bernstein, "Cuba," *Western Hemisphere Agricultural Situation: Review of 1976 and Outlook for 1977*, Foreign Agricultural Economic Report, no. 136 (Washington, D.C.: U.S. Department of Agriculture, May 1977), p. 8.

6. In January 1977 Cuba signed an agreement with the USSR to sell 1 million tons in addition to the yearly 2.5 million tons in the current agreement (ibid.).

7. *United States Commercial Relations with Cuba: A Survey* (Washington, D.C.: GPO, 1975), pp. 24–28. I have benefited from several ideas of this report in the preparation of this section of the chapter.

8. For divergent views on a potential U.S. market for Cuban cigars see Raymond Sokolov, "Havanas, Sí!" *New York Times Magazine*, September 28, 1975; Karen Rothmyer, "The New Havanas," *Wall Street Journal*, March 1, 1976, p. 30; and John A. Jones, "Best Cuban Cigars Aren't from Cuba, Maker Says," *Los Angeles Times*, May 2, 1977.

9. See "Citrus Growers Oppose New Trade with Cuba," *Los Angeles Times*, May 9, 1977; and "Keep Cuban Citrus Out of U.S.," *Miami Herald*, June 2, 1977.

10. *Christian Science Monitor*, October 1, 1975; and *Miami Herald*, October 11, 1975.

11. *Miami Herald*, October 15, 1975; Don Bohning, "Cuba Woos Book Tourists," *Miami Herald*, March 8, 1976; and "Cuba is Ready for U.S. Visitors, Island Tourism Director Says," ibid., March 12, 1977. The Cubans are also trying to attract more tourists from the USSR and Eastern Europe, thus the 11th Conference of Government Tourist Agencies was held in Havana in March 1976. Large distances and shortage of funds for travel make this task difficult.

12. *New York Times*, July 27, 1975, sec. 4, p. 3; and *Miami Herald*, August 24, 1975.

13. See *Miami Herald*, January 30, May 7, 17, and 26, 1977; and *New York Times*, April 29 and May 8, 1977.

14. Simon Malley, "20-Hour Interview with Fidel Castro," *Granma Weekly Review*, May 22, 1977, p. 3.

15. "Cuban Travel Ban Change is Only one Step Toward Business Opening," *Business Latin America*, March 23, 1977, p. 89; "Trade Ban Slows Cuban Tourism," *New York Times*, May 8, 1977; and *Washington Post*, May 14, 1977.

16. *Washington Post*, May 15, 1975.

17. *Miami Herald*, May 26, 1977.

18. James Nelson Goodsell, "Cuba Interested in U.S. Trade," *Christian Science Monitor*, April 28, 1977.

19. *Le Monde*, January 16, 1975, pp. 1, 4.

CARMELO MESA-LAGO

20. *Granma Weekly Review,* January 30, 1977, p. 1. See also chapter 12 in this volume.

21. Jerry Flint, "Cubans Admit their Economy is in Serious Trouble," *New York Times,* April 25, 1977; and Kirby Jones, statement at the International Conference on the Role of Cuba in World Affairs, University of Pittsburgh, November 17, 1976.

22. Benjamin C. Bradlee, "Conversation with Castro," *Miami Herald,* March 6, 1977.

23. *Anuario Estadístico de Cuba, 1972,* pp. 218–33. Subsequent data in the text on the origin of Cuban imports come from this source.

24. See Ramón C. Barquín, "Cuba, the Cybernetic Era," *Cuban Studies* 5, no. 2 (July 1975), 1–23. For a Cuban view see Balarmino Castilla, "Speech at the Opening Ceremony of the 15th Meeting of the Intergovernmental Commission on Data Processing," *Granma Weekly Review,* November 9, 1975, p. 4.

25. Cuba has increased the number of oil fields but without adding significantly to its crude output which remains at less than 3,000 barrels per day; present oil refinery output is about 120,000 barrels per day. Gas production, which reached nearly 2 MMcfd in 1974, is apparently falling. See Larry Auldridge, "Cuba's Oil Fields Now Add to Ten," *Oil and Gas Journal,* May 2, 1977, p. 305.

26. Although Cuba has been less affected by the oil crisis than other oil-consuming nations because of the Soviet subsidy, the island is nevertheless paying at least 54 percent more than it used to pay. Thus Fidel Castro has criticized the OPEC nations as selfish money-seekers that have worsened the world economic crisis, invested their wealth in capitalist countries, and indiscriminately taken advantage of developed and underdeveloped countries: "It is not the same to demand from the rich as to rob from the poor." To mollify somewhat this frontal attack, the Cuban president made a distinction between "progressive" and "fascist" countries within OPEC. See "Speech at the Solemn Session to Set Up the National Assembly of People's Power," *Granma Weekly Review,* December 12, 1976, pp. 2–3.

27. "Oil 'Triangle' for Supplying Cuba is Studied," *Miami Herald,* June 30, 1975.

28. *Latin America,* December 3, 1976, pp. 374–75.

29. Fernando Morais, "Quatro horas de entrevista com Fidel Castro," *Veja,* July 13, 1977, p. 46. For an exploration of Cuban potential in the nuclear field see Lewis Dunn and Herman Kahn, *Final Report Trends in Nuclear Proliferation 1975–1995* (New York: Hudson Institute, May 15, 1976). See the Cuban view in "Five Questions About Nuclear Research in Cuba," *Granma Weekly Review,* April 4, 1976, p. 4. The military dangers and safeguards of the Cuban nuclear program were discussed by the House Committee of International Relations in early 1977.

30. For Cuban imports of foodstuffs in 1973–1976 see Linda A. Bernstein, "Cuba's Agriculture, Led by Sugar, Shows Improvements in Key Crops," *Foreign Agriculture* 12, no. 21 (May 27, 1974), 6–7; "Cuba's Trade Horizons Widen as Diplomatic Ties Expand," ibid. 13, no. 17 (April 28, 1975), 2–4; and "Cuba," ibid., p. 8. See also Harold Boyer, "Canada and Cuba: A Study in International Relations," Ph.D. diss., Simon Fraser University, 1972. (My appreciation to Professor Maurice Halperin for calling my attention to this source.)

31. Information from Linda A. Bernstein, U.S. Department of Agriculture, and Maurice Halperin, Simon Fraser University.

32. *Miami Herald,* October 28, 1975.

33. *Miami Herald,* October 1, 1975.

34. Linda A. Bernstein, statement at the International Conference on the Role of Cuba in World Affairs, University of Pittsburgh, November 17, 1976.

35. Robert Keatley, "U.S. Businessmen Return from Cuba," *Wall Street Journal,* April 22, 1977, p. 10.

36. Lázaro Barrero Medina, "Development and Foreign Trade," *Direct from Cuba,* nos. 150–51 (August 1–15, 1976), p. 4. See also Business International, *Cuba at the Turning Point,* pp. 117–18.

37. As told to Senator Abourezk when he visited Cuba in August 1975. *Miami Herald,* October 11, 1975.

38. "Cuba Expands Merchant Fleet," *Latin American Economic Report* 3, no. 41 (October 17, 1975), 163. See also ibid. 4, no. 21 (May 28, 1976).

39. Barrero Medina, "Development and Foreign Trade," pp. 4–5.

40. Fidel Castro, "Speech at the Main Event in Commemoration of the Victory of Playa Giron," *Granma Weekly Review*, May 2, 1971, p. 6.

41. See Carmelo Mesa-Lago, *Cuba in the 1970s: Pragmatism and Institutionalization* (Albuquerque: University of New Mexico Press, 1974), pp. 11–12, 20–21.

42. I have reviewed the evaluations made in 1975 by some foreign banks that lent money to Cuba. Practically all of them had a favorable outlook on the Cuban economy; they estimated a large trade surplus for 1974 and ranked repayment as "good."

43. Business International, *Cuba at the Turning Point*, pp. 116–17. At the end of 1976, Cuba's credit reputation remained high among lenders not affected by suspensions of imports. In November 1976, the U.K. Morgan Grenfell lent Cuba $61 million, and the loan terms did not reveal any weakening in the assessment of Cuba's financial position. See "Cuba Economic Setback Threatens to Reduce Gains from any U.S. Opening," *Business Latin America*, February 2, 1977, p. 34.

44. Central Intelligence Agency, *The Cuban Economy: A Statistical Review, 1968–1976*, ER 76–10708 (Washington, D.C., December 1976), table 24. See table 2.2.

45. Banco Interamericano de Desarrollo, *El endeudamiento externo de América Latina: Situación actual y perspectivas* (Washington, D.C.: Departamento de Desarrollo Económico y Social, 1977). The Cuban estimate is based on figures from tables 9.1 and 10.3.

46. Cuba's debt/export proportion of 198 percent compares with 122 percent for Latin America and 110 percent for all developing countries. International Bank for Reconstruction and Development, *World Bank Annual Report 1975* (Washington, D.C., 1975).

47. Barbara Walters, "An Interview with Fidel," *Granma Weekly Review*, July 17, 1977, pp. 2–3. See also Morais, "Quatro horas," p. 40.

48. Fidel Castro, "Main Report Presented to the 1st Congress of the CPC," *Granma Weekly Review*, January 4, 1976, p. 8.

49. "Cuba: Crack in the Boycott," *Time*, September 1, 1975.

50. As reported by Jerry Flint, "Cuba Says Lifting Blockade Won't Bring Gush in Trade," *New York Times*, April 21, 1977, sec. 4, p. 1.

51. "Cuba Our Next Communist Trade Partner," *Industry Week*, March 24, 1975, pp. 89–90; *News Association of American Chamber of Commerce in Latin America*, May 6, 1971, p. 1.

52. *New York Times*, June 12, 1975, p. 40; *Wall Street Journal*, July 17, 1975, p. 1; ibid., August 22, 1975; *Latin American Times*, August 25, 1975.

53. *Journal of Commerce*, May 19, 1975; ibid., August 18, 1975; and *Miami Herald*, September 1, 1975.

54. "Statement of Arthur T. Downey Deputy Assistant Secretary for East-West Trade Before the Subcommittee on International Trade and Commerce of the House International Relations Committee," Washington, D.C., July 22, 1976, p. 4 and appendix B, table 3; and Business International, *Cuba at the Turning Point*, pp. 109–11. Rep. John Breaux criticized the Treasury Department's granting of a license for sale to Cuba of 90,000 to 100,000 tons of South American and Italian rice by a foreign subsidiary of Continental Grain Corporation as "blatant favoritism" toward multinational corporations and against domestic producers. *Miami Herald*, December 3, 1975.

55. The legal basis of the embargo was the Trading with the Enemy Act of 1917, the Foreign Assistance Act of 1961, Presidential Proclamation 3447 of 1962, and the Export Administration Act of 1969. For details see *U.S. Commercial Relations with Cuba*, pp. 19–20.

56. Ibid., p. 21. The best analysis of the impact of the embargo in its first decade is Maryanna Craig Boynton, "Effects of Embargo and Boycott: The Cuban Case," Ph.D. diss., University of California at Riverside, 1972.

57. See "U.S. Curb on Cuba Relaxed," *Washington Post*, August 22, 1975, sec. A, p. 1; and "U.S. to Allow Some Foreign Subsidiaries of American Firms to Trade with Cuba," *Wall Street Journal*, August 22, 1975, p. 4. For a discussion of the Quito meeting see "A Round Table on U.S.-Cuban Rapprochement," in *Latin America, Pitt Magazine* 30, no. 2 (May 1975), 31–38.

58. *Wall Street Journal*, August 23, 1975. On November 24, 1975, the Department of Commerce further reduced restrictions against Cuba by allowing Latin American and Caribbean countries

CARMELO MESA-LAGO

to sell goods to Cuba containing less than 20 percent of U.S.-made parts or materials except strategic ones. *Washington Post,* November 25, 1975, sec. A, p. 2.

59. "Excerpts from Press Conference Given by . . . Fidel Castro Ruz," *Granma Weekly Review,* August 31, 1975, pp. 7-9.

60. Walters, "An Interview with Fidel," pp. 2-3.

61. *United States Commercial Relations with Cuba,* pp. 34-35.

62. Ibid.

63. See "World Trade," *Journal of Commerce,* June 19, 1975.

64. See Lynn Darrell Bender, *The Politics of Hostility: Castro's Revolution and United States Policy* (Hato Rey, P.R.: Inter American University Press, 1975), pp. 101-10. Other recent studies on expropriation and compensation issues are Eric N. Baklanoff, *Expropriation of U.S. Investments in Cuba, Mexico, and Chile* (New York: Praeger Special Studies, 1975), chap. 2; and Cole Blasier, *The Hovering Giant: U.S. Responses to Revolutionary Change in Latin America* (Pittsburgh: University of Pittsburgh Press, 1976), chap. 4.

65. Business International, *Cuba at the Turning Point,* pp. 98-103. The assessment of the legal situation was given by participants in the State Department Colloquium on Cuba, May 22, 1975.

66. Jorge Domínguez, "A National Security Policy for Cuba," duplicated (Harvard University, September 1975), p. 24.

67. Ibid., pp. 21-24.

68. Fidel Castro, as quoted in Frank Mankiewicz and Kirby Jones, eds., *With Fidel: A Portrait of Castro and Cuba* (Chicago: Playboy Press, 1975), p. 140.

69. Abraham F. Lowenthal, "Cuba: Time for a Change," *Foreign Policy,* no. 20 (Fall 1975), pp. 65-86; and "Ending the Feud with Castro's Cuba," *Washington Post,* January 9, 1977, sec. C, p. 1.

70. David Binder, "U.S. and Cuba Discussed Links in Talks in 1975," *New York Times,* March 29, 1977, p. 1.

71. "Letter from Havana I: How Cubans View Prospects of U.S. Trade," *Business Latin America,* June 30, 1976, p. 202.

11

COLE BLASIER

COMECON in Cuban Development

The assistance the Soviet Union and other socialist countries have given to Cuba since 1960 is a historically unique transnational developmental effort. There has never been anything quite like it, not in the experience of developing countries in the Third World, nor of the socialist countries, most particularly the USSR.

Cuba has received far more comprehensive, sustained, and massive economic assistance from the USSR than any other developing country outside the Soviet Union's Eurasian orbit. The two other most favored countries, India and Egypt, appear to have received far less Soviet assistance than Cuba.[1] The number of Soviet technical assistance projects to these and other developing countries has also been far less than to Cuba (See table 11.3).

It is difficult to compare Soviet economic assistance to Cuba with that to other socialist countries. The number of Soviet projects completed in Cuba by 1975, for example, exceeds that to any other socialist country except Communist China, Mongolia, and North Vietnam. The Soviet figures on "Soviet assistance" to socialist countries in 1972 in table 11.2 suggest that Bulgaria, East Germany, Mongolia, and Poland all got more aid. But we do not know what those figures comprise, whether, for example, they are comparable with respect to Soviet price subsidies (in the Cuban case, for such commodities as sugar, nickel, and oil) or in monetary payments (in the Cuban case, suspension of payments on its Soviet debt). This is a question that is unlikely to be resolved because of the complexities of pricing arrangements within the planned economies and the unavailability of balance of payments data. In any case, Cuba is different from all the other socialist countries in her remoteness from the socialist Eurasian orbit.

In fact, the distinctiveness of the Cuban case is also broadly societal and cultural. Before Castro came to power, Cuba's ties with the USSR, while not nonexistent, were neglibible. Few countries were more distant, not only in a geographic sense, but also in a cultural, economic, and political sense. As I will attempt to show below, Cuba has experienced a remarkable integration with the distant and different socialist societies of Eastern Europe. Few historical cases of great integration with comparable societal and cultural contrasts come to mind.

Soviet aid to Cuba is also distinctive for its sheer magnitude. Its value, for example, appears to be far greater than some of the most generous U.S. programs to other small countries such as Chile and the Dominican Republic. In fact, although comparable figures are not available, it appears to approach in magnitude those exceptional beneficiaries of U.S. assistance, Israel and South Vietnam.[2]

The context of Soviet aid to Cuba differs from that of other socialist countries in that Soviet ties with Cuba appear to be looser than with the socialist countries of Eastern Europe. Castro, for example, is the former leader of a non-Communist political movement which took over the local Communist party; the Communist leaders of Eastern Europe, on the other hand, took over other political parties. No doubt this helps account, if only partially, for what appears to be Cuba's greater than average autonomy within the socialist family of nations. Cuba is also the only country benefiting from Soviet assistance that is literally under the very nose of the Soviet Union's leading rival, the United States. And Cuba is, of course, the first country in the Western Hemisphere to receive comprehensive Soviet aid.

The main purpose of this chapter is not to describe or evaluate the significance of socialist assistance to Cuba in its totality, that is, the grants, long-term loans, subsidized prices for Cuban exports (sugar) or imports (oil), and military assistance. This is dealt with in chapter 2, with respect to its calculation, volume, and overall significance, particularly as a burden on the Soviet economy. The subject of this chapter is technical assistance. Here I will attempt to describe and interpret the web of intersocietal and, especially, economic relations between Cuba and the European socialist countries.

The chapter's title, "COMECON in Cuban Development," is a form of shorthand. Most assistance to Cuba has been on a bilateral basis, more than half of it from the USSR. Much, but not all, of the bilateral aid from the other socialist countries has been coordinated and, sometimes, financed by the USSR. The Council for Mutual Economic Assistance (COMECON), the regional economic community whose members include European socialist countries, Mongolia, and, since 1972, Cuba, has only just recently begun to extend significant assistance, as an international organization, to Cuba. (An alternative acronym is CMEA.)

Since little is known or has been written on this subject in the West, the first section of the chapter describes my sources, partly as an aid to further research, but also because Soviet information policy with respect to this subject sheds light on its substance. The second section deals with Soviet assistance, including aid to different economic sectors; the third treats the aid programs of the other European socialist countries and the new COMECON program. The last two sections discuss the impact of socialist aid programs on Cuban public policy and present a general appraisal of socialist assistance.

Sources

Little has been published outside the socialist countries about Eastern European technical assistance to Cuba.[3] Much random detail is available in Cuban sources but there are few sectoral or comprehensive accounts.[4] There is, however, a growing literature in Eastern Europe, most of it in Russian. This largely descriptive treatment is found mainly in scholarly monographs, whose acquisition requires familiarity with Soviet bibliographic and publishing practices. The analysis of these indispensable sources is a formidable task for which the skills of a detective or prophet sometimes seem more desirable than those of a social scientist.

The Cubans do not appear to have tried to conceal Soviet assistance. On the contrary, Castro has often expressed his gratitude, and he correctly credits Soviet support with having saved the Revolution. There are frequent short items in the Cuban press about agreements with the Soviet Union, assistance in particular projects, and exchange visits between Cuba and Eastern Europe. Cuban statistical sources contain mainly trade data with no statistics on technical assistance or foreign aid.[5] Castro himself remains the principal authoritative interpreter of Cuban developments, particularly on such politically sensitive matters, and his speeches refer to Soviet aid only in general terms.

Comprehensive roundups of this scattered information have been made by Latin American specialists, most of them from Moscow. They are drawn from the cadres of specialists whose work, like that of their counterparts in the West, received impetus after Castro seized power in Cuba. No doubt part of the reason for the developing literature on Soviet-Cuban relations is the pride Soviet officials take in what they have been able to do for Cuba; it is a means of gaining recognition for the sacrifices this aid has entailed. Since the socialist countries have embarked on extensive operations there, more information must be kept generally available for the use of Soviet officials and to train specialists. Most important, the Soviet leaders consider socialist assistance to Cuba as a kind of window display of proletarian or socialist internationalism. The Soviet studies provide a data base for their political and ideological efforts to persuade Third World countries to adopt Soviet models and be responsive to Soviet influence.

The richest and most authoritative study on Soviet aid is *The Soviet Union and Cuba: Economic Cooperation* by A. D. Bekarevich and N. M. Kukharev of the Institute of Latin America in Moscow.[6] In addition to a lengthy description of Soviet assistance, the work contains many appendices: the text of some thirty-one agreements between the two countries, twenty pages of statistical tables, and a chronology of statements, communiques, agreements, and protocols. The same authors were major contributors to another volume in Russian, *The Soviet Union and Cuba: Fifteen Years of Fraternal Cooperation* in which Bekarevich presents a detailed description of the assistance of various other Eastern European socialist countries to Cuba.[7]

More recently I. G. Petushkov and E. Ia. Sheinin published in Russian for the Institute of Economics of the World Socialist System in Moscow a study entitled *The Economy of Cuba in the System of the International Socialist Division of Labor*.[8] Here socialist aid is described in the broader context of COM-

COLE BLASIER

ECON. Socialist assistance has been treated more briefly in other Soviet books and articles published under the auspices of the Institute of Latin America, the Institute of Ethnography, and others.[9]

Most of these works show great attention to detail, present systematic treatments, display a good command of the topic, and reflect personal commitments to the understanding of Soviet-Cuban relations. The USSR is rapidly developing a high level of scholarly competence about Cuba and Latin America. There is no absence of data. In fact, they are so massive as to be confusing and exhausting. The trouble is that they are often incomplete and sometimes misleading.

No figures are given, for example, on the total cost of technical assistance provided Cuba by a particular country in any given year, much less on a cumulative basis. Levels of credit extended in a particular agreement are announced, but we do not really know how much the technical assistance costs the USSR or other socialist countries in a given year. Western analysts can only estimate those costs through a variety of crude indices (see chapter 2 of this volume). Figures are given on trade, but balance of payments figures or levels of accumulated debt are not available. Nor is it possible to compare the volume of Soviet technical assistance to various economic sectors in any detailed way. Soviet figures on the sectoral distribution of Soviet aid are not sufficiently disaggregated so as to permit us to know how much went to the sugar industry or how much to fishing, and percentage figures or indices are frequently given instead of needed ruble or physical volume figures.

Politically sensitive data are often presented in such a way as to avoid adverse political repercussions. The figures, for example, comparing Soviet aid to Cuba with Soviet aid to other socialist countries (see table 11.2 below) suggest that such aid is roughly equivalent to that given to other countries of similar size, a conclusion impossible to check but most doubtful, nonetheless. Not surprisingly, there is also little data that could be used to drive a wedge between the Soviet and Cuban leaderships. Such treatment, however, may not be designed mainly to confuse or mislead opposition in the West. Equally or more important may be a desire not to cause political complications inside the Soviet Union or in COMECON countries.

Soviet interpretation of Soviet aid to Cuba shares the characteristics long familiar to readers of Soviet social science. Beyond that, Soviet treatment of Cuban affairs may be a more delicate matter still than, for example, the treatment of relations within Eastern Europe. Cuba has more autonomy than do the European socialist countries, and the Soviet position in Cuba in the long if not the short term is probably more precarious than in Eastern Europe.

Soviet scholars are constantly touching upon subjects related to sensitive negotiations and operations between the two governments, yet they know how dangerous it would be to them professionally to irritate the Cubans. Soviet Latin Americanists have readily confirmed my impression that research on Cuban affairs is more difficult than that on other Latin American countries. Far more is at stake. In fact, Soviet analysts have little choice in these matters since their publications, like virtually all Soviet publications, must pass multiple clearances. These handicaps are regrettable since otherwise Soviet publications could capture more vividly the social and human significance of this remarkable transnational effort.

Soviet Aid

Discussions in the West of Soviet aid to Cuba usually focus on the subsidies to cover Cuba's huge and continuing balance of payments deficits. For years the "fact" was bandied about that Soviet aid came to about $1 million per day; now the figure usually mentioned is $2 or $3 million. While the latter figures sum up neatly and not all that inaccurately the magnitude of Soviet assistance, it has become a cliché that conceals the significance of Soviet aid and leaves the impression that it is mainly a clearing operation.

What is more important is that Soviet assistance has become a motive force in Cuban life. Obviously, expenditures of that amount of money over nearly a generation involve tens of thousands of people and vast quantities of equipment and supplies. In addition, the USSR and other socialist countries have provided many of the scientific and technological resources that hold the society together and account for such material progress as Cuba has made since 1959 (see table 9.1). One Soviet scholar pointed out in the early 1970s that more than 70 percent of Cuba's economic ties and more than 80 percent of her capital investment were on the account of socialist countries.[10] In the economic crisis of the fall of 1976, Castro himself said that all new investment requiring imports would be suspended except for that which depended on socialist sources of supply.[11] The extent of the penetration of Cuban social processes and institutions by the socialist countries of Eastern Europe is not yet fully comprehended in the West.

Soviet assistance—initially of food, oil, and arms, and later of these items plus many of Cuba's other import needs—made possible the survival of the Cuban Revolution. Fidel Castro has frequently acknowledged this assistance, most particularly at the first congress of the Communist Party of Cuba (PCC) in December 1975:

> Without the decisive, steady, and generous aid of the Soviet people, our country could not have survived the confrontation with imperialism. They bought our sugar when our market was brutally suppressed by the United States; they supplied us with raw materials and fuel which we could not have acquired in any other part of the world; they caused to arrive free arms with which we opposed the mercenaries at the Bay of Pigs and equipped our Revolutionary armed forces in order to impose the highest price on any direct aggression by the United States; they supported our economy in extraordinary fashion in the critical years of the blockade. Thousands and thousands of military specialists and Soviet technicians helped in the instruction of our Armed Forces or supported

almost all branches of our economy. The effort of the Soviet people was seconded by the other socialist countries in accordance with their capacities.[12]

Unfortunately, the Soviet authorities have not released figures on the volume of Soviet technical assistance to Cuba. But they have released percentage figures showing how that assistance is distributed to various sectors of the Cuban economy and how the total amount compares with assistance to other socialist countries. The table below gives percentage figures on Soviet economic and technical assistance to Cuba from 1960 to 1973.[13]

Industry	76.1%
Agriculture	
(irrigation and drainage)	5.2
Geological surveys	8.3
Transportation and communication	8.2
Education and health	1.9
Other sectors	0.3

In the light of Soviet criticism of capitalist countries for keeping developing countries like Cuba in a kind of agricultural backwardness, it is not surprising that over three-quarters of Soviet assistance to Cuba has been reported in the industrial sector. The fact that aid to agriculture, shown as 5 percent, is attributed to irrigation and drainage suggests that probably all aid to the sugar industry must have been included in the "industry" figure. A breakdown of that figure, regrettably not available, would answer interesting questions about the distribution of assistance to the sugar, nickel, and other industries. The figure for geological surveys seems high and no doubt reflects preoccupation with Cuba's lack of oil resources, significant discoveries of which have not yet been made. It is also interesting that the USSR has apparently spent relatively little on the development of general education and in public welfare sectors such as health. It is possible that assistance for specialized education and training for specific industries is charged to the industry concerned.

Soviet figures are also available on the types of equipment provided Cuba. In table 11.1 the figures for Soviet deliveries are identical with Soviet exports for that year so that they must include exports to Cuba which are not in the narrower category of technical assistance. Moreover, the export total probably does not include technical assistance costs other than hardware, such as services. The table also indicates the share of equipment supplied to complete plants (*komplectnie predpriiatie*) which rose to over a third of all Soviet deliveries in 1969 and fell off sharply thereafter.

Further light is cast on the comparative magnitude of Soviet assistance to Cuba in table 11.2 where it is compared with that to other countries. The information accompanying the table does not make clear how Soviet assistance is defined and calculated. Almost two-thirds of Soviet "assistance" goes to the

TABLE 11.1
Growth of Soviet Deliveries to Cuba (year end)

	Growth of Economic and Technical Assistance (1960 = 100)	Soviet Deliveries (millions of rubles)	Machines and Equipment (millions of rubles)	Complete Plants (millions of rubles)	Complete Plants as a Percentage of Machines and Equipment
1960	100.0	67.2	5.79	—	—
1965	511.2	337.9	95.45	14.70	15.4
1967	557.6	506.8	145.80	27.22	18.4
1968	611.4	561.8	205.34	63.89	31.5
1969	635.0	561.6	213.98	80.25	37.5
1970	682.6	580.0	202.30	62.41	30.9
1971	730.8	602.0	176.00	20.86	11.9
1972	1,043.0	616.2	164.40	18.79	11.4

Source: A. D. Bekarevich and N. M. Kukharev, Sovetskii soiuz i Kuba: Economicheskoe sotrudnichestvo (Moscow, 1973), p. 267.
Note: Soviet deliveries are identical to Soviet exports for these years. For this reason I have changed the Russian title from "Some fundamental indicators of the economic and technical assistance of the USSR to Cuba" to "Soviet deliveries to Cuba."

socialist countries and about one-third to nonsocialist developing countries. Soviet assistance to Cuba between 1966 and 1974 hovers around 4 percent of total Soviet assistance. The volume of assistance to Cuba as defined in the table has tended to be less than that to East Germany and Poland and the lesser developed countries of COMECON—Mongolia, Bulgaria, and (except in 1972) Rumania. But Cuba has a much smaller population than any of the COMECON countries except Mongolia, Hungary, or Bulgaria. Only Bulgaria and Mongolia received more assistance on a per capita basis.

While table 11.2 may well reflect the comparative value of technical assistance in some narrow sense, it may be misleading about Cuba's comparative treatment if all Soviet aid to these countries were taken into account: Cuba may be a relatively heavier burden on the USSR than the figures indicate. To know for sure, one would need comparable disaggregated information for all the participating countries.

What perhaps may be a better indicator of Cuba's position with respect to Soviet assistance are comparative figures on Soviet enterprises shipped or built abroad, shown in table 11.3. In 1975, only Mongolia and Communist China had more such enterprises than did Cuba. (The figures suggest that the enterprises in Communist China were completed many years ago.) Cuba and Bulgaria were parties to agreements calling for the construction of 240 such enterprises each, with Cuba having 141 already in operation, Bulgaria 138. The country outside the socialist world with the most enterprises under agreement or in operation was Egypt with 148 and 86, respectively. The table does not indicate the capacities or capitalization of these enterprises.

COLE BLASIER

TABLE 11.2
Soviet "Assistance" to Foreign Countries
(percentage shares)

	1966	1969	1972
Socialist countries	61.38%	60.15%	62.23%
Bulgaria	11.20	11.73	12.28
Cuba	4.00	3.94	4.58
Czechoslovakia	0.98	1.08	1.77
Democratic Republic of Vietnam	2.45	2.55	2.44
German Democratic Republic	4.90	6.18	7.37
Hungary	2.30	2.29	3.14
Korean Popular Democratic Republic	3.06	3.55	3.29
Mongolia	4.64	4.90	5.29
Poland	5.65	5.28	4.81
Rumania	4.19	4.27	4.46
Yugoslavia	2.40	1.69	3.87
Other	15.61	12.68	8.93
Developing countries	38.20	39.13	36.51
Developed capitalist countries	0.42	0.72	1.26

Source: Bekarevich and Kukharev, Sovetskii soiuz i Kuba, pp. 9, 265, 266.
Note: Value figures are not available, nor do we know how "assistance" was calculated, that is whether items defined as assistance in the West are included here.

Study of Soviet assistance to Cuba is a reminder that the development process is a seamless web. Soviet assistance initially emphasized vital imports, but subsequently appears to have reached into nearly every corner and crevice of the economy. And in order to move the economy forward, Soviet assistance became necessary in science, technology, and education as well. As a result, relations have become complex and variegated. Some samples of Soviet assistance are:

Site surveys and feasibility studies
Project plans and engineering designs
Provision of seeds, fertilizers, insecticides, cultivating and irrigating
    equipment
Provision of complete plants, spare parts, and repair facilities
Provision of fuel, industrial and agricultural raw materials
Provision of power, construction, transport, and communication equipment
Technical advisors and operating teams
Training in Soviet secondary and higher educational institutions, ministerial
    institutes, scientific and technical institutes, and enterprises
Sponsorship of the strengthening or establishment of similar training and
    research programs in Cuba

Such assistance has also fanned out from the economy into cultural life, for example, in television, and into military, party, and, probably, internal security organizations.

TABLE 11.3
Projects Built or Scheduled for Construction by Intergovernmental Agreements with Technical Assistance of the USSR to January 1, 1975

	By Agreement	In Operation
Socialist countries	2,018	1,416
Albania	45	45
Bulgaria	240	138
Chinese People's Republic	256	256
Cuba	240	141
Czechoslovakia	40	19
Democratic Republic of Vietnam	220	167
German Democratic Republic	36	21
Hungary	89	61
Korean Popular Democratic Republic	73	46
Mongolia	393	269
Poland	157	112
Rumania	128	106
Yugoslavia	101	35
Developing countries	899	472
Afghanistan	89	67
Algeria	90	45
Egypt	148	86
India	68	40
Iran	81	43
Iraq	90	43
Somaliland	25	14
Syria	34	15
Yemen	21	8
Others	253	111
Total	2,929	1,894

Source: Tsentral'noe Statisticheskoe Upravlenie pri Sovete Ministrov SSSR, *Narodnoe khoziaistvo SSR v 1974 g.: Statisticheskii ezhegodnik* (Moscow, 1975), p. 774.

The structure of Cuban imports from the socialist countries as shown in table 11.4 must also reflect, though imperfectly, the emphases of Soviet assistance.[14] What stands out most may be the dependence of Cuba, whose economy is primarily agricultural, for the import of food and food products, which by 1973 constituted nearly a quarter of her imports from these countries. In view of the known absence of any significant oil resources, it is less surprising that fuels also constitute nearly a quarter of her imports from the East. The high level of Cuba's imports of food and oil is what most distinguishes the structure of her imports from socialist countries from the structure of her imports from all countries (see table 9.10). Note that imports of construction materials and manufactured consumer goods are relatively small.

Soviet technical assistance has also involved the exchange of many people, mainly Soviet specialists working in Cuba and Cubans studying in the USSR.

COLE BLASIER

TABLE 11.4
Cuban Imports from COMECON Countries

	1965	1970	1973
Machines, equipment, transport	36.3%	40.5%	29.0%
Fuel, minerals, and metals	22.6	18.7	22.5
Chemical products, fertilizers, rubber	6.9	6.1	6.0
Construction materials, metals	0.5	0.8	1.0
Crude and processed industrial raw materials	8.0	8.1	8.6
Raw foodstuffs	7.1	4.5	4.5
Food products	15.1	15.6	19.0
Manufactured consumer goods	3.1	5.4	7.5
Other goods	0.4	0.3	1.2

Source: I. G. Petushkov and E. Ia. Sheinin, *Ekonomika Kubi v sisteme mezhdunarodnogo sotsialisticheskogo razdeleniia truda* (Moscow, 1976), p. 54. For the structure of Cuban imports from the USSR from 1960 through 1970, see Bekarevich and Kukharev, *Sovetskii soiuz i Kuba,* p. 175.

Short official visits by high-ranking representatives have received much of the press attention, but there have been thousands of Soviet and Cuban citizens who have spent months or years in the other's country. In the years between 1967 and 1971 there were over seventy-five hundred specialists from COMECON countries working in Cuba, many of whom were Soviet citizens.[15] Cuba's relations with these countries are much improved since 1971 so that if that same rate has been continued, at least twenty thousand such specialists will have been in Cuba by 1977.

There have, of course, been many other kinds of exchanges. By 1972 the Soviet Academy of Sciences had sent some 312 specialists to the Cuban Academy. Other scientific exchanges included 51 agricultural scientists from a Soviet ministry at the Cuban Academy. In Soviet higher education, there were over seven thousand Cubans trained between 1962 and 1973 (see table 11.5). In the same period there were 889 Soviet scholars and specialists in Cuba on cultural exchanges.[16]

Since the early 1970s Cuban-Soviet cooperation has been coordinated by an Intergovernmental Soviet-Cuban Commission for Economic, Scientific, and Technological Cooperation. After the intergovernmental agreements of the 1960s expired and relations improved following Castro's support for the Soviet intervention in Czechoslovakia in 1968, the commission was established in an agreement signed on December 9, 1970. It had its first meeting in Havana in September 1971 and then alternated its annual meetings between the two capitals in the early 1970s.[17] The commission was designed to coordinate the work of planning organs; define the main directions of economic cooperation; reach joint decisions about trade, credit, and payments matters; prepare proposals to increase and improve the quality of trade; rationalize transport ties; and otherwise strengthen scientific-technical cooperation. Early meetings discussed mechaniza-

TABLE 11.5
Cubans Trained in Soviet Institutions of Higher Learning

	Preparatory Students	Undergraduates	Graduates	Nondegree Students	Total
1962–63	255	363	3	12	633
1963–64	237	509	6	29	781
1964–65	220	648	11	156	1035
1965–66	—	699	12	18	729
1966–67	—	655	14	42	711
1967–68	15	477	10	69	571
1968–69	14	423	10	22	469
1969–70	3	347	7	60	417
1970–71	54	355	6	39	454
1971–72	45	519	17	113	694
1972–73	37	736	30	87	890
Total	880	5731	126	647	7384

Source: Sovetskii soiuz i Kuba: 15 let bratskogo sotrudnichestva (Moscow, 1973), p. 62. Preparatory students were probably studying Russian and making preparations to transfer to other Soviet training institutions. Undergraduates include many students in professional training, such as engineers.

tion of the sugar harvests, completion of projects dealing with fertilizer production, irrigation, fishing, television, computers, merchant shipping, and so forth.

Carlos Rafael Rodríguez was appointed to head the Cuban delegation to the commission. As a leader of the pre-Castro Communist party (the PSP), Rodríguez had long-established ties to Moscow. At the same time he was one of the first of the old-guard Communists to throw his support to Castro and visited him in the Sierra Maestra before Batista's fall. Articulate and educated, Rodríguez's interest in economics further qualified him to lead the Cuban delegation. In fact, Rodríguez's appointments, not only to this job, but also as a deputy prime minister in charge of international matters, signaled Castro's adoption of more conventional economic policies and closer relations with the USSR. The deputy chairman of the Soviet council of ministers, V. N. Novikov, was appointed to head the Soviet delegation.

Soviet technical assistance to Cuba is extremely large and varied. Some impression of its scope and importance can be gained by examining the highlights in selected sectors.

Sugar. The assistance of the USSR and other socialist countries has probably been most massive in the sugar industry. This is not surprising since sugar constitutes Cuba's main export and nearly one-quarter of her national income. Sugar is, moreover, Cuba's principal means of payment to the socialist countries. The USSR has provided Cuba with technical assistance in virtually all stages of the sugar industry: planting, cultivating, harvesting, milling, and transport. Soviet scientists have collaborated with the Cubans in protecting sugar cane from disease and developing the best yielding strains suitable for Cuban soil and climate. The two other main concerns of Soviet assistance have been to mechanize the harvest and to boost sugar milling capacities.

Harvesting has been mechanized in order to increase the efficiency of the industry and solve manpower shortages, especially of cane cutters. According to Soviet sources, there were 425,000 professional cane cutters in 1958 and by 1973 that figure was cut to 39,000.[18] Soviet specialists were deeply involved with the Cubans in the invention of automatic loaders for collecting cut cane. By the early 1970s, there were 10,000 Soviet automatic loaders in service.[19] In addition, the USSR took the lead in the design of harvesting combines to cut as well as load cane. As a result of discussions in the Intergovernmental Committee for Economic and Scientific-Technological Cooperation, the USSR undertook to assist Cuba in the production of its own trailers to transport cane and combines to harvest it. Ambitious production goals were set at 3,000 trailers and 600 combines a year.[20] Twenty-one Soviet advisors were at work in early 1976 helping Cubans build a plant in Holguín to produce the KTP-1 combine.[21] Motors and certain other parts are to be supplied initially by the USSR, but Cuba is eventually to produce many of these parts herself. Before the Revolution almost all the cutting and loading of cane was done by hand. By 1974 reportedly only 4 percent was still cut and loaded by hand, 77 percent was cut by hand and loaded automatically, and 19 percent was cut and loaded by combine.[22] The plan for 1980 seeks to harvest 80 percent of Cuban cane by combine, a goal since revised downward.

The second major thrust of Soviet assistance in the Cuban sugar industry involved the renovation and expansion of existing mills. When Castro took over Cuba, all mills dated from before the Great Depression. Renovation was urgent, and the Cubans sought Soviet help. The costs of the renovation, together with improvements to associated rail transport, truck transport, and to storage and port facilities, were estimated at 800 million pesos.[23] In helping the Cubans shoulder this huge task, the USSR assumed responsibility for supplying technical assistance, supplies and transport, the assignment of specialists for designing, building, and operating these enterprises. The USSR also provided financing in the amount of 150 million rubles.[24]

Five other socialist countries participated in the renovation, particularly in the provision of particular types of equipment.[25] Although the Soviet share was not the largest, the USSR had the responsibility for financing the entire project[26] and the other countries' enterprises acted as subcontractors. The USSR reportedly sent 350 specialists to help renovate the mills between 1965 and 1970 and fulfilled all its obligations to provide equipment for the renovation of 114 mills by early 1970.[27] I have been unable to find, however, a critical evaluation of the sugar-mill renovation and the Soviet role in the renovation in socialist sources. Such an evaluation would be most interesting in the light of the failure to reach the ten-million-ton sugar harvest goal in 1970. The USSR was also heavily involved in renovating rail transport and improving port facilities for storing and loading refined sugar.

Other Agriculture. As in the sugar industry, Soviet and other East European assistance to Cuban agriculture has emphasized the transfer of technology: the sending of technical assistance teams; the training of Cuban workers, technicians, and agronomists; and the provision of heavy equipment. Soviet attention to agriculture in general has been focused on helping Cuba improve irrigation and draining of soil. An agreement for these purposes was made in 1963 and has subsequently been extended several times up to the mid-1970s.[28] Soviet topographers and soil scientists have surveyed the country's water and land resources and have made comprehensive recommendations for their improvement, including designs for some twenty reservoirs and ninety-five dams.[29] Soviet specialists also have participated in the training of technicians and engineers in these fields which from 1963 to 1969 alone came to 778 topographers, hydrogeologists, hydrologists, and so on. Many Cubans have also been sent to study in these fields in the USSR and in Poland, Bulgaria, and East Germany. According to Soviet sources, the water capacity of Cuban dams increased seventy-five times from 1959 to 1973, and the area of irrigated land has increased more than seven times. The USSR has also supplied Cuba with much equipment for construction work related to water resources, such as tractors, excavators, bulldozers, scrapers, tractors, trucks, cranes, and compressors.[30] From 1968 to 1972, for example, COMECON countries provided Cuba with 83 percent of her tractors, that is, 26,108 units.[31]

Fishing. Soviet-Cuban collaboration in the fishing industry has been especially successful, no doubt in part because Soviet fishing enterprises could advance their own interests measurably while helping the Cubans. The Cuban catch rose rapidly from twenty-two thousand tons in 1958 to nearly one hundred sixty-five thousand tons in 1974, or more than seven times.[32]

Collaboration began in 1962 when five Soviet trawlers and two smaller Polish trawlers served as the nucleus of a modern fleet to which was shortly added five Japanese ships. Initially, almost all the commanders of these ships were Soviet fishermen. Other fishing fleets were formed and the number of Cuban ships grew rapidly, many but not all of Soviet manufacture.

Meanwhile, specialists from the USSR in collaboration with Cubans began to explore not only local waters but also the Gulf of Mexico, the western Atlantic north of the Bahamas, and father points in the Caribbean basin. Together the two countries published scientific reports on their joint endeavors. The major purpose of these efforts was to locate the best fishing grounds, establish the best season for catches, and identify the most effective fishing methods. The Soviets, for example, claim to have introduced the Cubans to fishing with electric lights. As indication of Cuban progress, the Soviets report having sent nine scientists to the first joint conference and the Cubans two; a year later the Soviets again sent nine and the Cubans twenty.[33]

As a result of a 1963 agreement, the USSR helped Cuba build a large fishing base in Havana harbor with mooring, refrigeration, storage, dry dock, repair, and radio facilities. The USSR itself provided large dry docks for ship repair. In exchange for Soviet assistance, the Cubans agreed to service Soviet fishing vessels for a period of ten years. In 1972 the harbor served as a base for thirty-nine Soviet fishing ships, most of which also were repaired or cleaned there.[34]

Schools of the Ministry of the Fishing Industry and other Soviet institutions trained hundreds of Cubans in relevant trades and professions for fishing. The Leningrad Nautical School, for example, trained the faculty for a similar Cuban institution named in honor of González Lipez. Soviet fishermen employed on Cuban ships have passed on recommendations to the Cubans about the organization of their fishing fleets, instructions on the use of fishing equipment, and recommendations for training.[35]

Nickel. Next to sugar, nickel is Cuba's most valuable export product. Since Cuba has some of the largest reserves in the world, nickel also holds much promise as a source of increased foreign exchange. After the Castro government seized the nickel mines at Nicaro and Moa Bay from U.S. owners in 1960, the American engineers and other administrative staff left the island, and U.S. sources of supply dried up. As a result, the processing plants closed down for six months. In order to get the mines working again, the Cubans signed an agreement in 1961 with the USSR to receive up to thirty-three specialists to operate the plants and supply the necessary imported raw materials, equipment, and spare parts to operate the mines.

Another agreement was signed with the USSR on December 23, 1972, for an expansion of technical cooperation through the modernization of the plants at Nicaro and Moa Bay with a proposed new combined annual capacity of forty-seven thousand tons of nickel-cobalt concentrate. The USSR has also taken responsibility for the design and exploratory work required to build a new nickel mining facility at Punta Gorda with a capacity of thirty thousand tons a year. In addition, the members of COMECON, except Mongolia, plan a second facility of Soviet design to produce thirty thousand tons of nickel-cobalt concentrate annually. When the existing facilities are modernized and the two new facilities are in operation, it is hoped that Cuba will have nearly tripled her output of these minerals.[36] Cuba hopes thereby to provide increased and more secure supplies to COMECON markets as well as to have surpluses for sale in the West.

In the meantime, Cuba's production of nickel has not been increasing. Output reached a peak of thirty-seven thousand metric tons in 1968, a figure it has not surpassed and has only intermittently reached since that time, including the latest year, 1975, for which figures are available. Nor was evidence available in 1977 of substantial progress in expanding nickel output. Socialist technical assistance is also planned for the future production of special steels which require nickel, chrome, and other residual ores from nickel production.[37]

An important issue in Cuba's future is whether Soviet technology and the technology of other socialist countries will be sufficient to permit Cuba to capitalize fully on its huge nickel and related mineral resources. Cuban and Soviet authors frequently point out that Cuba's production of nickel has doubled since the Revolution and that Soviet technical assistance helped get the Cuban nickel industry back on its feet after the departure of the U.S. companies in 1960.[38] While Cuban and Soviet sources explain that one of two of the nickel facilities was built on the eve of the Revolution and did not begin production until just after Castro took power, they ordinarily do not make clear that the doubling is mainly due to the product of the new plant, that is, a plant planned, financed, and largely built before Castro. Nor have I seen reference to the fact that British as well as Soviet technical assistance has benefited Cuban output (see chapter 12 of this volume).

Soviet authors have assigned a productive capacity to the Nicaro and Moa Bay plants of forty-seven thousand tons annually[39] so that even by 1975, when output was thirty-seven thousand tons, Cuba had not fully realized the capacity of the two plants inherited from pre-Castro times. In view of Cuba's long and continuously urgent need for foreign exchange and the persisting trade deficits with the USSR, it seems likely that if Cuban or Soviet technology were capable of increasing nickel production substantially it would have occurred by 1975.

Manufacturing. Soviet assistance has been extensive in many branches of Cuban manufacturing, including steel, machine building, chemical products (particularly fertilizer), and construction (the USSR gave the Cubans a factory for producing prefabricated dwellings).[40] It is interesting that there was relatively little Soviet cooperation in textile manufacturing until after 1972 when Soviet enterprises, on what appears to have been a turnkey basis, supplied Cuba with a complete textile factory for cotton and synthetic materials.

Communications and Transport. Soviet specialists have been intimately involved in the development of communications in Cuba since the beginning of the Revolution. One of the first steps, based on an agreement in late 1962, was to establish direct telephonic and telegraphic contact between Havana and Moscow using Soviet radio equipment. Assistance was also given to strengthen Cuba's communications elsewhere in the world, apparently with a marked increase in shortwave transmissions. Poland helped Cuba build a factory to produce radios, and the Soviets constructed repair facilities to service these and other communication equipment. Plans went forward in the early 1970s for Soviet cooperation in the mass production of television sets and transistorized radios. At about the same time, arrangements were made for Cuba to establish her own transmission and receiving facilities for telephonic, telegraphic, and television transmission via satellite, including exchanges of television programming between Moscow and Havana. With respect to transport, the USSR sent to Cuba on the latter's request 110 specialists to advise on the development of roads, bridges, air strips, and railroads. Under an agreement in late 1973 the USSR also undertook technical assistance for Cuban railways.[41]

Power. Soviet specialists began to cooperate with the Cubans in the early 1960s in the construction of new power stations and in the integration of the national power system.[42] After Soviet geologists made early but apparently unsuccessful efforts to find oil reserves in Cuba, the USSR supplied Castro with oil which, according to Soviet sources, came to about fifty million tons from 1966 to 1974.[43] Soviet specialists also attempted to improve Cuba's refining capacity which has been about five million tons a year. In 1967 Cuba and the Soviet Union signed an agreement for cooperation in the field of atomic energy, and the latter supplied Cuba, as a gift, with a reactor for experimental and teaching purposes.[44] Soviet assistance provided the needed expertise for the foundation of the Cuban Institute for Nuclear Research. In the mid-1970s Cuba began plans for a nuclear power station with capacity of 880 megawatts.[45]

Aid from Eastern Europe and COMECON

The Soviet Union quickly mobilized the support of other socialist countries for the Cuban Revolution. All of the USSR's allies in Eastern Europe recognized Cuba and concluded trade agreements in 1960 and 1961. By the end of the latter year they had extended Cuba credits totaling $157 million. Enterprises from these countries also extended commercial credit at low rates. By 1973 there were some 220 technical assistance projects from these countries. The USSR provided over half the technical assistance to Cuba, and these countries provided most of the remainder (see table 11.6).[46]

Czechoslovakia has been characterized as having the most noteworthy economic relations with Cuba, possibly because this technical cooperation involved some of the heaviest equipment and most complex technologies. In the early 1970s the Czech government kept about one hundred experts and advisors resident in Cuba, especially in mining and the sugar industry.[47] The Czechs have helped the Cubans modernize old power plants or build new ones. They cooperated in building a hydroelectric station in the province of Las Villas and thermal electric stations in Camaguey, Las Villas, and Oriente. Czech assistance had also been given by 1973 in the construction of a dozen enterprises including factories for the production of diesel motors, tractor assembly, and motorcycle assembly. In addition, Czechoslovakia was heavily involved in helping Cuba build factories to produce consumer goods such as refrigerators, kitchenware, tableware, pencils, and milk.[48]

The German Democratic Republic has been active in the industrial field, particularly in mining, textiles, cement, machine building and metal working, food, and milling. It has also collaborated in the Institute of Tropical Research, in establishing an Experimental Institute for Weights and Measures, and has provided specialists and equipment for sports, physical culture, and orthopedic care. East Germany's trade with Cuba has exceeded Czechoslovakia's trade with Cuba since 1909.[49]

Bulgaria occupies a unique place among Cuba's socialist partners because she has many characteristics in common with Cuba. Bulgaria is a smaller, poorer, and more agriculturally oriented economy than the other socialist countries. Apparently there is a notable rapport between the citizens of the two countries. Castro singled out Bulgaria for especially favorable comment in his

TABLE 11.6
Cuban Trade with COMECON Countries
(millions of pesos)

	1965			1970			1974		
	Export	Import	Total	Export	Import	Total	Export	Import	Total
Bulgaria	20.8	15.9	36.7	28.8	23.3	51.4	77.4	41.0	118.4
Czechoslovakia	45.5	35.8	81.3	49.2	30.2	79.4	80.8	55.2	136.0
East Germany	28.1	24.8	52.9	48.8	49.9	98.7	105.0	47.2	152.2
Hungary	1.6	7.8	9.4	3.5	4.9	8.4	21.3	9.7	31.0
Mongolia	—	—	—	0.0	0.2	0.2	1.0	0.5	1.5
Poland	4.1	8.3	12.4	5.4	3.4	8.8	21.5	13.2	34.7
Rumania	0.5	3.9	4.4	12.9	22.9	35.8	35.3	10.8	46.1
USSR	322.5	428.4	750.9	529.1	690.6	1219.7	787.6	1018.7	1806.3
Total	423.1	524.9	948.0	647.7	825.4	1503.1	1129.9	1196.3	2326.2

Source: Petushkov and Sheinin, Ekonomika Kubi, p. 53.

speech to the first party congress noting that the strong ties between the two countries are based on similar "patriotic and revolutionary traditions" as well as size of territory and population. According to Castro, Bulgaria has sent more technicians to Cuba than has any other country except the USSR; the Bulgarians have been especially helpful in the development of agriculture, water resources, roads, and, by 1972, had helped build or renovate thirty-five enterprises. Bulgaria has in recent years been providing Cuba with about a quarter or more of her medicines.[50] Cuban trade, with Bulgaria, particularly exports, has been large considering that Bulgaria's economy is much smaller than Cuba's more important trading partners, East Germany and Czechoslovakia.

Rumania has focused technical cooperation on the extractive industries. In 1968 Rumania agreed to provide oil-drilling rigs and technical assistance for oil exploration, and more than fifty specialists arrived to work in Cuba in that year. As Castro made clear in late 1975, no significant oil strikes have yet been made. The Rumanians also agreed to provide assistance in other extractive industries, including the mining of copper.[51]

Poland has been less active in technical cooperation and in trade with Cuba than have other socialist countries of comparable size, population, and industrial development, such as Czechoslovakia and East Germany. Nevertheless, Poland has offered technical assistance in shipbuilding, metallurgical and glass industries, metal working, radio, and agriculture. The Poles helped the Cubans build the large ship repair facility in Havana harbor. More recently, Cuba has also secured from the Poles heavy industrial and transport equipment including ships and automotive and mobile construction equipment.[52]

Hungarian technical assistance has been important in the development of Cuban communications, especially telephone (new, large automatic facilities) and radio. Hungarians have also taken the lead in helping develop the Cuban glass industry.[53]

Since figures for the level of technical cooperation of Eastern European countries are not available, trade figures serve as a gross reflection of levels of cooperation. Czechoslovakia, which was the largest trading partner within this group in the 1960s, was superseded by East Germany in 1969. Bulgaria was gaining on Czechoslovakia in the early 1970s and even surpassed her in 1974.[54] No doubt the high level of exports to Bulgaria reflects in part the Cuban effort to finance Bulgarian technical assistance.

Throughout the 1960s Cuba tended to have substantial trade deficits with these Eastern European countries, again with the exception of Bulgaria. In the 1970s, however, and especially in 1974, the latest year for which figures are available, Cuba enjoyed a trade surplus. As would be expected, however, western and Japanese sources supplied more industrial equipment and projects of all kinds than East Germany and Czechoslovakia did. Czechoslovakia was a leading supplier of "complete factories." Bulgaria supplied large quantities of canned meat, cheese, and medicines. East Germany provided more diesel motors than the USSR, one of the few cases where a small Eastern European country edged ahead of imports from the USSR.[55]

Cuba's capacity to reciprocate in her relationships with Eastern Europe depend partly on the extent to which it needs sugar. Table 11.7 shows COMECON's production and consumption of sugar and the level of sugar imports from Cuba. It is interesting that the three countries other than the USSR that have the largest programs of technical assistance with Cuba (Czechoslovakia, East Germany, and Bulgaria) are also the countries that import the most Cuban sugar. The fact that Poland produces more sugar than it needs for local consumption may go far to explain why as one of the larger and more industrialized socialist countries it has a relativel small technical assistance program in Cuba.

While the Soviet Union has been heavily committed to helping finance Cuban development, most particularly by covering recurring annual trade deficits, only three of the socialist countries of Eastern Europe have exported more to Cuba between 1959 and 1974 than they have imported: Rumania, Hungary, and East Germany (see table 9.7). The other COMECON countries during those years had greater imports from Cuba than exports: Poland, Czechoslovakia, and Bulgaria. In fact, Cuba has exported more to the whole of the COMECON countries, except the USSR, than she has imported. This favorable balance was, however, only a tiny fraction of her deficit with the USSR.

The pattern of socialist assistance to Cuba also has interesting political implications. The USSR not only has provided well over half of such assistance but also appears to have been the sponsor of other socialist assistance. One of the most complex and variegated of the socialist aid programs in which many countries took part has been the reconstruction and mechanization of the sugar industry, both its agricultural and industrial aspects. This effort was coordinated by the

TABLE 11.7
Annual Production and Consumption of Sugar in COMECON Countries, 1969–1973

	National Production (1,000 tons)	National Consumption (1,000 tons)	Cuban Imports (1,000 tons)	Cuban Share of Consumption (%)
Bulgaria	217.0	540.0	202.8	37
Czechoslovakia	739.3	582.0	190.9	32
East Germany	476.0	483.8	289.1	59
Hungary	331.7	450.2	36.6	8
Mongolia	—	23.5	2.7	11
Poland	1738.9	1462.0	31.9	2
Rumania	510.0	504.0	85.7	17
USSR	9332.2	10487.2	1759.2	17
Total	13315.1	14532.7	2598.9	17

Source: Petushkov and Sheinin, Ekonomika Kubi, p. 133.

USSR which subcontracted various aspects of the work to enterprises in different countries. The percentage share of the various countries participating in the provision of equipment for that purpose is as follows:

German Democratic Republic	28.70%
Rumania	24.00
USSR	21.50
Czechoslovakia	15.50
Hungary	8.35
Poland	1.95

It is significant that the USSR took responsibility for "the long-term financing" of this project.[56] The distribution in this particular case does not reflect the distribution of socialist technical assistance generally, particularly because of the large participation here of Rumania and the absence of Bulgaria.

One has the impression that the countries where Soviet political influence is strongest, namely East Germany and Czechoslovakia, have tended to be the heaviest participants in socialist cooperation with Cuba, whereas Poland and Hungary, which have been able to take a more independent line, have tended to be less active. This point should not be exaggerated since the complementarity of the economies of the various bilateral sets varies too. An interesting aspect of the economic relationship is that in spite of the technical assistance and credits offered Cuba by these countries, most of Cuba's exports of consumer goods, including luxury items such as canned fish and tobacco, go to hard currency markets in the West.

These brief summaries attempt only to touch on the high points of the various bilateral relationships. As a general rule, they have been conducted on the basis of trade and payments agreements and long-term credits under the supervision of joint committees for economic and scientific-technical coopera- tion. The academies of sciences also have joint agreements under which there has been a variety of international exchanges in scientific fields, including large conferences, many of which have taken place in Cuba. The Eastern European countries have also had a variety of educational exchanges and training programs there and in Cuba.

As the above country-by-country description shows, the participation of the member governments of COMECON in Cuba's economic development has been primarily through bilateral relationships. In the reconstruction and development of the sugar industry in the 1960s, Cuba relied primarily on the Soviet Union to coordinate and finance the participation of other socialist countries. As result, the participation of COMECON as a regional organization in Cuban development has not been large. Nonetheless, plans are now underway for more active partici- pation by COMECON itself in economic relations with Cuba.

Cuba began attending meetings of COMECON as an observer in East Berlin in November 1962.[57] It was not until 1972, however, that Cuba was admitted as a full member, the only one in the Western Hemisphere. Cuba has assumed a position, together with Mongolia, as an underdeveloped country in COMECON. In view of the fact that Cuba, like Mongolia, has a lower level of industrialization, she is entitled to "preferential" conditions in economic collaboration.[58] Cuba now sits on most of the COMECON committees such as trade, transport, statistics, science and technology, and planning.[59] The seventy-ninth meeting of the Executive Committee was a big event for Cuba when high-ranking socialist officials from all the member governments met in Havana for the first time on January 18, 1977.[60]

Cuba's participation is closely linked to her first five-year plan for 1976–1980, coordinated with the plans of other COMECON members. All of these plans are supposed to be harmonized so as to achieve the best results in "the world system of socialist division of labor." In the negotiations, Cuba succeeded in securing commitments from COMECON for development assistance. COMECON's major organizational commitment is to help develop Cuba's nickel industry by providing technical assistance for the construction of a plant to produce nickel-cobalt concentrate in Punta Gorda as described above.

COMECON is also committed to assist the Cubans in the development of cellulose and paper by-products from sugar cane. Cuba produces far less paper per capita than do any of the European socialist countries, shortages that must be met by imports. Producing paper from sugar cane requires further research, in which the Cubans, Russians, and Poles are engaged. Cuba is also supposed to be included in the COMECON system of standardized shipping containers.[61]

Impact of COMECON on Cuban Policy

Soviet diplomacy has not always been at its best in dealing with developing countries, witness the hasty Soviet departure from Egypt. In fact, a case might be made that the USSR has been less effective in dealing with the Third World than has the United States, which is saying a good deal. With respect to Cuba, however, Soviet leaders have justification for taking real pride, whether it be for their decisive aid to Castro in 1960 or for the close and influential relations they have with Cuba today.

What may not be fully appreciated in the West is that in the interim Castro probably posed a greater challenge to the USSR as an ally and presumed friend, than he did to the United States as a presumed enemy. Surely during the 1960s Cuba's policies must have been irritating to the Soviet leaders. One of the most flamboyant and popular Communist leaders since Lenin and Trotsky was refusing to toe the Soviet mark. Mao Tse-Tung was recalcitrant, too, but he was the leader of a great power which the Soviet leadership was not forced to subsidize in such a huge way and which proved its capacity to stand on its own feet. In dealing with Castro and his small island, Soviet officials in the end felt forced to contain their frustration, hold their tempers, and swallow their pride.

The catalogue of tensions and conflicts between the two governments needs to be recalled only briefly here: Castro's high-handed treatment of the old-guard

Cuban Communists; his romantic and ill-conceived support for national liberation movements in Latin America; his freewheeling operations elsewhere in the
Third World; and not least, his economic policies often diametrically opposed to
Soviet practice. Castro's first experiments with socialist economic policies sent
him on an industrialization binge that caused severe damage to the economy and
which he later came to regret. In repudiating that policy, the Cuban government
sent the pendulum swinging wildly in the other direction in an overly ambitious
and unsuccessful campaign to produce 10 million tons of sugar in 1970. To
achieve that goal, Castro emphasized mass mobilization, voluntary labor and a
campaign of moral rather than material incentives in conflict with hard-earned
socialist experience that material incentives work best. And throughout the
1960s, he refused to delegate authority or establish orderly mechanisms for the
conduct of the economy, while intervening in the economy erratically and whim-
sically himself. What other Communist leader has exercised such freedom of
action, caused the USSR so much irritation, and still remained within the Soviet
fold?

Moscow has had to deal with recalcitrant ruling Communists before. But in
Eastern Europe the USSR has had the advantage of occupation troops or nearby
garrisons and an established police network. Nor has the USSR been forced to
subsidize such a large part of a foreign economy in Eastern Europe. Subsidiza-
tion posed the great dilemma. On the one hand, economic measures were the
strongest weapon Moscow had to keep Castro in line. But their use meant
damaging the Cuban economy, thereby defeating the objective of keeping a
Marxist-Leninist regime in Cuba. Castro's wasteful and ill-conceived economic policies must have caused special hurt. Like anxious parents, the Russians
put up with Castro's erratic behavior, political excesses, and one economic
failure after another for about a decade, paying the bill for the consequences
while maintaining a publicly accommodating posture.

Castro had to learn his economic lessons for himself, justifying first the
negative impact of the early industrialization campaign and later the dislocations
of the sugar campaign. Nonetheless, the Soviet leaders deserve credit for helping
Castro see the light. By late 1967 Castro's independent domestic and foreign
policies were becoming literally unsupportable, partly because they defied Soviet
interest, partly because, in the Soviet view, they were leading Cuba into a blind
alley.

In 1967, as in previous years, Cuba's need for oil, almost all of which was
imported from the USSR, continued to grow rapidly. In 1967, for example,
Cuba's consumption of oil rose 8 percent while supplies increased only 2 percent. As a result, the nation had to draw down on its reserves, including those
held back for the armed forces. To relieve the adverse effect on military security,
Cuba requested some 115 tons of advance oil deliveries, but received only 80
from the USSR.[62] Trucks and cars began to line up at Cuban gas pumps, industrial shutdowns were threatened if tankers arrived late in port, and gas rationing
was tightened. Meanwhile, Soviet production of oil continued to rise, thereby

making it clear that the Cubans, not the Soviets, were the victims of a squeeze. The USSR was using its control over oil exports to Cuba to make Castro more tractable.

At the same time, January 1968, a policy dispute erupted among party members in Cuba. Castro and his brother Raúl purged the party of the so-called microfaction, nine party members led by Aníbal Escalante, an old guard Communist from the pre-Castro era. The leadership's ire was focused on Escalante and his associates when the true opposition must have been the USSR with whom the Escalante group was accused of intriguing. Many of the allegedly mistaken views attributed to the microfaction were held by Castro's critics in Moscow: insufficient party influence on policy (meaning that Castro was too personalistic); too much emphasis on moral incentives, "voluntary" labor, and the like; failure to be responsive to Soviet recommendations. They also charged that the sugar goal of 10 million tons was not practical; supported the Soviet leaders in the missile crisis, although they failed to clear the removal of the missiles in advance with the Cubans; and expressed their criticism of efforts to eliminate the old Communists, of Ché Guevara for being "romantic, adventuristic, and anarchistic," and of the pro-Chinese currents in Cuba.[63] It is of great interest that the views attributed to Escalante not only tended to correspond with the Soviet critique of Cuban policies but, in large measure, they became the views and policies that Castro ultimately adopted. In his speech to the first congress of the PCC in December 1975, for example, Castro admitted that Cuba had followed utopian and unrealistic ideas and had not known how to benefit from the rich experience of other socialist countries.[64]

Although meticulous effort was made in the attacks on the microfaction not to impugn the Soviet authorities, there was little reason for the party to make such a fuss about Escalante and the admittedly few people linked to him. He was discredited and made harmless in 1962. Moreover, two of the major decisions made by the Central Committee which met to deal with the microfaction involved conserving fuel oil and not sending representatives to the forthcoming meeting of Communist parties in Budapest, two decisions unmistakenly taken in response to Soviet pressure.[65] By then, 1968, domestic economic difficulties and the failure of his campaign in support of national liberation movements, symbolized by the death of Ché Guevara, forced Castro badly off balance. At the same time the USSR was crowding him economically.

In his speech following the invasion of Czechoslovakia by the Warsaw Pact powers in August 1968, Castro revealed how vulnerable he was to Soviet sanctions and U.S. arms. That speech was an anguished and bitter cry, deeply opposed in principle to Soviet armed action against the Czech people, but painfully aware of how much he would need Soviet armed support himself if Cubans organized opposition against him. On the one hand, Castro knew the widespread popular support that the Dubcek regime had in Czechoslovakia, but at the same time he felt obliged to build an elaborate case that Czech revisionism was an instrument of capitalism and imperialism. Whistling in the dark, he said that he would never need to suffer the humiliation of asking for foreign support against his own people. But he quickly made the case justifying such support if it were linked to imperialist aggression. Fearful that the Czech invasion might prompt the United States to take compensatory military action against Cuba, Castro bitterly acknowledged how much he needed Soviet military as well as economic support. And the bitterness was revealed in his complaints about the Czechs' stinginess in selling Cuba military "junk" at high prices. In a candid but contorted presentation, Castro ultimately had to approve the Soviet invasion as essential to the protection of the integrity of the East European socialist regimes, a politically realistic gesture that marked a turning point in his relations with the USSR.[66] The coup de grace which ultimately led to the sharp reversal of his domestic and foreign policies was the failure of the Cuban effort to produce 10 million tons of sugar in 1970.

Through it all, Soviet leaders appear to have remained flexible and patient, a costly tactic in the short term but which eventually brought Castro around. They combined the carrot of Soviet aid with the stick of economic sanctions in a setting of Cuban military vulnerability. In the end, the USSR got its way without an irreparable break between the two countries. Castro agreed to institutionalize the Cuban system and rationalize the economy largely along the lines of the Soviet model. He did so because of Soviet blandishments and warnings, but also because hard-earned experience taught him that the new Soviet-sponsored arrangements were better suited to his regime's long-term interests.

Soviet guidance of Castro has proved effective partly because Soviet leaders and scholars have carefully avoided offending the Cubans in public forums. Soviet disagreements with Castro's former economic policies are implicit in Soviet writing, but the Cubans would be hard put to find explicit statements about which they could complain. The Soviet position is made clear through their selective quotes of Castro, by what is praised, and by what is ignored. One Soviet device for dealing with sensitive subjects of Cuban internal affairs is not to criticize the past but to stress in general but unmistakeable terms what needs to be done in the future. On other occasions, the Soviet critique of Cuban policy and success in influencing are rather more explicit. One Soviet author explained in late 1976:

> In the life of every party and country there are crises as a result of which social development receives new impetus and is infused with qualitatively new content. Such a crisis occurred in Cuba in 1970 when, as a result of a profound analysis of the process of social development of the country, huge unutilized potentialities and reserves were discovered, yielding the appropriate conclusions about past mistakes and shortcomings. . . . In 1970 an uninterrupted process of improvements in all aspects of the revolution began . . . , the Party grew and was strengthened . . . , functions of the party and state organs were clearly delineated . . . , the system of the administration of the economy was

completed . . . , attention to the study of the experience of the USSR and other socialist countries grew.[67]

The USSR and the other socialist countries have not, of course, been concerned only with Cuban interests in their efforts to persuade the Cubans to develop a viable economic system and to adopt more effective economic policies. No less important is making sure that their Cuban debtor pays off her huge debts. Now that Cuba, a member of COMECON, is locked into many long-term commodity and other trade agreements and is coordinating its first five-year plan with the plans of the other COMECON countries, Cuban economic policies must be shaped in part by the ''world socialist system'' and the principles of the ''socialist division of labor.'' In these complex relationships many delicate issues arise. Not the least of these are the relationships within COMECON between the more-developed and less-developed members. These relationships are burdened by much ideological baggage, most particularly by the long-established Marxist criticisms of capitalist expolitation of ''colonial and semicolonial'' countries. Soviet leaders and scholars have criticized the capitalist countries for years for perpetuating the agrarian economies of the poorer countries, by encouraging their emphasis on one or two agrarian or mineral exports, and for imposing inequitable terms of trade between their raw material exports and manufactured imports.[68] U.S.-Cuban relations before Castro have provided a rich source of illustrations for this line of attack. Soviet authors traditionally begin discussions of relations between Cuba and other socialist nations by comparing the benevolence of Soviet policies with the supposedly exploitative character of U.S. policies. Most often mentioned in support of this contention are the important distinctions that the USSR does not have capital invested in Cuba, and therefore takes out no profits related thereto, and that the USSR provides Cuba with long-term agreements for the purchase of assured volumes of sugar and nickel at high and stable prices.

Soviet arguments not withstanding, conflict between developing and developed economies persists in COMECON just as it does among the free-market economies. In his not infrequent references to socialist internationalism, Castro insists on a high standard of conduct on the part of the more developed socialist nations, but the Cubans have been disappointed more than once. Ché Guevara, for example, once complained about Cuba selling her raw materials cheap and paying high prices for manufactured goods from socialist countries.[69] Such complaints are also known in Eastern Europe where Rumania has objected to being forced to export grain she needed herself to supply the deficits of more advanced socialist countries, asking how that squares with leveling up economic development and the supposed benevolent character of socialist cooperation.[70] It is not surprising that the more industrialized socialist countries may have a different view of socialist internationalism than Castro does, especially when aid to Cuba must come out of their already scarred hides.

What makes this all rather awkward for the parties is that Cuba's fundamental economic problems are about the same as they have always been: how to produce enough at home to pay for the imports needed from abroad. As much as Castro might like the socialist countries to be a never ending font of generosity, Cuba will have to pay eventually for what she buys. And to do that, she will have to capitalize on her natural economic advantages. After the political rhetoric is cleared away, Cuba, under socialism as under capitalism, must continue to emphasize agriculture and the export of raw materials, namely, sugar and nickel. And it is precisely such an economic emphasis that COMECON espouses and Castro at long last has approved. To take some of the sting off that, COMECON has agreed to promote industrial applications in agriculture, such as the more efficient use of sugar cane in paper and pulp manufacture and the use of mineral by-products of nickel ores in steel production.

Soviet and Cuban authorities have reached agreement on Cuba's general development goals for the balance of the decade. Writing from a Soviet perspective, two Cuban specialists from the Institute of Economics for the World Socialist System, the leading Soviet scholarly institute for the affairs of the socialist countries, expressed the official COMECON view, carefully balancing the conflicting forces and interests within the socialist family:

> On the basis of a profound study and comprehensive evaluation of economic and natural resources and of the potentialities of the country, of its own domestic needs as well as of the needs of the other fraternal socialist countries, the Communist party and the revolutionary government of Cuba have given great attention to the rapid development of the export branches of agriculture and industry as a first priority: to the sugar industry by completely utilizing the by-products of sugar production; to tobacco, citrus fruits, and to the production of other tropical fruits, as well as to mining.[71]

According to these authors, this statement sums up the participation of Cuba in the international division of labor. What this boils down to is that Cuba must develop her natural resources to the full for export in order to pay her way and finance the further development of the country even though this might mean sacrifices in the consumer sector and less industrialization in sectors where she does not have a natural economic advantage.

In his speech on the Cuban economic crisis in the fall of 1976, Castro emphasized these same priorities. He said, for example, that Cuba's first obligation is to fulfill her international economic obligations and maintain her credit.[72] Since the bulk of Cuba's economic relations are with the COMECON countries and it is they who hold most of her debt, Castro's statement means that Cuba's first priority is to produce exports to meet commitments to these countries. Significantly, he put expenditures for health, education, employment, and essential supplies as a second priority. In taking this position, Castro is simply facing up to the realities of Cuba's economy and of her international economic relations.

The Nature of Socialist Assistance

Comprehensive evaluations of socialist assistance to Cuba must be made cautiously because the available data are incomplete.[73] Not surprisingly, Soviet and Cuban sources do not make penetrating analyses of its shortcomings or failures. Without these, and appraisals by independent specialists based on site visits, conclusions are necessarily preliminary.

Socialist assistance must, in all fairness, be considered in the light of the desperate situation the Castro government faced in mid-1960. The Eisenhower administration and many members of Congress did not think Castro had a chance to survive after the U.S. government ended purchases of Cuban sugar, persuaded the oil companies to refuse to refine Soviet crude oil, and began arming a counterrevolutionary force.[74] Beginning in 1960 the roots and branches of the Cuban economy were severed. This could have been a mortal blow because of her dependence on foreign sources for most of her raw materials, including virtually all of her fuel and some of her food, and for equipment, spare parts, and technology. Few governments could have survived such radical surgery. Nor could Castro had it not been for Soviet assistance. His survival was the ultimate proof of the efficacy of that assistance. It is difficult to identify any economy so dependent on its foreign economic relations that has ever experienced such radical economic surgery in peacetime. The simple facts that the Cuban economy still functions and Castro is in power are for him and the USSR an economic and political triumph.

In addition, the Castro government has made much progress in promoting social welfare: eliminating the worst consequences of unemployment, fighting illiteracy, strengthening education, and promoting public health. Although Soviet assistance has tended to emphasize projects directly related to agriculture and industry, the USSR deserves to share in the credit for achievements in promoting social welfare.

In other respects, socialist technical assistance has had mixed results. Its main thrust has been in industries already or potentially the best sources of exports. It is not surprising, nor improper, that socialist assistance has emphasized sectors where the socialist countries had most to gain, that is those industries which promised the most reciprocal benefits.

Tables 9.2 and 9.3 contain the most useful indicators of Cuban economic progress under Castro. The record in the two most important export products, sugar and nickel, where socialist attention has been focused, is only fair at the best. Cuban sugar output in 1975 was not much above prerevolutionary levels although it is important to note that socialist sponsorship of mechanization of the harvest has helped overcome manpower shortages. Although nickel output has doubled, Cuba already had the unused capacity to double output at the beginning of the Revolution, a time which coincided with the completing of a second large nickel refining plant. The gains since that time were mainly putting that capacity to use. In the light of Cuba's large nickel reserves and the pressing need for foreign exchange, the fact that capacity is not yet appreciably above 1960 levels represents an unimpressive record.

The economy's best performance in export sectors has been in citrus fruits and fishing, the latter being truly impressive. And in fishing, of course, Soviet technical assistance has been important, and Soviet fishing enterprises have themselves directly engaged in their own operations.

Cuba's future economic relations with the socialist countries, including technical assistance, will depend in part on the extent to which the Eastern European countries can put her exports to good use. Soviet sources predict that the sugar consumption of COMECON countries (except Cuba) will exceed production in 1980 by about four million tons and in 1985 by about five to six million tons.[75] If these figures prove correct, then Cuba will continue to be assured of substantial demand for sugar in these countries.

Much attention has recently been devoted in Cuban and Soviet publications to socialist technical assistance in the development of Cuba's nickel industry, whether this be the bilateral Soviet project or the Soviet-sponsored multilateral COMECON project. If Cuba does not begin to show progress soon on increasing her output of nickel, whether the required technical assistance comes from the East or the West, the socialist countries will be embarrassed. Cuba needs foreign exchange so badly and her reserves of nickel are so large and valuable, that inability to exploit this resource will become increasingly obvious with painful repercussions for the socialist countries.

While the consequences of failures in socialist technical assistance for Cuba would be domestic and economic, at least initially, the consequences for the USSR would be broadly political. Cuba is the Soviet model par excellence of proletarian or socialist internationalism, that is, one of the best examples of the relationship between a relatively developed socialist country and a developing socialist country. In order to keep the Castro government viable, the USSR has been forced to expend huge sums in assistance. No wonder the Soviet government seeks to capitalize on what has been an exemplary model of Soviet generosity, whatever the motives. Not withstanding detente, or perhaps partly because of it, the USSR continues its political and ideological competition with the West. What this has meant in the Third World is attempting to demonstrate that socialism is the model to emulate and that the interests of the developing countries lie with the USSR rather than with the United States and other western powers. As a result of the Soviet Union's long-standing commitment, Soviet pride and prestige, as well as her political interests, are engaged in maintaining a viable Marxist-Leninist government in the Western Hemisphere.

The gravest handicap of socialist technical assistance in the long term is beyond the remedy of its authors. The important ties established between Cuba and Eastern Europe arose out of U.S. ineptness and Castro's necessity, not out of natural advantage. The relationships which have been laboriously forged at great cost are partly artificial. In many ways Cuba's natural economic allies are among other American and free-market economies—not in Eastern Europe. And her most natural trading partner is the United States, not the Soviet Union.

Both Soviet and Cuban leaders are aware of the importance of Cuba's ties in the Americas. In a recent authoritative Soviet study of Cuba's role in COMECON, the authors stress this, quoting Fidel Castro on the necessity that Cuba's COMECON ties not interfer with Cuba's eventual integration with the rest of Latin America.[76] Castro himself has given the ultimate verdict on that subject. Since Cuba can hardly integrate herself into the economy of Latin America as it is now constituted, he has explained that integration with the Eastern European socialist economies has made sense in the medium term. However, he maintains that "our fatherland of the future is Latin America... a Latin America of revolutionaries."[77]

NOTES

1. Cumulative Communist credits and grants for the period 1954 to 1975 to India and Egypt were $2.4 billion and $2.2 billion, respectively. See Central Intelligence Agency, *Communist Aid to Less Developed Countries of the Free World, 1975* (Washington, 1976), p. 33. Cumulative repayable Soviet aid to Cuba for the period 1961–1975 (not to mention other forms of assistance) came to more than twice that, that is, $4.4 billion. Central Intelligence Agency, *The Cuban Economy: A Statistical Review, 1968–76* (Washington, 1976), p. 14.

2. Soviet economic assistance to Cuba is estimated at over $8 billion since 1958. This amount is greater than U.S. economic aid to Israel and Vietnam as shown in U.S. official statistics, but the two sets of figures are not comparable. For further details see chapter 2.

3. Leon Gouré and Julian Weinkle were among the first to exploit Soviet sources on a closely related topic in "Cuba's New Dependency," *Problems of Communism*, March–April 1972, pp. 68–79. Professor Edward A. Hewlett of the Department of Economics of the University of Texas presented a paper, "Analysis of Cuba's Membership in the CMEA," at the Ibero American Language Center, New York University, at a conference on October 31–November 1, 1975.

4. Among the rare documents is a paper prepared under the direction of Lic. Oneida Alvarez Figueroa for a conference in Moscow in April 1974 entitled "Conferencia Internacional por el aniversario del CAME: Ponencia de Cuba," *Economía y Desarrollo*, no. 28, 1975, pp. 186–209.

5. See *Anuario Estadístico de Cuba*, various years.

6. *Sovetskii soiuz i kuba: Ekonomicheskoe sotrudnichestvo* (Moscow, 1973). An earlier study, which I have not seen, is A. D. Bekarevich, *Kuba: Vneshneekonomicheskie otnosheniia* (Moscow, 1970).

7. *Sovetskii Soiuz i Kuba: 15 let bratskogo sotrudnichestva* (Moscow, 1973), hereafter cited as *15 let*. In addition to articles by Bekarevich and others, this volume contains contributions on economic relations by V. I. Bondarchuk and E. A. Kosarev. See also a similar earlier volume, *Kuba: 10 let revoliutsii* (Moscow, 1968).

8. *Ekonomika Kubi v sisteme mezhdunarodnogo sotsialisticheskogo razdeleniia truda* (Moscow, 1976).

9. *Vneshniaia politika stran latinskoi ameriki posle vtoroi mirovoi voini* (Moscow, 1975); *Vneshneekonomicheskoe sviazi sotsialisticheskikh stran* (Moscow, 1974); *Rossiiski-Kubinskie i Sovetsko-Kubinskie sviazi XVIII–XX vekov* (Moscow, 1975).

10. *15 let*, pp. 146–47.

11. *Granma Weekly Review,* October 10, 1976, p. 4.

12. Fidel Castro, *La Primera Revolución Socialista en América* (Mexico, 1976), pp. 55-56.

13. Bekarevich and Kukharev, *Sovetskii soiuz i Kuba,* p. 7. The figures probably cover the period to January 1, 1973.

14. The structure of *Soviet* exports to Cuba for 1966, 1970, and 1971 may be found in *15 let,* p. 39. Soviet exports to Cuba in 1975 and 1976 are listed in Ministerstvo vneshnei torgovli, *Vneshniaia torgovlia SSSR v 1975 g.: Statisticheskii sbornik* (Moscow, 1976), pp. 296-302. The figures are not completely aggregated by major category.

15. *15 let,* p. 147.

16. Ibid., pp. 24, 54.

17. Bekarevich and Kukharev, *Sovetskii soiuz i Kuba,* p. 12.

18. Petushkov and Sheinin, *Ekonomika Kubi,* p. 123. Carmelo Mesa-Lago informed me that the figure 425,000 is too high. The highest figure published in prerevolutionary Cuba was 350,000.

19. Bekarevich and Kukharev, *Sovetskii Soiuz i Kuba,* p. 83.

20. Ibid., p. 84. Carmelo Mesa-Lago informs me that 200 to 300 machines were produced in 1976.

21. *Granma Weekly Review,* April 4, 1976, p. 7.

22. Petushkov and Sheinin, *Ekonomika Kubi,* p. 126.

23. Bekarevich and Kukharev, *Sovetskii soiuz i Kuba,* p. 87. The peso was pegged at $1.00 until the U.S. devaluation.

24. Ibid., p. 87. See the appendices, documents 19 and 22. See also *Latinskaia Amerika,* no. 1, 1975, p. 18.

25. Bekarevich and Kukharev, *Sovetskii soiuz i Kuba,* p. 89. See also the section on East European aid below.

26. Ibid., p. 90.

27. *Economía y Desarrollo,* no. 28, p. 199; Bekarevich and Kukharev, *Sovetskii soiuz i Kuba,* pp. 86-90, 231-34, and 238-39. See also Carmelo Mesa-Lago, ed., *Revolutionary Change in Cuba* (Pittsburgh: University of Pittsburgh Press, 1971), p. 307, for problems in the renovation.

28. The agreement is contained in document 11 in the appendix of Bekarevich and Kukharev, *Sovetskii soiuz i Kuba,* p. 213 ff.

29. Petushkov and Sheinin, *Ekonomika Kubi,* p. 78

30. Bekarevich and Kukharev, *Sovetskii soiuz i Kuba,* pp. 123-26.

31. Petushkov and Sheinin, *Ekonomika Kubi,* p. 73.

32. Chapter 9, table 3. See also chapter 3.

33. Bekarevich and Kukharev, *Sovetskii soiuz i Kuba,* pp. 107-08.

34. Ibid., p. 111.

35. Ibid., p. 112.

36. Petushkov and Sheinin, *Ekonomika Kubi,* pp. 134-36; *Granma Weekly Review,* January 30, 1977; Castro, *La Primera Revolución,* p. 111.

37. Petushkov and Sheinin, *Ekonomika Kubi,* pp. 136, 137.

38. Bekarevich and Kukharev, *Sovetskii soiuz i Kuba,* pp. 34 ff.

39. Ibid., p. 29.

40. Ibid., p. 76.

41. Ibid., pp. 129, 131, 133 ff. See also Carmelo Mesa-Lago, *Cuba in the 1970s* (Albuquerque: University of New Mexico Press, 1974), p. 156, n. 51.

42. Ibid., pp. 16 ff.

43. Petushkov and Sheinin, *Ekonomika Kubi,* p. 62.

44. Bekarevich and Kukharev, *Sovetskii soiuz i Kuba,* p. 27.

45. Petushkov and Sheinin, *Ekonomika Kubi,* p. 58. See text of chapter 10, note 29.

46. *15 let,* pp. 137, 147, 148.

47. *Latinskaia Amerika,* no. 2, 1974, p. 109.

48. *15 let,* 148-53.

49. Ibid., pp. 153–57.

50. Ibid., pp. 157–61.

51. Ibid., pp. 161–64.

52. Ibid., pp. 164–67. See also Ewa Legomska Dworniak, *Polska-Kuba gospodarka wspolpraca* (Warsaw, 1975), p. 231.

53. *15 let,* pp. 167–69.

54. República de Cuba, Junta Central de Planificación, Dirección Central de Estadística, *Anuario Estadístico de Cuba 1974,* pp. 186–87.

55. Ibid., pp. 212–27.

56. Bekarevich and Kukharev, *Sovetskii soiuz i Kuba,* p. 90. A graph showing the shares of the various socialist countries in the provision of equipment for the sugar industry is on p. 89.

57. *East Europe,* January 1963, p. 40. See also Daniel Tretiak, "Perspectives on Cuba's Relations with the Communist System," (Ann Arbor, Mich.: University Microfilms, 1975), p. 241; and Michael Kaser, *Comecon: Integration Problems of the Planned Economies* (London, 1967), pp. 68, 103. Edward Hewlett in "Analysis of Cuba's Membership in the CMEA" concludes that the USSR urged the Cubans to join COMECON (CMEA) to put Cuba's relations within the socialist family on the same basis as other members, to encourage Cuba to model her economic and political system after the Eastern European countries, and to spread the costs of socialist assistance to Cuba. He believed Cuba responded affirmatively because the costs of admission were not particularly high and there were continuing benefits from the associations with the USSR.

58. "La Integración económica: Las posibilidades de los diferentes sistemas político-sociales," *Economía y desarrollo,* no. 27, 1975, p. 219.

59. *15 let,* pp. 172–73.

60. *Granma Weekly Review,* January 30, 1977, p. 3.

61. Petushkov and Sheinin, *Ekonomika Kubi,* pp. 163, 141–42; Iu. P. Zhuravlev, "Latinskaia Amerika—CEV: Tendentsii vsaimootnoshenii," *Latinskaia Amerika,* no. 4, 1976, p. 22.

62. *Granma Weekly Review,* January 3, 1968, p. 3. See also Gouré and Weinkle, "Cuba's New Dependency," p. 73.

63. The Central Committee documents were carried in installments in *Granma* beginning January 28, 1968. See also *Informe Raúl Castro: ¿Por qué están presos Aníbal Escalante y otros ex-dirigentes del P.C. Cubano?* (Montevideo, 1968), pp. 7 ff.

64. Castro, *La Primera Revolución,* pp. 116, 117.

65. *Granma Weekly Review,* January 28, 1968, p. 1.

66. *Granma Weekly Review,* August 25, 1968, pp. 2 ff.

67. V. Kh. Man'ko, "Osnovnye napravlenie ideino-politicheskoi rabota Kompartii Kuby," *Latinskaia Amerika,* no. 5, 1976, pp. 37–38.

68. Ibid., pp. 9–11, 81 ff. Also Bekarevich and Kukharev, *Sovetskii soiuz i Kuba,* pp. 3–5.

69. Tretiak, "Perspectives on Cuba's Relations," p. 275.

70. Kaser, *Comecon,* pp. 217, 218.

71. Petushkov and Sheinin, *Ekonomika Kubi,* p. 86.

72. *Granma Weekly Review,* October 10, 1976, p. 4.

73. For example, lines of credit are reported without figures on the amounts actually drawn down; plans and goals are often described without authoritative reports on current or final status; comprehensive figures on technical assistance (as distinct from foreign trade), balance of payments, and foreign indebtedness are not available; there is an absence of comprehensive indicators and evaluations of performance.

74. See Cole Blasier, "The Elimination of U.S. Influence" in *Revolutionary Change in Cuba,* ed. Carmelo Mesa-Lago (Pittsburgh: University of Pittsburgh Press, 1971), pp. 66 ff.

75. Petushkov and Sheinin, *Ekonomika Kubi,* p. 134.

76. Ibid., p. 147.

77. *Granma,* July 28, 1972, p. 3.

12

THEODORE H. MORAN

The International Political Economy
of Cuban Nickel Development

Cuba possesses the fourth largest nickel reserves in the world. If developed at a rate that is easily feasible from an engineering point of view, these reserves would offer the country an opportunity to diversify its export base, strengthen its economy, earn hard currency, fortify its ties with the industrial nations of the West, and reduce its dependence upon the Soviet Union. The cautious estimation documented in this chapter suggests that foreign exchange receipts from nickel exports could equal 50 percent of the hard currency earnings from sugar before 1985, could grow more rapidly, and could be less vulnerable to the capitalist business cycle or to declining terms of trade. However, Cuban laterite ores are difficult to process. To make them commercially competitive in world markets requires technology that neither the Cubans nor the Soviets possess—a point that is recognized by Cuban technicians and at least some political leaders. And they require a political environment for large-scale development and marketing that presupposes a fundamental restructuring of U.S.-Cuban relations.

The attractiveness of developing Cuban reserves will probably rise in the short run, if Cuban sites are compared to alternative laterite deposits in the tropics, and decline over the middle term as the possibilities of deep seabed mining are probed offshore. This places the successful implementation of a Cuban strategy to expand nickel exports under a definite time constraint, with a margin for success that will narrow as the price of Cuba's petroleum imports, needed for energy-intensive processing, rises from the present subsidized rate to world levels.

What are the prospects for the development of the Cuban nickel industry? Can multinational mining companies be incorporated successfully into Cuba's militantly socialist society? What are the political implications of nickel for the evolution of U.S.-Cuban relations? This chapter is divided into three parts. The first explores the structure of the international nickel industry and tests some hypotheses about how a host country might best maximize its bargaining power vis-à-vis various types of foreign corporations. The second part examines Cuban mining needs and outlines a possible Cuban strategy designed to pursue its economic self-interest, narrowly defined. But Cuban policy toward its mining sector will not be determined exclusively by its economic self-interest, ''narrowly defined.'' The third section of this chapter tries to place the prospects for   257

THEODORE H. MORAN

Cuban nickel development within the context of the broader evolution of U.S.-Cuban relations.

Oligopoly Strategy in Natural Resources

Nickel is the most highly concentrated major natural resource industry in the world. As recently as the 1950s the International Nickel Company of Canada (Inco) had a near monopoly in the "Free World" market, controlling 85 percent of the total output.[1] In the first two decades after the war, the position of Inco gradually eroded, as the company refused to participate in the U.S. government's plan to stockpile critical war materials. The resulting vacuum offered an assured market to other companies willing to risk the large amounts of capital necessary to enter the industry. As a consequence, Inco's share of noncommunist production capacity dropped steadily to a level of about 43 percent in the mid-1970s. But the degree of concentration has remained high, with three companies controlling more than 60 percent of capacity outside the Soviet Union in 1975.[2] The six largest aluminum companies, in contrast, account for "only" 60 percent of that industry's capacity. And one must include all Seven Sisters of the petroleum industry to reach more than 60 percent of world oil output.

Like petroleum and bauxite-aluminum producers, nickel companies can be divided into "majors" and "independents," with the crucial distinction being whether a company's share of the market is large enough that a given expansion of production will reduce the total profit (unit margin times volume) accruing to the firm. Such a calculation depends upon the price and income elasticities of demand for the product in the target price range and the response of one's competitors to the hypothetical production increase. In the international nickel industry, three companies—Inco, Falconbridge of Canada, and Société le Nickel of France—clearly have to weigh the impact of any production increase against the lower price they will receive for their already substantial market sales. These three are the majors of the international nickel industry. For other producers, the independents, the wisest corporate strategy is to expand production as fast as possible until marginal revenue equals marginal cost and leave it to the majors to balance supply and demand (that is, cut back supply) to capture oligopoly rents in the industry. In the nickel industry, as in other mining industries, new entrants are more likely to be found among natural resource companies involved in the extraction of minerals other than nickel and among users, such as steel companies, anxious to integrate backward to their own secure sources of supply.[3] These companies tend to have the experience, technology, marketing networks, and reputation in credit markets necessary to hurdle the barriers that protect the oligopoly rents from outsiders.

This industry structure offers opportunities as well as dangers to a country with large quantities of untapped reserves. The danger arises from the fact that the oligopoly rents of the majors come from keeping price above marginal cost—that is, from restricting supply.[4] The majors typically control reserves far in excess of what would be needed to meet demand for the foreseeable future. They may prefer, therefore, that vast new ore bodies not be proved up, developed, or brought to the market—or that they be proved up, developed, and brought to the market no faster than is consistent with maintaining their own corporate market share.[5] Frequently, the majors in a mining industry will keep large tracts under lease, ostensibly for their own future use, but mainly to prevent exploitation by others. From this perspective, the interests of the major nickel-mining companies might be best served if Cuban reserves were never brought to the market in commercially viable form.

But the independents, if they can be attracted to a new ore body, are motivated by no such desire to restrict production. They want to seize the possibility of using a vast discovery to expand their market share as rapidly as possible; they have nothing to lose by doing so. Thus, their corporate interests coincide with those of a host country that wants to develop its mineral resources with dispatch. The independents are not without their drawbacks, however: first, since they have less experience than the majors, they may be less successful; second, since they face great risk and great uncertainty, they must be actively enticed and generously rewarded. In contrast to the majors, however, for whom generous treatment is unlikely to alter behavior to a great degree, assurance of reward to independents is likely to be cost-effective in producing the speedy results desired by the host country.

The greatest opportunity for a host government comes, however, not from relying upon independents alone but from playing the independents against the majors: The possibility that "greedy," "reckless" independents might rush to expand their market shares so fast as to undermine the position of the large producers and upset the oligopoly equilibrium for everybody can create extreme anxiety among the majors, for whom fear of broad loss is stronger than desire for marginal gain.[6] Consequently, to take no chance, they must be willing to jump where independents threaten to jump, to bid against and indeed underbid any new competitors.

The general phenomenon of oligopolistic competition, of "follow-the-leader" behavior, has been observed across a broad spectrum of international industries.[7] In the natural resource sector, its most noticeable demonstration has taken place in petroleum, with Libya offering the clearest example of a host country successfully playing the independents and the majors off against each other.[8] In the late 1950s, Libya sought the advice of a consultant group of retired petroleum executives for a formula to increase the level of exploration in the country, accelerate the development of proved reserves, and speed the penetration of the European market with the country's low-sulfur crude. The consultants pointed out that the majors (the Seven Sisters) already had carefully balanced shares within Europe, already possessed abundant reserves for future exploitation in the Persian Gulf, and were reluctant to cut prices (thereby lowering the margin on established sales) to move more crude to France, Germany, or Great Britain. They recommended that Libya mount an active search to attract some of the independents, such as Continental Oil and Occidental Petroleum. The result was not only successful exploration and development by the independents, but a vigorous kindling of interest by the majors, who feared that Continental and Occidental, if left alone, might use the new source as the base to grow to "major" size themselves, much as Gulf had done earlier in Kuwait.[9] Thus the Libyan government was successful in manipulating the tension within the petroleum oligopoly to its own advantage.[10]

In the past decade the nickel industry has evolved in many respects like the petroleum industry, placing Cuba, with its vast reserves and potential for upsetting the entire nickel oligopoly, in a position not dissimilar to that of Libya in the mid-1960s. While Inco and Falconbridge have maintained their dominance over the world's major deposits of sulfide ores, mining companies with experience in minerals other than nickel have tried to chip away at their market by developing the technology needed to work the more abundant but more difficult laterite ores of the type Cuba possesses. Freeport pioneered in laterite metallurgy to work Cuban ores during the Second World War (Nicaro) and Korean War (Mao Bay). Besides Freeport (now working laterite ores at Greenvale in Australia), Amax, Marinduque, Asarco, Anaconda, Newmont, Pechinery, and perhaps others among companies that have not traditionally produced nickel have the technology to process laterites. Among the smaller producers within the nickel industry, Hanna and Sherritt Gordon could be potential bidders for Cuban contracts.[11] At the consumer end of the industry, U.S. Steel, Thyssen, Hoogovens, and at least three Japanese trading companies have explored the possibility of integrating backward to their own sources of supply. Outside the industry, Union Oil, Chevron, and Petroles D'Aquitaine have formed partnerships to try to enter the nickel business. All of these occupy the same structural position as the independents in the international oil industry.

Does the same potential for oligopolistic competition exist in the nickel industry as has been demonstrated in the petroleum industry? An investigation of the extent of interest among companies that could, hypothetically, contribute to the development of Cuban ores suggests that it does. Ten large U.S. and Canadian companies (majors and independents), representing at least thirteen corporations including nonaffiliated associates, were surveyed in the last quarter of 1975 and first quarter of 1976. (Time constraints and a limitation of research funds precluded a more extensive sample that would include European and Japanese firms, as well as other North American companies.) All interviews were conducted at the senior operational level (chairman, president, or senior vice-president). One of the two majors surveyed expressed no interest in mining in Cuba. Seven of the independents (representing at least ten corporations if one includes nonaffiliated associates) showed a serious interest (defined below) in pursuing the possibility of developing Cuban ores. The second of the majors surveyed showed only mild interest when Cuban projects were first discussed but, when informed of the outcome of the interviews with the independents, expressed the intent to bid against any investment offer or technology-sharing proposal made by any other company at any time in Cuba. The results of these interviews were reported to the Cuban government, to the U.S. government, and to U.S. business and academic audiences (including, of course, the companies involved).[12] In sum, as of June 1976, four U.S. and Canadian companies had conveyed to the Cuban government a desire to establish direct contact with Cuban representatives and had expressed willingness to send a senior corporate team to Havana as soon as commercial visas could be arranged to discuss participation in the island's nickel development. In addition, three companies (representing at least seven U.S. and Canadian corporations if one includes nonaffiliated associates) had sought to be kept directly informed by the Cubans about the possibilities for discussing concrete proposals but were unwilling to commit themselves to seeking commercial visas at the earliest possible opportunity.[13]

The Cuban Position

Cuba's nickel deposits rank behind only those of New Caledonia, the Soviet Union, and Canada (see table 12.1). Concentrated in a mountainous belt approximately 150 kilometers long on the north coast of Oriente Province, with additional deposits in Pinar del Rio and Camaguey, Cuban reserves (4.2 million tons) are more than half as large as Canada's (8.0 million tons) and almost twice as large as Australia's (2.5 million tons). They are equal to 8.6 percent of the world total and 12.1 percent of the non-Soviet-bloc total. (These estimates may be too low, since the country's geological endowment has been shut off from modern evaluation methods for nearly two decades.)

TABLE 12.1
World Nickel Production and Reserves
(thousand short tons)

	1973		1974		
	Production	Exports	Production	Exports	Reserves
Canada	269	91	290	87	8,000
Soviet Union	152	—	155	—	10,000
New Caledonia	109	52	115	61	15,000
Cuba	35	34	35	34	4,200
Australia	44	—	—	—	2,500
United States	18	22	17	34	200
Other "Free World"	99	—	145	—	9,100
World total	726		757		49,000

Sources: U.S. Bureau of Mines, Commodity Data Summaries, 1975, p. 111; and "The Cuban Nickel Industry: History, Prospects, and Implications for the World Market," study supplied by Arthur T. Downey, Deputy Assistant Secretary for East-West Trade, U.S. Department of Commerce, to Congressman Edward G. Biester, Jr., August 1975.
Note: These estimates do not include seabed reserves.

THEODORE H. MORAN

If Cuba were to reach its announced goal for 1985 of 90,000 tons of nickel production, that would equal 7 percent of world consumption or 8 percent of non-Soviet-bloc consumption, assuming (as the U.S. Bureau of Mines does) a 2.6 percent per year growth in world demand. Cuba would be the fourth largest producer and the second or third largest exporter in the world. With an output of 90,000 tons, nickel pproduction could equal 30 percent of the value of the nation's entire sugar production at free-market prices; nickel exports, after commitments to CMEA (Council for Mutual Economic Assistance) countries were covered, could equal half of the hard currency value of sugar exports.[14] Moreover, since the nickel industry is highly oligopolistic whereas the sugar industry is highly competitive, nickel prices are likely to perform better relative to the price of imported manufactures and to be less cyclical than sugar prices— problems that have bedeviled Cuban development both before and after the Revolution.

Yet Cuba's lateritic nickel-bearing ores are, and always have been, difficult to process metallurgically. Laterites, which account for approximately 80 percent of the world's nickel reserves, have the advantage over sulfides of being easy to mine: Cuban deposits are essentially raked off the land surface (after a thin overburden has been removed) in a large strip-mining operation; sulfides in Sudbury, Ontario, in contrast, come from relatively deep underground mines. But processing costs for laterites are much higher: They are mixed in complex fashion with other minerals, and the smelting and refining necessary to extract the nickel content is eight to ten times as energy-intensive as that used for sulfides.[15]

Cuba currently has two nickel mining-processing operations, at Nicaro and Moa Bay, and a third facility is scheduled for completion by 1980 at Punta Gorda. The Nicaro plant was built in 1943 by the Freeport Sulphur Company, with capital supplied by the Reconstruction Finance Corporation.[16] The ores that enter the Nicaro plant are high in water, silica, alumina, and magnesia content. Freeport designed the plant, which has a capacity of about 23,000 tons, to use a theretofore largely experimental hydrometallurgical processing technology, based on atmospheric-pressure leaching with ammonia. The high-cost operating technology forced the plant to close in 1947. It was reopened during the Korean War in 1952 under the ownership of the Nickel Processing Corporation (74 percent of whose shares were held by the National Lead Company and 26 percent by Cuban nationals). The plant was nationalized in 1960. Since that time, two new ore bodies have been opened, ample water supplies developed, and some modern British instrumentation introduced into the plant. With about four thousand workers (including service personnel), Nicaro currently produces about 18,000 tons of nickel in the form of 76 percent nickel oxide and 90 percent nickel sinter. Both products can be marketed directly to final consumers. By 1980 the Cubans would like to lower the level of dust emission and recapture the lost nickel, incorporate a new oven, extend the milling process and the electrical generation capacity, renovate the system of pumps and compressors, add levitation tanks, and install a new water filter and treatment facility (much of the equipment at Nicaro has been in place since 1943). The production goal is 22,000 tons by 1980.

The construction of Moa Bay began in 1953, also under the direction of Freeport Sulphur, with a capacity of 25,000 tons contained nickel.[17] The Moa Bay ores are of the limonitic type, low in magnesia, and require an enormously corrosive pressurized sulfuric acid treatment process. The plant had begun operations with no more than experimental runs when it was nationalized in 1960, and it was brought into regular operation in 1961 only with extreme difficulty. (An engineer who had worked at Moa Bay since the nationalization recalled a recurrent nightmare from the early 1960s: he would drive to the plant in the morning and find it had spontaneously blown up, but neither he nor anybody else would ever know why, and he would have to design a new plant exactly like the old one!) Current production is approximately 19,000 tons of nickel contained in a slurry of nickel (55 percent) and cobalt (4.5 percent) sulfides. There is no commercial market for such a slurry. Originally, it was shipped to Port Nickel, Louisiana, for refining by Freeport. Now it is shipped to the Soviet Union. Present plans call for additional equipment, including a conveyor belt from the mining area, a fourth steam boiler, new facilities for making sulfuric acid, a third acid line, electric power backup, and port expansion. The target for production capacity in 1980 is 24,000 tons. Moa Bay employs about 2,000 workers, including service personnel.

Punta Gorda comprises a vast expanse of ore bodies to the southeast of Moa Bay. Cuban plans call for the construction of one plant with a capacity of 30,000 tons by 1980, using an ammonia leaching process similar to Nicaro's and two additional 30,000-ton plants thereafter.[18]

The Cubans signed a protocol in September 1974 with the Soviet Union to modernize the Nicaro and Moa Bay operations and to begin production at Punta Gorda.[19] Total investments of $600 million were contemplated from CMEA sources (perhaps via the group's International Bank for Economic Cooperation), with the goal of increasing Cuba's nickel output to 77,000 tons by 1980. The country's first comprehensive five-year National Economic Plan, which was to be unveiled at the first Cuban Communist party congress in December 1975, should include the details of the nickel development program.[20] As of July 1976, the plan had not yet been published, perhaps owing to some reassessments of the future evolution of sugar prices.

A visit to the mining district in Oriente Province and interviews with technical, supervisory, and policy-making personnel suggest the following observations about the Cuban nickel industry.[21] First, Cuban managers have developed an extraordinary degree of skill and confidence in managing the traditional processing technologies at both Nicaro and Moa Bay. Whether compared to similar operations in the Third World or in North America, the technical mastery, operational competence, and apparent productivity of the work force at Nicaro and Moa Bay are immediately impressive.[22] Second, despite this, the Cubans want and need newer and more advanced technology to expand their operations and make them more efficient. This was stated in unequivocal terms at both the supervisory level in the mining district and at the political level in Havana. Third, the Cubans have concluded, unambiguously, that the Soviets cannot provide them with the technology they want; only the private corporations of the West can.[23] In making this judgment, Cuban experts are well informed about what kinds of operations the various international mining companies are undertaking, what their problems have been, and where their successes lie. Fourth, one gains the impression that the Cubans are confident that they could deal firmly and successfully with foreign mining multinationals if it came to negotiations or participation. The hesitancy, uncertainty, and anxiety that frequently accompany host-country representatives to the negotiating table in the Third World appear notably absent in Havana. Indeed, the theme of being weak and dependent that pervades discussions elsewhere in Latin America is not common in Cuban analyses of possible relations with transnational corporations.[24] In sum, there is a clear interest and desire on the part of the Cubans to incorporate Western technology into their nickel industry, and a remarkable confidence that they could do so quickly and successfully without damaging themselves socially or economically.

There appears to be a much less clear appreciation, in contrast, of the opportunity cost of passivity and delay in approaching the companies. They do not have to take an activist stance vis-à-vis private investors, they assert, because, first, they "know" that the "foreign monopolists" are anxious to gain access to Cuban ores. And, in any case, they argue, they have their own mining expansion program in progress which will allow them, on their own if necessary, to expand their penetration of the international nickel market surely and steadily. The first assertion is inaccurate: the "foreign monopolists" in the nickel industry, if by that one means the majors, are the firms *least* interested in speeding the development of Cuban ores. Their interests would best be served by Cuban supplies remaining off the market indefinitely. Rather, it is the smaller members of the oligopoly or the outsiders that could use Cuba as a base to expand their market share. And it is only by actively manipulating the potential rivalries within the mining oligopoly that Cuba can create the push to enter the island that will put it in the best bargaining position. On this point, the rhetorical trappings of Marxist theory may be leading Cuban decision makers astray. On a more general level, Cuban planners, like their counterparts elsewhere in the Third World, seem to underestimate the lack of information, the misinformation, and the organizational lethargy that impede the typical foreign investment decision. The image of the giant transnational company scanning the globe with perfect, instantaneous knowledge of commercial opportunities hides the real search costs, uncertainty costs, and bureaucratic inertia that must be overcome to produce corporate movement in a new direction.[25] The evidence shows that host countries which make a concerted effort (however discreet) to attract the attention and arouse the interest of potential investors create a stronger position for themselves than those which do not.[26]

With regard to the second assertion—that Cuba will in any case penetrate the international nickel market slowly and surely on its own—the outlook is opaque. On the one hand, Cuban officials report that their production costs compare favorably with published figures for Inco and other producers, and are substantially below world prices. On the other hand, Cuban estimates of their own production costs do not include a charge for the use of capital,[27] nor do they reflect input prices (especially energy and sulfur) at world levels. The director of Cuba's nickel development program, Felipe Perez, asserted, without qualification, that the Cubans could never expand their production competitively unless the capital for such expansion came in the form of aid.[28] The Cubans already market a certain amount of their oxides and sinter (between 9,000 and 13,000 metric tons) in Spain and Italy at world market prices.[29] For the rest (or at least for the 17,500 metric tons they sell to the Soviet Union) they receive a price about 38 percent higher than world market quotations.[30] In the absence of competitive factor markets in Cuba and a freely convertible exchange rate, it is difficult to tell whether the Cubans could expand their hard currency sales of nickel with a net gain or a net loss of real resources. But the outlook, especially as Cuban energy costs rise, is not something to be confident about.[31]

Thus, from a point of view limited to economic self-interest, Cuba would probably best be served by an active campaign to play upon oligopoly rivalry among the international mining companies and incorporate Western technology as rapidly as possible into the Cuban nickel industry. "Western technology" could in fact include many things: improved ammonia leaching processes for Nicaro and Punta Gorda, help with the pressurized sulfuric acid treatment at Moa Bay, and techniques for capturing and recycling nickel dust at Nicaro and for the separation of cobalt. It could include access to specially designed refineries in Louisiana, Canada, or Great Britain for Moa Bay's sulfide slurry. It could include managerial and engineering skills to improve the efficiency of operating facilities and to improve the design of new facilities. It could include capital in the form of equipment and credits: the senior executives of the companies surveyed discussed projects in which their own capital contribution could run from $20 million to $100 million.[32] Finally, it could include a marketing outlet via the established corporate global networks at world prices.

The time sequence in which both sides (the companies and Cuba) could explore the costs and benefits of working with each other is favorable: low-cost, low-risk, high-payoff opportunities coming first, with larger commitments following after. Within one or two years, the foreign companies could provide important technical services to improve the efficiency of ongoing operations at Nicaro and Moa Bay. Within two to four years, they could help in the engineering and redesign of new as well as renovated facilities. Beyond four years, they could contemplate participating in major new expansions at Punta Gorda or the construction of a complete refinery at Moa Bay. Neither side has to be prepared for a major commitment under high uncertainty until it has built up experience and confidence in working with the other.

But Cuban decisions about how to develop the nickel industry will not be based upon economic self-interest alone. They will be political and cannot be evaluated except as part of broader Cuban strategy toward the evolution of U.S.-Cuban relations.

Nickel Development and U.S.-Cuban Relations

What is the relation between the incorporation of Western technology into the Cuban nickel industry and the broader evolution of U.S.-Cuban relations?

If the United States and Cuba find their policies in other areas sufficiently compatible to want to explore the possibilities of rapprochement, the interest of the international mining companies in the island's ore bodies could play a central role in easing and speeding the process. At the present time U.S. business interest in Cuba appears to be broad but diffuse—agricultural equipment manufacturers, food-processing companies, spare-parts salesmen—with no major U.S. industrial or financial groups hoping to alter their market position with the normalization of U.S.-Cuban relations.[33] If the U.S. mining industry could be mobilized with the expectation of gain and the disquiet of fearing that their competitors might lock things up first, it would constitute a potent political interest group with influence in Congress and in the executive branch. Moreover, the enthusiasm of the mining, metal-processing, and metal-consuming groups could have an important spillover effect on other outstanding issues between the United States and Cuba. With regard to past nationalizations, for example, the American Mining Congress has taken a very tough stand publicly on the principle of compensation for expropriated properties.[34] But, almost without exception, the sample of ten companies I talked with asserted that they would take the lead in helping to work out a compromise arrangement.[35] At the same time, they asserted that under the proper circumstances they would be willing to use their contacts in Congress to stimulate positive movement on the embargo and most-favored-nation status.

If the United States and Cuba continue to pursue policies that will rekindle basic antagonisms, such as the recent activities in Africa, it is difficult to be optimistic about the speed and effectiveness with which Cuba could penetrate the international nickel market. Lacking formal State Department approval, U.S. mining firms have very little room to maneuver with regard to Cuba. They might, in theory, attempt to provide some technical services, via foreign subsidiaries, to the existing plants at Nicaro and Punta Gorda, analogous to the product sales that subsidiaries of U.S. firms in Argentina and Canada have carried out.[36] But U.S. mining companies are particularly sensitive to U.S. tax laws affecting depletion and the expensing of development costs, to stockpile purchases and price controls, and to U.S. policy affecting expropriation overseas. They are thus unlikely to want to antagonize a U.S. president or a U.S. Congress hostile to the easing of relations with Cuba. The U.S. companies sampled all affirmed that their participation in the Cuban mining industry would be dependent upon explicit approval by the U.S. government.

Without the push of U.S. companies to get into the Cuban nickel industry, the task of churning up oligopolistic rivalry is considerably more difficult. Three of the most experienced nickel miners outside the United States—Inco and Falconbridge of Canada, and Société le Nickel of France—are already majors and thus have little incentive to go on their own. The Japanese have very limited direct expertise in mining, especially nickel mining, preferring to finance others and buy up the resulting output with long-term contracts.[37] Perhaps, with concentrated effort, Cuba could stir up some enthusiasm among the smaller Canadian, European, and Japanese firms, but in the absence of U.S. corporate participation, the possibilities of creating serious anxiety among the majors are limited. This is all the more true since as long as U.S. borders remain closed to Cuban products, Cuban ores lose attractiveness in comparison to other Caribbean sites. (The "natural market" for a heavy bulk material like nickel from the Caribbean is Pittsburgh or Gary.) Thus, even if Cuba and the United States did no more than retain the present, relatively frigid status quo, the prospects for expanding Cuban nickel production via Western technology are dim. If, moreover, there were an evolution in the direction of active hostility between the two countries, the United States might go so far as to seek writs of attachment against shipments of nickel landed in Europe or Japan, much the same way Kennecott did in the case of Chile.[38] With such a possibility on the horizon, few firms or financial intermediaries (even of non-U.S. origin) would be likely to take the risk of developing a large, expensive new property like Punta Gorda.[39]

Finally, if for one reason or another, U.S.-Cuban relations remain in limbo for six to ten more years, the opportunity to use the nickel industry to broaden the economy and diversify exports may largely pass the Cubans by. No one can be sure how the production costs of seabed mining will ultimately compare to onshore mining for nickel. But by the end of the decade many of the one-time costs to develop the appropriate extraction and refining technology for manganese nodules will have been sunk, and many of the international mining companies will be much more committed to continuing in that direction than they are now. That will be the focus of oligopoly anxiety. If the United Nations has not, by then, produced an acceptable seabed mining code, the pressures for unilateral OECD action will probably have been more than enough to produce results. Thus it is doubtful that time is on the side of the Cubans.

NOTES

The background research on structure and strategy in the international nickel industry and on the implications of nickel development for U.S.-Cuban relations was supported by a grant from the Ford

Foundation. The study of the Cuban mining industry and of the prospects for incorporating Western technology into Cuba's socialist economy was carried out on a trip to Cuba in January 1976, paid for by the Cuban government. The views in this chapter are solely the responsibility of the author.

1. See "Inco: A Giant Learns How to Compete," *Fortune*, January 1975, p. 105.

2. Estimates of capacity and production are particularly difficult to acquire for individual companies since they immediately indicate market shares in an industry as concentrated as nickel. This capacity estimate comes from private industry sources. Figures for sales show lower concentration, reflecting, as one would predict in an oligopoly, the willingness of the larger members to hold spare capacity. From industry and U.S. government sources, 1974 nickel sales for the non-Soviet bloc countries are 701,000 short tons; for Inco, 274,000 short tons (39 percent); for Falconbridge, 45,000 short tons (6 percent); and for Société le Nickel, 67,000 short tons (9 percent). The total market share of these three companies is 55 percent.

One would also get a larger figure for the Seven Sisters of the oil industry if one used capacity rather than sales, although the recent "nationalization" in Saudi Arabia, Venezuela, and so on would cloud the interpretation considerably.

3. For a general analysis of the sources of new entry into natural resource industries, and of the dynamics of "backward" and "forward" vertical integration, see Theodore H. Moran, *Multinational Corporations and the Politics of Dependence: Copper in Chile*, published under the auspices of the Harvard Center for International Affairs (Princeton, N.J.: Princeton University Press, 1974), chap. 2.

4. Not that the majors want to generate oligopoly rents for anybody but themselves if they can help it. Indeed, for short periods of time they might drop prices deliberately to drive out competitors or discourage new entrants. But, over the longer term, an imperfectly competitive industry will keep supply more constricted than a more perfectly competitive one.

5. As an important sidelight, since a production increase would under some circumstances *lower* the aggregate revenue to a company with a large market share, the indiscriminate proffering of tax breaks and other subsidies by a host government in the hope of stimulating rapid mineral development may result in nothing more than a giveaway of public revenues. That is because, from the firm's point of view, the high return on the new project is not enough to offset the lower average return on all of its outstanding investment. In short, a "good investment climate" represented by tax breaks and subsidies may not function as neoclassical theory would lead one to expect if the conditions assumed in neoclassical theory (for example, perfect competition) are not met.

6. The Seven Sisters of the international oil industry used to refer to petroleum outside their control as "oil in weak hands."

7. See Frederick T. Knickerbocker, *Oligopolistic Reaction and Multinational Enterprise* (Cambridge, Mass.: Harvard University Press, 1973).

8. On the Libyan example, see Edith T. Penrose, *The Large International Firm in Developing Countries: The International Petroleum Industry* (London: George Allen and Unwin, 1968); Mira Wilkins, *The Maturing of Multinational Enterprise: American Business Abroad from 1914 to 1970* (Cambridge, Mass.: Harvard University Press, 1974); M. A. Adelman, *The World Petroleum Market* (Baltimore: Johns Hopkins University Press for Resources for the Future, 1972); and Raymond Vernon, *Sovereignty at Bay: The Multinational Spread of U.S. Enterprises* (New York: Basic Books, 1971).

For suggestions of a similar dynamic in the copper industry, see *Bougainville Copper Ltd. (B)*, Case Study 4-174-104 (Boston: Harvard Business School, 1974); and Raymond F. Mikesell, *Foreign Investment in Copper Mining: Case Studies of Mines in Peru and Papua New Guinea* (Baltimore: Johns Hopkins University Press for Resources for the Future, 1975).

Almost without exception, every major host country advance in the Persian Gulf was accomplished through the successful manipulation of independent-major rivalry, with Iran using Mattei's ENI (Ente Nazionale Idrocarburi) and the Standard Oil Company of Indiana and Saudi Arabia using J. Paul Getty's Pacific Western Oil Company and Japan's Arabian Oil Company, for example, to break the solidarity of the Seven Sisters. For sources, see Penrose, *Large International Firm*, Wilkins, *Maturing of Multinational Enterprise*, and Adelman, *World Petroleum Market*.

9. Cuba has an advantage that Libya did not have in that the extent of its nickel reserves is already well known (although the structure of production costs is not). Cuba's disadvantage is that the future treatment of private foreign corporations is considered highly problematic.

10. The effort to pull the independents into Libya required the promise of substantial gain if the companies' efforts proved commercially successful. After Occidental and Continental were allowed to enjoy their lucrative position for a few years, however, the host country had no difficulty in tightening the squeeze on the returns accruing to the investors. Independents pose a relatively simple problem in this respect because, unlike the majors, they typically do not have a diversified resource base and thus are highly susceptible to a host-country threat of a production cutback or the revocation of a lease.

11. Sherritt Gordon (as well as Inco) has already held direct talks in Cuba about the possibility of participating in the country's nickel development program.

12. Some of the discussions with corporate officials were remarkably specific with regard to possible processing technologies and engineering techniques, size of capital "investment" required, sources of financing, and the legal form that corporate participation might take. But no specific proposals, of course, were carried between the companies and the Cuban government, or vice versa. I have neither sought nor received any fees or other honoraria from any interested party while carrying out this research.

13. This corporate interest is all the more striking since it was recorded in the period February–June 1976, when U.S.-Cuban relations reached a point of extraordinary tension due to Angola and the U.S. presidential primary in Florida.

14. The first calculations assume arbitrarily that Cuba produces an average of 6.5 million tons of sugar in the mid-1980s with a world price for sugar of 10 cents per pound (1976 prices) for $1.3 billion and a world price for nickel of $4,000 per ton for $360 million. The second calculation further assumes that Cuba is able to export for hard currency 2 million tons of sugar (for $400 million) and 50,000 tons of nickel (for $200 million). The exact nature or amount of Cuban payback commitments after its debts to the Soviet Union become due in 1986 are not known. To the extent that Cuba relies on private international companies rather than CMEA support to expand nickel production, it may have more than 50,000 tons available for hard currency sales, although the country would of course have to pay whatever fees the companies charge out of those hard currency receipts.

15. The latter estimate comes from talks with nickel experts at the College of Mineral Economics, Pennsylvania State University. The U.S. Bureau of Mines offers an even more striking comparison: sulfide smelters using electric furnaces consume 387 kilowatt hours per ton of concentrate; oxide smelters (for laterites) use 29.5 kilowatt hours per pound of nickel. Thus the ratio of energy intensity for smelting is 1 to 17. "Nickel," a preprint from Bulletin 667, U.S. Department of the Interior, 1975, p. 10.

16. For the background on Nicaro, see P. H. Royster, "Cuban Ore as a Source of Nickel," mimeo, U.S. Bureau of Mines, August 20, 1951; "Nicaro Proves Lateritic Nickel Can Be Produced Commercially," *Engineering and Mining Journal,* June 1954, pp. 80–83; "Nicaro Expands Nickel Capacity," *Engineering and Mining Journal,* September 1975, pp. 82–89; "The Cuban Nickel Industry: History, Prospects and Implications for the World Market," report of Arthur T. Downey, Deputy Assistant Secretary of Commerce for East-West Trade, to Congressman Edward G. Biester, Jr., August 5, 1975; and interviews with Nicaro's current manager, Antonio De Los Reyes, Nicaro, January 1976.

17. For the background on Moa Bay, see "New Nickel Process on Stream," *Chemical Engineering,* September 7, 1959, pp. 145–52; "Freeport Nickel's Moa Bay Puts Cuba Among Ranking Ni-Producing Nations," *Engineering and Mining Journal,* December 1959, pp. 84–92; Downey, "Cuban Nickel Industry"; and interviews with Rafael Rivero, chief engineer, Moa Bay, January 1976.

18. Interviews with Felipe Perez, director of Cuban nickel development, Punta Gorda, January 1976.

19. U.S. Department of Commerce, *United States Commercial Relations with Cuba: A Survey* (Washington, D.C.: GPO, August 1975); and Downey, "Cuban Nickel Industry." *American Metal Market,* October 20, 1976, reports that Cuban plans call for an upgrading of Nicaro and Moa Bay to

46,500 metric tons and the construction of a 30,000 metric ton operation at Punta Gorda, but quotes Felipe Perez as saying that the 1980 completion date will probably be delayed by two or three years.

20. In 1976 all the CMEA governments were, for the first time, to coordinate their five-year plans so as to maximize, in their words, the benefits of the international division of socialist labor.

21. The most senior policy-making official with whom I spoke (for three hours) was Ernesto Melendez, vice-president of the Commission for Economic and Technical Cooperation. These observations are based on a survey of fifteen to twenty middle-level officials from the Ministry of Foreign Relations, the Office of the Prime Minister, the Communist party, and the departments concerned with nickel production.

22. For a good example, the observer should interview Antonio De Los Reyes, manager, Nicaro.

23. For example, in discussing the problems Freeport has encountered with Green Vale (Australia) and Amax with Selebi-Pikwe (Botswana), a senior Cuban engineer committed perhaps the only indiscretion of the interview by turning to a colleague and saying, "It doesn't matter. No matter how bad they are, they can't offer us anything worse than the Russians!" This is surprising, since the Soviets have the reputation for excelling in heavy industry and metallurgy. See John W. Kiser, II, "Technology: Not a One-Way Street," *Foreign Policy,* no. 23 (Summer 1976), pp. 131–48. Inco and Amax had previously briefed me on the defects of Soviet nickel technology, which I had cavalierly discounted as a mixture of ideology and jealousy.

This judgment about Soviet technology should be tempered, however, by two additional observations about the Soviet presence. First, Cuban officials seemed genuinely grateful for Soviet financial assistance (capital, credits, a subsidized price for nickel, cheap oil) to the industry. Second, on a personal level, Soviet technicians (about one hundred) seemed well integrated into the Cuban mining community. On the basis of a handful of examples, it appears that the Russians are there with their families, speak Spanish, and avoid the "ugly Russian" characterization.

24. The Cubans are, however, sensitive to the form that foreign corporate participation could take—"technology contracts" and "service contracts" being the acceptable form, "direct ownership" and "equity" being unacceptable. But they were not hesitant to acknowledge the corporate need for stability and generous fees.

25. This is one reason why some analysts argue that fear of loss (for example, of an established market) is a stronger motivation than desire for gain in determining the strategy of multinational corporations.

26. On the corporate dynamics of, and impediments to, foreign investment decisions, see Yair Aharoni, *The Foreign Investment Decision Process* (Boston: Division of Research, Harvard Business School, 1966).

27. Whether this is because of a Marxist disinclination to attribute a "return" to capital, or a simple mistaking of marginal for average costs, is not known.

28. This observation was not only made in conversation with the author but was subsequently confirmed in discussions with Eugene Dimario of *American Metal Market.*

29. The U.S. Commerce Department estimates that about half of Cuba's production of 35,000 tons (1972) goes to the Soviet Union. Inco estimates that 50 percent of the remainder goes to Eastern Europe (U.S., Congress, House of Representatives, Committee on International Relations, Subcommittees on International Trade and Commerce and International Organizations, *U.S. Trade Embargo of Cuba, Hearings* [Washington, D.C.: GPO, 1976], pp. 173, 491). *American Metal Market* (October 19, 1976) reports, however, that approximately 70 percent of Nicaro's output is marketed in the noncommunist world (a total of about 13,000 tons).

30. According to the U.S. Commerce Department, the Soviets were paying $6,050 per ton for Cuban nickel, with the world price at $4,400 (July 1976). Statement of Arthur T. Downey, Deputy Assistant Secretary of Commerce for East-West Trade, before the Subcommittee on International Trade and Commerce of the House International Relations Committee, July 22, 1976, p. 9

31. The U.S. Commerce Department estimates that Soviet petroleum exports to Cuba in 1974 were priced at about one-half world levels and were increased in 1975 to about $7.50 (with OPEC prices in the Persian Gulf at about $11.50). If Soviet policy toward Cuba parallels its announced

intentions toward the Eastern European countries, it will steadily reduce the difference between its oil sales price and world market prices.

Industry sources indicate that energy constitutes about 50 percent of the cost of processing laterite ores.

32. Several of the corporations surveyed indicated that they would strongly prefer equity investment to any other form but, upon seeing Cuba in an Eastern European rather than a Latin American context, nearly every company asserted that management or service contracts would be an acceptable alternative to direct ownership.

33. This observation is based on the author's experience in discussing the prospects of U.S.-Cuban rapprochement with U.S. corporations and financial institutions.

See also *U.S. Trade Embargo of Cuba,* pp. 127 et seq., and testimony of Kirby Jones, Subcommittee on International Trade and Commerce and International Organizations, U.S. House of Representatives, July 22, 1976.

34. Letter from J. Allen Overton, president, American Mining Congress, *U.S. Trade Embargo of Cuba,* p. 547.

35. The most widely discussed formula was that established under the Nixon administration by the Greene Mission to Peru. In the Cuban case, two plenipotentiaries named by the respective governments would negotiate claims and counterclaims in one bundle, leaving the disposition of final awards to the public authorities in each country. (To offset the $1.8 billion recognized as valid by the U.S. Foreign Claims Settlement Commission, the Cuban government argues that it should be compensated for damage done during the Bay of Pigs invasion and by the U.S. economic blockade.)

Such a compensation formula might be sabotaged, however, by one company (Amax) if that company is left out of the development of Cuban nickel. According to its chairman, Ian MacGregor, Amax has tried to position itself to be able to give Cuba "an offer it can't refuse." Not only has the company acquired the Port Nickel refinery (originally constructed to process Cuban ore) from Freeport, but it has bought up the shares of the nationalized Moa Bay mining company. The aim of the first acquisition was to have a plant in place to serve as an outlet for the slurry from Moa Bay as soon as the United States and Cuba seemed on the road to rapprochement. The aim of the second acquisition was to be able to gum up any movement toward normalization of commercial relations if Amax were cut out of participation in the Cuban nickel industry. The net result was to ensure that "neither Fidel Castro nor Henry Kissinger could settle with each other without settling with [Ian MacGregor] first." The latter individual was prepared to be quite "reasonable," however, on both the question of participation and the question of compensation.

This strategy was related to the author in a private conversation with MacGregor at the Links Club, New York, November 17, 1975. But since the essential ingredients are well known to the U.S. government, the Cuban government, and the other mining companies, there seems to be no reason to keep it a secret from the academic community.

36. But it is hard to see how a Peruvian or Botswani government, for example, could force Asarco or Amax to provide services to Cuba the way the Argentinian or Canadian governments "forced" U.S. subsidiaries to export to Cuba.

37. For an analysis of Japanese strategy in natural resource development, see Theodore H. Moran, C. Fred Bergsten, and Thomas Horst, *American Multinationals and American Interests* (Washington, D.C.: The Brookings Institution, 1978).

38. Kennecott Copper Corporation, *Expropriation of the El Teniente Copper Mine by the Chilean Government,* supplements 1-4, 1971-73.

See also Theodore H. Moran, "Transnational Strategies of Protection and Defense by Multinational Corporations: Spreading the Risk and Raising the Cost for Nationalization in Natural Resources," *International Organization* 27, no. 2 (Spring 1973), 273-87.

The current position of the U.S. government is that attachment is permissible only within U.S. boundaries. Fidel Castro, however, has claimed that "the United States follows our own nickel all over the world to stop its commercial use." For the U.S. position, see *U.S. Trade Embargo of Cuba,* pp. 162, 172, 175, 559, and letter of Arthur T. Downey, Deputy Assistant Secretary of Commerce for East-West Trade, to Congressman Edward G. Biester, Jr., April 8, 1976. For Fidel Castro's

THEODORE H. MORAN

quotation, see *U.S. Trade Embargo of Cuba*, p. 133. Treasury officials report that the U.S. government is vigilant in preventing imports of products containing Cuban nickel (such as specialty steels) into the United States. This appears to have hurt Cuban sales to Japan and France. See *American Metal Market*, October 21-22, 1976.

39. Kennecott was less than successful in the courts of Italy, France, and Germany against the government of Chile, but the prospect of impounded cargoes and blocked payments creates enough delay and harassment to make a large new investment unattractive.

13

JORGE F. PÉREZ-LÓPEZ

Sugar and Petroleum in Cuban-Soviet Terms of Trade

Sugar and petroleum play a pivotal role in contemporary Cuba. Sugar is the main export, and petroleum is the fuel that keeps the economy going. In 1973–1974, sugar and petroleum were in the limelight as the world market price for both commodities rose to unprecedented highs. The world market price for sugar peaked in November 1974 and has fallen dramatically since then, while the world market price for petroleum has continued to climb steadily, with no prospect of trend reversal in the immediate future. Since the beginning of the 1960s Cuban-Soviet relations have been deeply entangled in sugar-petroleum exchanges: The Soviet Union has been the main purchaser of Cuban sugar, while Cuba has relied almost completely on Soviet petroleum. In view of the role of sugar and petroleum in the Cuban economy, it is of considerable significance to study the impact that recent fluctuations in the world prices of these two commodities have had on Cuban-Soviet commercial relations.

This chapter first examines briefly the importance of sugar and petroleum both in the Cuban economy and in Cuban-Soviet relations since 1960. It then summarizes the literature on price-setting in the external trade of socialist nations and on Soviet terms of trade with other socialist trading partners. Finally, the chapter analyzes Cuban-Soviet terms of trade with respect to the exchange of sugar and petroleum, emphasizing the period 1973–1976. [Readers who are interested in the extent to which exchanges in sugar and petroleum resulted in Soviet subsidies to Cuba may consult table 2.2 prepared on the basis of estimates by the U.S. Central Intelligence Agency, Ed.]

Sugar and Petroleum in the Cuban Economy

The importance of sugar and petroleum in the Cuban foreign sector, and hence in the Cuban economy, may be partially seen from data in table 13.1. During the selected years shown for 1963 to 1974, sugar exports accounted for 70 to 90 percent of the value of Cuban exports. Petroleum and petroleum products, meanwhile, accounted for less than 10 percent of total imports for the same years. The true importance of petroleum in the Cuban economy, however, cannot be learned from these figures alone.

274

JORGE F. PÉREZ-LÓPEZ

TABLE 13.1
Relative Importance of Sugar and Petroleum in Value of
Cuban Exports and Imports, Selected Years, 1963–1974

	Sugar as Percentage of Total Exports [a]	Petroleum as Percentage of Total Imports [b]
1963	84.5	8.6
1964	86.0	8.2
1965	85.0	9.4
1966	83.3	9.6
1969	72.7	8.4
1972	71.2	9.5
1973	79.0	9.2
1974	89.1	n.a.

Sources: Based on República de Cuba, Junta Central de Planificación, Dirección Central de Estadística, BE Boletín estadístico 1966, 1968, 1970, and 1971, and Anuario estadístico de Cuba 1972, 1973, and 1974 (Havana, 1968– 1976).
Note: Percentages calculated from trade figures in million current pesos.
a. Raw and refined sugar. Exports f.o.b.
b. Includes crude petroleum, fuel oil, gas oil, gasoline, and lubricants. Imports c.i.f.

As a result of its geological formation and its shape, Cuba is not well endowed with energy resources. The narrow and elongated shape of the island precludes the existence of large water masses for significant amounts of hydroelectric power.[1] Despite considerable exploration, deposits of native hydrocarbons (coal, mineral oil, petroleum, paraffin, the fossil resins, and the bitumens occurring in rocks) large enough for self-sufficiency have not been found.[2] Thus, the Cuban economy has traditionally depended on imported petroleum and petroleum products and on domestic noncommercial fuels, such as bagasse, fuel wood, and other vegetable wastes, to meet its energy needs.

Table 13.2 shows estimates of total consumption of energy in Cuba during 1961, 1970, and 1973, by energy source. Although these figures should be considered only rough estimates, they point out the large and increasing role of petroleum and petroleum products in Cuban energy supplies. The large contributions of noncommercial fuels to total energy consumption indicated by the table need to be qualified, since the bulk of these fuels (in the form of sugar cane bagasse) are used in the industrial stages of sugar production.[3] Thus, while data for 1973 indicate that petroleum and petroleum products accounted for about 63 percent of total energy consumed in Cuba in 1973, this figure probably underestimates the true importance of petroleum and its products in the Cuban economy for that year. Petroleum and petroleum products are the source of energy in almost all electricity generation, transportation, and nonsugar industrial activi-

TABLE 13.2
Cuban Consumption of Energy by Source
(thousand metric tons of petroleum equivalents, 10,700 Kcal/Kg)

	Total	Coal	Crude Petroleum and Petroleum Products	Natural Gas	Hydro-electricity	Noncommercial Fuels
1961	7,114	—	3,855	—	—	3,259
1970	10,129	—	6,600	—	—	3,259
1973	10,947	—	6,850	—	30	4,067

Sources: 1961, 1970: estimate by United Nations, Economic Commission for Latin America, *La Producción y el consumo reciente de energía en la América Latina,* mimeo (November 1973), table A-1, p. 47. 1973: estimate by Organización Latinoamericana de Energía, *Estructura actual de la demanda de energía en la América Latina y sus proyecciones hasta 1990* (Quito, Ecuador, n.d.), unnumbered page, annex 1.
Note: These figures should be considered estimates only. They are included here as an indication of the relative importance of different energy sources in total energy consumption. The two sets of estimates do not seem to match, particularly since the data for 1961 and 1970 ignore hydroelectric power generation and imports of coke are not included in either of the estimates.

ties, and they play a significant role even in the sugar industry. President Osvaldo Dorticós has summarized the importance of petroleum in the Cuban economy:

> Without petroleum there is no sugar. Without petroleum the sugar mills cannot operate.... Without petroleum there is no transportation; without petroleum sugar cane cannot be transported, because there would not be gasoline for trucks, for agricultural equipment, and sugar cane lifters.... Our economy begins with petroleum, continues with electricity and goes on from there.... Without petroleum there is no economy. There is nothing left. There would not even be food, because there would not be fuel for the transportation sector to carry the beans [foodstuffs] from one place to another. The country would be paralyzed immediately.[4]

Although petroleum deposits have been found in different parts of the island and some have been exploited commercially, Cuban production of petroleum has been insignificant when compared with consumption. As a result, imports are responsible for the bulk of the petroleum consumed. As table 13.3 indicates, during 1963–1966 the share of domestic production in apparent supply of crude petroleum and products was about 1 percent. In 1968, the domestic share rose to about 3 percent, to fall again to around 2 percent during 1967 and 1969–1972. Available data indicate that Cuban crude petroleum production for the period 1973–1975 has remained around the level reached in 1970–1972,[5] while imports of crude petroleum and petroleum products have continued to increase. Thus, there is no evidence that the participation of domestic crude in apparent supply for the period 1973–1975 diverged from the average participation during the previous decade.

JORGE F. PÉREZ-LÓPEZ

TABLE 13.3
Production, Trade, and Apparent Supply of Petroleum and Petroleum Products in Cuba
(thousand metric tons)

	Crude Petroleum Production	Imports (Petroleum and Petroleum Products)	Apparent Supply	Domestic Production as Percentage of Apparent Supply
1963	31	4,086	4,117	0.75
1964	37	4,571	4,608	0.80
1965	57	4,569	4,626	1.23
1966	69	5,057	5,126	1.35
1967	113	5,107	5,220	2.16
1968	160	5,232	5,392	2.97
1969	123	5,695	5,818	2.11
1970	118	6,030	6,148	1.92
1971	118	6,834	6,952	1.70
1972	117	6,691	6,808	1.72

Sources: Production: 1963–1967, Cuba Economic News 4, no. 34 (1968), 4; 1968–1972, U.S. Department of the Interior, Bureau of Mines, International Petroleum Annual 1974 (March 1976), table 7, p. 24. (Conversion factor of 6.652 barrels per metric ton used to calculate figure in terms of metric tons.) Imports: 1963–1966, C. Paul Roberts and Mukhtar Hamour, eds., Cuba 1968, Statistical Abstract of Latin America Supplement 1 (Los Angeles: UCLA Latin American Center Publications, University of California, 1970), p. 181; 1967–1972, República de Cuba, Junta Central de Planificación, Anuario estadístico de Cuba 1973 (Havana, 1975), pp. 216–17.

Cuban-Soviet economic relations began in earnest with the signature of a bilateral trade and payments agreement on February 13, 1960. The Soviet Union agreed to purchase 425,000 metric tons of Cuban sugar during 1960 (in addition to 575,000 metric tons purchased earlier in the year), and 1 million metric tons for each of the years 1961 through 1964. The price at which the sugar was to be sold was not specified, although it was believed to be the world market price. The Soviet Union would compensate Cuba partly with convertible currencies (20 percent) but mostly with Soviet machinery and equipment, industrial replacement parts, wheat, petroleum, fertilizers, and so on.

On April 9, 1960, the Cuban press reported the arrival of the first Soviet tanker carrying 75,000 metric tons of Soviet crude petroleum to be processed at a small refinery in Cabaiguán operated by the Cuban Petroleum Institute (ICP). The international oil companies operating refineries in Cuba (Texaco, Esso, and Royal-Dutch Shell) continued to import petroleum from their affiliates. On May 17, 1960, the Cuban National Bank informed the international oil companies that they would each have to purchase (and process) 300,000 metric tons of Soviet crude oil during the remainder of 1960. The rationale for the government's decision was that the crude petroleum imported by the oil companies, paid for in dollars, was a burden to Cuba's dwindling dollar balances. The Soviet crude, on the other hand, was bartered for Cuban goods and, therefore, did not have a negative effect on the dollar balances.[6] In addition, Ernesto Guevara, then president of the Cuban National Bank (BNC), defended the decision to purchase Soviet crude petroleum, indicating that the landed price of Soviet crude oil was 33 percent lower than the price at which the international oil companies operating in Cuba imported crude.[7]

On June 29, 1960, the Cuban government seized the refineries operated by the oil companies on the grounds that they had violated the law by refusing to purchase and process Soviet crude petroleum. From then on, Cuban-U.S. relations deteriorated rapidly. On July 6, 1960, the United States retaliated for the seizure of the refineries by cutting the Cuban sugar quota for 1960 by 700,000 metric tons. The socialist countries moved in quickly to purchase the Cuban sugar refused by the United States, and to subscribe commercial and credit agreements with Cuba. Cuba then nationalized U.S.-owned industries and banks, and President Dwight D. Eisenhower set the Cuban quota at zero for the first quarter of 1961. Finally, Cuba and the United States broke diplomatic and consular relations on January 3, 1961.

By 1961, Cuba's trade patterns had changed drastically, so that the socialist countries were now its primary trade partners. Among the socialist countries, the Soviet Union became the main purchaser of Cuban sugar while at the same time becoming, for all practical purposes, Cuba's sole supplier of petroleum and petroleum products.

Pricing in Socialist Foreign Trade

Socialist countries follow different pricing practices in trading with Western nations and with other socialist nations. In dealing with Western countries, the socialist nations as a rule accept and adjust to world market prices. In intra-socialist trade, however, external prices are related to world market prices according to "principles vague enough to leave room for bargaining."[8]

In practice, commercial relations among socialist countries are conducted through bilateral agreements. These agreements, arrived at through negotiations, provide the framework within which the conditions of trade (including prices, quantities, delivery terms, and form of payment) are specified. Prices generally refer to average world market prices for an extended earlier time period, typically five years. These average prices may be adjusted to account for such factors as quality differences and differentials in transportation costs by mutual consent. The official rationale for the use of averages of world market prices of earlier periods to determine intra-socialist external prices is the desire to delete the influences of speculation, business cycles, and monopoly, all connected with the capitalist system, from the pricing system.

The negotiating procedure for price determination is cumbersome and time-consuming. Documentation of the different possible world market prices for products and adjustments to be made to these prices are subject to bargaining. As Paul Marer has pointed out, the term "average world market price" is ambiguous because (1) it could refer to different capitalist markets; (2) actual transaction

JORGE F. PÉREZ-LÓPEZ

prices are nearly impossible to ascertain because of discounts, rebates, and so on; (3) average values or unit values of product categories can reflect differences in such things as quality, transportation costs, and conditions of payment; and (4) there are numerous alternatives for averaging component prices.[9] In addition to all these economic factors, there is some evidence that political considerations, in the form of special terms, also enter into the pricing decision. As a result, prices of identical goods exported by a socialist country to two other socialist countries may be different because independent negotiating sessions are held.

Over the last two decades, a number of investigators have attempted to analyze the terms of trade between socialist countries and between socialist countries and Western economies. The pioneer in this area, Horst Mendershausen, used Soviet trade statistics for the period 1955–1958 to test whether prices charged by the Soviet Union in trade with other socialist countries were in line with prices of comparable goods exported to Western Europe. His studies indicated that the Soviet Union discriminated against socialist trading partners by exporting to them at higher prices, and importing from them at lower prices, than it did in trade with Western Europe.[10] Frederic Pryor analyzed the terms of trade of the Soviet Union with Eastern European socialist nations and Western developing countries also for the period 1955–1958 and concluded that certain Eastern European countries were relatively discriminated against, while others were favored in the exchange relations.[11]

Franklyn Holzman disagreed with Mendershausen's use of Soviet-Western prices as proxies for world prices and questioned their use as a standard of fairness. In his view, socialist nations usually had difficulty trading with Western nations, so they often had to sell below market prices in order to break into and hold Western markets and buy at higher prices in order to get Western firms to deal with them. This amounts to Western discrimination against the Eastern European socialist nations and explains the disparities between prices in Soviet trade with socialist partners and Western nations.[12]

Finally, Marer found that foreign trade prices among socialist nations were substantially higher than world market prices, while foreign trade prices of COMECON (Council for Mutual Economic Assistance) exports to the West were often lower than world prices. During the 1960s, the Soviet Union's terms of trade with COMECON countries deteriorated as a result of significant decreases in the export prices of fuels, raw materials, and semimanufactures, and smaller declines in prices of manufactures.[13] Edward Hewett's analysis essentially supports Marer's conclusions concerning the deterioration of Soviet terms of trade vis-à-vis COMECON nations in the 1960s.[14]

None of the statistical studies on terms of trade among socialist nations surveyed above deals explicitly with Cuba. Thus, very little can be said concerning the terms of trade between Cuba and the Soviet Union or between Cuba and any other COMECON member. There have been references, apparently impressionistic and unconfirmed, suggesting that Cuban-Soviet terms of trade may have not favored Cuba. For example, with reference to Soviet exports to Cuba, Leon

Gouré and Julian Weinkle state that ''an estimate by the National Bank of Cuba places the total cost of the Soviet goods supplied to Cuba at about 50 percent above what Cuba would have had to pay if it had been able to purchase the same quality and types of goods from non-Communist countries.... Soviet goods were... overpriced by world standards.''[15] No additional information beyond the quote is available. The time period to which the statement refers is not mentioned.

Sugar and Petroleum Prices in Cuban-Soviet Commercial Relations

This study is primarily concerned with analyzing the behavior over time of the ratio of the price of Cuban sugar exports to the Soviet Union to the price of Cuban petroleum imports from the Soviet Union. Changes over time in this ratio, called here the Cuban-Soviet terms of trade for exchanges of sugar and petroleum, may be used to indicate relative improvement or deterioration in the conditions of trade and in the distribution of income from sugar-petroleum exchanges between the two countries.[16] For example, a decrease, or deterioration, in the ratio is tantamount to saying that Cuba is worse off than before in the exchange since it must now use more units of sugar exports to obtain the same number of units of petroleum imports. An increase, or improvement, in the terms of trade implies the reverse.

The concept of the terms of trade is generally developed for the totality of exports and imports between two countries or regions and, therefore, export and import price indexes representative of trends in prices of all exports and imports are used. However, owing to the nature and limitations of the price data available, this study is limited to the terms of trade between Cuba and the Soviet Union with reference to sugar and petroleum only.

The primary problem faced by the analyst attempting to examine Cuban-Soviet terms of trade is that there are no price data available that refer to trade between the two countries. The only information available is average values of exports or imports for individual trade categories calculated from trade data by dividing the cumulative value of trade in a category by the cumulative number of units exchanged in each category. Changes over time in these average values (generally called export or import unit values), however, reflect not only pure price changes of the commodities traded, but also changes in the product composition within each category, changes in the quality of the products, or in the circumstances of transaction (for example, size of shipment, frequency of purchase, or discounts). Thus, changes in unit values compound unknown changes in any, or all, of these factors in such a way that the effect of each individual factor cannot be discerned.

The problems in using changes in unit values as proxies for price changes are particularly severe in the case of broadly defined categories that contain a large number of fairly heterogeneous commodities (such as manufactured goods, machinery, and transportation equipment). For other trade categories, generally called "homogeneous" commodities categories (such as narrowly defined groupings of agricultural commodities or raw materials), where quality changes may not be significant and there is a very limited number of commodities in each category, changes in unit values may be reasonable proxies for price changes.[17]

In view of the problems inherent in the use of unit values as proxies for actual prices, particularly for categories containing a large variety of goods, the analysis here deals strictly with exchanges between Cuba and the Soviet Union in two homogeneous commodities categories, sugar and petroleum. Since these two products are of great importance to the Cuban economy and are significant items in Cuban-Soviet commercial exchanges, changes in the relative prices of these two products have far-reaching implications for the Cuban economy and for Cuban-Soviet commercial relations.

The data used in the calculation of the sugar and petroleum unit values originate from Soviet foreign trade yearbooks (*Vneshniaia Torgovlia SSSR*) for the period 1960–1975. In the case of sugar, the data refer to f.o.b. Cuban port value, while for petroleum the basis is f.o.b. Soviet port. Soviet rather than Cuban trade data have been used to calculate the unit values because of data availability. Cuban foreign trade data, although more disaggregated than Soviet data for petroleum and petroleum products,[18] and conceptually more appropriate for this study, were not used because of time-lag problems. While at the time of this study the Soviet Union had already published complete foreign trade data for 1975, Cuba had just released preliminary data for 1973.[19]

The use of Soviet unit values for petroleum and petroleum product exports to Cuba to approximate unit values of Cuban petroleum imports assumes implicitly that commodity mix in the category has remained invariant and that trends in the cost of insurance and freight associated with the transportation of the crude and products from the Soviet Union to Cuba have moved at the same rate as those of Soviet petroleum and petroleum products unit values for shipments to Cuba. On the first assumption, fragmentary trade data seem to indicate that the proportion of crude petroleum to total crude petroleum and petroleum products exports probably remained essentially constant over the period. The second assumption, open to empirical investigation, has not been pursued here because of the lack of appropriate data.

Table 13.4 presents Soviet trade data on Cuban-Soviet exchanges of sugar and petroleum and petroleum products for the period 1960–1975. Table 13.5 shows unit values for these exchanges, calculated from data in table 13.4. For sugar, the data represent Cuban export unit values to the Soviet Union in terms of rubles per metric ton and U.S. cents per pound. For petroleum and petroleum products, the data refer to Cuban import unit values from the Soviet Union, in terms of rubles per metric ton and U.S. dollars per barrel.

Results

Table 13.6, column 1, presents the terms of trade of Cuban-Soviet exchanges of sugar and petroleum and petroleum products for the period 1960–

TABLE 13.4
Soviet Imports of Cuban Raw Sugar and Soviet Exports of Petroleum
and Petroleum Products to Cuba

	Sugar Imports from Cuba[a]		Petroleum and Petroleum Products Exports to Cuba[b]	
	Quantity (1,000 mt)	Value (1,000 rubles)	Quantity (100 mt)	Value (1,000 rubles)
1959	132.5	6,675	—	—
1960	1,467.8	93,400	2,164.8	24,909
1961	3,345.0	270,369	4,028.6	44,250
1962	2,233.2	183,589	4,384.4	46,466
1963	996.0	123,187	4,219.9	50,574
1964	1,859.0	223,090	4,559.3	53,574
1965	2,331.0	273,368	4,726.6	55,847
1966	1,841.0	225,774	5,090.4	59,800
1967	2,480.0	302,316	5,286.2	61,561
1968	1,749.0	212,706	5,303.2	62,590
1969	1,332.0	161,947	5,759.5	66,694
1970	3,000.0	364,339	5,987.0	69,175
1971	1,500.0	185,642	6,400.0	73,542
1972	1,100.0	131,465	7,000.0	92,208
1973	1,603.0	323,058	7,435.0	114,185
1974	1,858.0	610,782	7,643.0	135,778
1975	2,964.0	1,344,312	8,060.0	248,230

Sources: Vneshniaia Torgovlia SSSR v 1960 g. (Moscow, 1961), and issues for 1959–1963, 1965, 1967, 1969, 1970, 1972, 1974, 1975.
Note: Imports recorded f.o.b. Cuban port; exports recorded f.o.b. Soviet port.
a. Quantity rounded in original source for 1963–1975.
b. Quantity rounded in original source for 1970–1975.

1975. Columns 2 and 3 present the same information in index number form using 1965 and 1970 as the respective base periods. Since the choice of base period can, on the surface, affect the results of the comparisons, the reader may wish to use the data in column 1 to compute series of index numbers using time periods different from the ones used here.

1960–1963. Cuban terms of trade vis-à-vis the Soviet Union for sugar and petroleum improved significantly between 1960 and 1963. This can be taken as a favorable development for the Cuban economy, since it received a higher price for its exports with the same price for imports; that is, Cuba had to export fewer units of sugar during 1961, 1962, and 1963 to obtain the same number of units of petroleum and petroleum products as it did in 1960.[20] This result came about because average values of sugar exports to the Soviet Union almost doubled between 1960 and 1963, while average values of imported petroleum and petroleum products rose much more modestly.

During this period, Cuba neglected production of sugar in favor of rapid industrialization. As a result, Cuban production and deliveries of sugar to the

JORGE F. PÉREZ-LÓPEZ

TABLE 13.5
Unit Values of Cuban Exports of Sugar to the Soviet Union and of Cuban Imports
of Petroleum and Petroleum Products from the Soviet Union

	Sugar Export Unit Values		Raw Sugar World Price [a]	Petroleum and Petroleum Products Import Unit Values		Petroleum World Price [b]
	(rubles/mt)	(cents/lb)	(cents/lb)	(rubles/mt)	($/bbl)	($/bbl)
1960	63.63	3.20	3.14	11.51	1.74	1.92
1961	80.83	4.07	2.91	10.98	1.66	1.86
1962	82.21	4.14	2.98	10.60	1.60	1.80
1963	123.68	6.23	8.50	11.99	1.81	1.80
1964	120.01	6.04	5.87	11.75	1.77	1.80
1965	117.28	5.90	2.12	11.82	1.78	1.80
1966	122.64	6.17	1.86	11.75	1.77	1.80
1967	121.92	6.14	2.03	11.65	1.76	1.80
1968	121.62	6.12	1.98	11.80	1.78	1.80
1969	121.58	6.12	3.37	11.58	1.75	1.80
1970	121.45	6.11	3.75	11.55	1.74	1.80
1971	123.76	6.23	4.53	11.49	1.74	2.19
1972	119.51	6.61	7.43	13.17	2.19	2.46
1973	201.53	12.34	9.63	15.36	2.82	3.29
1974	329.09	19.70	29.96	17.77	3.19	11.58
1975	453.55	28.60	20.50	30.80	5.82	11.53

Sources: Unit values: calculated from table 13.4. World market prices: International Monetary Fund, *International Financial Statistics,* May 1976, pp. 38–41.
    Notes: Conversion for sugar from mt to lbs made using 1 mt = 2204.62 lbs. Dollar/ruble exchange rates were as follows: 1960–1971: 1 r = $1.11; 1972: 1 r = $1.22; 1973: 1 r = $1.35; 1974: 1 r = $1.32; 1975: 1 r = $1.39. Conversion factor of 7.35 bbl/mt for Soviet crude from *International Petroleum Annual.*
    a. Raw sugar, f.o.b. Caribbean ports.
    b. Saudi Arabian light, 34° API, f.o.b. Ras Tanura.

Soviet Union declined markedly (see table 13.4). Since world market prices for raw sugar more than doubled between 1962 and 1963, a Cuban-Soviet trade protocol established a price of 6 centers per pound for sugar exports during 1963.

1964–1970. After the failure of the rapid industrialization development strategy became evident in 1963, Cuba reoriented its economy to emphasize sugar production once again. An ambitious long-term plan for the development of the sugar industry for the period 1965–1970 was drawn up and implemented during the late 1960s. The culmination of the plan would be a sugar crop of 10 million metric tons in 1970. In January 1964, Cuba and the Soviet Union entered into a new long-term commercial agreement (to replace the one subscribed in February 1960) which stipulated a new schedule of Cuban deliveries of sugar to the Soviet Union during 1965–1970 and established the price of sugar at 6.11 cents per pound for the entire period.

Cuban-Soviet terms of trade with reference to sugar and petroleum and petroleum products were essentially stationary over this period, turning slightly

TABLE 13.6
Cuban-Soviet Terms of Trade with Reference to Sugar and
Petroleum and Petroleum Products, 1960–1975

	Sugar/Petroleum Terms of Trade		
	Ratio	1965 = 100	1970 = 100
1960	5.53	55.7	52.6
1961	7.36	74.2	70.0
1962	7.76	78.2	73.8
1963	10.32	104.0	98.1
1964	10.21	102.9	97.1
1965	9.92	100.0	94.3
1966	10.44	105.2	99.2
1967	10.47	105.5	99.5
1968	10.31	103.9	98.0
1969	10.50	105.8	99.8
1970	10.52	106.0	100.0
1971	10.77	108.6	102.4
1972	9.07	91.4	86.2
1973	13.12	132.3	124.7
1974	18.52	186.7	176.0
1975	14.72	148.4	139.9

Source: Calculated from table 13.5.

against Cuba in 1964–1965, and then recovering modestly during 1966–1970. The average value of Cuban sugar exports to the Soviet Union hovered around 6.11 cents per pound, the contracted price, although world market prices were well below this level. Unit values of imported crude petroleum and petroleum products remained virtually unchanged at 11.5 to 12 rubles per metric ton during this period. Note that the world market price for crude petroleum remained at $1.80 per barrel during 1962–1970.

1971–1975. Despite a general mobilization of productive resources into the sugar industry, Cuba was unable to meet its goal of a 10 million metric ton sugar crop in 1970. As a result of the concentration of productive resources in sugar production, nonsugar industrial and agricultural production also suffered severely. Beginning with 1971, a process of rationalization of the economy was initiated, with a deepening of Soviet influence in economic decision making.

During the period 1971–1974, Cuban-Soviet terms of trade with reference to sugar and petroleum underwent significant fluctuations: After a small movement favorable to Cuba in 1971 compared with 1970, they turned against Cuba in 1972, only to improve strongly in 1973–1974. The terms of trade turned sharply against Cuba in 1975.

Unlike the period 1964–1970, when average values of sugar and petroleum and petroleum products in Cuban-Soviet exchanges were fairly stable, the period 1971–1975 was characterized by significant fluctuations. This period marks the

JORGE F. PÉREZ-LÓPEZ

total breakdown of the system of reliance on fixed prices for a five-year period in intra-socialist trade and the adoption of more flexible pricing policies, including that of annual price adjustments. The behavior of average values of sugar and petroleum and petroleum products in Cuban-Soviet trade during this period illustrates this new price flexibility.

The price of Cuban sugar exports to the Soviet Union remained fixed at 6.11 cents per pound during 1971 and 1972, but by the end of 1972, the world market price of sugar had gone above the contracted price. A new Cuban-Soviet agreement, subscribed in December 1972, set the price for 1973 at 12.02 cents per pound.[21] World market prices continued to increase through 1973, so that by December 1973, they had once again risen above the Cuban-Soviet contracted price (see table 13.7). The climb continued through 1974, peaking at about 57 cents per pound in November 1974. A Cuban official publication has indicated that the agreed delivery price for Cuban sugar to the Soviet Union for 1974 was 19.64 cents per pound (the average world price was 29.96 cents per pound), and about 30 cents per pound for 1975–1980 (the average world price for 1975 was about 20.5 cents per pound).[22]

While sugar prices fluctuated severely during 1973–1975, the Arab oil embargo of October 1973, and the subsequent increases in posted prices of crude petroleum exported by members of the Organization of Petroleum Exporting Countries (OPEC), led to roughly a fourfold increase of the world market price for crude petroleum between 1972 and 1974 (see table 13.5). Countries that depended on OPEC for petroleum supplies faced a quadrupling of their oil bill and serious balance-of-payments problems.[23]

Cuba and the rest of the socialist nations did not feel at once the impact of the large rises in the world market price for petroleum since they received the bulk of their supplies from the Soviet Union, presumably at fixed prices, under long-term contracts. For example, in his first major speech after the oil embargo, Fidel Castro alluded to the rise of petroleum prices in the world market, but did not indicate how, if at all, these increases would affect Cuba.[24] On December 21, 1973, *Granma* conspicuously carried a report from the Soviet news agency Tass of a press conference held in Moscow by the vice-minister for foreign trade of the Soviet Union. The official, Ivan Semichastnov, was quoted as saying, "The Soviet Union will fulfill completely its commitments with the Socialist countries regarding deliveries of crude petroleum and petroleum products *and it will not increase prices despite the sharp rise of prices in the world market.*"[25]

Although theoretically they should not have varied at all, in practice Soviet export prices of petroleum and petroleum products to socialist countries apparently rose modestly in 1974 over 1973. In September 1974, Fidel Castro boasted that Cuba "with the generous help of the Soviet Union, has not known the energy crisis."[26] But the Cuban leadership admitted that the prices of products imported by Cuba from Western Nations had risen sharply in 1974 and they affected Cuba's ability to import.[27] The Federation of Cuban Women decided, in late November 1974, that each citizen would donate one pound of sugar from the

TABLE 13.7

Monthly Averages of Spot Prices for Cane Sugar, 96° Polarization, f.o.b. and Stowed Port of Origin (Caribbean) (U.S. cents/lb)

	1973		1974		1975		1976	
	To World Market[a]	To U.S. Market[b]	To World Market[a]	To U.S. Market[b]	To World Market[a]	To U.S. Market[b]	To World Market[a]	To U.S. Market[b]
Annual average	9.59	10.29	29.99	29.50	20.49	22.47	11.72	13.17
January	9.40	9.38	15.32	12.63	38.32	40.15	14.04	15.42
February	9.06	9.14	21.26	17.09	33.72	36.07	13.52	15.04
March	8.89	9.45	21.27	18.11	26.50	28.52	14.92	16.27
April	9.06	9.65	21.77	19.25	24.06	26.07	14.06	15.58
May	9.67	10.06	23.65	23.05	17.38	19.27	14.58	15.97
June	9.77	10.25	23.67	26.50	13.83	15.96	12.99	14.40
July	9.86	10.25	25.40	28.35	17.06	19.89	13.21	14.59
August	9.09	10.75	31.45	32.60	18.73	21.11	9.99	11.32
September	8.98	10.97	34.35	33.71	15.45	17.36	9.80	8.16
October	9.56	11.15	39.62	38.82	14.09	15.45	8.03	10.65
November	10.15	11.10	57.17	57.30	13.40	15.03	7.91	10.46
December	11.83	11.34	44.97	46.74	13.29	14.80	7.54	10.22

Source: Organización de los Estados Americanos, Secretaría General, Boletín de precios internacionales de productos básicos, no. 34, SG/Ser. G/39 (February 1977), 8, and earlier issues.
  a. New York, immediate delivery, contract no. 11.
  b. New York, immediate delivery, contract no. 10.

JORGE F. PÉREZ-LÓPEZ

assigned per capita consumption quota to be used for export purposes. By export-ing this additional amount of sugar at very high world market prices, Cuba could finance the added cost of its imports from Western nations.[28]

In late January 1975, the executive committee of COMECON met in Moscow to review issues dealing with trade and cooperation among members. The communiqué of the session indicated that "measures to stabilize prices in commercial contracts among members for the five-year period 1976–1980 [were adopted] ... to create favorable conditions for the development of external trade."[29] The thrust of the new measures was to create a new policy whereby prices in intra-socialist trade would be adjusted annually rather than only during the first year of each five-year-plan period as had been customary. This modifica-tion of the existing COMECON external pricing policies, apparently forced by the Soviet Union, caught most of the members by surprise, since the new policies affected only selected commodities, utilized a three-year average as the reference pricing period, and were made retroactive to January 1, 1975. Price adjustments had been expected for 1976–1980, but not for 1975, the last year of the 1971–1975 plan period.[30]

It is not clear that for COMECON importers of Soviet petroleum and petro-leum products the shift to annual price adjustments came as a complete surprise, since unit values of Soviet exports of these commodities to socialist trading partners had been gradually increasing through the 1970s (see table 13.8). What

TABLE 13.8
Unit Values of Exports of Soviet Crude Petroleum and Petroleum Products to Socialist and Selected Western Countries
(rubles/mt)

	1972	1973	1974	1975	1972–1975 Increase (%)
Bulgaria	14.93	14.56	15.15	34.24	129.3
Cuba	13.17	15.43	17.17	30.80	133.9
Czechoslovakia	16.31	16.44	16.32	30.85	89.2
East Germany	14.09	14.23	18.77	28.18	100.0
Hungary	16.96	17.94	20.93	40.98	141.6
Mongolia	36.54	37.43	35.96	36.10	− 1.2
North Korea	34.65	28.64	26.24	23.98	− 30.8
North Vietnam	44.96	43.29	38.65	35.33	− 21.4
Poland	16.47	17.35	20.57	39.50	139.8
Yugoslavia	15.11	25.52	65.60	61.32	305.8
France	13.98	17.17	61.91	58.23	316.5
West Germany[a]	14.35	36.60	66.77	62.26	333.9

Source: Calculated from data in *Vneshniaia Torgovlia SSSR v 1975g.* (Moscow, 1976).
   a. Excluding Berlin.

may have come as a surprise, however, was the magnitude of the increases, since they were substantially larger than would have been obtained had the export prices been adjusted to reflect changes in petroleum world market prices for 1970–1974. (This point is analyzed in more detail below.) This new pricing practice for Soviet crude petroleum and petroleum products exports during 1975 meant substantially higher prices for the oil importers, although it should be pointed out that the export prices of Soviet petroleum and petroleum products to COMECON members were still significantly below world market prices. While the Cuban press carried a summary of the main topics discussed at the COMECON session where these changes were adopted, it did not report that prices of imported petroleum and petroleum products would rise during 1975. Instead, *Granma* chose to stress the positive by printing a story in which Victor Slovtsov, vice-president of the Soviet petroleum exporting firm Soyuzneftexport, was quoted as stating that "the volume of Soviet petroleum exports to the Socialist countries will be increased this year [1975], at prices much lower than those currently in the world market."[31]

An examination of unit values of Soviet exports of crude petroleum and petroleum products to socialist and Western countries for 1972–1975 bears out the increases and suggests an interesting pattern of Soviet price-raising. Unit values for Soviet exports to the socialist countries (Rumania and Communist China did not import crude petroleum and petroleum products from the Soviet Union during this period), France, and West Germany are given in table 13.8. Soviet exports of crude petroleum and petroleum products to Eastern Europe, Cuba, France, and West Germany averaged 13 to 17 rubles per metric ton in 1972. The average value for Mongolia, North Korea, and North Vietnam was much higher, about 35 to 45 rubles per metric ton. This disparity can probably be explained in terms of the composition of the exports. Soviet exports to the first group are composed primarily of crude petroleum to be refined in the importing countries, with higher-priced petroleum products occupying a secondary place. Soviet exports to Mongolia, North Korea, and North Vietnam appear to contain a higher proportion of the relatively higher-priced finished products, probably because of lack of refining capacities in these countries.

Assuming that the composition of Soviet crude petroleum and petroleum products shipments to each of the countries listed in table 13.8 remained unchanged between 1973 and 1975, the following patterns emerge. Unit values of exports to Eastern Europe (excluding Yugoslavia) and Cuba rose modestly during 1972–1974, despite the large increments in world market prices during this period. Unit values of shipments to France and West Germany and to Yugoslavia rose very rapidly during 1972–1974, to over 60 rubles per metric ton in 1974, an average value well in line with prices of crude petroleum exported by OPEC members in the world market.[32] The conclusion here is, of course, that while the Soviet Union did not pass the world market price increases to its socialist trading partners during 1973 and 1974, it did so in its trade with Western countries.

JORGE F. PÉREZ-LÓPEZ

Yugoslavia was treated as a Western nation in this case, apparently to remind that country of the benefits of intra-socialist trade and to gain a larger share of Yugoslavian imports.[33]

Average values of Soviet crude petroleum and petroleum products exported to Eastern Europe and Cuba during 1975 showed the results of the pricing formula adopted in January 1975. Export unit values to these countries approximately doubled for 1975 over 1974, while average values to the two Western countries and Yugoslavia underwent a minor downward adjustment. (Note in table 13.5 that the price for the OPEC marker crude also declined slightly in 1975 over 1974.) The behavior of these average values is consistent with descriptive materials on Soviet crude petroleum price-setting for 1975 discussed earlier.

Average values of Soviet exports of crude petroleum and petroleum products to Mongolia, North Korea, and North Vietnam during 1972–1975 present another interesting aspect of Soviet pricing. During 1972–1975, average values of Soviet exports of crude petroleum and petroleum products to North Korea and North Vietnam decreased significantly (from about 45 rubles per metric ton to 35 rubles per metric ton for North Vietnam; from about 34 rubles per metric ton to 24 rubles per metric ton for North Korea), while unit values to Mongolia remained basically unchanged. This is significant in view of the opposite trends in export unit values to other socialist and Western nations and in trends in petroleum market prices. A possible explanation may be that the Soviet Union chose not to apply the price increases to all countries, but rather decided to aid these three countries, the most underdeveloped in the socialist bloc with the exception of Cuba and Communist China, by maintaining prices of crude petroleum and petroleum products at a fraction of world market prices.

The apparent selectivity of the Soviet Union in administering price increases for crude petroleum and petroleum products to socialist and Western nations during 1972–1975 raises interesting questions concerning the role of Cuba in the socialist bloc. In general, Cuba is considered a developing country within the socialist bloc, and as a result it is grouped with Mongolia, North Korea, and North Vietnam. These four countries are generally the *recipients* of economic, technical, and scientific assistance (euphemistically called "cooperation") from the more industrialized East European socialist countries and the Soviet Union.[34] It is significant, then, that the Soviet Union apparently treated Cuba as one of the East European partners in the matter of increasing petroleum export prices, while subsidizing more heavily exports to Mongolia, North Korea, and North Vietnam. A plausible hypothesis may be that since the Soviet Union had contracted with Cuba to purchase sugar (and nickel) at prices well above world market prices, it felt that Cuba was in a position to afford the higher prices for crude petroleum and petroleum products.

The severe fluctuations in the world market prices for sugar and petroleum during 1973–1975 outlined earlier, and their impact on the prices for these commodities in Cuban-Soviet trade, had a great deal of influence on the behavior of the Cuban-Soviet terms of trade for exchanges of sugar and petroleum over this period. Thus, the large rise in world market prices of sugar during 1973 and 1974, which led to contracts with the Soviet Union at rising prices, coupled with more slowly increasing unit values for Soviet crude petroleum and petroleum products prices, gave rise to a phenomenal improvement of the Cuban-Soviet terms of trade in 1973 and 1974. During 1974, Cuba relived the "Danza de los Millones" of 1920, since, besides maintaining sales of sugar to the socialist countries, it was able to take advantage of the very high world market prices for sugar to make additional sales to Western countries. Much like the earlier dance, however, it was short-lived, although in this instance economic viability was preserved by obtaining a Soviet commitment to purchase sugar during 1975–1980 at prices extremely favorable to Cuba. Still, the large increment in Soviet petroleum and petroleum product prices during 1975 created a deterioration in the sugar-petroleum terms of trade for 1975 over 1974, although the overall level in 1975 with reference to 1970 was still highly favorable.

1976–1980. The Cuban-Soviet trade agreement signed in 1975 presumably fixed the price of Cuban sugar exports to the Soviet Union at 30 cents per pound for the period 1975–1980. However, the price of sugar in the world market slipped considerably during 1975 and 1976 so that it stood at 7.54 cents per pound in December 1976. World market prices for petroleum, meanwhile, have remained relatively stable over this same period, with no tendency to fall in the immediate future. In fact, OPEC crude petroleum prices effective January 1, 1977, were reported to average out at 8 to 8.3 percent higher than for 1976.[35] In view of these developments, what are the prospects for the Cuban-Soviet terms of trade for exchanges of sugar and petroleum for the rest of the decade?

Soviet foreign trade data for 1976 indicate that the unit value of Soviet exports of petroleum and petroleum products to Cuba for 1976 was 32.72 rubles per metric ton (about $6.01 per barrel), an increase of about 6.2 percent over 1975, while the unit value of Soviet imports of raw sugar from Cuba was 455.62 rubles per metric ton (about 27.9 cents per pound), an increase of about 0.7 percent over 1975.[36] Thus, the resulting Cuban-Soviet terms of trade with reference to sugar and petroleum exchanges for 1976 show a decrease of 5.4 percent from the 1975 level. Considering the level and trends of prices of sugar and petroleum in the world market, contractural agreements between Cuba and the Soviet Union and the new formula to determine future prices of Soviet petroleum and petroleum products shipments to socialist countries, we can speculate that Cuban-Soviet terms of trade for sugar and petroleum exchanges will continue to deteriorate or at best remain unchanged in the second half of the 1970s. The basis for this speculation is given below.

The first necessary step in analyzing the prospects of the Cuban-Soviet terms of trade with reference to sugar and petroleum in the second half of the 1970s is to understand the pricing formula for Soviet exports of crude petroleum and petroleum products and its application to world market price data. Table 13.9 illustrates the mechanism of price adjustments that appears to be in effect. Data in column 2 represent index numbers of an indicator of the world market price for

JORGE F. PÉREZ-LÓPEZ

TABLE 13.9

World Market Prices for Crude Petroleum and Increases in the Price of Soviet Crude Petroleum Exports to East European COMECON Members

	Index of World Petroleum Market Price[a] (1965 = 100)	COMECON Multi-year Reference Period	Multi-year Average Price	Percentage Increase from Previous Period
1969	100.0			
1970	100.0			
1971	121.7			
1972	136.7			
1973	182.7			
1974	643.3	1969–1973	128.2	
1975	640.6	1972–1974	320.9	150.3
1976	687.6	1971–1975	345.0	7.5
1977	739.2[b]	1972–1976	458.2	32.8
1978	n.a.	1973–1977	578.7	26.3

a. Based on Saudi Arabian light, 34° API, f.o.b. Ras Tanura, from International Monetary Fund, *International Financial Statistics,* various issues.

b. Estimate based on price increase of 5 percent for the first half of 1977 and 10 percent for the second half.

crude petroleum, rebased to 1965=100; column 3 indicates the time period presumably used as the reference period to calculate the price of Soviet crude petroleum exports to COMECON members for recent years; and column 4 shows the result of the application of the pricing formula to data in column 2. Finally, column 5 presents year-to-year changes in the hypothetical price levels obtained by the formula and given in column 4.

The first tentative conclusion that emerges from the table is that the Soviet Union appears to have switched to annual adjustments of petroleum export prices to COMECON members based on moving five-year averages of world market prices even before 1974. If this had been the case, the Soviet crude petroleum export price for 1974 would have been about 28 percent higher than that obtained had the 1965–1969 average world market price been used. Movements of unit values for Soviet crude petroleum and petroleum products exports to several socialist countries in table 13.8 seem to bear this out. Although these variable annual prices represented a departure from customary intra-COMECON pricing practices, they were probably accepted by the importing countries without much difficulty since the price increases were rather modest. However, the very large petroleum world market price increases of late 1973 and early 1974 and the decision to use average world market prices for the period 1972–1974,[37] rather than 1970–1974, as the basis for determining 1975 export prices had a dramatic impact on the oil export price. As seen in column 5, the 1975 price, using the 1972–1974 world market average price as reference, was 150.3 percent higher than that in 1974. This compares with actual increases of 131 percent in the price of imported Soviet crude petroleum reported by Hungary and other COMECON members for 1975.[38] It should be noted that the shift of reference period for determining 1975 petroleum export prices from 1970-1974 to 1972-1974 had the effect of magnifying the price increase for 1975, which otherwise would have been about 84 percent.

Following table 13.9, Soviet petroleum export prices to socialist countries should have been 7.5 percent higher in 1976 than in 1975. This figure compares with reported increases of about 8 percent for unit values of crude petroleum exports to East European trading partners[39] and actual increases in unit values for petroleum and petroleum products exports to these same countries ranging from 6.4 to 13.8 percent.[40] As indicated earlier, unit values of Soviet exports of crude petroleum and petroleum products to Cuba rose by 6.2 percent in 1976. Thus, the data suggest that the Soviet Union closely adhered to the new COMECON pricing policy for shipments of crude petroleum and petroleum products during 1976, and further, that Cuba continued to be treated on equal terms with East European COMECON members in this respect.

If the policy of annual petroleum price adjustments remains unchanged, and if it continues to be rigidly applied, data in table 13.9 may be used to project the magnitude of annual adjustments to prices of Soviet crude petroleum exports to COMECON trading partners in 1977 and 1978. Since Cuba has heretofore been treated on a par with East European COMECON members with respect to adjustments of petroleum prices, it is reasonable to expect that this treatment will continue in the future. Under these assumptions, table 13.9 indicates that prices of Soviet crude petroleum exports to East European COMECON members and to Cuba should have risen by 32.8 percent in 1977 and will rise by about 26 percent in 1978. Provided that OPEC nations either maintain or raise crude petroleum export prices during 1978 and 1979, Soviet crude petroleum export prices to Cuba can be expected to continue to rise throughout the rest of the decade.

The risks of attempting to predict the magnitude of Soviet petroleum price increases following a formula approach are illustrated by the situation for 1977. Press reports from Hungary have indicated that Soviet crude petroleum prices for 1977 were 22.5 higher than in 1976.[41] Another report, indicating that the 1977 price of Soviet oil delivered to COMECON members increased by 22.6 percent over 1976, explicitly states that 1977 prices were "based on the average world price of oil for the last five years."[42] There are no explanations to account for the differences between the projected and actual price increases, although one author speculates that lower transportation costs or refinements in the pricing formula may be responsible.[43] In this light, projections of Soviet oil price increases for the rest of the decade should be considered as tentative, although it is quite clear that adjustments, if effected, will be upward.

The prospects for the price of Cuban sugar exports to the Soviet Union are very difficult to evaluate because of puzzling statements by Cuban leaders and inadequate information. As noted earlier, the Cuban-Soviet trade agreement of 1975 presumably fixed the price of Cuban sugar exports to the Soviet Union at 30 cents per pound for 1975–1980. However, on April 14, 1976, Carlos Rafael Rodríguez, deputy prime minister of the Cuban government, signed a long-term agreement on economic and scientific-technical cooperation with the Soviet Union covering the period 1976–1980. In a press conference in Moscow following the signing of the agreement, Rodríguez stated that Cuba had secured from the Soviet Union all the liquid fuel it would need for the period 1976–1980, at favorable terms, through an agreement which related sugar prices to oil prices. Rodríguez further stated that "at present, Cuba delivers a smaller amount of sugar for a ton of oil than it did in 1965. So, the relation between our main export and our most important import is extremely favorable."[44] These statements by Rodríguez are puzzling for two reasons. First, they seem to indicate that Cuba has obtained an indexation agreement with the Soviet Union whereby the price of Cuban sugar exports to the Soviet Union would be adjusted periodically to account for Soviet petroleum export price increases, and second, Rodríguez compares the terms of sugar-petroleum exchanges in 1976 to those in 1965, a year when the terms of trade with reference to these two products were unfavorable to Cuba (see table 13.6).

There is very little that can be added to clarify these statements by Rodríguez. Soviet trade data for 1976 are inconclusive as to whether or not the price indexation agreement was in force in 1976. While the unit value of Soviet imports of Cuban sugar rose only by 0.7 percent during 1976 (as against an increase of 6.2 percent in the unit value of Soviet petroleum and petroleum products exports to Cuba in 1976), the trade data apparently include, in addition to sugar imported under the conditions of the trade protocol, additional purchases of Cuban sugar for hard currencies at then prevailing world market prices. Given that the 1976 world market price of sugar (about 12.7 cents per pound) was substantially lower than the presumed contracted prices, the inclusion of these additional transactions in the trade data result in lower unit values.

Based on the information currently available, it appears that the Cuban-Soviet terms of trade with reference to sugar and petroleum exchanges will not favor Cuba during the remaining of the 1970s. We can speculate that they will continue to deteriorate through 1980, although under one scenario they would remain unchanged. This latter situation will occur if, in effect, Cuba has been able to obtain an indexation scheme linking changes in the prices of all sugar exports to the Soviet Union to forthcoming increases in the prices of all Soviet petroleum exports to Cuba. However, the levels of Soviet import prices of Cuban sugar necessary to accomplish this appear to be unrealistic, particularly considering depressed world market prices for sugar at the present time and poor prospects for their recovery through 1980. Using the base price of Cuban sugar exports to the Soviet Union as 30 cents per pound for 1975 and applying to it indexing factors based on expected changes in the price of Soviet petroleum exports to COMECON members from table 13.9, we can estimate sugar export prices to the Soviet Union as high as 32.3 cents per pound for 1976, 42.8 cents per pound for 1977 and 54.1 cents per pound for 1978. Prices for 1979 and 1980 would be even higher, but it cannot be expected that the generosity of the Soviet Union will have no upper limit.

Conclusion

This study analyzed Cuban terms of trade vis-à-vis the Soviet Union in the exchange of sugar and petroleum during the period 1960–1976. Because of the unavailability of price data necessary to carry out the examination, average values (unit values) of Soviet exports of petroleum and petroleum products to Cuba and of Soviet imports of sugar from Cuba have been used to approximate trends in prices paid and received by Cuba for these products. Certain restrictive assumptions have been necessary concerning the composition of these trade categories over time and the behavior of the unit values.

The main finding of the study is that during the period 1960–1974, Cuban-Soviet terms of trade with reference to sugar and petroleum and petroleum products were generally favorable to Cuba, although minor fluctuations occurred. These results appear, on the surface, to be consistent with some of the findings of Marer and Hewett indicating reductions in the export price of Soviet fuels to socialist countries through the 1960s. These reductions in the cost of Cuban imports of petroleum and petroleum products, coupled with favorable fixed prices for Cuban sugar exports to the Soviet Union determined by means of long-term agreements, resulted in favorable terms of trade for Cuba during most of the period. Focusing on the more recent period 1973–1976, Cuban-Soviet terms of trade with reference to sugar and petroleum and petroleum products were strongly in favor of Cuba in 1973 and 1974, as a result of booming export prices for sugar and modest rises in the import price of liquid fuels. Upward adjustments in the export price of Soviet crude oil as of January 1975 reversed the trend, with the terms of trade becoming unfavorable to Cuba in 1975 and 1976. The prospects for the remainder of the 1970s are that the terms of trade with reference to these two products will continue to be unfavorable to Cuba.

It is important to stress that this study has dealt strictly with the net barter terms of trade for sugar and petroleum and petroleum products between Cuba and the Soviet Union. Thus, the results should not be interpreted to mean that Cuba (or the Soviet Union) was better or worse off in some larger sense as a result of the exchanges. The net barter terms of trade compare only the prices of the commodities exchanged and do not take into account the volume of the transactions, changes in productivity and so on.

Moreover, the results of this study should not be taken as indicators of the global terms of trade between Cuba and the Soviet Union. As pointed out by Holzman, in socialist economies, where foreign trade monopolies are responsible for import and export decisions, there is often a tendency to take a barter approach to foreign trade rather than to approach export and import transactions independently, as is the case with private enterprise.[45] Thus, profitability may often be assessed on the basis of the global terms of trade, that is, the ratio of the

JORGE F. PÉREZ-LÓPEZ

price of all exports to the price of all imports. Traders may be willing to pay a large price for an import (or offer an export at a lower price) if they can make up for it in another area of commercial relations. As a result, it is possible that Cuban gains or losses in sugar and petroleum exchanges with the Soviet Union may be compensated for by matching gains or losses in other areas of trade between the two countries.

NOTES

The views expressed here are strictly those of the author and do not represent the views of the Bureau of Labor Statistics. I wish to thank Russ Swanson, Leonardo A. da Silva, and Val Zabijaka for their help in obtaining some of the data used in the study. Carmelo Mesa-Lago, René Pérez-López, and Russ Swanson read an earlier draft and made helpful comments.

1. The first (and only) hydroelectric plant constructed in Cuba, at the Hanabanilla River, in Las Villas Province, was near completion in 1960. Generating capacity was 28.4 megawatts. See Grupo Cubano de Investigaciones Económicas, *Un estudio sobre Cuba* (Coral Gables, Fla.: University of Miami Press, 1963), pp. 1170–72.

2. For an interesting overview of petroleum exploration in Cuba, see Herbert J. Sawyer, "Latin America After 1920," in Edgar Wesley Owen's *Trek of the Oil Finders: A History of Exploration for Petroleum* (Tulsa, Okla.: American Association of Petroleum Geologists, 1975), chap. 20. In addition to petroleum deposits, asphalt and naphtha deposits have been found. Peat deposits have been known to exist in the Ciénaga de Zapata, but there is no evidence that they have been exploited commercially.

3. See Cuba, Junta Central de Planificación Revolucionaria, Departamento de Recursos Naturales, *Estudio de producción y consumo de energía eléctrica y uso de combustibles en los centrales azucareros* (Havana, 1960).

4. Osvaldo Dorticós, "El combustible: factor esencial para el mantenimiento de la actividad económica," *Economía y Desarrollo* (Havana), no. 12 (July–August 1972), 78.

5. Production data from U.S. Department of the Interior, Bureau of Mines, *World Crude Oil Production Annual 1975* (Washington, D.C., June 9, 1976), p. 2.

6. Edward Boorstein, *The Economic Transformation of Cuba* (New York: Monthly Review Press, 1968), p. 28.

7. Ernesto "Che" Guevara, conference on national television, program "Universidad Popular," March 20, 1960. Reproduced as "Soberanía política, independencia económica" in *Ernesto Che" Guevara; Obra Revolucionaria,* ed. Roberto Fernández Retamar, 4th ed. (Mexico: Ediciones Era, S.A., 1971), p. 303. On this point see also statement by Alfonso Gutiérrez, who was at the time the chief of the ICP, in *El Mundo* (Havana), April 3, 1960, pp. A1, A8.

8. Paul Marer, "Foreign Trade in the Soviet Bloc," *Aste Bulletin,* Fall 1968, p. 2, and *Postwar Pricing and Price Patterns in Socialist Foreign Trade* (Bloomington: Indiana University Press, 1972), p. 4.

9. Marer, *Postwar Pricing,* p. 5.

10. Horst Mendershausen, "Terms of Trade Between the Soviet Union and Smaller Communist Countries, 1955-1957," *Review of Economics and Statistics* 61, no. 2 (May 1959), 106–18; and "The Terms of Soviet-Satellite Trade: A Broadened Analysis," *Review of Economics and Statistics* 62, no. 2 (May 1960), 152–63.

11. Frederic L. Pryor, *The Communist Foreign Trade System* (Cambridge, Mass.: MIT Press, 1963), pp. 144–53, 180–87.

12. Franklyn Holzman, "Soviet Foreign Trade Pricing and the Question of Discrimination," and "More on Soviet Bloc Trade Discrimination," in his *Foreign Trade Under Central Planning* (Cambridge, Mass.: Harvard University Press, 1974). On this see also J. Wilczynski, *The Economics of Socialism* (London: George Allen and Unwin, 1970), pp. 179–80.

13. Marer, *Postwar Pricing,* pp. 57–59, 33.

14. Edward A. Hewett, *Foreign Trade Prices in the Council for Mutual Economic Assistance* (London: Cambridge University Press, 1974), chap. 3, esp. pp. 91–114.

15. Leon Gouré and Julian Weinkle, "Cuba's New Dependency," *Problems of Communism* 21, no. 2 (March–April 1972), 75. As another example, Wilson, referring presumably to the period 1966–1967, points out that "the Soviets are reported to be stiffening their terms of trade with the Cubans." See Desmond P. Wilson, Jr., "Cuban-Soviet Relations: Conditions and Constraints," in *Aspects of Modern Communism,* ed. Richard F. Staar (Homewood, Ill.: Richard D. Irwin, 1968), pp. 73–77.

16. The expression "terms of trade," despite its frequent use, does not have an unambiguous meaning. For purposes of this chapter, this expression refers to the commodity or net barter terms of trade. For a useful presentation of the concept of terms of trade, its uses, and limitations, see Gerald M. Meier, *International Trade and Development* (New York: Harper and Row, 1963), chap. 3, pp. 40–63; and Charles P. Kindleberger, *International Economics* (Homewood, Ill.: Richard D. Irwin, 1968), pp. 73–77.

17. It should be pointed out that even in the case of "homogeneous" commodities categories, changes in composition of trade within the category, such as shifts from a high-priced variety of grain or fruit to a lower-priced variety, may give rise to changes in unit values even if actual transaction prices of each variety have remained unchanged.

18. Cuban foreign trade data show different categories for crude petroleum and petroleum products imports. Beginning with 1968, Soviet trade yearbooks ceased to publish data on crude petroleum exports to Cuba (or to any other country). Instead, crude petroleum and petroleum products, theretofore two separate categories, were combined. No satisfactory reason for this change in Soviet statistics has been found. The unit value used here to approximate Cuban petroleum import prices is actually the unit value of Soviet crude petroleum and products exports to Cuba.

19. Ministerstvo Vneshnei Torgovli SSSR, *Vneshniaia Torgovlia SSSR v 1975 g.* [USSR Foreign Trade in 1975] (Moscow, 1976); Cuba, Junta Central de Planificación, *Compendio del Anuario Estadístico de Cuba 1974* (Havana, 1976). The latter contains preliminary quantity data on imports of petroleum and petroleum products for 1973, but no disaggregated data. Since this chapter was originally written, the 1976 Soviet data have become available and are used in later analyses.

20. Note that the statement does not imply that Cuba's capacity to import was improved, since the quantities exchanged are not considered. In fact, Cuban sugar production and exports to the Soviet Union (and to the world) were small during this period.

21. Cuban National Bank, *Development and Prospects of the Cuban Economy* (Havana, September 1975), p. 32. Leon Gouré and Morris Rothenberg, *Soviety Penetration of Latin America* (Coral Gables, Fla.: University of Miami Press, 1975), p. 51, give the contracted price as 11 cents per pound. This latest figure, although accurate in terms of the contracted price, did not turn out to be the actual price, since the U.S. dollar was devalued in 1972. Thus, although the contracted price was 11 cents per pound, the actual received price was about 12.02 cents per pound after the devaluation.

22. *Development and Prospects of the Cuban Economy,* pp. 31–32.

23. Edward R. Fried and Charles L. Schultze, eds., *Higher Oil Prices and the World Economy: The Adjustment Problem* (Washington, D.C.: The Brookings Institution, 1975).

24. For the text of the speech see *Granma,* November 17, 1973, pp. 2–6.

25. "Cumplirá la URSS compromisos de suministros petroleros con los países socialistas," *Granma,* December 21, 1973, p. 8. Emphasis added.

26. For the text of the speech see *Granma,* September 30, 1974, p. 2.

27. Osvaldo Dorticós, speech at the ceremony honoring workers who had participated in the sugar industry for fifty years, text given in *Granma,* October 11, 1974, pp. 2–3; Roberto Alvarez Quiñones, "El alza de precios en el mundo capitalista," *Granma,* December 13, 1974, p. 5.

JORGE F. PÉREZ-LÓPEZ

28. *Granma*, November 29, 1974, p. 1; see also Alvarez Quiñones, "El alza de precios."

29. "Adopta el Comité Ejecutivo del CAME medidas para estabilizar los precios en contratos comerciales," *Granma*, January 24, 1975, p. 8.

30. "Comrade Sheik," *Economist*, January 25, 1975, pp. 79–80; Harold Horstmeyer, "Soviet Oil Price Hikes Hitting Eastern Europe," *Journal of Commerce*, March 25, 1975, pp. 1, 4; "Pay Up Comrade," *Economist*, March 1, 1975, p. 77; *Platt's Oilgram News Service*, October 22, 1975, p. 1; "Soviet Exports to Reflect OPEC Hike," *Oil and Gas Journal*, October 13, 1975, p. 48.

31. *Granma*, January 27, 1975, p. 8.

32. The average values of Soviet exports to France and West Germany were $11.62 per barrel and $11.99 per barrel, respectively. The posted price for Arabian light crude, the OPEC marker crude, averaged $11.58 per barrel in 1974 (see tables 13.5 and 13.8).

33. "Now You See, Now You Don't," *Economist*, May 10, 1975, p. 100.

34. For a preliminary analysis of the position of Cuba in the donor-recipient relationship for 1973, see Jorge F. Pérez-López and René Pérez-López, "A Calendar of Cuban Bilateral Agreements 1959–1975: Description and Uses," *Cuban Studies/Estudios Cubanos* 7, no. 2 (July 1977), 167–82.

35. *Middle East Economic Survey* 20, no. 9 (December 20, 1976), supp., p. 1.

36. Calculated from data in *Vneshniaia Torgovlias SSR v 1976 g.* (Moscow, 1977), with conversion factors as given in table 13.5. For 1976, 1 ruble = $1.35.

37. Harry Trend, "Prices in Intra-COMECON Price Puzzle Falling Into Place," RAD Background Report/34 (Eastern Europe), *Radio Free Europe Research*, February 28, 1975, pp. 1–2; Harry Trend, "Some Effects of COMECON's Revised Price System," RAD Background Report/27, *Radio Free Europe Research*, February 20, 1975.

38. Horstmeyer, "Soviet Price Hikes"; "Oil Still a 'Bargain' in the East Bloc," *Journal of Commerce*, March 26, 1975, p. 2; and "Soviets' Oil Price Hike to Hit Trade," *Journal of Commerce*, March 27, 1975, p. 1.

39. "USSR Hikes Crude Prices to Hungary," *Journal of Commerce*, January 19, 1976, p. 26; Harry Trend, "Soviet Crude Oil Price to COMECON May be a Third Higher in 1977," RAD Background Report/18 (Eastern Europe), *Radio Free Europe Research*, January 20, 1976, p. 1.

40. The actual percent changes, calculated from *Vneshniaia Torgovlia SSSR v 1976 g.*, are as follows: Bulgaria, 9.6; Czechoslovakia, 10.5; East Germany, 13.8; Hungary, 9.2; and Poland, 6.4. Differences are probably attributable to differences in product composition and in transportation charges.

41. Harry Trend, "First Announcement of Price to be Paid for Soviet Oil in 1977," RAD Background Report/7 (Eastern Europe), *Radio Free Europe Research*, January 11, 1977, p. 1.

42. Report from *Borba* (Belgrade), February 25, 1977, as reported in *IMF Survey*, March 21, 1977, p. 96.

43. Trend, "First Announcement," p. 3.

44. *Granma*, April 15, 1976, p. 8. Reference to a procedure for establishing prices in Cuban-Soviet trade where the price of Cuban sugar would be adjusted according to the price of imports from the Soviet Union appears in *Development and Prospects of the Cuban Economy*, p. 32.

45. Holzman, *International Trade Under Communism*, pp. 23–24.

14

STEVEN L. REED

Participation in Multinational Organizations and Programs in the Hemisphere

Cuban bilateral and multilateral relations with Latin American countries entered a new era in the 1970s. While at the end of the 1960s only Mexico had diplomatic and trade relations with Cuba, in 1977 eleven Latin American and Caribbean nations had reestablished relations with the island. Cuba has trade missions in seven of these countries, and regular air flights now link Cuba with several Latin American nations. In 1975 the Organization of American States (OAS) modified its policy to permit member countries to determine their own attitudes toward Cuba, thus bolstering the prospects for rapprochement. Clearly the political and economic isolation of the 1960s has given way to greater interaction between Cuba and the rest of the hemisphere.

The magnitude of the transformation in Cuban–Latin American relations is perhaps most dramatically demonstrated by Cuba's new and active role in Latin American regional organizations. Cuba has been an active supporter of the Latin American Economic System (SELA), the Caribbean Committee of Development and Cooperation (CCDC), the Latin American Energy Organization (OLADE), the Latin American and Caribbean Sugar Exporting Group (GEPLACEA), and the Caribbean Multinational Shipping Company (NAMACUR).[1] This chapter examines Cuban participation in these organizations and analyzes the political and economic implications of Cuba's multilateral relations with the hemisphere. In most cases these organizations have been in existence less than two years and have only recently begun actual operations, so the impact of their activities is only now being felt. Cuban interaction with these organizations has been limited, and any assessment of Cuba's present and future role must therefore be somewhat impressionistic.

The chapter is divided into three sections. The first summarizes the foundations and objectives of Cuba's Latin American foreign policy. In the second section, the evolution of Cuba's multilateral affiliations is described and the potential economic and political consequences of these affiliations are analyzed. The final section evaluates briefly the major implications of Cuba's multilateral affiliations with the hemisphere and attempts to indicate the future course of Cuban hemispheric relations.

STEVEN L. REED

Foundations and Objectives of Cuba's Latin American Foreign Policy

The evolution of Cuban-Latin American relations in the 1970s and Cuba's participation in hemispheric organizations in particular is most clearly understood in the light of previous policy failures and current foreign policy objectives. The roots of current Cuban foreign policy were nurtured in the changing domestic and international economic and political environment of the late sixties and early seventies, but their origin was in the policy failures of the early sixties.

In 1962 the OAS banned Cuba after Castro's pronouncement of a Marxist-Leninist revolution. Two years later, after Venezuela accused Cuba of sponsoring an armed expedition against it, the OAS approved sanctions requiring member states to sever diplomatic, economic, and transportation links with Cuba. Throughout the sixties, only Mexico maintained diplomatic relations with Cuba. In an effort to break this isolation, Cuba increased guerrilla activities in Latin America and, for most of the decade, a basic goal of Cuban foreign policy was the revolutionary overthrow of Latin American governments supporting the OAS sanctions. Rather than creating new alliances and support within Latin America, however, "exporting the revolution" only generated greater animosity and further isolation.[2]

In the late 1960s a number of events induced Cuba to terminate armed guerrilla activities abroad and to reduce overt support for revolutionary movements. Ernesto "Ché" Guevara, the principal symbol and leader of Latin American guerrilla movements, was killed in Bolivia in 1967. Moreover, ambitious and unattainable economic goals had led to the misallocation of resources, declining worker productivity, and the subsequent deterioration of the Cuban economy which forced an inward orientation and a drastic curtailment in the exportation of the revolution. From 1969 on, Cuba's foreign policy gradually shifted to a more flexible and moderate stand aimed at breaking its isolation from Latin America. The emergence in the region of some progressive nationalist government practicing independent foreign policies toward the United States aided Cuba in breaking its regional isolation and favored the new direction in Cuban foreign policy. As a result of these changes, Cuba reestablished diplomatic relations with one democratic socialist government (Chile under Allende), three autocratic military regimes (Argentina, Panama, and Peru), and seven representative democracies (Barbados, Colombia, Costa Rica, Guyana, Jamaica, Trinidad-Tobago, and Venezuela).

The deterioration of the Cuban economy in the second half of the 1960s and in 1970 increased Cuban dependency on the Soviet Union. Approximately 50 percent of total Cuban trade is with the USSR, and since 1962 the Cuban-Soviet trade balance has shown a large and continuous deficit. The USSR is Cuba's major supplier of oil, capital goods, and manufactures and is the principal market for Cuban sugar and other exports. Preferential pricing for both imports and exports insulates the Cuban economy from the vagaries of international markets, but it also increases Cuba's vulnerability to Soviet influence in domestic and foreign affairs. A reduction of Soviet dependence is probably a major objective of Cuba's international economic policy, and increasing relations with the Western Hemisphere is a potential way to achieve more independence.

During the 1970s domestic economic performance improved significantly, with a 12.7 percent annual growth rate of gross social product (GSP) from 1970–1974. Paradoxically, however, economic growth has generated new requirements for foreign trade and technology to ensure future economic progress. Cuba is caught in the proverbial vicious cycle: In order to maximize comparative advantage and expand output, the Cubans must modernize their industry with technology not currently available in the socialist world. However, in order to purchase Western technology, Cuba must expand output and generate higher export revenues. Limited natural resources and manpower constraints also mean that further development of the nickel and sugar industries and of the economy as a whole depends to a large extent on increased productivity. Capital-intensive technology seems to be the only viable and acceptable alternative for the Cuban leadership.[3] Similarly, development of its nickel resources, the fourth largest reserves in the world, is potentially extremely advantageous for Cuba (see chapter 12 of this volume). However, the markets, technology, and political environment needed to exploit these ores profitably require a restructuring of international relations. Domestic economic realities have therefore necessitated changes in Cuban foreign relations.

Although economic considerations are crucial in explaining the transformation and composition of Cuban foreign policy, the aspirations and perceptions of Cuban leaders cannot be overlooked in analyzing present trends. Identification with Latin America has been a consistent theme of Cuban leadership in recent years.[4] For Cuba, the most odious manifestation of U.S. domination in Latin America is the OAS, specifically the economic and political sanctions against Cuba ratified in 1964. Havana's new dialogue with the hemisphere is an effort to break its economic isolation and forge alliances which nullify the OAS sanctions, reduce U.S. influence in the hemisphere, and give Cuba greater international prestige and leverage. Cuban participation in regional and subregional organizations in the short run, and integration with Latin America in the long run, are major objectives of Cuban foreign policy. In 1972 Castro declared, "We are in this hemisphere, on this side of the Atlantic. We are Latin Americans. . . . In the future, we will be economically integrated with Latin America."[5]

Multilateral Affiliations in the Hemisphere: Political and Economic Effects

The expansion of Cuban bilateral relations within the region has been accompanied by a proliferation of multilateral regional affiliations. These affiliations can be categorized into two types: broad regional cooperative organizations and limited groupings centered on a specific purpose.

The first type of affiliation includes the Latin American Economic System (SELA) and the newly created Caribbean Committee of Development and Cooperation (CCDC), a subregional committee of the Economic Commission for Latin America (ECLA). Both organizations seek to promote cooperation and integration through a broad range of endeavors: the promotion of multicountry economic projects such as Latin American multinational corporations; agricultural development; industrial complementarity; coordination of production, marketing, and stockpiling of basic commodities; support for commodity producer organizations; and formulation of unified Latin American positions at international economic forums.

The second type of affiliation includes organizations whose objectives are much more narrowly focused, seeking cooperative action and solutions to problems in a single area such as energy, maritime transportation, or commodity production and marketing. Cuban participation in groups of this nature includes the Latin American Energy Organization (OLADE), the Latin American and Caribbean Sugar Exporting Group (GEPLACEA), and the Caribbean Multinational Shipping Company (NAMACUR).

Latin American Economic System (SELA)

In July 1974 former Mexican president Luis Echeverría identified the need for a genuinely Latin American forum to examine common problems and to formulate global, sectoral, and regional development strategies to channel Latin American resources into collective efforts.[6] In particular Echeverría said, "Latin America cannot return to bilateralism with the United States. . . . If we realize that our problems have a common origin and that we should make common efforts to resolve them, nationalism is converted into a principle of action, en route to economic liberation."[7] The immediate impact of this initiative was a joint resolution by Mexico and Venezuela proposing the creation of the Latin American Economic System. Both governments agreed to send delegations to various countries, including Cuba, to seek backing for the proposal. At the end of 1974, Horacio Flores, a top official in the Mexican government, reported Castro's response of support for the SELA concept.[8] A ministerial meeting of twenty-five Latin American nations was held in Panama in August 1975, producing a draft resolution to create SELA. In October 1975, less than a year and a half after the original suggestion, the charter establishing SELA was signed in Panama by the official representatives of twenty-three nations.[9]

From the beginning, SELA's purpose has been to attempt to solve Latin American economic problems collectively and to reduce Latin American economic dependence on the United States; the organization can be interpreted as an important challenge to U.S. economic interests and influence in the hemisphere. Moreover, for the first time, Cuba and other countries in the Caribbean are represented in an exclusively Latin American forum designed to address a broad range of topics.

SELA's constitution offers a broad definition of the organization's function, describing it as a "permanent regional agency for joint consultation, coordination, cooperation, and economic and social promotion."[10] A clearer indication of the group's future activities emerged at the first meeting of the Latin American Council (SELA's supreme organ) held in Caracas in January 1976. The group acted quickly to establish joint positions on international issues, to fund an operating budget, and to define future areas of cooperative endeavor. The guidelines established in Caracas emphasized the promotion of specific cooperative efforts outlined in a series of "action programs." Essentially, SELA's activities are intended to improve the terms of trade and competitive stance of member nations and to increase intraregional efforts at economic development.[11]

Other major areas of discussion dealt with the determination of unified stands on international economic issues. Three events were significant in this regard. First, all twenty-five members supported a resolution condemning the U.S. Foreign Trade Act of 1974, which excluded Venezuela and Ecuador, among others, from most-favored-nation status because of their membership in OPEC. SELA members were also fearful that this type of provision could be expanded to other commodity cartels. Second, SELA strongly supported a greater rapprochement with the centrally planned economies in order to obtain more technical and financial aid. Increasing Latin American exports of raw materials and manufactures in addition to cooperation with COMECON (Council of Mutual Economic Assistance) countries in the establishment of industrial enterprises will be the principal thrusts of future negotiations with socialist countries. Finally, the Latin American position at upcoming meetings of the group of 77 and UNCTAD was defined through guidelines on basic commodities, manufactured and semimanufactured goods, GATT negotiations, reform of the international monetary system, transfer of funds for development, the transfer of technology, and cooperation among developing countries.[12]

In the short run, probably the most significant decision in Caracas concerned SELA's first-year budget and activities. The conference agreed on a budget of $1.9 million for the first year.[13] In addition, it was decided that the first year would be spent establishing SELA's regulations and determining its future work program. At the second meeting, in June, the work program was further elaborated. SELA members agreed to set up a number of "action committees" to implement the plans for continental cooperation in a number of specific areas and in most cases assigned these projects to specific countries. Mexico is the designated center for cooperative efforts in fertilizer manufacture; Venezuela is the center for high-protein foodstuffs; Honduras, the center for timber, pulp, and paper industries. The establishment of a multinational news agency and the development of aluminum, pharmaceutical, and capital-goods industries were also slated for future SELA action.

Cuba's response to SELA has been assertive and positive. At the inaugural meeting Cuba came prepared with thirteen specific projects for consideration, ranging from the manufacture of machinery for sugar mills to the provision of worker housing. Only the housing provision was positively acted upon, and another country, Ecuador, was designated the center for this activity. In addition, Cuba and Venezuela clashed over the question of state versus private capital in the proposed multinational corporations.[14] On the whole, though, the reaction of Cuban officials has been favorable. Cuba provides 7 percent of the annual budget and in 1975 contributed $133,000. Cuba's financial support is relatively greater than that of other countries such as Colombia and Venezuela, who, with substantially larger economies, also provide 7 percent of the annual budget.[15] Late in 1975, Cuban Foreign Trade Minister Marcelo Fernández Font cited Cuban-Mexican efforts to increase sugar production and manufacturing equipment as specific examples of the significant benefits potentially achievable through the cooperative efforts of SELA members. In addition, he stressed the political significance of Cuban participation in SELA: "It is a fact that the continent has made gigantic progress in political affairs and international relations and in Cuba's case, it is evident that the Revolution, already consolidated and with great strength and prestige, is an irreversible, incontestable and unparalleled fact within the Latin American Economic System."[16] In the short run it is difficult to imagine Cuba achieving any significant economic benefits from SELA. Initial funding is extremely limited, although the work program is extensive and ambitious. One encouraging development in this regard is the pledge of World Bank financial assistance for multinational enterprises created by SELA.[17] Cuba could acquire financial and technological assistance through cooperative development programs among SELA nations. However, Latin America's recent history in the field of economic cooperation and integration does not augur well for future cooperation. LAFTA (Latin American Free Trade Association) has at best made minimal progress, and the recent withdrawal of Chile from the Andean Pact casts doubt on the long-run viability of that organization as it was originally conceived. In addition, the Central American Common Market, after an encouraging start, was blocked by the Honduras–El Salvador war. Latin America's real commitment to SELA is itself doubtful. As late as June 1976 only fourteen countries had actually ratified the Panama declaration. This delay suggests a reluctance on the part of some countries, particularly the governments of the "southern cone" to commit themselves to the new organization.

The short-run political and symbolic benefits of Cuban participation in SELA are more obvious. First of all, Cuban membership in this Latin American forum is a concrete sign that the member nations have accepted the Cuban revolution as a political reality. Second, SELA's goals of relative economic independence from the United States are, in many ways, a reaffirmation of Cuban foreign policy toward Latin America and the United States. Moreover, since SELA wishes to reap the political and economic benefits of a bipolar world, Cuba plays an important role in that relationship as the only Communist government in the Western Hemisphere. Finally, Cuba's vigorous support for rapid and constructive cooperation with SELA has been applauded by the other small member nations and has increased Cuba's prestige with those nations.[18]

In the long run the outlook for significant Cuban influence in SELA appears limited. Venezuela and Mexico, the principal supporters of the group, are themselves vying for the leadership of Latin America. Cuba, in comparison, lacks the economic resources to play a major long-term role in Latin American development efforts. Essentially, Cuba's importance in SELA has stemmed from its nearly twenty-year effort to attempt to reduce the influence of the United States in the hemisphere. If and when Cuban-U.S. political and economic relations improve, Cuba's fairly well-defined role and importance in SELA may be diminished.

Caribbean Committee of Development and Cooperation (CCDC)

Cuba's reemergence in the hemisphere is particularly notable in the Caribbean, where bilateral and multilateral contacts have flourished since 1972, when the English-speaking Commonwealth countries established diplomatic relations with Cuba. Since then the Cubans have actively campaigned to develop relations and contacts with these countries. In 1973 Castro made short visits to Trinidad-Tobago and Guyana in addition to meeting with Caribbean prime ministers in Port-of-Spain. Forbes Burnham, Eric Williams, and Michael Manley, the prime ministers of Guyana, Trinidad-Tobago, and Jamaica, have all paid official visits to Cuba.[19] The joint communiqués issued following these diplomatic exchanges indicate a convergence of Cuban and Caribbean views and highlight the prospects for future expansion of bilateral contacts and development efforts. Cuban leaders have strongly supported Caribbean government attempts to obtain greater control of their material resources and have endorsed the initiatives of the International Bauxite Association, which includes Jamaica and Guyana, to increase prices and tax revenues. In addition, Guyana and Cuba held open the possibility of joint foreign policy actions, while all three leaders joined with Cuba in hailing the activities of the nonaligned nations.[20]

For Cuba, one of the obvious advantages of increased interaction with the Caribbean community is greater prominence and influence within the Caribbean. An indication of Cuba's growing prestige and leadership in the area is illustrated by the formation in May 1975 of ECLA's Caribbean Committee of Development and Cooperation. The first meeting of this group, composed of Cuba and eight other Caribbean nations, was held in Havana in November 1975.[21] The objectives of the CCDC are broadly defined to include "the promotion of development in the subregion" and "the coordination and harmonization of activities designed to fortify cooperation of the countries of the Caribbean with the other member countries of ECLA."[22] The principal outcome of the Havana meeting was a declaration which enunciated the common aspirations and goals of the members of the new committee. Like SELA's action program, the scope of CCDC's objectives is broad and includes a wide range of economic as well as social cooperative activities; foremost among the purposes are the cooperative development of agricultural technology, of maritime transportation, and of regional trade, and the creation of multinational cooperatives.[23]

Although the Havana meeting produced little in the way of tangible results, the creation of the committee itself and Cuba's role as host at the first meeting have some significance. The CCDC is the first attempt to organize cooperative economic efforts among all Caribbean countries. Other subregional organizations, such as the Caribbean Common Market (CARICOM) and the Caribbean Development Bank, to which Cuba does not belong, have goals in common with the CCDC, but their memberships are not as inclusive. Moreover, the committee represents the first effort by Cuba in many years to develop closer economic and political ties with neighboring countries. Finally, the fact that the initial meeting was held in Havana is symbolic of Cuba's growing influence and leadership in the Caribbean. Whether real economic changes develop as a result is, however, an open question.

Latin American Energy Organization (OLADE)

Cuba's more conventional, pragmatic dealings with Latin America in the seventies are illustrated by its reemergence in regional affairs as a member of the Latin American Energy Organization. OLADE began informally in two meetings of Latin American energy and petroleum ministers prompted by Venezuela. In August 1972 and again in April 1973, energy ministers discussed a Venezuelan proposal advocating the creation of an organization to coordinate regional policies on pricing and development of energy resources. What emerged at the April meeting in Quito was a recommendation to form OLADE in an effort to conserve and allocate the region's energy supplies with the prospect of establishing an energy common market. Cuba, not represented at the first two meetings, was present at the October 1973 meeting held in Lima. At that time, energy ministers from twenty-one Latin American nations, including Cuba, signed the Lima convention that formally created OLADE.[24]

The Lima agreement only faintly resembled the ambitious proposals for energy cooperation advocated in Quito. A majority of countries, basically energy deficient, sought agreements whereby members would enjoy special pricing privileges on imports within the region and would establish direct negotiations between Latin American exporting and importing countries. Venezuela and Ecuador opposed these proposals, clearly asserting their allegiance to OPEC and their opposition to breaking international pricing agreements in favor of Latin American countries. The agreement established OLADE as a consultative organization with limited prospects for real cooperation. The agreement provides for a framework for voluntary joint development projects without providing a means to finance such efforts.

In subsequent meetings, member nations have made little progress in realizing the aims of the organization: to create an autonomous fund to finance OLADE projects intended to integrate the Latin American energy market, to produce an inventory of regional energy resources, and to support members faced with threats to their sources of energy from outside the region. Formal ratification of the agreement proceeded slowly. As late as December 1975, only fifteen of the original signatory nations had ratified the agreement. Venezuela did not ratify it until 1976. No permanent executive secretary was appointed until September 1975, almost two years after the Lima agreement. More important, though, member nations have been unable to reach a consensus on the two most critical issues: the creation of a Latin American energy market and the setting up of an autonomous fund to finance OLADE activities.

Despite the lack of any real progress, Cuba, one of the early ratifiers of the Lima convention, has continued to endorse OLADE and to encourage the continuation of cooperative efforts in the energy field. However, Cuban representatives have urged more far-reaching and concrete solutions to Latin America's energy problems, and, at the close of the sixth ministerial meeting in Mexico City in September 1975, the Cuban delegate reaffirmed the need for more substantive cooperative efforts.[25]

Since 1975, however, political relationships among the member nations have deteriorated (for example, Cuba and Venezuela are at present critical of the Bolivian executive secretary, Carlos Miranda, who was reluctant to sign a declaration against Gulf Oil), and the future of the organization is seriously in question. In addition, from Cuba's point of view, the leadership of OLADE has ignored the original supporters of the organization, Mexico, Venezuela, and Cuba, seeking support from Brazil, Argentina, and Chile. As a result, continued Cuban support of OLADE is doubtful at this time.[26]

Although the prospects for genuine economic benefits from OLADE are rather remote, Cuba's participation is notable for several reasons. OLADE was the first regional organization to be established which is genuinely Latin American, excluding the United States and including Cuba. In addition, at OLADE's fourth meeting, Cuba's minister of mines and metallurgy, Manuel de Céspedes, was elected a vice-president of the organization.[27] Moreover, Cuba's participation was the first sign of its willingness to cooperate with a diverse range of Latin American political regimes, including countries that have not reestablished diplomatic relations with Cuba and that Cuba opposes, such as Chile and Brazil.

Latin American and Caribbean Sugar Exporting Group (GEPLACEA)

Cuba is highly dependent on the foreign sector to generate income and provide resources for the development of other sectors of the economy. The most critical element dictating the performance of the Cuban economy is the sugar sector, which accounted for approximately 80 percent of annual export earnings from 1964 to 1974. Cuba's balance of trade and its national economic performance are highly dependent on domestic sugar production and international sugar prices. A recent study indicates that the average annual percentage change in international sugar prices was almost 27 percent between 1950 and 1972, the second highest rate of annual variation among all the raw materials studied.[28] Widely fluctuating international sugar prices and an overwhelming dependence on foreign sugar earnings are two obvious reasons for participation in the Latin American and Caribbean Sugar Exporting Group.

At the initiative of Mexico, Cuba and eighteen other Latin American sugar-producing countries, accounting for 61 percent of world sugar exports, formed GEPLACEA in November 1974 to act as an advisory and coordinating body for issues related to sugar production and marketing.[29] The initial reluctance of participating countries to agree to substantive resolutions in 1974 diminished in subsequent meetings in 1975 and 1976 as international sugar prices fell sharply from the record high in 1974. At the group's third meeting in September 1975, the twenty-two members agreed to coordinate action to defend international sugar prices, adopt provisions to strengthen technological cooperation among members, establish permanent ties with SELA, and coordinate action at international meetings, particularly during negotiations for a new International Sugar Agreement. In an effort to strengthen cooperation and develop a unified marketing strategy, a number of specific measures were adopted; fixing a minimum world export price and establishing common norms for selling sugar in the world market—for example, announcing auctions with not more than forty-eight hours' notice—were the principal thrusts of the proposals. However, there is no doubt that the major purpose of the organization is to defend export prices at a "fair, stable" level.[30]

From the Cuban viewpoint, perhaps the most notable aspect of the third meeting in Lima was the election of a Cuban, Jorge Brioso Domínguez, as secretary general. Although the choice was not surprising, since Cuba is the largest sugar exporter in the world, the nomination had been strongly opposed by Brazil, a major ideological opponent and the region's second largest exporter.[31]

Although GEPLACEA's short history makes it difficult to evaluate its ability to stabilize world prices or at least to negotiate a more favorable international agreement, recent events do not portend immediate success. Attempts to negotiate a long-term agreement with the European Economic Community in 1975–1976 failed to establish prices acceptable to both parties. Late in 1975 the EEC suggested that the price would be $520 per ton, but with sharply declining world prices in 1976 their offer fell to $353, a level unacceptable to the sugar producers.[32] In addition, preliminary estimates indicate that 1976 recorded a record world sugar harvest of approximately 88 million tons, complicating the group's efforts. However, at a February-March 1977 meeting, GEPLACEA nations developed a consolidated bargaining position for the UNCTAD negotiations, evidence that members view GEPLACEA as a necessary and viable mechanism.[33]

There are very distinct advantages of continued Cuban participation in GEPLACEA. One is symbolic: Cuba as the identifiable leader in a Latin American economic organization. The fact that the February–March meeting referred to earlier was held in Havana reinforces Cuba's leadership position.[34] Moreover, the group is composed entirely of Third World nations, so Cuba's symbolic leadership is not compromised by participation of developed countries such as the United States. Finally, any success in stabilizing or increasing world sugar prices has obvious and immediate economic benefits for Cuba.

Caribbean Multinational Shipping Company (NAMACUR)

Since 1959 the development of a merchant fleet has been a major priority of the Cuban government. Cuba now has the fourth largest merchant fleet in Latin

America, with an estimated 670,000 tonnage.[35] The fleet has increased ninefold since 1959 and will continue to expand throughout the decade, according to development plans. Agreements for construction and delivery of new ships point to an expansion of fourteen ships, or 161,000 tons, in 1976 alone.[36] Cuba is now constructing its own shipyards with Polish assistance and has signed drydock and repair agreements with a Curaçao firm to eliminate the long and expensive trips to Asia and Europe where repairs were formerly made.[37]

Cuba's partnership in the Caribbean Multinational Shipping Company is consistent with Cuban shipping interests and indicative of a desire to play a more substantial role in the economic life of the Caribbean area. Cuba, along with Mexico, Venezuela, and Costa Rica, has been one of the major proponents of the enterprise. Even prior to the May 1975 meeting of incorporation in Costa Rica, Cuba announced its intention to join. Signatories to the final agreement were the four original sponsors, together with Jamaica, Nicaragua, Panama, and Trinidad-Tobago. El Salvador has also agreed to participate.

Unlike Cuba's other multinational affiliations, NAMACUR is not a consultative group but a multinational company designed to reduce dependence on extraregional transnational corporations. NAMACUR's general purposes are to increase trade flows within the Caribbean, stimulate regional integration, and eliminate trade barriers caused by a lack of adequate communication and transportation. Although NAMACUR may eventually operate outside the Caribbean area, its primary function is to transport regional trade.

NAMACUR began operations in March 1976, starting with an initial authorized capital of $100 million; $30 million is subscribed, paid-in capital contributed in equal shares by member countries, while the remainder is authorized capital. Shares will be issued in two series; the A shares can be acquired only by participating governments or state-owned companies; the B shares, which carry no voting privileges, may be subscribed by individuals, governments, or companies outside the member states.[38]

Rather than build its own fleet immediately, the company at first used existing fleets in a coordinated fashion. In 1976 the chartered ships carried 10 to 11 percent of the 1 million tons of goods transported among NAMACUR's principal customers, a much larger percentage than was originally anticipated. Alvaro Fernández Escalante, NAMACUR's permanent secretary, attributed the large volume of trade to Cuba's intensive trade flows with Mexico and other zonal countries.[39] In fact, the venture has been successful enough for the Cuban government, at a NAMACUR meeting in Havana in November 1976, to advocate that the group actually purchase and operate its own fleet, beginning with three ships in 1977.[40]

It seems unreasonable to assume that NAMACUR will significantly reduce Cuban shipping or freight costs in either the short or long run. Although extraregional shipping was not excluded from the company's plans, the principal area of operations will be within the hemisphere. At present less than 5 percent of Cuba's total trade transactions are with Latin America and prospects for greater trade with the region are limited, implying that the savings for Cuba will be minimal. The potential for real economic benefits for Cuba exists, but only if NAMACUR expands its shipping routes to include Europe and Japan. Any possibility of that occurring is of course pure conjecture, but NAMACUR's first-quarter operations yielded a profit of $30,000, so a glimmer of optimism is not completely unwarranted.

There are some immediate advantages of Cuba's participation in NAMACUR, primarily symbolic. Participation allows Cuba to play a very active and visible role in leading Caribbean integration efforts. Cuba has a large and growing fleet as well as technical expertise in maritime affairs which enhances its prominence and influence in the firm and the region. Cuban vessels as well as technical personnel will most likely be used, providing a constant reminder that Cuba has a visible and viable role to play in Caribbean and Latin American economic development.

Evaluation of Current Policy and Exploration of Future Course

In reviewing Cuban participation in hemispheric organizations in the 1970s, several observations seem to ben order. First of all, Cuba did not initiate the formation of any of the organizations; even the sugar group, GEPLACEA, was formed at Mexico's suggestion. Whereas in the sixties Cuba could be said to be a revolutionary activist in hemispheric affairs, in the seventies a more pragmatic and perhaps cautious approach is evident. Cuba will join and attempt to utilize multilateral organizations which are consistent with its foreign policy objective of reducing Latin American economic dependence on the United States, but Cuba has not been the catalyst in the formation of these organizations.

Cuban participation has had some benefits for ther country, although few can be measured in economic terms. From virtually complete ostracism throughout Latin America, Cuba has emerged as a potential leader of the Caribbean countries and as a spokesman and advocate of Latin American economic integration and independence from the United States. The costs of membership, such as contributions to various secretariats and toward the shares of the shipping organization, are probably outweighed by the good will and enhanced prestige Cuba currently experiences among various Latin American nations. It would appear that the pragmatic approach of the seventies has produced effects much more potentially fruitful for Cuba than the "export of the revolution" of the sixties.

Besides emphasizing its economic and political independence from the United States and encouraging economic integration of Latin America, another probable reason for Cuban participation in hemispheric organizations is the desire to become more self-sufficient, not relying so heavily on the Soviet Union for support. However, the benefits of the shipping group, NAMACUR, in this respect are limited. Moreover, OLADE does not appear to provide an alternative to Cuba's dependence on the USSR for energy. And, given the fact that most Latin American countries have competitive rather than complementary economic structure—for example, sugar is exported by many Latin American countries in addition to Cuba—economic integration via organizations such as SELA and CCDC cannot hold the long-term answers to Cuba's need for economic development and desire for economic independence.

If the sugar group were able to obtain an agreement with consumer nations on a "fair, stable price," an important step in Cuba's economic development would have been taken; without the significant revenue vagaries of an economy relying heavily on a single agricultural good, Cuba could plan for needed capital development. However, the experience of GEPLACEA to date has not been encouraging, nor has the experience of other commodity groups been successful from the producers' viewpoint, except for oil. Groups attempting to control the supply of renewable agricultural products face even more difficulties in achieving a stable revenue picture than do cartels of nonrenewable resources. It is very difficult to control supply because of the large number of potential producers and because of the political and economic difficulties in assigning and following production quotas. In addition, producer groups have little control over demand, and a combination of a bumper harvest and depressed levels of demand because of recession, conditions experienced in 1976, can be disastrous. In such a fluctuating environment it is unlikely that a settlement will ever be reached which is advantageous to a commodity producer such as Cuba.

Thus, it appears that multilateral and bilateral relations with Latin America do not hold the key to Cuban economic independence. Unless Cuba wishes to and is able to develop economic relations with the United States or perhaps other developed countries, it is not likely that the reliance on Soviet assistance will be reduced. Moreover, the technology provided by the USSR is not necessarily the best choice in all cases (for example, the capital required for more efficient sugar production is available in the West, not in the socialist world), and the ability to utilize other technologies would certainly enhance Cuban economic development prospects. The sugar example reflects Cuba's double bind: Because Cuba relies on one agricultural product for the generation of foreign exchange, it is very difficult to implement a capital development strategy using technology not available in the Soviet Union. Without that development, however, Cuba will probably continue to remain extraordinarily dependent on that agricultural product, with the consequent vagaries described above. If Cuba is to break out of the vicious cycle of underdevelopment, the provision of loans and grants through agencies such as the Caribbean Development Bank and the Inter-American Development Bank would appear to be a desirable strategy.

Cuba has not applied to the Caribbean Development Bank for membership, although in November 1975 Carlos Rafael Rodríguez, a prominent Cuban minister, in his formal address to the opening session of the Caribbean Committee of Development and Cooperation, spoke warmly of the Caribbean Development Bank and made a special point of greeting the president of the bank.[41] It is possible that we may see a shift in Cuban policy toward this bank in the future.

Participation in the Inter-American Development Bank is limited to members of the OAS, which Castro has declared Cuba will never join. In addition, because the United States is a major participant in the bank, any real assistance to be provided by the bank is dependent upon improved political relations between the United States and Cuba.

Moreover, there are very real ideological and symbolic constraints on Cuban participation in organizations such as the Inter-American Development Bank. Socialist countries under Soviet influence generally do not participate in international monetary organizations; only Rumania is a member of the World Bank, for example. More relevant to this discussion is the fact that Cuba has so far refused to participate in Latin American organizations with the United States, except for regional United Nations organizations such as the Pan American Health Organization and the Economic Commission for Latin America. Cuba is also opposed to weighted voting, particularly when the weights are a function of financial involvement; this, of course, reflects the desire of a small country not to be dominated by a larger one such as the United States.

As the Cuban leadership has reiterated, Cuba has undergone a radical ideological and political transformation that it does not wish to have subverted by the United States. Given the desire of the Soviets to maintain a Communist government in the Western Hemisphere and their consequent willingness to provide considerable assistance to Cuba, it is not likely that Cuba will reverse its stand on organizations such as the Inter-American Development Bank unless capital requirements become extraordinarily severe.

It is possible, especially given Cuba's more pragmatic view of hemispheric organizations in the seventies, that circumstances such as the tremendous decline in sugar prices in 1976, which caused Cuba to restrict imports from countries such as Canada and Argentina, may force another policy shift toward participation in such organizations.

NOTES

I gratefully acknowledge the comments and assistance of Carmelo Mesa-Lago, Richard Thorn, and Marie C. Reed in the preparation of this chapter.

1. The Spanish acronyms stand for Sistema Económico Latinoamericano (SELA); Comité de Cooperación y Desarrollo del Caribe (CCDC); Organización Latinoamericana de Energía (OLADE); Grupo de Países Latinoamericanos y del Caribe Exportadores de Azúcar (GEPLACEA); and Empresa Naviera Multinacional del Caribe (NAMACUR).

2. For a more complete discussion of this policy, see Ernesto R. Betancourt, "Exporting the Revolution to Latin America," in *Revolutionary Change in Cuba,* ed. Carmelo Mesa-Lago (Pittsburgh: University of Pittsburgh Press, 1971), pp. 105–25.

3. Osvaldo Dorticós, "Third National Conference of the Technical Youth Brigade," *Granma,* September 14, 1974.

4. Fidel Castro, "The Nineteenth Anniversary of the Attack on the Moncada Garrison," *Granma Weekly Review,* August 6, 1972.

5. Ibid.

6. See "Presidential Visit to South America and the Caribbean," *Mexican Newsletter,* no. 42, August 31, 1974.

7. *El Universal,* (Caracas), July 7, 1974.

8. *Washington Post,* January 4, 1975, p. 10.

9. The twenty-three original signers of the agreement were Argentina, Bolivia, Brazil, Chile, Colombia, Costa Rica, Cuba, Ecuador, El Salvador, Guatemala, Guyana, Haiti, Honduras, Jamaica, Mexico, Nicaragua, Panama, Paraguay, Peru, Dominican Republic, Trinidad-Tobago, Uruguay, and Venezuela. Barbados and Grenada signed in November 1975, bringing the total to twenty-five.

10. See "Constitution of the Latin American Economic System," *Mexican Newsletter,* no. 56, October 31, 1975.

11. See "Activities of the Latin American Economic System," *Mexican Newsletter,* no. 60, February 29, 1976.

12. See "Latin American Economic System," *Comercio Exterior de* México, 22, no. 3, (March 1976), 99.

13. *Latin American Economic Report,* June 25, 1976.

14. Ibid., October 24, 1975.

15. SELA uses a four-tier budget allocation system. Cuba is in the second group, which includes Venezuela, Peru, Chile, and Colombia; all five contributed 7 percent of the budget for the first year. Venezuela made a voluntary special contribution, however, which increased its contribution to about 10 percent.

16. *Granma Weekly Review,* November 11, 1975.

17. See "SELA: The World Bank Will Back Multinational Enterprises," *Comercio Exterior de México,* 21, no. 10 (October 1975), 167–68.

18. *Latin American Economic Report,* October 24, 1975.

19. *Granma Weekly Review,* April 20, 1975; ibid., June 20, 1975; ibid., July 20, 1975.

20. Ibid., joint communiqués: Guyana, April 20, 1975; Trinidad-Tobago, July 6, 1976; Jamaica, July 20, 1975.

21. The members are the Bahamas, Barbados, Cuba, Dominican Republic, Grenada, Guyana, Haiti, Jamaica, and Trinidad-Tobago.

22. Comisión Económica para América Latina, *Notas sobre la economía y el desarrollo de América Latina,* no. 204, December 1975.

23. Ibid.

24. *Latin American Economic Report,* November 9, 1973.

25. Ibid., November 19, 1975.

26. *Latin American Political Report,* January 28, 1977.

27. *Diario de las Américas* (Miami), August 20, 1974.

28. Alton D. Law, *International Commodity Agreements* (Lexington, Mass.: Lexington Books, 1975), p. 15.

29. See "Organization of Sugar Exporting Countries," *Comercio Exterior de México,* 21, no. 5 (May 1975), 154. In addition to Cuba and Mexico the members of the organization include Argentina, Barbados, Brazil, Colombia, Costa Rica, Dominican Republic, Ecuador, El Salvador, Guatemala, Guyana, Honduras, Jamaica, Nicaragua, Panama, Paraguay, Peru, Trinidad-Tobago, and Venezuela.

30. See "Group of Sugar Exporting Countries," *Comercio Exterior de México,* 21, no. 12, (December 1975), 503.

31. *Latin American Economic Report,* October 10, 1975.

32. Ibid., April 30, 1976.

33. *Granma Weekly Review,* March 13, 1977.

34. Ibid., February 27, 1977.

35. *Latin American Economic Report,* October 17, 1975.

36. *Granma Weekly Review,* May 30, 1976; *Latin American Economic Report,* May 28, 1976.

37. *Granma Weekly Review,* February 23, 1975.

STEVEN L. REED

38. *Latin American Economic Report,* June 6, 1975.

39. See "Latin American Multinational Enterprises," *Comercio Exterior de México,* 23, no. 2 (February 1977), 67.

40. *Latin American Economic Report,* January 7, 1977.

41. Carlos Rafael Rodríguez, "Comité de Desarrollo and Cooperación del Caribe: unión de esfuerzos para el desarrollo," *Economía y Desarrollo,* no. 33 (January–February 1976), 35.

15

ARCHIBALD R. M. RITTER

The Transferability of Cuba's Revolutionary Development Models

Since the early days of the Revolution, the Cuban leadership has displayed a strong missionary impulse and implicitly or explicitly conveyed the message that Cuba's developmental experience is relevant to, and worthy of careful consideration by, any other country striving toward social justice and economic abundance.[1] There can be little doubt that some of the positive results of Cuba's developmental experience (reduced inequality, elimination of open unemployment, eradication of illiteracy, improvements in public health, and substantial economic growth in 1971-1975) have strong appeal to broad varieties of individuals in elite, counterelite, academic, labor, religious, and other groups in developing countries as well as in developed market economies. There are also some lessons which can be derived from Cuba's negative developmental experiences. What is debatable, however, is the extent to which some of the various sets of interrelated strategies and institutions, that is, the Cuban "models of socioeconomic development," are appropriate and transferable to other developing countries.

The first objective of this chapter is to analyze and evaluate the suitability of two basic Cuban models of socioeconomic development for other developing countries. To perform this task fully would require a careful analysis of each developing country and the relevance of the Cuban models to each. Unfortunately, it is not possible to adopt such an approach in the brief space of this chapter. Therefore, the emphasis is placed upon identifying some factors that determine the appropriateness of the two Cuban models within the context of other developing countries in more general terms. A second objective is to survey the methods the Cubans have used to transfer their "developmental models" to the rest of the world and to gauge the success of these efforts.

It should be stressed that any explanation of why an individual, group, political party, or governing elite adopts or evolves an ideology and vision of the "good society," and builds a particular set of institutions and development strategy, is most complex. To understand this requires the insights of a variety of disciplines, such as history, political science, social psychology, and economics. Moreover, ideological biases and the interplay of sectional interests and political

ARCHIBALD R. M. RITTER

forces are of obvious importance in determining which developmental model is adopted in a particular developing country. Nevertheless, developmental models have objective merits and demerits for different countries, as will be argued later. It should therefore be possible to arrive at some meaningful generalizations concerning the determinants of the suitability of Cuba's main socioeconomic developmental models for other developing countries.

In the last decade, there has been a rapid expansion in the literature dealing first with the appropriateness of production (and consumption) technology transferred from developed to developing countries, and second, with the relative merits of different mechanism by which technology can be transferred (direct foreign investment versus joint ventures, licensing schemes, turnkey investments, management contracts, education abroad, and so on.)[2] Similar tasks are attempted here.

In the first section of this chapter, two major types of Cuba's institutional technology, or socioeconomic development models, are examined. In the second section some criteria are identified to judge the "appropriateness" or viability of the major Cuban models in other developing countries. In the third section, some of the mechanism used by the Cubans to accelerate the transmission of these models are surveyed and briefly assessed. Finally, the major findings of the chapter are summarized and some conclusions drawn.

Cuba's Socioeconomic Development Models

As used in this chapter, the term *socioeconomic development model* refers to a set of political, social, and economic institutions which, together with a package of strategies or policies, shape the mobilization and allocation of natural, human, and capital resources and the distribution of goods, services, and status for the achievement of societal objectives. Such a model would have a variety of component parts which might include: institutions and policies for resource allocation (such as the central planning and economic administration system, and strategies for the inter- and intrasectoral allocation of investment); institutions and policies involved in the mobilization of human energies directed toward the economy (such as incentive structures, trade unions, ideologies, and the Vanguard Workers Movement); institutions and policies affecting the distribution of goods and services (such as the health system and the rationing system, all of which are also parts of the structure of incentives); and institutions and policies pertaining to national integration and maintenance of support for the political system (such as the party, the military, the mass organizations, the media, and educational institutions).

Since 1959, the components of Cuba's development model have changed several times, but not simultaneously. For this reason, a considerable number of models could be defined for particular points in time.[3] The temptation to elaborate series of such models is avoided here because the analysis of the transferability of several of those models could not be carried out adequately in a brief essay.

Besides, some of the models have proved to be unviable even in Cuba, making irrelevant the analysis of their transferability.

In this chapter, I examine the two models of Cuban socioeconomic development that I consider to be of greatest relevance to other developing countries. The first, which is here labeled the "basic dynamic model," refers to the overall sequence of goal priorities pertaining to redistribution and growth. The first model focuses not on institutional and policy detail at a point in time, but on the timing of Cuba's developmental orientations. The second model, the "emerging model of the 1970s" then focuses on the specific configuration of institutional arrangements and policy substance which appears to have taken shape so far in the 1970s.

The Basic Dynamic Model

One of the more interesting features of Cuba's development experience has been the dynamic sequence of distributional and growth priorities. A majority of developing countries, at least until recently, have given first priority to economic growth, assuming that some of its gains would eventually accrue to all or most groups in society, in other words, that distribution would more or less take care of itself. All too frequently growth gains have accrued disproportionately to specific elites or social groups, leaving large proportions of the population with reduced shares of the national income and, in some cases, with absolutely reduced levels of material well-being. Worsening unemployment has too often been an additional result of this type of development strategy in many developing countries. A few have tried to give higher priority to income distribution and employment creation, but without sacrificing growth. This optimal combination has proved to be difficult, but not impossible, to achieve.

The Cuban case contrasts sharply with these experiences. The essence of the Cuban dynamic sequence was, first, a concentration upon income distribution and access to opportunities in the early years of the Revolution. Then, after 1961, economic growth became the primary objective, although it was not to be achieved at the expense of distributional equity.

Paradoxically, the institutional and policy changes of 1959 to 1961, which successfully redistributed income and opportunity, were also partly responsible for significant increases in output in this early period, because high incomes in the hands of the less advantaged increased the demand for less complex Cuban-produced commodities. This in turn led to increased use of installed capacity, as well as running down of inventories of final, intermediate, and raw materials, and of foreign exchange holdings.[4] Productive capacity did not increase much, if at all, in these years, however.

Following the redistribution priority, and particularly when production problems intensified, economic growth became the overriding priority. For many reasons, all now well known, Cuba's economic growth from 1962 to 1970 was highly unsatisfactory. However, it must be emphasized that while consumption levels were sacrificed in order to increase investment, the degree of equality of

ARCHIBALD R. M. RITTER

income distribution was never sacrificed for growth. The policies affecting income distribution were to a minor extent responsible for poor growth performance through their impact on relations with the United States, on the structure of material incentives, and on emigration of technicians, professionals, and skilled workers.

But the long-run growth potential of the economy was undoubtedly increased by the improvements in human resources arising from expanded education in all levels, better health services (particularly in the countryside), improved nutrition for much of the population (due in part to income redistribution as well as the rationing system),[5] and the massive "learning-by-doing" experience with the new economic system which much of the population went through. These improvements were an important factor behind the rapid growth in the 1970s.[6]

An additional aspect of Cuba's development experience, the eradication of open unemployment, is of interest in view of the serious unemployment problem and the "spurious absorption" of the labor force in marginal sectors faced by other developing countries. Cuba's "full employment" was largely achieved through hoarding of labor by enterprises which did not have to pay their employees (so that labor productivity fell sharply, open unemployment being converted into covert or disguised unemployment) as well as by the expansion of bureaucracies, the armed forces, and employment in social services.[7] There was some semantic sleight of hand involved as well, as evidenced by the 101,000 workers (approximately 3.5 percent of the labor force) who returned to work in 1971 before the Anti-Loafing Law came into effect, despite official assertions that unemployment did not exist at the time. But Cuba has successfully eliminated unemployment as a major source of poverty, destitution, and decay of human capital.

The Emerging Socioeconomic Model of the 1970s

The current Cuban socioeconomic development model is still evolving.[8] For a while in the early 1970s, at least, it appeared that the essential outline of the "model" was becoming clearer. However, more recent clarifications of the nature of the new economic administration and of the Organos de Poder Popular (Organs of Popular Power) raise more questions regarding the functioning of the emerging system than they answer.[9] Once again, the Cuban Revolution appears to be moving into terrain uncharted by East European and Soviet precedents. Now, however, the major features of the experiment appear to be movement toward greater economic decentralization and the introduction of some political changes which may be "democratizing." It is most difficult to predict how the "model" will function in its "mature" configuration. It also is impossible to forecast how conflicting tendencies will ultimately be resolved. Most important of these will be the continuing antagonism between the maintenance of centralized economic control and greater autonomy for productive enterprises and the probable clash of democratization moves with continuing central control of the media, and with continuing central orchestration of civil organs such as youth movements, women's organizations, and farmers' associations. It is possible that the decentralizing and democratizing tendencies will prevail, although I would not estimate the probabilities of this to be particularly high, for a number of reasons which are not germane to the argument here.

Despite the unpredictability and obscurity of the current economic and political trends, I would judge the following to be the major features of the emerging socioeconomic model of the 1970s.

The economic administration. The most significant feature of the model continues to be demarketization, that is, the replacement of the price system as a major instrument for the social control of economic activity (and as an important medium for government intervention) by a centrally planned economic system (of more recent Soviet vintage). The new "Economic Management System" to be installed by 1980 is an attempt to insert some rationality into the unworkable system of the late 1960s.[10] It involves a continuation of centralized control over inter- and intrasectoral investment, pricing, decision-making concerning product mix at the enterprise level and choice of technology, and major aspects of interenterprise and interindustry materials flows. But it will also establish financial accountability and financial responsibility at the enterprise level, and will involve reliance upon prices and interest rates as instruments for the determination of enterprise profitability.[11] However, the structure of prices will not be market-generated, but will be determined by the central planning authority on the basis of political and tax-collection criteria. Enterprise "self-financing" and the use of a set of prices and an interest rate should make possible a more efficient allocation of investable resources.[12]

Centrally planned economies have exhibited a number of advantages, including "macroflexibility" in the allocation of resources; the possibility of emphasizing public consumption; and the possibility of achieving equity in income distribution and high employment levels. The current move toward relative economic decentralization is designed to counter the traditional shortcomings of central planning, which became severe in Cuba in the 1960s.[13] Those included micro*in*flexibility, pervasive micro*in*efficiencies, the suppression of initiative, the hoarding of productive factors (labor, capital, new materials, and component parts) by enterprises, and cumbersome communication and the traditional bureaucratic vices within the planning administration.

Developmental priorities. A second feature of the Cuban model of the 1970s is the strong emphasis given to economic growth. Economic growth has probably taken priority over equality of income distribution (if material incentives continue to intensify) and also over increased economic independence (if the economy continues to become more closely intertwined with that of the Soviet Union). As Dudley Seers has pointed out, however, growth is probably a more meaningful surrogate for welfare in Cuba than elsewhere because the gains from growth are distributed more equally there than in almost any other country in the world.[14]

Growth strategy. The current socioeconomic development model incorporates a growth strategy—or grand design for the intersectoral allocation of investable resources—which appears to be quite reasonable, in contrast to the instant-industrialization strategy of 1961–1963 and the sugar-centered strategy of 1964–1970. The current strategy (1976–1980) emphasizes interlinked complexes of industrial and primary-sector investment, a reasonably balanced set of foreign-exchange-generating export investments and import-substituting projects, and consumer-goods-producing industries.[15]

International interrelations. Cuba appears to be pursuing an export-oriented development strategy, although traditional exports continue to dominate. So far, international specialization in industry has been highly constrained owing to the nature of protection through bureaucratic control of trade flows. Cuba also has had a unique relationship with the Soviet bloc, as a preferred trading partner, aid recipient, and COMECON member. Cuba's policies affecting the importation of production technology (that is, the prohibition of such transfer under the aegis of the multinational corporation) is of interest, as are policies shaping Cuban interaction with the rest of the world in shipping, tourism, migration, and capital flows.

The political component. While this is not the place for a detailed examination of the structure and functioning of Cuba's political system, some discussion is appropriate because of its very close interrelationship with the functioning of the economy. In general terms, it might be argued that centralized economic control both permits and necessitates centralized political control, although it is clearly possible to have the latter without the former—witness the majority of countries in South America. A centrally planned economy facilitates the functioning of a centrally controlled political system through central control over all communications media; over the incomes of journalists, authors, cinematographers, and so on; over all income-earning opportunities, and hence over the economic base of any potential political opposition.[16] In other words, political monopoly can be buttressed by the economic monopoly inherent in a high degree of centralized economic control. Similarly, and again in general terms, centralized political control facilitates the functioning of a centrally planned economy in that criticism of basic institutions, strategies, and policies is avoided (although constructive criticism of plan directives is a necessity).[17] Moreover, potential dissatisfaction with the economy or with specific plans, policies, or directives is fragmented, isolated, co-opted, or manipulated by means of often "corporatist" types of penetration and control of organizations such as trade unions, farm or peasant associations, and youth and women's organizations.

In Cuba's experience more specifically, these interrelationships between centralized economic control and centralized political control lasted into the early 1970s. However, by 1977 it appeared that significant changes might be commencing with the emergence of democratization (through the Organos de Poder

Popular and in the unions) and with the move toward greater economic decentralization.

The Viability of Cuban Development Models in Other Developing Countries

A careful examination of the viability of the two Cuban development models considered in this essay would require detailed country-specific analyses. Because of the great differences among developing countries, simple generalizations concerning the applicability or inapplicability of the Cuban models to other developing countries cannot usefully be made. Differences in geography, resource base, economic structure, levels of income, political systems, goal priorities, and the objective problems faced make it unlikely that such models could be installed in their totality. Therefore, emphasis is placed here upon identifying some factors which determine the general appropriateness of the two Cuban models within the context of other developing countries.

The Transferability of the Basic Dynamic Model

A variety of powerful arguments can be marshaled to support the case for adopting the basic Cuban redistribution-growth sequence in other developing countries. The first and most potent argument is simply that existing poverty and unequal access to opportunity in developing countries cannot be tolerated on ethical or humanitarian grounds. A second argument is somewhat economistic but nonetheless important. Income maldistribution results in severe poverty, malnutrition, ill health, and short life expectancy. These, in turn, reduce on-the-job productivity and the amount of time that people can actually work. Reduced life expectancy and debility of the labor force lower the returns to the investment which goes into bringing up, educating, and training citizens. Malnutrition also has a serious negative effect on the mental and physical development of young children, which amounts to a partial destruction of the most valuable resource, human beings.

A successful income redistribution policy, which increases the incomes of lower-income groups (and reduces the share of higher-income groups), may facilitate economic growth in the short run in certain important ways: (1) the demand for locally produced necessities may be increased (the import content of relatively simple commodities consumed by the lower-income groups is less than that of the luxuries and durables consumed disproportionately by the rich); (2) the size of the market for simpler commodities may increase, thereby stimulating certain industries, in part at the expense of imports; (3) balance-of-payments problems may be alleviated if the demand for imported commodities, or for local commodities with high import content, is reduced; (4) unemployment may fall, as the luxuries and consumer durables purchased by high-income groups are probably less labor-intensive than the commodities of popular consumption; (5) terms of trade of the agricultural sector may experience a relative improvement, given the higher propensities to consume foodstuffs of the poor, resulting in a rise in rural living standards, a reduction in the large gap between urban and rural income levels, and, under some conditions, a slowdown of rural-to-urban migration.

The case for income distribution as a development priority has been made in general terms. The actual Cuban experience with income-redistributive changes was less clear-cut than a priori reasoning would suggest. This was due in large part to the concurrent effects of the U.S. embargo, the emigration, the organizational restructuring of the economy, and misguided growth strategies. In the Cuban case, the early redistributive measures such as nationalizations, land reform, urban reform, increased government expenditures on social services, wage increases, and (later) central control over income and price structures were all part of a larger "package" characterized by international reorientation, demarketization, and economic and political centralization. This world complex of policies was the source of the difficulties as well as the achievements of the Cuban experience in the 1960s.

While the Cuban distribution-growth sequence is significant, it is just one of a number of possible basic sequences. Of the alternative approaches, that of Taiwan is of special interest.[18] While aiming primarily at rapid economic growth, Taiwan has achieved not only rapid growth but a high degree of equality in income distribution and low rates of unemployment, all within the framework of a mixed market economy participating fully in the international economic system.[19] The Taiwanese experience is highly unusual: few other mixed market economies have successfully achieved growth with equity, for political and economic reasons which are well known. At any rate, the Taiwanese example demonstrates that the Cuban approach is not the sole alternative.

There are undoubtedly important negative lessons from the Cuban developmental experience of the 1960s which have been transmitted more or less imperfectly to other developing countries. First, the unhappy experience with what might be labeled the instant-industrialization and agricultural-diversification strategy pursued from 1961 to 1963 suggests that, at least under some circumstances, the most viable strategy for achieving industrialization, economic diversification, and enhanced economic independence in the long run may be to earn foreign exchange from traditional exports which can then be plowed into investment in diversified ranges of industry and agriculture.

Second, the problems created by the drive for the 1970 ten-million-ton sugar harvest demonstrated to Cuba and the world that will power, enthusiasm, and exhortation were no substitute for economistic calculation of costs and benefits, good organization, and careful plan implementation.

The third lesson from Cuba's development experience of the 1960s was that the "parallel construction of socialism and communism" was, under existing circumstances, unviable and perhaps impossible.[20] To develop the "New Man" morality and to use "communist conscience, consciousness, and conscientiousness" as the primary input for the tasks of the economy (for enforcing consumption austerity in order to raise investment levels and to elicit greater work efforts from the population) turned out to be unfeasible. (Reliance upon altruism and nationalism as activators complementary to material incentives may be valuable in countries with different socioeconomic systems, and under varying circumstances.)

A fourth negative feature of the Cuban experience, and one closely related to the others, is that a moderately complex economy cannot be operated as a single giant enterprise with no internal accounting system. This attempt at extreme centralization and "demarketization" produced serious distortions and economic losses, and has, of course, been reversed. Clearly, an economic administration cannot be structured on the assumption that *conciencia* is a viable substitute for financial accountability and cost-revenue consciousness at the level of production units.[21]

The Transferability of the Model of the 1970s

It is difficult to estimate the appropriateness of the emerging Cuban model of the 1970s for other developing countries because neither the precise nature of that model nor how it will eventually operate is yet known. In this section, the transferability of some of the key features of the model of the 1970s is examined. The features included are the economic administration, developmental priorities, growth strategy, international economic relations, and the political component. No attention is paid to certain components of the model that are in the embryonic stage, such as the profit-sharing scheme and the increased decision-making role of the enterprise.

The economic administration. Cuba's economic administration holds considerable attraction for other developing countries anxious to mobilize and re-channel resources quickly. In attempting to assess its transferability, we should consider it not in isolation, but in comparison with other types of economic systems. This raises the whole question of institutional choice, more specifically, choice of "the market" versus bureaucratic forms of economic administration, versus particular blends of these.[22] Choice among alternative economic institutions is a broad issue overladen with ideological preconceptions and ethnocentric biases. Because that issue cannot be dealt with adequately here, an analysis is presented of those factors which influence the appropriateness of Cuban economic administration for other developing countries. There is no doubt that a Cuban set of economic institutions could be implanted anywhere, but they would work better in some situations than others, and transitional costs would vary greatly for different countries.

A Cuban-style economic administration (that is, a centrally planned economic system) will function most effectively and can be installed with least transitional cost in an economy which is small, little diversified, with a relatively homogeneous resource base, and in which production units are large and concentrated, and use similar technologies. As mentioned earlier, the major feature of Cuba's economic system is "demarketization," or the elimination of spontaneously functioning markets as a means of harmonizing resource allocation and as an instrument for the social control of industry. Demarketization, which is virtually complete in Cuba, requires that planning bureaucracies perform the functions previously performed by markets. The dimension of the coordination or harmonization task which must be performed by a planning bureaucracy in the absence of markets varies directly with the size of the economy, the number of production units, and the degree of heterogeneity of the production units. By these criteria, Cuba was relatively well adapted to demarketization in that there was a high degree of concentration in the sugar sector, in mining, and in industry; the agricultural resource base was quite homogeneous (in comparison with Guatemala or Mexico, for example, where extreme ecological differences may require different agricultural technologies even within the same *municipio* or county), and the structure of the economy was not too complex in 1959. The task of harmonization of economic activity that the planning bureaucracy had to perform was of relatively manageable dimensions.

On these grounds, countries such as Trinidad and Tobago, Jamaica, and Guyana (all small, with high degrees of concentration in agriculture and industry, and with relatively simple economies) are likely to provide economic structures which could be fitted into a demarketized central planning framework more easily than countries such as Chile, Brazil, or Mexico. This, of course, is not to imply that countries such as the latter could not be demarketized. However, the dimension of the task of establishing planning bureaucracies to replace imperfect markets would be disproportionately difficult.

Alternatively, for larger, more complex, and heterogeneous countries, demarketization would have to be confined at first to those specific sectors or activities which were concentrated (for example, plantation agriculture, the "commanding heights" industries, energy, and mineral extraction), rather than to sectors in which there were already myriads of different productive enterprises.

A second factor which affects the adaptability of an economy to a Cuban-style centrally planned economic system is the availability and collectibility of the relevant information on the functioning of the economy. Central bureaucratic control over the operation of an economy requires large volumes of information on such matters as enterprise input-output relationships, interindustry commodity flows (in their sectoral, geographic, and temporal dimensions), relative rates of return of investment in different industries and firms, and the varieties, sizes, and so forth of consumer commodities. This information must be collected, aggregated, transmitted up the planning hierarchy, and used as the basis for resource allocation decisions.

The immense volume of information required for centralized economic control can be collected most easily when the economic structure is characterized by high levels of concentration, with production units which function as "modern" organizations with formal systems of account-keeping, and with the codification of procedures. In those countries or sectors where economic structures are highly unconcentrated, where production units are small-scale with no formalized accounts or codified procedures, the collection of the relevant information may be most difficult. This is because the required information on input sources, production techniques, marketing, and so on may exist only in the minds of small peasant farmers, craftsmen, small-scale manufacturers, retailers, and street vendors. Such data may not be susceptible to collection by bureaucrats.

To incorporate small-scale production units into a central planning system may require that they be reorganized, rationalized, or collectivized, in order to reduce the dimensions of the task of information collection—as well as the task of control. Such rationalization may involve high transitional costs as exemplified by the demarketization of the approximately 56,000 small enterprises during the 1968 Revolutionary Offensive in Cuba.

A second relevent factor with respect to data collection is the administrative capability of the statistics gathering apparatus. Where this network can be easily established, that is, where the appropriate blend of skilled manpower is readily available, a centralized planning bureaucracy can incorporate a broader range of economic activities than where suitable manpower is unavailable. This brings us, however, to a third general factor determining the applicability of the Cuban-style centrally planned economic system to other countries.

To staff a set of planning bureaucracies which perform economic functions previously performed under nonbureaucratized markets requires huge numbers of skilled personnel: accountants, statisticians, filing clerks, general administrators, secretaries, data collectors, and so on.[23] The availability of large numbers of such people, or people able to acquire the appropriate skills rapidly because of relatively high levels of education, is a significant determinant of the applicability of the Cuban model.[24] The greater the availability of this type of personnel, the easier it should be to install a Cuban type of planning bureaucracy. It is therefore likely that a country could set up a planning bureaucracy more readily if it had a higher level of formal education among broad strata of the labor force, more "modern" forms of economic organization and hence many workers with skills relevant to the functioning of larger-scale organizational hierarchies, and a larger public sector. Countries such as Uruguay and Chile, which have large public sectors, plentiful "modern" organizations, and relatively plentiful bureaucrats or potential bureaucrats, clearly provide a more hospitable human infrastructure for Cuban-style central planning than countries such as Haiti or Honduras, where such personnel are notably lacking.[25]

Elite, counterelite, and popular perceptions concerning existing socioeconomic difficulties and perceived developmental priorities may be significant determinants of the receptivity of particular groups in developing countries to the Cuban model. In a developing country experiencing rapid growth, perceived equity in the distribution of the gains from this growth, and low unemployment, there may be little dissatisfaction with existing institutions. On the other hand, in countries where these objectives do not seem to be achievable within existing institutions, it is natural that radical alternative institutional frameworks, such as that of Cuba, would appeal to many people. On occasion, established elite groups may see considerable merit in aspects of Cuban economic organization. More often, existing political elites, usually closely interlocked with economic elites, will perceive the Cuban model as threatening their position. In such cases, "counterelites," perhaps labor, academic, or religious groups, or legal or clandestine leftist political parties, would be more attracted to the Cuban institutional alternative. At any rate, it is likely that more people in a mixed-market developing country which is not achieving the primordial developmental objectives are likely to favor exploration of nonmarket institutional arrangements than would be the case for a developing country which is more successful.

Cultural traditions and political preferences also may be relevant in some cases. Where small-scale entrepreneurship has deep historical roots, for example in the small peasant sectors of Taiwan or of some African countries such as Ghana, there may be strong cultural biases, translating into political preferences of large portions of the population against collectivization and centralized bureaucratic control. On the other hand, in those plantation economies in which first slaves and then landless laborers constituted the labor force, and in which large-scale and often foreign-owned enterprises have prevailed, there may be a popular preference for nationalization or collectivization, and for more centralized national mechanisms of economic control.

Developmental priorities. It is probably appropriate that economic growth be a dominant objective in Cuba at present in view of the equitable incidence of its benefits among all sectors of the population. However, the emphasis upon growth is likely to be inappropriate for the majority of developing countries. Most such countries in much of the postwar era implemented growth-oriented development strategies which led to high and rising rates of unemployment and worsening relative positions for lower-income groups. Indeed, the conventional wisdom among development-oriented international organizations and aid agencies (such as the World Bank, the International Labour Organization, the Canadian International Development Agency, and the U.S. Agency for International Development), among developmental social scientists, and increasingly among policymakers in developing countries is that income distribution and employment creation should receive greater emphasis in the design of development strategies.[26] Alternatively, development strategies should be—and clearly can be— constructed so that growth on the one hand and employment and distributional objectives on the other do not conflict, but are instead mainly complementary goals. The task, then, is not to improve income distribution at the expense of growth, but to achieve a particular type of growth which will produce disproportionately large benefits for the poor. Even in Brazil, for example, there is growing recognition that in the face of lagging foreign demand for manufactured exports owing to the international recession, redistributional policies may broaden the domestic markets for manufactures, providing an internal dynamic for continued growth.[27] Whether recognition of complementarities between distributional and growth objectives will actually lead to significant redistributive measures in Brazil or other developing countries is, of course, highly problematic, fairly improbable, but not impossible. In sum, Cuba can and should emphasize growth as the means of further improving the material levels of living of the population. But many other developing countries now need to put much greater emphasis on redistribution and employment creation as paramount objectives.

Growth strategy. The current Cuban growth strategy emphasizes interlinked industrial and primary-sector investments rather than a forced choice between industry and primary sectors. This key feature of the growth strategy is highly relevant for other developing countries. Of course much current conventional wisdom on the issue favors this type of approach. Indeed it might be said that the old agriculture versus industry, and import-substituting industrialization versus primary-export promotion debates—which were prominent in the literature on development in much of the postwar period—are no longer considered to be particularly fruitful. Instead, any industrialization program must generate rather than consume foreign exchange, and this likely involves some types of import-substituting industrialization projects, but also some industries which concentrate, process, fabricate, or otherwise add value to indigenous primary resources. On the other hand, any growth strategy focusing on agriculture must also emphasize the related industrial activities (for example, dairies, yogurt production, ice cream plants, and distribution systems as well as dairy cattle; vegetable processing and packaging as well as cultivation). Perhaps because of the nature of sugar production as a complex of agroindustrial activities, Cuban planners have always been aware of the significance of industrial-agricultural linkages, although insufficiently in the 1960s. The current emphasis on such linkages and the balance which seems to have been struck between foreign-exchange-generating investment and import-substituting industrialization constitute reasonable examples for other countries. The specific mix of industrial-primary sector and import-substituting or export-promoting investments obviously must be custom designed to fit the specific conditions of each developing country.

International relations. It is especially difficult at this time to judge the appropriateness for other developing countries of the ways in which Cuba is integrated into the international economy. We still lack comprehensive and careful evaluations of Cuban commercial and exchange rate policies from the standpoint of their interaction with industrial development; Cuban policy with respect to the importation of technology; the unique relationship with the USSR and COMECON; and policies pertaining to international migration, capital flows, tourism, and shipping. Such studies are only beginning to appear, or have not yet been conducted. (Chapters 9, 10, 12 and 13 in this volume constitute valuable contributions to such a literature.) When more such studies have been completed it should be possible to estimate with some accuracy the transferability of these types of policies to other developing countries.

A number of useful insights may be derived from Cuban experience in some

ARCHIBALD R. M. RITTER

of these areas. For example, on the basis of hearsay evidence concerning the current nature of tourism in Cuba, I would guess that the industry has been structured to minimize income leakages, to maximize positive internal economic linkages from tourist expenditures, and to minimize the potential social disruption from the sector. Cuba's experience so far appears to be in sharp contrast with that of most other developing countries, and especially those in the Caribbean, where tourism developed as an outgrowth of tourism in the Miami area and followed its pattern and institutional structure. The standard criticisms of tourism in other parts of the Caribbean have been first that the impact on domestic income levels has been slight (due to high propensities to import for tourist consumption, together with foreign ownership of tourist facilities and the employment of expatriate personnel), and second, that the impact on the internal economy and society has had some serious negative features (such as importation of alien consumption habits and values, and harmful effects on agriculture because labor in some cases—notably in Antigua—has left agriculture for employment in tourism).[28] There may be some valuable lessons from Cuban tourism policy for other developing countries, though once again it cannot be expected that Cuban policy could be transferred in toto to other countries.

There may also be useful insights to be gleaned from Cuban policy concerning technological importation and shipping. On the other hand, other policy areas may have been less successful and are perhaps inappropriate for other developing countries. One might guess that the very high, indeed prohibitive, levels of industrial protection inherent in the bureaucratic control of importation may have reduced significantly the incentive for Cuban manufacturing to become internationally competitive, and may therefore have impeded the penetration of foreign markets by Cuban manufacturing industries, thereby choking off an important avenue for industrialization and foreign exchange generation. (Cuban exports of nontraditional manufactures were still negligible in 1974).[29] But any such tendency presumably can be overcome by decisions from the planning apparatus to expand nontraditional manufactures exports, as has been done by some of the countries of Eastern Europe. (Likely candidates for exportation in the future may be sporting equipment, sugar cane cultivation machinery, cane transport equipment, and perhaps some durable consumer items now being produced for mass internal markets.)

The political component. Certain elements of the political component of Cuba's development model are highly transferable. Indeed, some elements are so transferable that they have been adopted more or less spontaneously by many developing countries. Many developing countries, right-wing and left-wing, revolutionary and counterrevolutionary, "capitalist" and "communist," are characterized by political monopoly, that is, by some or all of the following: prohibition of all political parties but a single official party or quasi party; prohibition of all unsanctioned political assemblies; central political control of the media; prohibition of any elaboration or dissemination of world views, opinions, policy proposals, or criticisms which fall outside officially circumscribed limits; suppression of dissent by measures of varying sophistication; and penetration and control of civil organizations.

In developing countries where political elites have as a major objective the maintenance of an inequitable and exploitative socioeconomic system, some or all of the characteristics of political monopoly, buttressed by the monopoly of coercive power of the military apparatus, may be necessary for the exclusion of broader "popular" strata from meaningful participation in political decision-making and from major shares of the benefits resulting from policy interventions of the state. Needless to say, the ideological content and the broader economic institutional framework of the Cuban model are anathema to such regimes.

For more radical regimes or counterelites, the specific ideological content and institutional framework of the Cuban model are doubly appealing, first, because they give some promise of providing a means for dealing with problems of unemployment and inequity, and second, because they provide a powerful rationale for the elimination of a political opposition. The Cuban model also provides a moral rationalization for either the incorporation or elimination of all civil organizations such as unions and organizations of women, youth, and farmers, so that they become corporatist institutions linking individuals to the state in dependent state-sponsored groupings rather than potentially antagonistic, sectional interest organizations.

The possible emergence of a type of representative democracy inside Cuba's one-party system may alter the appeal of the political component of Cuba's development model. It is interesting to speculate what might happen if meaningful participatory democracy were perceived to develop and flourish within Cuba, and if this were eventually accompanied by elements of political liberalization, such as reduced monopolistic control of the media and of civil organizations. In this case, the appeal of the Cuban model for developing countries might be broadened considerably for those who in the past have objected to the highly centralized and antipluralistic nature of Cuba's political system.

Accelerating the Transmission of Cuba's Development Models

Cuban-style economic and political institutions are pivotal components of the type of society that the revolutionary elite would like to assist in constructing in the rest of the world. While in the view of the revolutionary elite, socialism and finally full communism must ultimately and inevitably prevail throughout the world, it is thought that the process can be accelerated by a variety of means. These range from military intervention to "making the Cuban model work"; from speeches in international meetings to demonstrations of athletic prowess.

Cuba has attempted in many ways to market its developmental model to the rest of the Third World. However, while the Cuban model can be consciously purveyed by the Cubans, it is important to note that knowledge of the Cuban model is disseminated automatically and spontaneously through the communications media, through academic or religious groups, and in some cases through labor unions or political organisms or parties (clandestine or officially tolerated) in other countries, or in a few cases by ruling political elites. (Of course, much misinformation as well as information, pro and con, is disseminated.) Most of the channels through which information on Cuba is transmitted in the rest of the world are beyond Cuba's control. However, the Cuban revolutionary elite has tried to utilize these channels as effectively as possible to create a positive international image.

Perhaps the most basic means of exporting the Cuban model is to ensure that the model itself is functioning effectively. As long as the Cuban economy was experiencing the severe contortions of the 1960s, and despite achievements in income redistribution and the elimination of open unemployment, the Cuban economic model was widely perceived abroad as being fundamentally flawed. Moreover, growing perceptions abroad of internal militarization, bureaucratization, one-man rule, and lack of meaningful political participation apparently came to be considered by the revolutionary elite as an additional stain on Cuba's international image. It is likely that the current dedication to participation and *poder popular,* and on making the Cuban economy function efficiently from the standpoint of production and growth, is to some extent part of an attempt to make the Cuban model more attractive internationally.

Second, the Cubans have attempted to influence the nature of the information disseminated through international media, so as to present the Cuban experience in a more favorable light. A variety of techniques has been used at various times for this purpose, including extreme official secrecy and release of selected information or statistics; limitations on research by foreign academics; use of such publications as *Cuba Internacional* and *Granma;* formation of the international news agency Prensa Latina to compete with such agencies as Reuters and the Associated Press; dissemination of revolutionary art, movies, and literature; and provision of revolutionary experiences for foreign students.

Third, the Cubans have undertaken certain projects which have had as an important subsidiary objective the portrayal of Cuba as a superior, efficient, humanistic, and solidaristic society. The large and successful investment in Olympic athletics has shown the superiority of Cuban institutions in athletics as well as in discipline, competitiveness, health, nutrition standards, and education.[30] Cuba also provided prompt and generous medical and other assistance following the earthquakes in Peru and Nicaragua, which conveyed an image of a humanitarian society willing to show solidarity regardless of ideological differences. Cuba has provided technical assistance to regimes as diverse as those of Vietnam and Jamaica. Presumably, the demonstration of "proletarian internationalism" has been a by-product of these aid activities.

A wide range of more direct interventions into the affairs of other countries have been used in an attempt to accelerate the "revolutionary process." The guerrilla actions in Bolivia undertaken by Cuban initiative, the military intervention by Cuban troops in Angola, and the prospective role in the conflict in Southern Africa need no comment. President Castro played a significant role in

Chile during the Allende administration through his visit in 1971 and through the activities of the embassy and advisors of various kinds (a role which further alienated the opposition to Allende, gave moral support to the Movimiento Izquierdista Revolucionario, and probably made the task of governing more difficult for Allende). A less direct form of influence is exercised through various youth organizations (Organización Continental Latino Americana de Estudiantes), labor movements, "friendship" organizations, and, of course, communist parties. This is not to say that such organizations in other countries "take orders" from Cuba, although it is conceivable that a few might. But a variety of such organizations share closely Cuba's ideology and "institutional technology." Symbiotic cooperation with Cuba assures them of moral and, in some cases perhaps, financial support, and gives the Cubans some promise of the fulfillment of their revolutionary "grand design."

The success of the various attempts to disseminate ideology and "institutional technology," to "win friends and influence people," or to "market the development model" is difficult to evaluate. There is substantial literature on revolutionary strategy. However, there does not appear to be a corpus of empirical work, or even a theoretical framework, which would permit a comparative evaluation of the less direct or "softer" techniques of transferring the Cuban model or of influencing attitudes and decision-making in other countries. Such evaluation would require a major research effort to probe and assess the mechanisms through which Cuba may exert influence upon attitude formation, the interplay of internal sociopolitical forces, and decision-making in other developing countries.

It appears that the Cubans have been following a highly pragmatic and flexible strategy for "transferring their development model." As the occasion has demanded, they have used a wide variety of modes of intervention ranging from direct political and military intervention to soft-sell molding of international opinion. Mechanisms which ostensibly have been relatively ineffective in moving the world closer to Cuba's normative vision for the future have been quietly dropped (for example, the cessation of the program providing foreign students with revolutionary experiences and of direct guerrilla intervention in Latin America under Cuban leadership). Other presumably more effective schemes have been intensified (notably at the diplomatic level). Furthermore, it appears that the Cubans have been prepared to respond rapidly and effectively, as well as flexibly, to opportunities for shaping external events. This is demonstrated by the Angolan intervention, the expansion of the Cuban role in Africa, and the moral and technical support in 1976 for the Peoples National Party government of Jamaica led by Michael Manley.

Summary and Conclusions

This chapter has attempted to evaluate the appropriateness of two of Cuba's development models in the context of other Third World countries, and to examine and assess the ways in which the Cubans have attempted to transmit these models. Of the numerous possible socioeconomic development models which could be employed to delineate the varied Cuban developmental experiences, two were selected for examination. These were the ''basic dynamic sequence'' of the 1960s (emphasizing an initial redistributive priority followed by a growth priority) and the ''emerging model of the 1970s.''

Both tasks were more difficult than originally expected. While there is abundant literature on ''comparative economic systems,'' socialism in specific countries, and alternative organizational forms, there is relatively little theoretical or empirical work on the appropriateness of different institutional technologies in different developing countries. For this reason, this chapter only attempted to determine the useful criteria for gauging the relevance of the Cuban development models for different countries. Research on a country-specific basis is necessary to evaluate the relative effectiveness of the various methods used by the Cubans to influence attitudes and decision making in other countries.

A number of conclusions did emerge from the study. The first was that despite ethnocentric and ideologically based prescriptions and panaceas concerning the appropriateness of different types of institutions, it is impossible to arrive at simple recommendations of supposedly universal applicability. Because of the great differences among countries with respect to such factors as resource base, economic structure, culture, political preferences, nature of the available human resources, availability of usable data, existing patterns of ownership, and the specific nature of the development problems confronted, it is not possible to find a single institutional model and set of strategies optimal for all times and places. Instead, varying blends of institutions—notably various forms of ownership, centralized versus decentralized organizations, comprehensive central plan versus market—will be appropriate at different times and in different places. The useful occupation for social scientists and, of course, for institutional entrepreneurs or architects in developing countries—and in developed market economies as well—should not be to invent or impose institutional nostrums but, instead, to devise mixes of institutional forms optimal for the specific countries at specific times. It would be only a coincidence if the Cuban model of the 1970s as an integrated organic unit were applicable to any other developing country.

Second, some components or more detailed subcomponents of the model of the 1970s may provide useful insights or examples for other developing countries. Among these might be the current emphasis in the growth strategy of industrial–primary-sector linkages, and perhaps some aspects of Cuban policy shaping the interaction with the international economy. On the other hand, other features of the current model, such as the emphasis upon growth as a development priority, may be appropriate for Cuba now, but highly inappropriate for many other developing countries in which redistribution of opportunity, assets, and income should constitute the major priority in designing development strategies. Unfortunately, it is impossible at this time to evaluate the effectiveness of a variety of Cuban's policies affecting Cuba's integration in the world economy (for example, policies on foreign commerce, exchange rates, importation of technology, capital flows, migration, tourism, and shipping) and to estimate their relevance and transferability to other developing countries.

Third, the "basic dynamic sequence" followed by Cuba in the 1960s was seen to be of particular interest and relevance to other developing countries in view of the common patterns of income maldistribution and unemployment. Many of the specific changes which brought about the egalitarian income distribution and the elimination of open unemployment in Cuba would be applicable elsewhere only in broad outline. It was also mentioned that there are other development models which have achieved favorable developmental results.

Finally, after surveying the methods by which the revolutionary leaders have attempted to disseminate and implement their world view and its institutional components, it was suggested that the strategy employed for this purpose has been highly pragmatic and flexible. Unfortunately, it has not yet been possible to specify the conditions under which different techniques would have a comparative advantage in disseminating the Cuban model or, indeed, any development model. This is an area in which further research would be useful.

NOTES

I am very grateful to Carmelo Mesa-Lago for valuable comments on an earlier draft of this chapter. Needless to add, the interpretation and any defects in the chapter are my own responsibility.

1. "The triumphs of Cuba will not be Cuba's triumphs, but . . . an example for the underdeveloped countries of the world, a solution and a road to be followed by those who suffer from hunger, misery, unemployment, and exploitation." Fidel Castro, "Discurso pronunciado al conmemorarse el X Aniversario del Triunfo de la Rebelión," January 2, 1969, *Granma*, January 3, 1969. See also idem, "Report of the Central Committee of the Communist Party of Cuba to the First Congress," December 17, 1975, *Granma Weekly Review*, December 28, 1975; and ibid., January 4, 1976.

2. See, for example, G. K. Helleiner, "The Role of Multinational Corporations in the Less Developed Countries' Trade in Technology," *World Development* 3, no. 4 (April 1975), 161–89; C. Cooper, "Science, Technology and Production in the Underdeveloped Countries: An Introduction," *Journal of Development Studies* 9, no. 1 (October 1972), 1–18; United Nations, UNCTAD Secretariat, *Transfer of Technology* (TD/106), November 1971; S. J. Patel, "The Technological Dependence of Developing Countries," *Journal of Modern African Studies* 12, no. 1 (1974), 1–18.

3. There are a number of delineations of Cuba's socioeconomic development models. See Carmelo Mesa-Lago, *Cuba in the 1970s: Pragmatism and Institutionalization* (Albuquerque: University of New Mexico Press, 1974); and A. Ritter, *The Economic Development of Revolutionary Cuba: Strategy and Performance* (New York: Praeger, 1974).

4. F. Pazos, "Comentarios a dos artículos sobre la Revolución Cubana," *El Trimestre Económico* 30, no. 13; and Ritter, *Economic Development*, chap. 3.

5. This generalization is not based on hard evidence such as a nutritional survey of the population. Instead, it is reasoned that the universally applied rationing system guaranteed all strata of the population a fairly well-balanced diet. Shortages were shared by all. With lower levels of open unemployment and increased monetary incomes of groups that had very low incomes before 1959, access to the basic bundle of rationed commodities became universal.

ARCHIBALD R. M. RITTER

6. For one perspective on growth performance in the 1970s, see National Bank of Cuba, *Development and Prospects of the Cuban Economy* (Havana, 1975); and F. Castro, "Report of the Central Committee," December 28, 1975.

7. In Cuba, employment in services increased by approximately 275,000 from 1958–59 to 1964, or from 25.4 percent to 33.2 percent of the total labor force. Between these dates, employment in industry and mining was unchanged in absolute terms. The total labor force increased by about 311,000, from 2,197,000 to 2,508,000. While a significant proportion of the increase in service employment is accounted for by education (± 65,500) and health (± 20,300), it is likely that a major portion of the remaining 189,000 were absorbed in the network of planning bureaucracies. See B. A. Pollitt, "Employment Plans, Performance and Future Prospects in Cuba," Department of Applied Economics, Cambridge University, Reprint No. 349, 1971; Carmelo Mesa-Lago, *The Labor Force, Employment, Unemployment and Underemployment in Cuba: 1899–1970* (Beverly Hills: Sage Publications, 1972); and JUCEPLAN, *Boletín estadístico de Cuba 1970* (Havana, 1971).

8. For a discussion of the economic administrative system in the 1970s, see Mesa-Lago, *Cuba in the 1970s* chaps. 2 and 3; and F. Castro, "Report of the Central Committee," January 4, 1976, p. 2.

9. On the new economic administrative system, see F. Castro, "Report of the Central Committee," and "The Nature of Socialist Enterprises in Cuba," *Granma Weekly Review,* January 30, 1977, p. 8. Concerning the emergence of greater popular participation, see L. Casal "On Popular Power: The Organization of the Cuban State During the Period of Transition," in *Latin American Perspectives* 2, no. 4 (1975), supp., pp. 78–88; D. Barkin, "Popular Participation and the Dialectics of Cuban Development," ibid., pp. 42–59; "Cuba: la institucionalización histórica," special supplement of *Cuba Internacional,* 1977; and Mesa-Lago, *Cuba in the 1970s,* chap. 3.

10. F. Castro, "Report of the Central Committee," January 4, 1976, p. 2.

11. "Among those laws is the law of value, the need to have receipt and disbursement relations among all the enterprises including those of the state, and that in those relations, and on the various economic relations in general, money, prices, finances, budget, taxes, credits, interest, and other commodity categories should function as indispensable instruments to allow us to measure the use we make of our productive resources." Ibid.

12. In the new system, enterprises are to be given greater decision-making power than they possessed in the 1960s. They are now to receive revenues from the sale of their output and to pay for their inputs (at prices and wage rates set by the planners). The difference between revenues and costs ("profits" is the term used by the Cubans) are then divided into (1) taxes paid to the state budget; (2) interest payments on loans, fines, and the enterprise share of social security costs; (3) an "economic incentive fund" for the enterprise; and (4) contribution to the state budget of any profits still remaining. The "economic incentive fund" is determined not only by the amount of profits less items (1) and (2), but also by over- or underfulfillment of a variety of indices relating to quality, assortment, and quantity of output, and "production costs, productivity . . . and profitability." The incentive fund can then be used "[to improve] the socio-cultural conditions of the workers in the enterprise; [to provide] individual material rewards for the workers, including management according to the success of the enterprise; [to develop] the technical and productive conditions of the enterprise." See *Granma Weekly Review,* January 30, 1977, p. 8.

13. See Ritter, *Economic Development,* pp. 245–53.

14. D. Seers, "Cuba," in H. Chenery et al., *Redistribution with Growth* (London: Oxford University Press, 1974).

15. See, for example, F. Castro, "Report of the Central Committee," December 28, 1976, p. 8. A large proportion of the investment projects listed for the 1976–1980 five-year-plan period involve either the production of inputs for use in agriculture or further processing, fabricating, or otherwise adding value to natural materials, including agricultural, mineral, forest, and fisheries outputs. Listed among the former were ten plants for producing animal protein from molasses, farm implement production, a plant to produce cane harvesters (600 per year), and a new nitrogenous fertilizer plant. Among the latter were completion of automatic handling and bulk loading of sugar, two new cement plants, new textile mills, dairy plants, candy factories, expanded fish-processing

capacity, expanded nickel extraction and concentration, other food-processing plants, furniture factories, sawmills, and expanded paper production.

16. In some cases, notably Czechoslovakia since 1968, central control of the economy and of income-earning opportunities has been used to curtail those individuals who continue to oppose the prevailing political power of the regime.

17. See P. J. D. Wiles, "Economics Activation, Planning and the Social Order," in *Action Under Planning,* ed. B. M. Gross (New York: McGraw-Hill, 1968). As Wiles states: "It is very impressive how invariably men lose their non-economic freedoms where the command economy rules, and how any partial restoration of the market in a Communist country seems to be accompanied by relaxation elsewhere."

18. For discussions of the Taiwanese case, see B. Johnson and P. Kilby, *Agricultural and Structural Transformation* (London: Oxford University Press, 1975), chap. 6; M. C. Yang, *Socioeconomic Results of Land Reform in Taiwan* (Honolulu: East West Center Press, 1970); and G. Ranis, "Annex: Taiwan," in H. Chenery et al., *Redistribution with Growth.*

19. While it is difficult to explain precisely this amazing experience, it appears that a number of factors are relevant. Included among these would be widely based ownership of productive resources (due to land reform under the Japanese and later in the early 1950s); a set of economic policies and an environment of prices and taxes which have compelled strict allocation of capital to the most productive uses, and the development of capital-saving labor-intensive technologies; networks of infrastructure in rural areas and agriculture (especially agricultural research and technological dissemination); an open economy such that the most efficient industries have expanded to provide for international markets; and a "special relationship" with the United States (concerning aid and market access). The example of Taiwan, while unique, is also relevant here because it demonstrates that a mixed-marked economy participating in the international economy can move toward social justice (as interpreted by the international development community).

20. Before: "The route . . . is not to create *conciencia* with money or material incentives, but to create abundance with *conciencia* and continuously greater collective wealth with greater collective *conciencia*" (Fidel Castro, July 26, 1968). After: "We cannot fall into the idealism of thinking that because we want communism . . . and because consciousness is the most important factor that must be developed, that consciousness has been developed and that we already have the necessary foundation for the communist society" (Fidel Castro, May 1, 1971).

21. Before: "Under socialism, commodities should not be sold on the basis of their cost of production, but according to the social function they fulfill" (Fidel Castro, August 29, 1966). "In the future we will have to free ourselves from money" (Fidel Castro, May 18, 1967). After: "On the other hand, it must be taken into account that the fact that we base ourselves on the profitability criterion does not mean we are going to close down necessary factories. The profitability criterion shows us which factory is the most backward in technology, which the costliest" (Fidel Castro, December 17, 1975).

22. Some of the relevant studies are Gross, *Action Under Planning,* chaps. 2, 6, and 7; W. F. Stolper, *Planning Without Facts* (Cambridge, Mass.: Harvard University Press, 1966); O. Sik, *Plan and Market Under Socialism* (White Plains, N.Y.: International Arts and Science Press, 1967); and T. Balogh, "Economic Policy and the Price System," *Economic Bulletin for Latin America,* 1961, pp. 41–53.

23. See note 7.

24. While a Cuban-style centrally planned economy may be "bureaucracy-intensive," market economies, and especially high-income market economies, tend to require large numbers of salesmen, advertisers, marketing agents, purchasers, and so on. Presumably, centrally planned economies require fewer of these, since some of their functions are performed in large part by bureaucrats.

25. The establishment of planning (or other) bureaucracies may divert qualified personnel from directly productive enterprises where their productivity is likely to be higher than in paper-shuffling activities, or from bureaucratic activities which perform functions that cannot be performed by markets at all. This is likely a serious cost of centralized economic control.

26. Major articulations of this new conventional wisdom are the International Labour Office

ARCHIBALD R. M. RITTER

reports on Kenya and Colombia: *Towards Full Employment: A Programme for Colombia* (Geneva, 1970); and *Employment, Incomes and Equality: A Strategy for Increasing Productive Employment in Kenya* (Geneva, 1972); and the World Bank study by H. Chenery et al., *Redistribution with Growth*.

27. For some official discussions of the problem of severe income inequality in Brazil, see Embassy of Brazil, *Social Aspects of Brazilian Economic Development* (London, 1974), pp. 6–12; and *Second National Development Plan 1975–1979* (Rio de Janeiro, 1974).

28. For some discussion of tourism and development, see L. Turner, *The Golden Hordes: International Tourism and the Pleasure Periphery* (London: Constable, 1975); J. Bryden, *Tourism and Development: A Case Study of the Commonwealth Caribbean* (Cambridge: Cambridge University Press, 1973).

29. National Bank of Cuba, *Development and Prospects,* p. 33.

30. F. Castro, "Report of the Central Committee," January 4, 1976, p. 4.

BIOGRAPHICAL NOTES
INDEX

Biographical Notes

COLE BLASIER, professor of political science and former director of the Center for Latin American Studies at the University of Pittsburgh, is author of *The Hovering Giant: U.S. Responses to Revolutionary Change in Latin America*. He was a career foreign service officer in the 1950s, serving in Bonn, Belgrade, and Moscow.

JORGE I. DOMINGUEZ, an associate professor of government and research fellow at the Center for International Affairs at Harvard University, has written extensively on Cuban affairs. He is the author of *Cuba: Order and Revolution in the Twentieth Century*. Born in Cuba, he is now a citizen of the United States.

EDWARD GONZALEZ is professor of political science at the University of California at Los Angeles. His many publications on Cuba include *Cuba Under Castro: The Limits of Charisma* and *Post Revolutionary Cuba in a Changing World* (with David Ronfeldt). Professor Gonzalez visited Cuba in 1967 and 1968.

RONALD E. JONES is a graduate student in political science at the University of Pittsburgh. He was a member of the initial Marine Corps landing force in the Dominican Republic in April 1965 and later served in Vietnam. Subsequent to military service he traveled to Cuba as a member of the Venceremos Brigade.

ROZITA LEVI is a research fellow in the Department of Regional Studies of the Institute for International Politics and Economics in Belgrade, Yugoslavia. She was a visiting scholar at the University of Pittsburgh in 1976–1977.

AUSTIN LINSLEY is a doctoral candidate in political science at the University of Pittsburgh. As a Peace Corps volunteer from 1973 to 1975, he spent three months in Puerto Rico and two years in Venezuela.

CARMELO MESA-LAGO is professor of economics and director of the Center for Latin American Studies, University of Pittsburgh. He was the organizer and chairman of the 1976 international conference, The Role of Cuba in World Affairs, at which the initial versions of the papers that constitute this volume were presented. He is the author of six books and twenty articles on Cuba, including *Revolutionary Change in Cuba* (editor) and *Cuba in the 1970s: Pragmatism and Institutionalization,* and the editor of the journal *Cuban Studies/Estudios Cubanos*.

THEODORE H. MORAN is a visiting professorial lecturer at the Johns Hopkins School of Advanced International Studies and has recently been appointed to the Policy Planning

Staff of the U.S. Department of State, focusing on North-South issues. He holds a Ph.D. in government from Harvard. His most recent book is *American Multinationals and American Interests* (with C. Fred Bergsten and Thomas Horst).

JORGE F. PEREZ-LOPEZ is an economist in the Division of International Prices, Bureau of Labor Statistics. He holds the M.A. and Ph.D. in economics from the State University of New York at Albany. He is the author of various articles on Cuba including "Cuban Industrial Production 1930–1958" in *Caribbean Studies* and "A Calendar of Cuban Bilateral Agreements 1959–1975: Description and Uses" (with René Pérez-López) in *Cuban Studies/Estudios Cubanos*.

STEVEN L. REED is an economist in the international research section of the First National Bank of Chicago. He holds the M.P.I.A. in international relations and the M.A. in economics from the University of Pittsburgh. As a graduate teaching fellow at the Center for Latin American Studies, he conducted research on international commodity cartels and assisted Carmelo Mesa-Lago with a number of economic studies on the Cuban economy.

ARCHIBALD R. M. RITTER is associate professor in the department of economics and the School of International Affairs, Carleton University, Canada. He has conducted field research on Cuba and is the author of several articles, co-editor of *Latin American Prospects for the 1970s: What Kinds of Revolutions,* and author of *The Economic Development of Revolutionary Cuba: Strategy and Performance*.

YORAM SHAPIRA is the acting head of the department of Spanish and Latin American studies at the Hebrew University of Jerusalem. He has written on Latin American political topics as well as on Israeli relations with the continent. He is the co-author (with E. Kaufman and J. Barromi) of *Israel-Latin American Relations*.

NELSON P. VALDES, associate professor of sociology at the University of New Mexico, has written a number of articles and books on Cuba. He is an editor, with Rolando Bonachea, of *Revolutionary Struggle: The Selected Works of Fidel Castro*. He visited Cuba in 1978.

Index

Argentina in the Twentieth Century
  David Rock, Editor
Army Politics in Cuba, 1898–1958
  Louis A. Pérez, Jr.
Authoritarianism and Corporatism in Latin America
  James M. Malloy, Editor
Barrios in Arms: Revolution in Santo Domingo
  José A. Moreno
Beyond the Revolution: Bolivia Since 1952
  James M. Malloy and Richard S. Thorn, Editors
Bolivia: The Uncompleted Revolution
  James M. Malloy
Constructive Change in Latin America
  Cole Blasier, Editor
Cuba, Castro, and the United States
  Philip W. Bonsal
Cuba in the World
  Cole Blasier and Carmelo Mesa-Lago, Editors
Cuban Sugar Policy from 1963 to 1970
  Heinrich Brunner
Essays on Mexican Kinship
  Hugo G. Nutini, Pedro Carrasco, and James M. Taggart, Editors
Female and Male in Latin America: Essays
  Ann Pescatello, Editor
Gaitán of Colombia: A Political Biography
  Richard E. Sharpless
The Hovering Giant: U.S. Responses to Revolutionary Change in Latin America
  Cole Blasier
Intervention, Revolution, and Politics in Cuba, 1913–1921
  Louis A. Pérez, Jr.
My Missions for Revolutionary Bolivia, 1944–1962
  Victor Andrade
The Overthrow of Allende and the Politics of Chile, 1964–1976
  Paul E. Sigmund
Panajachel: A Guatemalan Town in Thirty-Year Perspective
  Robert E. Hinshaw
The Politics of Social Security in Brazil
  James M. Malloy
Puerto Rico and the United States, 1917–1933
  Truman R. Clark
Revolutionary Change in Cuba
  Carmelo Mesa-Lago, Editor
Selected Latin American One-Act Plays
  Francesca Colecchia and Julio Matas, Editors and Translators
Social Security in Latin America
  Carmelo Mesa-Lago
Society and Education in Brazil
  Robert J. Havighurst and J. Roberto Moreira
The United States and Cuba: Hegemony and Dependent Development, 1880–1934
  Jules Robert Benjamin

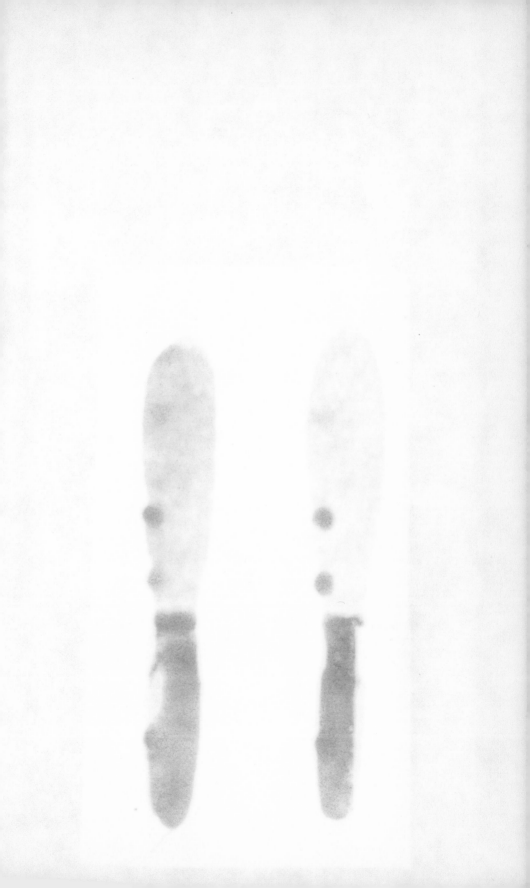